Never Wink at a Worried Woman

Other *For Better or For Worse®* Collections

Striking a Chord
Reality Check
With This Ring
Family Business
Graduation: A Time for Change
The Big 5-0
Sunshine and Shadow
Middle Age Spread
Growing Like a Weed
Love Just Screws Everything Up
Starting from Scratch
"There Goes My Baby!"
Things Are Looking Up . . .
What, Me Pregnant?
If This Is a Lecture, How Long Will It Be?
Pushing 40
It's All Downhill from Here
Keep the Home Fries Burning
The Last Straw
Just One More Hug
"It Must Be Nice to Be Little"
Is This "One of Those Days," Daddy?
I've Got the One-More-Washload Blues . . .

Retrospectives

Suddenly Silver: 25 Years of For Better or For Worse®
All About April
The Lives Behind the Lines: 20 Years of For Better or For Worse®
Remembering Farley: A Tribute to the Life of Our Favorite Cartoon Dog
It's the Thought That Counts . . . Fifteenth Anniversary Collection
A Look Inside . . . For Better or For Worse®: The 10th Anniversary Collection

Gift Books

So You're Going to Be a Grandma!
Isn't He Beautiful?
Isn't She Beautiful?
Wags and Kisses
A Perfect Christmas
Graduation: Just the Beginning!

With Andie Parton

Leaving Home

Never Wink at a Worried Woman

A *For Better or For Worse*® Collection by Lynn Johnston

**Andrews McMeel
Publishing**

Kansas City

For Better or For Worse® is distributed by Universal Press Syndicate.

Never Wink at a Worried Woman copyright © 2005 by Lynn Johnston Productions, Inc.
All rights reserved. Printed in the United States of America. No part of this book may be used or reproduced in any manner whatsoever without written permission except in the case of reprints in the context of reviews. For permission information, write Andrews McMeel Publishing, an Andrews McMeel Universal company, 4520 Main Street, Kansas City, Missouri 64111.

05 06 07 08 09 BBG 10 9 8 7 6 5 4 3 2 1

ISBN-13: 978-0-7407-5444-9
ISBN-10: 0-7407-5444-0

Library of Congress Control Number: 2005925093

www.andrewsmcmeel.com

www.FBorFW.com

For Nancy

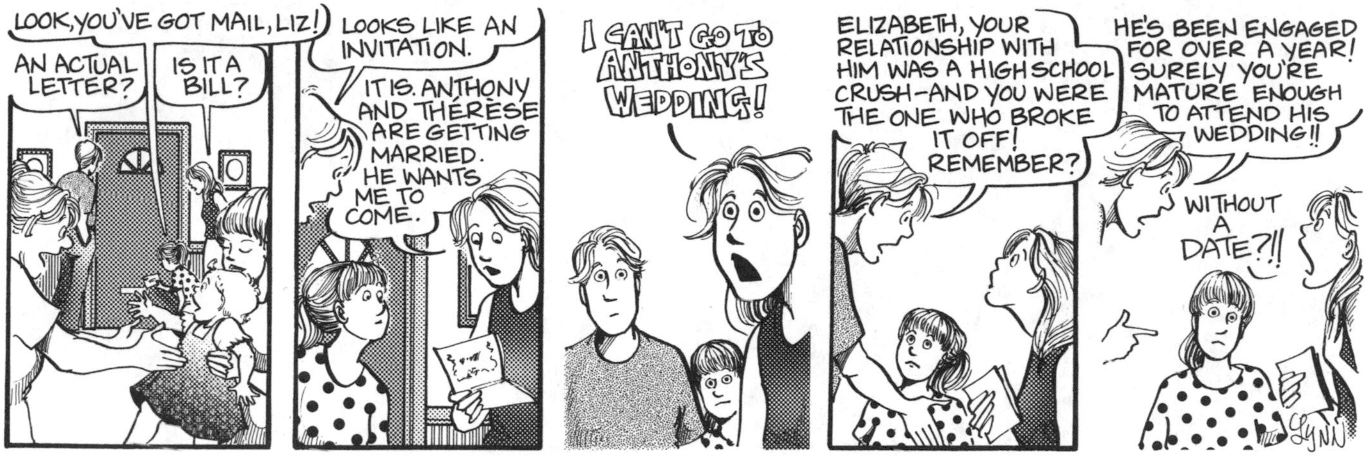
LOOK, YOU'VE GOT MAIL, LIZ!
AN ACTUAL LETTER?
IS IT A BILL?
LOOKS LIKE AN INVITATION.
IT IS. ANTHONY AND THÉRÈSE ARE GETTING MARRIED. HE WANTS ME TO COME.
I CAN'T GO TO ANTHONY'S WEDDING!
ELIZABETH, YOUR RELATIONSHIP WITH HIM WAS A HIGH SCHOOL CRUSH–AND YOU WERE THE ONE WHO BROKE IT OFF! REMEMBER?
HE'S BEEN ENGAGED FOR OVER A YEAR! SURELY YOU'RE MATURE ENOUGH TO ATTEND HIS WEDDING!!
WITHOUT A DATE?!!
LYNN

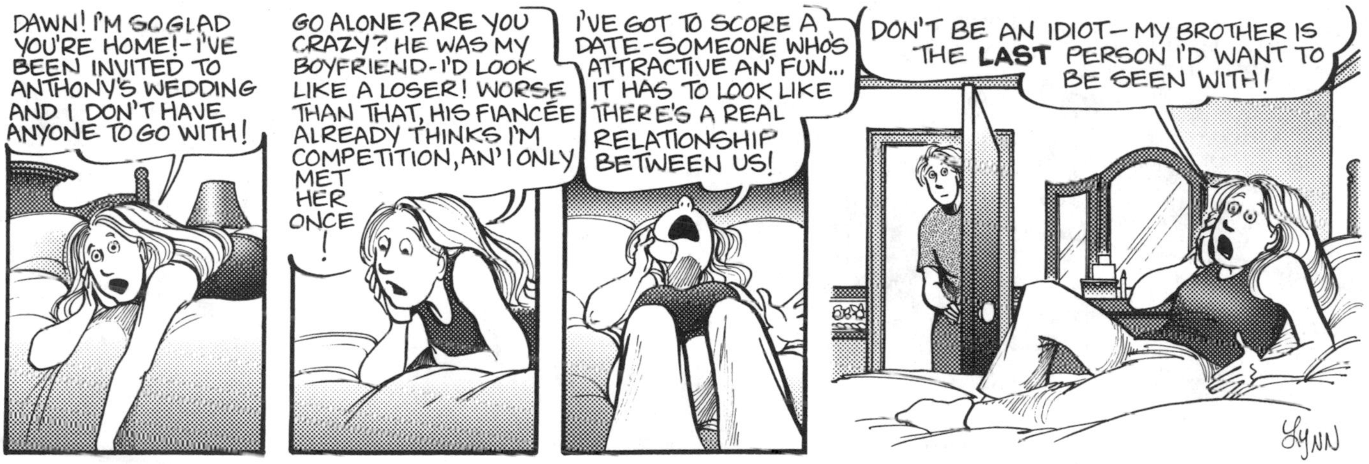
DAWN! I'M SO GLAD YOU'RE HOME!–I'VE BEEN INVITED TO ANTHONY'S WEDDING AND I DON'T HAVE ANYONE TO GO WITH!
GO ALONE? ARE YOU CRAZY? HE WAS MY BOYFRIEND–I'D LOOK LIKE A LOSER! WORSE THAN THAT, HIS FIANCÉE ALREADY THINKS I'M COMPETITION, AN' I ONLY MET HER ONCE!
I'VE GOT TO SCORE A DATE–SOMEONE WHO'S ATTRACTIVE AN' FUN... IT HAS TO LOOK LIKE THERE'S A REAL RELATIONSHIP BETWEEN US!
DON'T BE AN IDIOT–MY BROTHER IS THE LAST PERSON I'D WANT TO BE SEEN WITH!
LYNN

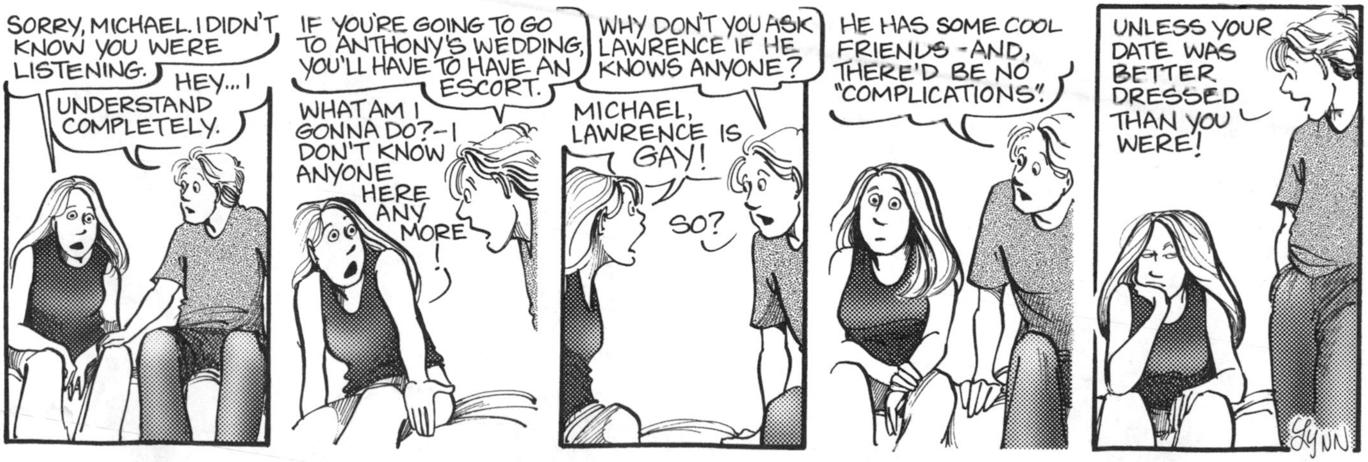
SORRY, MICHAEL. I DIDN'T KNOW YOU WERE LISTENING.
HEY... I UNDERSTAND COMPLETELY.
IF YOU'RE GOING TO GO TO ANTHONY'S WEDDING, YOU'LL HAVE TO HAVE AN ESCORT.
WHAT AM I GONNA DO?–I DON'T KNOW ANYONE HERE ANY MORE!
WHY DON'T YOU ASK LAWRENCE IF HE KNOWS ANYONE?
MICHAEL, LAWRENCE IS GAY!
SO?
HE HAS SOME COOL FRIENDS–AND, THERE'D BE NO "COMPLICATIONS".
UNLESS YOUR DATE WAS BETTER DRESSED THAN YOU WERE!
LYNN

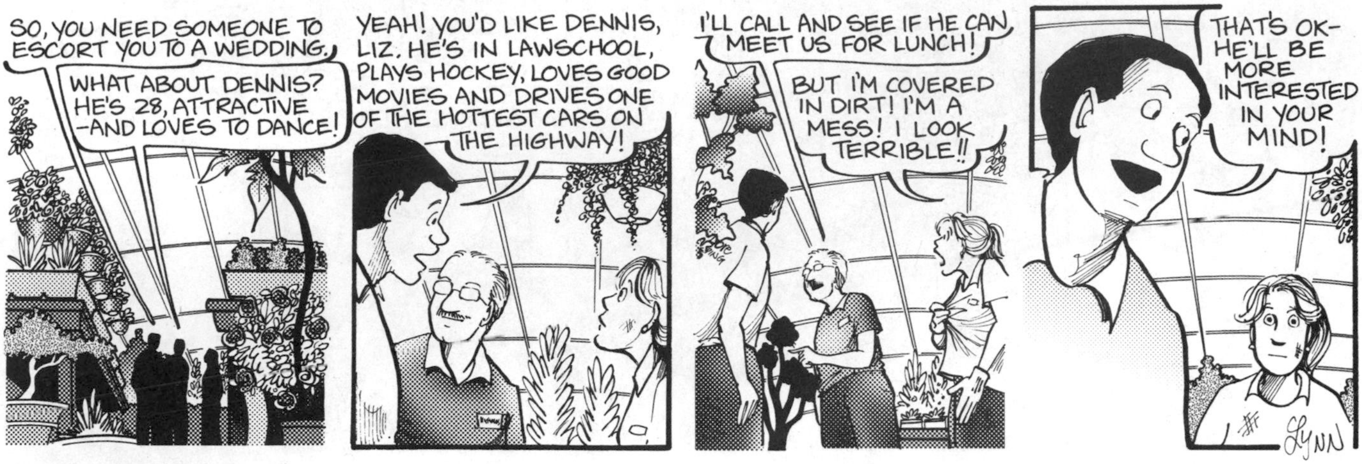
SO, YOU NEED SOMEONE TO ESCORT YOU TO A WEDDING.
WHAT ABOUT DENNIS? HE'S 28, ATTRACTIVE -AND LOVES TO DANCE!
YEAH! YOU'D LIKE DENNIS, LIZ. HE'S IN LAWSCHOOL, PLAYS HOCKEY, LOVES GOOD MOVIES AND DRIVES ONE OF THE HOTTEST CARS ON THE HIGHWAY!
I'LL CALL AND SEE IF HE CAN MEET US FOR LUNCH!
BUT I'M COVERED IN DIRT! I'M A MESS! I LOOK TERRIBLE!!
THAT'S OK- HE'LL BE MORE INTERESTED IN YOUR MIND!
LYNN

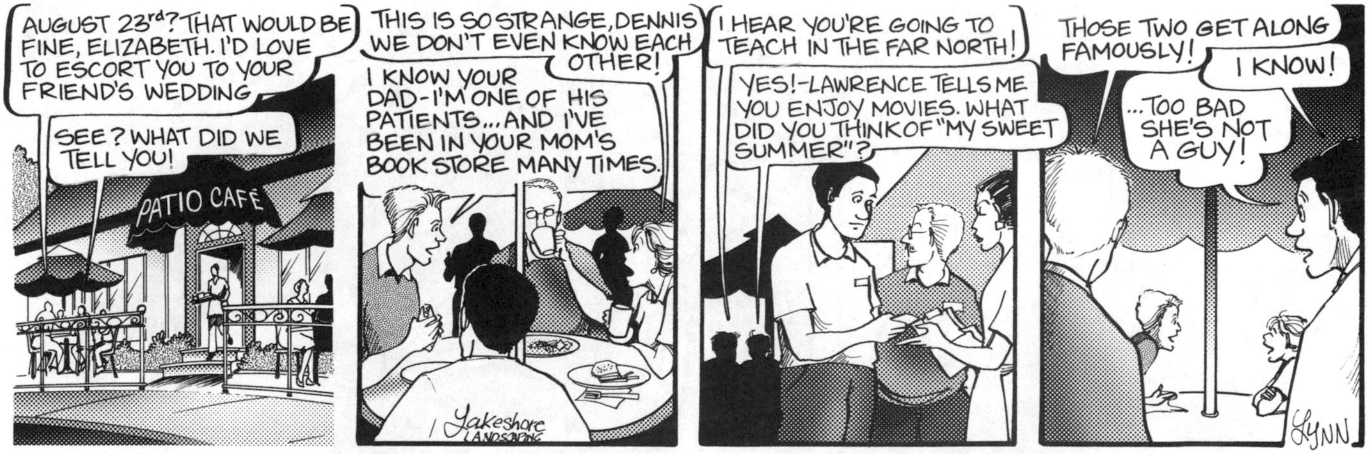
AUGUST 23rd? THAT WOULD BE FINE, ELIZABETH. I'D LOVE TO ESCORT YOU TO YOUR FRIEND'S WEDDING
SEE? WHAT DID WE TELL YOU!
PATIO CAFÉ
THIS IS SO STRANGE, DENNIS WE DON'T EVEN KNOW EACH OTHER!
I KNOW YOUR DAD-I'M ONE OF HIS PATIENTS... AND I'VE BEEN IN YOUR MOM'S BOOK STORE MANY TIMES.
I HEAR YOU'RE GOING TO TEACH IN THE FAR NORTH!
YES!-LAWRENCE TELLS ME YOU ENJOY MOVIES. WHAT DID YOU THINK OF "MY SWEET SUMMER"?
THOSE TWO GET ALONG FAMOUSLY!
I KNOW!
...TOO BAD SHE'S NOT A GUY!
LYNN

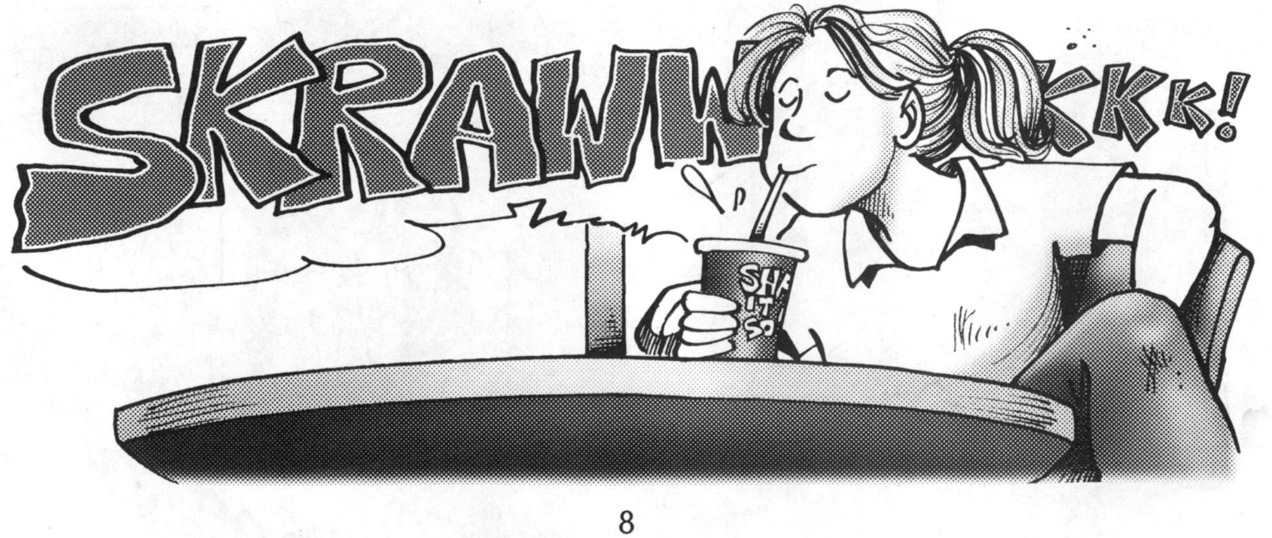
SKRAWW
KKK!

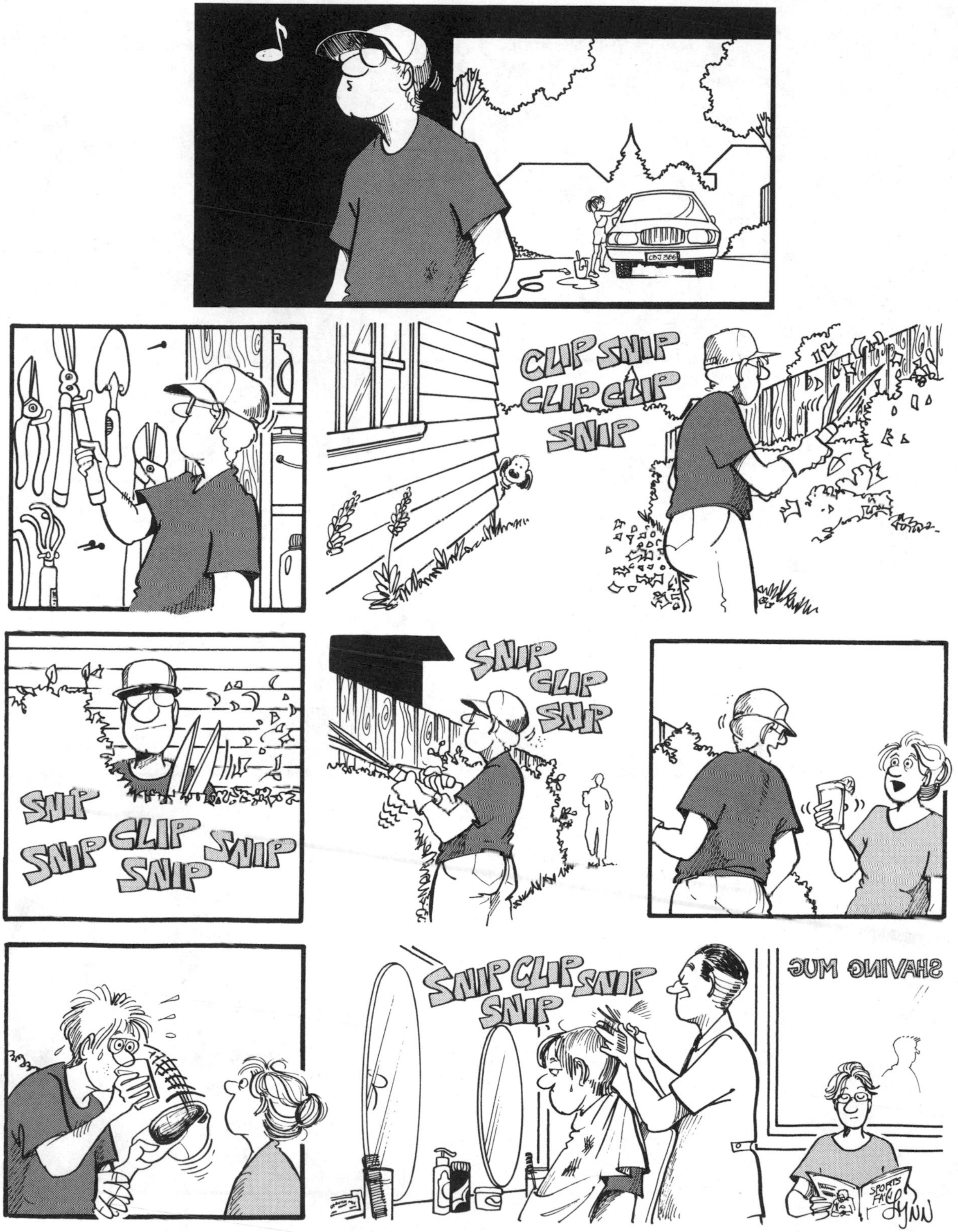

CLIP SNIP
CLIP CLIP
SNIP
SNIP
SNIP CLIP SNIP
SNIP
SNIP
CLIP
SNIP
SNIP CLIP SNIP
SNIP
SHAVING MUG
LYNN

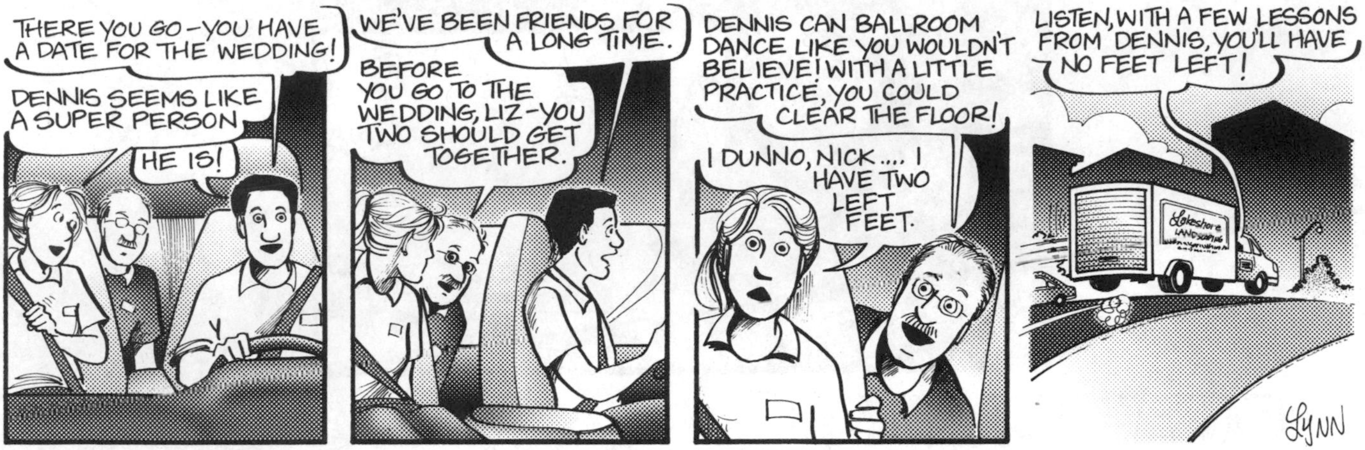
THERE YOU GO—YOU HAVE A DATE FOR THE WEDDING!
DENNIS SEEMS LIKE A SUPER PERSON
HE IS!
WE'VE BEEN FRIENDS FOR A LONG TIME.
BEFORE YOU GO TO THE WEDDING, LIZ—YOU TWO SHOULD GET TOGETHER.
DENNIS CAN BALLROOM DANCE LIKE YOU WOULDN'T BELIEVE! WITH A LITTLE PRACTICE, YOU COULD CLEAR THE FLOOR!
I DUNNO, NICK.... I HAVE TWO LEFT FEET.
LISTEN, WITH A FEW LESSONS FROM DENNIS, YOU'LL HAVE NO FEET LEFT!
LYNN

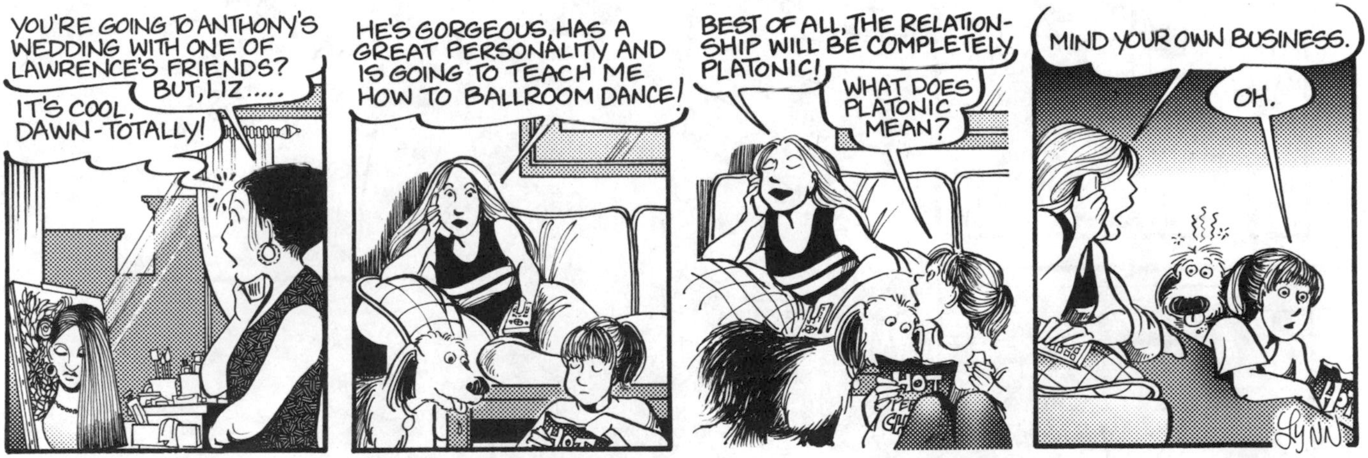
YOU'RE GOING TO ANTHONY'S WEDDING WITH ONE OF LAWRENCE'S FRIENDS?
BUT, LIZ.....
IT'S COOL, DAWN-TOTALLY!
HE'S GORGEOUS, HAS A GREAT PERSONALITY AND IS GOING TO TEACH ME HOW TO BALLROOM DANCE!
BEST OF ALL, THE RELATIONSHIP WILL BE COMPLETELY PLATONIC!
WHAT DOES PLATONIC MEAN?
MIND YOUR OWN BUSINESS.
OH.
LYNN

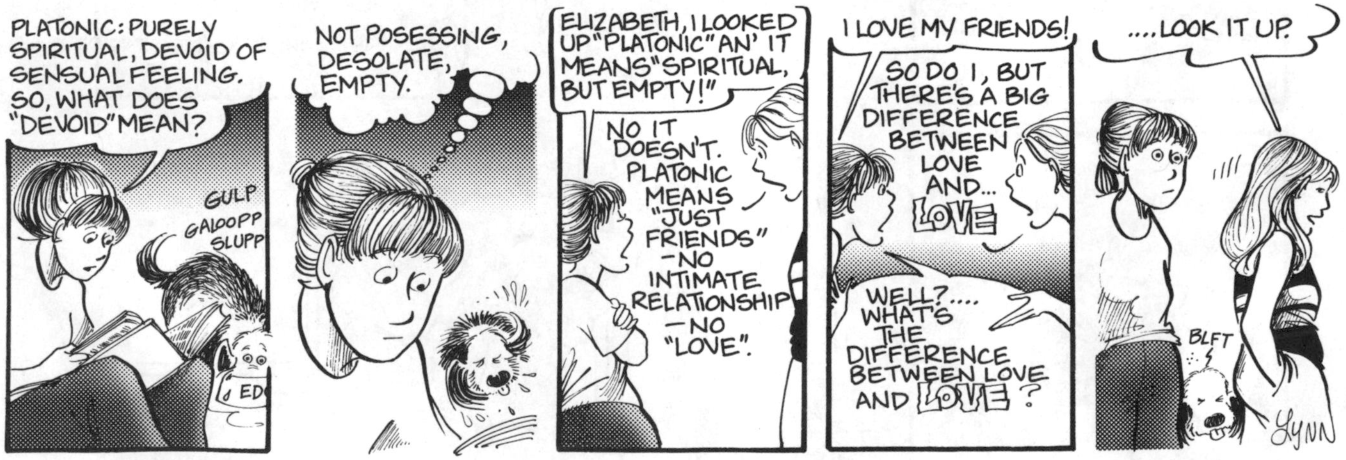
PLATONIC: PURELY SPIRITUAL, DEVOID OF SENSUAL FEELING. SO, WHAT DOES "DEVOID" MEAN?
GULP
GALOOPP
SLUPP
NOT POSESSING, DESOLATE, EMPTY.
ELIZABETH, I LOOKED UP "PLATONIC" AN' IT MEANS "SPIRITUAL, BUT EMPTY!"
NO IT DOESN'T. PLATONIC MEANS "JUST FRIENDS" —NO INTIMATE RELATIONSHIP —NO "LOVE".
I LOVE MY FRIENDS!
SO DO I, BUT THERE'S A BIG DIFFERENCE BETWEEN LOVE AND... LOVE
WELL?.... WHAT'S THE DIFFERENCE BETWEEN LOVE AND LOVE?
....LOOK IT UP.
BLFT
LYNN

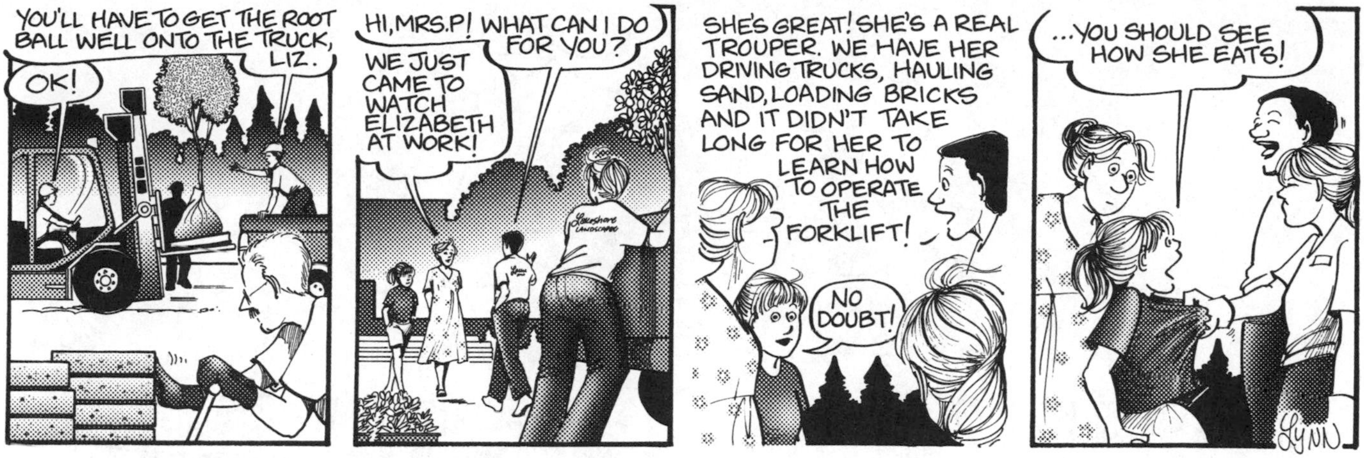
YOU'LL HAVE TO GET THE ROOT BALL WELL ONTO THE TRUCK, LIZ.
OK!
HI, MRS. P! WHAT CAN I DO FOR YOU?
WE JUST CAME TO WATCH ELIZABETH AT WORK!
SHE'S GREAT! SHE'S A REAL TROUPER. WE HAVE HER DRIVING TRUCKS, HAULING SAND, LOADING BRICKS AND IT DIDN'T TAKE LONG FOR HER TO LEARN HOW TO OPERATE THE FORKLIFT!
NO DOUBT!
...YOU SHOULD SEE HOW SHE EATS!
LYNN

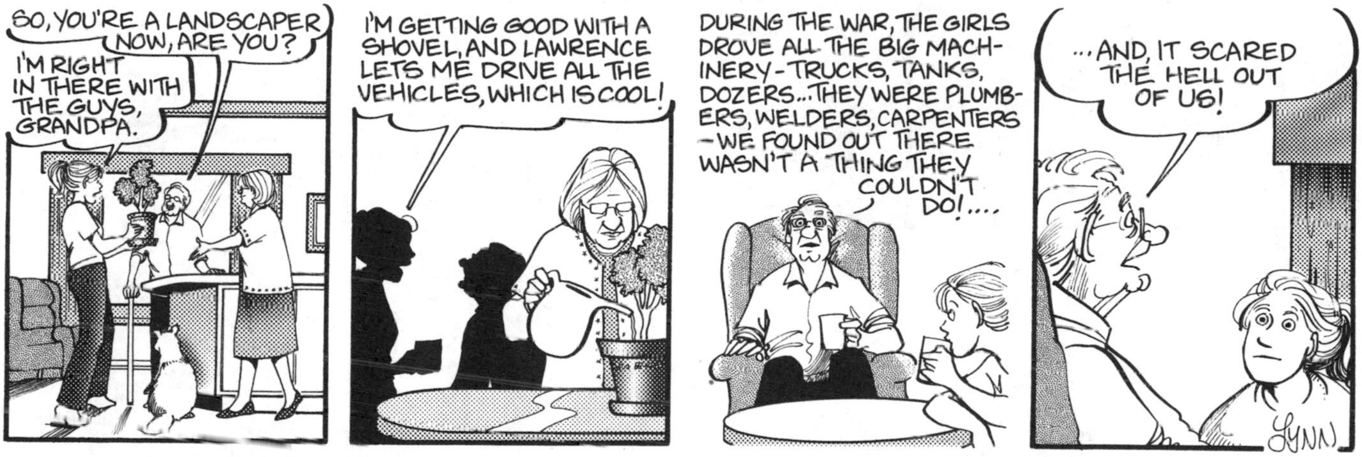
SO, YOU'RE A LANDSCAPER NOW, ARE YOU?
I'M RIGHT IN THERE WITH THE GUYS, GRANDPA.
I'M GETTING GOOD WITH A SHOVEL, AND LAWRENCE LETS ME DRIVE ALL THE VEHICLES, WHICH IS COOL!
DURING THE WAR, THE GIRLS DROVE ALL THE BIG MACHINERY - TRUCKS, TANKS, DOZERS... THEY WERE PLUMBERS, WELDERS, CARPENTERS - WE FOUND OUT THERE WASN'T A THING THEY COULDN'T DO!....
...AND, IT SCARED THE HELL OUT OF US!
LYNN

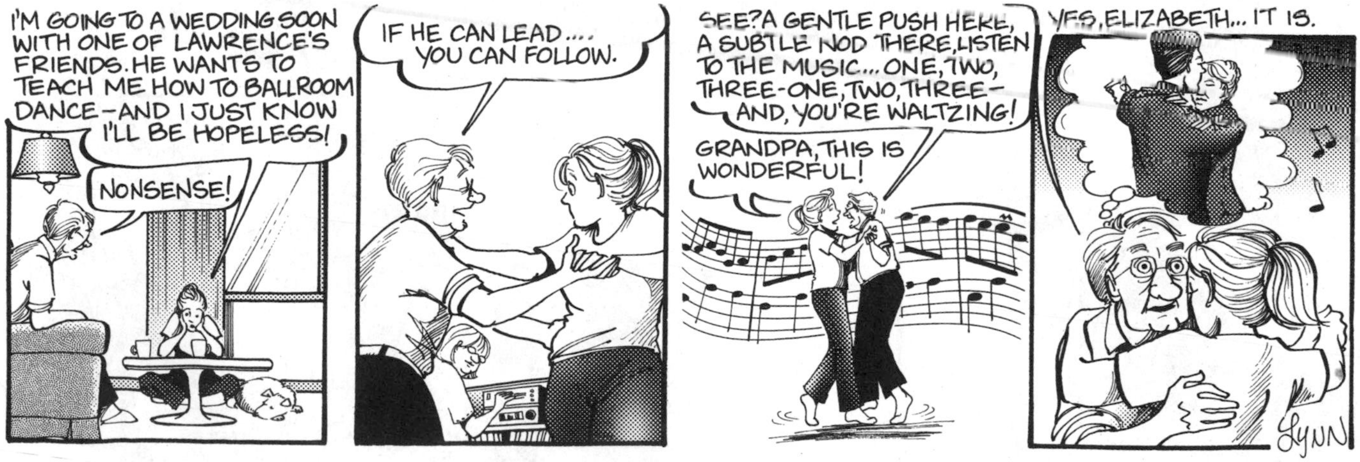
I'M GOING TO A WEDDING SOON WITH ONE OF LAWRENCE'S FRIENDS. HE WANTS TO TEACH ME HOW TO BALLROOM DANCE - AND I JUST KNOW I'LL BE HOPELESS!
NONSENSE!
IF HE CAN LEAD.... YOU CAN FOLLOW.
SEE? A GENTLE PUSH HERE, A SUBTLE NOD THERE, LISTEN TO THE MUSIC... ONE, TWO, THREE - ONE, TWO, THREE - AND, YOU'RE WALTZING!
GRANDPA, THIS IS WONDERFUL!
YES, ELIZABETH... IT IS.
LYNN

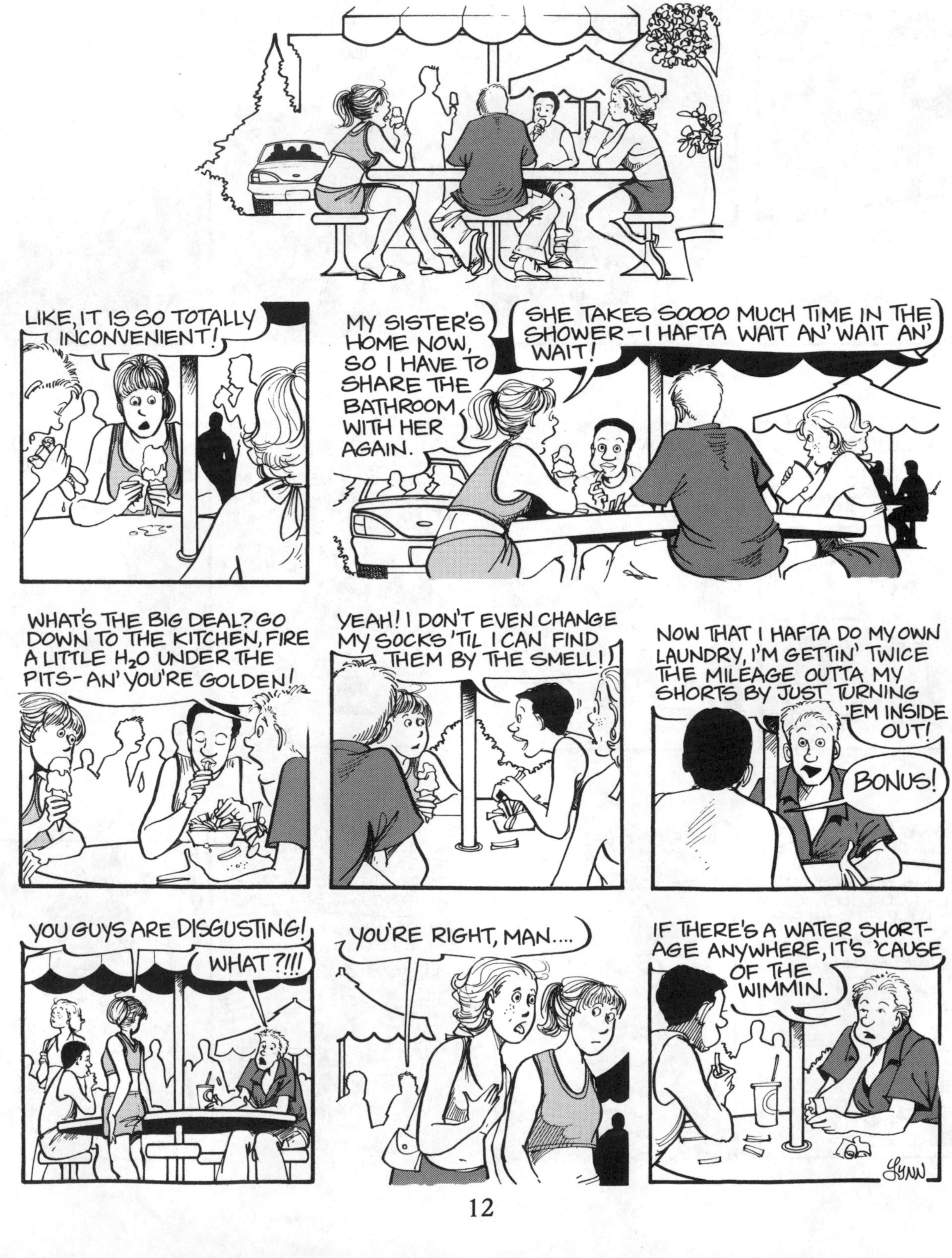
LIKE, IT IS SO TOTALLY INCONVENIENT!
MY SISTER'S HOME NOW, SO I HAVE TO SHARE THE BATHROOM WITH HER AGAIN.
SHE TAKES SOOOO MUCH TIME IN THE SHOWER—I HAFTA WAIT AN' WAIT AN' WAIT!
WHAT'S THE BIG DEAL? GO DOWN TO THE KITCHEN, FIRE A LITTLE H2O UNDER THE PITS—AN' YOU'RE GOLDEN!
YEAH! I DON'T EVEN CHANGE MY SOCKS 'TIL I CAN FIND THEM BY THE SMELL!
NOW THAT I HAFTA DO MY OWN LAUNDRY, I'M GETTIN' TWICE THE MILEAGE OUTTA MY SHORTS BY JUST TURNING 'EM INSIDE OUT!
BONUS!
YOU GUYS ARE DISGUSTING!
WHAT?!!!
YOU'RE RIGHT, MAN....
IF THERE'S A WATER SHORTAGE ANYWHERE, IT'S 'CAUSE OF THE WIMMIN.
LYNN

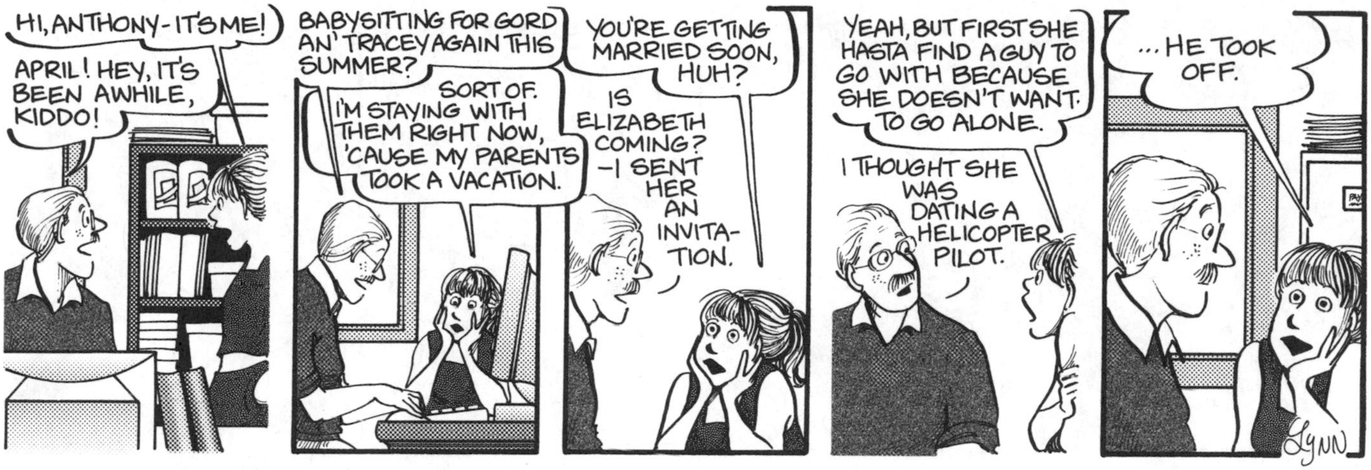
HI, ANTHONY - IT'S ME!
APRIL! HEY, IT'S BEEN AWHILE, KIDDO!
BABYSITTING FOR GORD AN' TRACEY AGAIN THIS SUMMER?
SORT OF. I'M STAYING WITH THEM RIGHT NOW, 'CAUSE MY PARENTS TOOK A VACATION.
YOU'RE GETTING MARRIED SOON, HUH?
IS ELIZABETH COMING? — I SENT HER AN INVITA-TION.
YEAH, BUT FIRST SHE HASTA FIND A GUY TO GO WITH BECAUSE SHE DOESN'T WANT TO GO ALONE.
I THOUGHT SHE WAS DATING A HELICOPTER PILOT.
...HE TOOK OFF.
LYNN

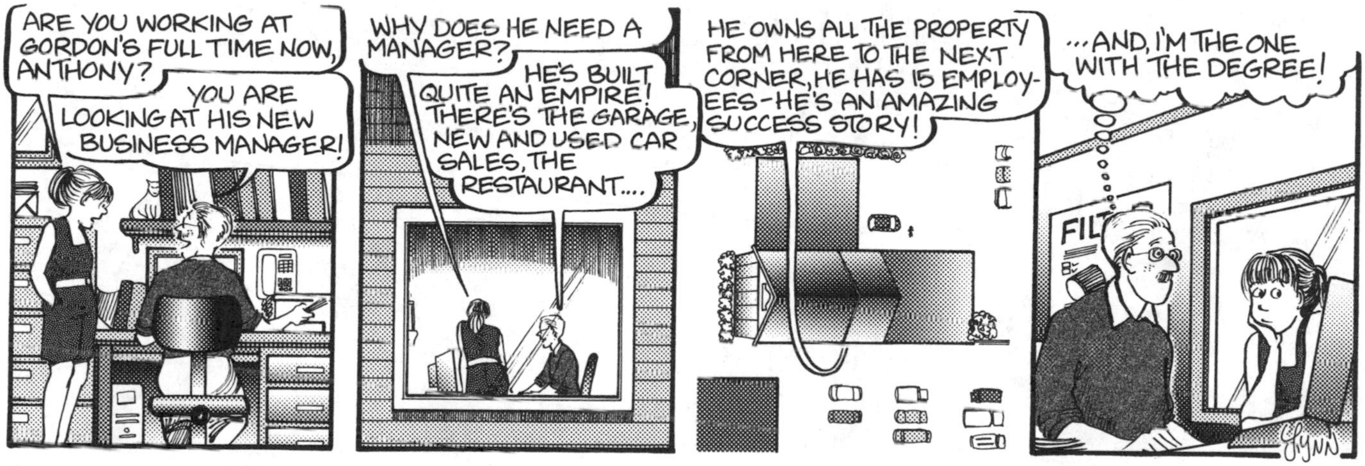
ARE YOU WORKING AT GORDON'S FULL TIME NOW, ANTHONY?
YOU ARE LOOKING AT HIS NEW BUSINESS MANAGER!
WHY DOES HE NEED A MANAGER?
HE'S BUILT QUITE AN EMPIRE! THERE'S THE GARAGE, NEW AND USED CAR SALES, THE RESTAURANT....
HE OWNS ALL THE PROPERTY FROM HERE TO THE NEXT CORNER, HE HAS 15 EMPLOY-EES - HE'S AN AMAZING SUCCESS STORY!
...AND, I'M THE ONE WITH THE DEGREE!
LYNN

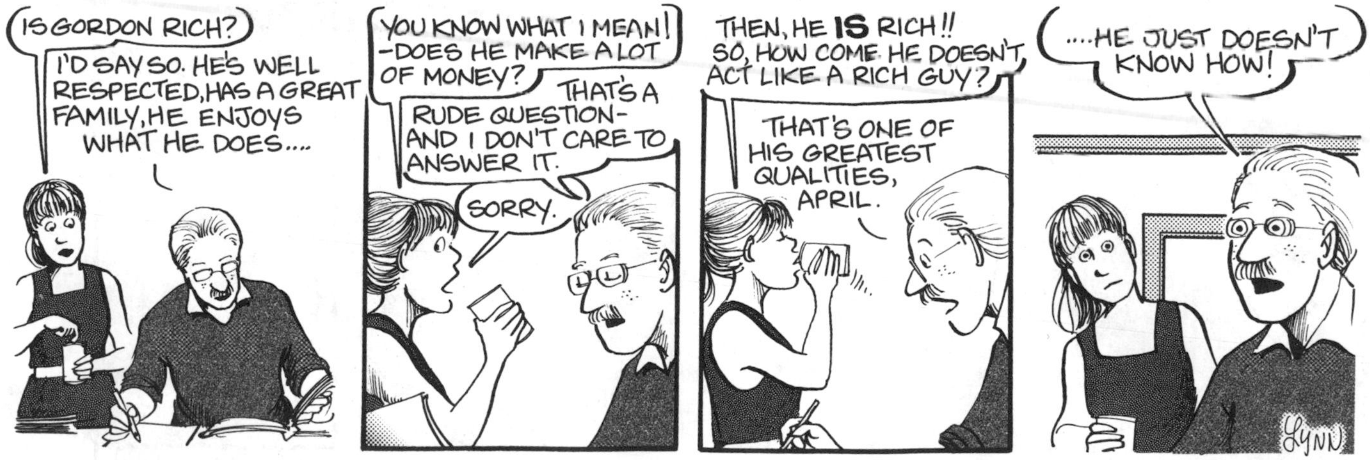
IS GORDON RICH?
I'D SAY SO. HE'S WELL RESPECTED, HAS A GREAT FAMILY, HE ENJOYS WHAT HE DOES....
YOU KNOW WHAT I MEAN! - DOES HE MAKE A LOT OF MONEY?
THAT'S A RUDE QUESTION - AND I DON'T CARE TO ANSWER IT.
SORRY.
THEN, HE IS RICH!! SO, HOW COME HE DOESN'T ACT LIKE A RICH GUY?
THAT'S ONE OF HIS GREATEST QUALITIES, APRIL.
....HE JUST DOESN'T KNOW HOW!
LYNN

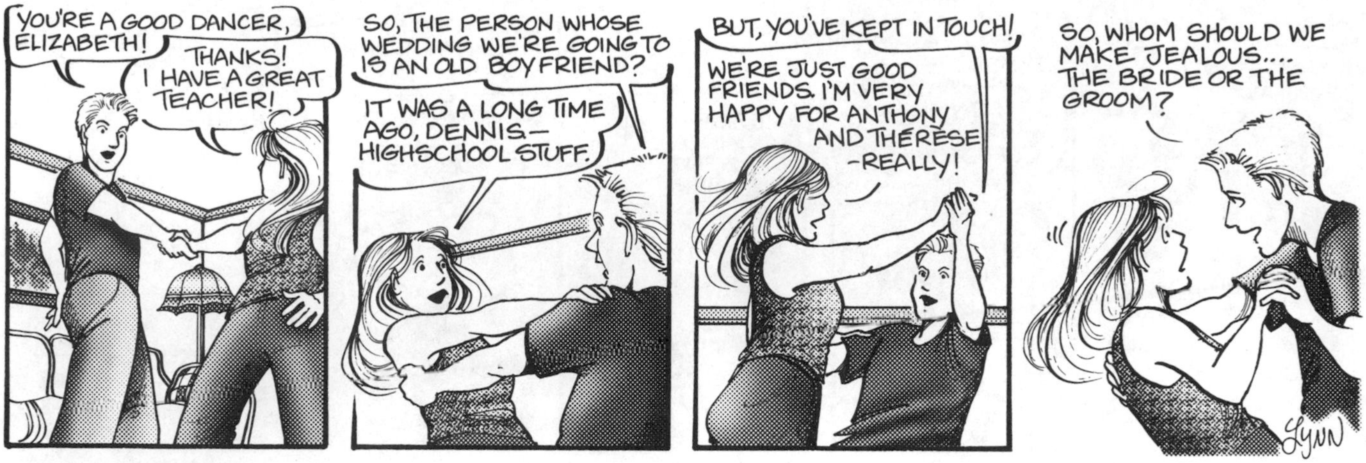
YOU'RE A GOOD DANCER, ELIZABETH!
THANKS! I HAVE A GREAT TEACHER!
SO, THE PERSON WHOSE WEDDING WE'RE GOING TO IS AN OLD BOYFRIEND?
IT WAS A LONG TIME AGO, DENNIS.— HIGHSCHOOL STUFF.
BUT, YOU'VE KEPT IN TOUCH!
WE'RE JUST GOOD FRIENDS. I'M VERY HAPPY FOR ANTHONY AND THÉRÈSE -REALLY!
SO, WHOM SHOULD WE MAKE JEALOUS.... THE BRIDE OR THE GROOM?
LYNN

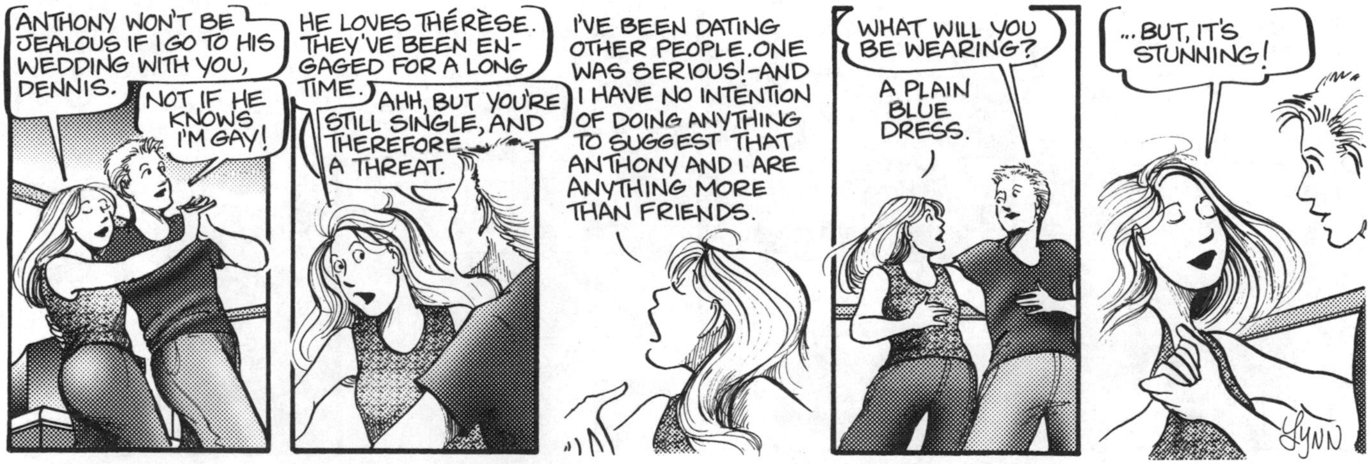
ANTHONY WON'T BE JEALOUS IF I GO TO HIS WEDDING WITH YOU, DENNIS.
NOT IF HE KNOWS I'M GAY!
HE LOVES THÉRÈSE. THEY'VE BEEN ENGAGED FOR A LONG TIME.
AHH, BUT YOU'RE STILL SINGLE, AND THEREFORE A THREAT.
I'VE BEEN DATING OTHER PEOPLE. ONE WAS SERIOUS!-AND I HAVE NO INTENTION OF DOING ANYTHING TO SUGGEST THAT ANTHONY AND I ARE ANYTHING MORE THAN FRIENDS.
WHAT WILL YOU BE WEARING?
A PLAIN BLUE DRESS.
...BUT, IT'S STUNNING!
LYNN

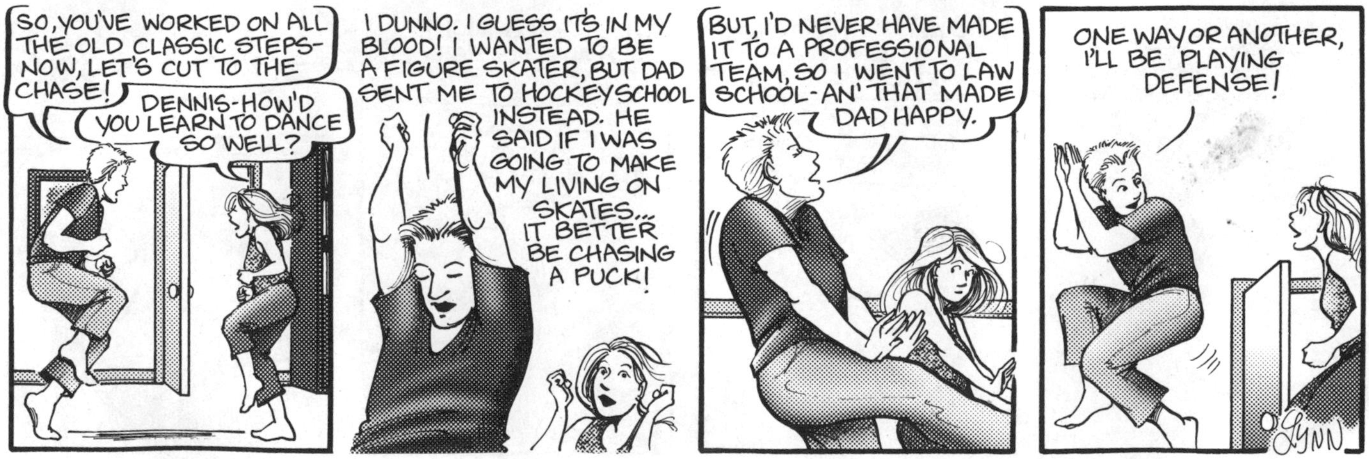
SO, YOU'VE WORKED ON ALL THE OLD CLASSIC STEPS- NOW, LET'S CUT TO THE CHASE!
DENNIS-HOW'D YOU LEARN TO DANCE SO WELL?
I DUNNO. I GUESS IT'S IN MY BLOOD! I WANTED TO BE A FIGURE SKATER, BUT DAD SENT ME TO HOCKEYSCHOOL INSTEAD. HE SAID IF I WAS GOING TO MAKE MY LIVING ON SKATES... IT BETTER BE CHASING A PUCK!
BUT, I'D NEVER HAVE MADE IT TO A PROFESSIONAL TEAM, SO I WENT TO LAW SCHOOL- AN' THAT MADE DAD HAPPY.
ONE WAY OR ANOTHER, I'LL BE PLAYING DEFENSE!
LYNN

THE ARCTIC HARE IS ALMOST INVISIBLE AGAINST THE SNOWY LANDSCAPE

BUT, A SLIGHT MOVEMENT OF HIS BLACK-TIPPED EARS CATCHES THE EYE OF A FOX, EQUALLY WELL CAMOUFLAGED

THE HARE HAS FOUND A SMALL PATCH OF EDIBLE FOLIAGE. THE STEALTHY FOX MOVES CLOSER....

TOO LATE FOR HIS POWERFUL LEGS TO PROPEL HIM FROM DANGER, THE HARE BECOMES A MEAL FOR THE HUNGRY FOX.

HIGH ON THE SLOPES, A YOUNG MOUNTAIN GOAT JUMPS SURE-FOOTEDLY ALONG THE CRAGGY HILLSIDE

DOWNWIND AND HIDDEN BY THE LIMBS OF A FALLEN TREE A COUGAR WAITS IN SILENCE.

IN FLAWLESS MOTION, THE COUGAR LANDS, CLAWS EXTENDED. RAZOR SHARP TEETH CLOSE DOWN.....

WOW, YOU'RE LIKE, WALKING ALONG, MINDING YOUR OWN BUSINESS AN' SUDDENLY **WHAM!** YOU BECOME SOMEBODY'S LUNCH!!

I WOULD SO NOT WANT TO BE A WILD ANIMAL!

ANIMALS PREY ON OTHER ANIMALS 'CAUSE IT'S THE ONLY WAY TO SURVIVE, APRIL.

CLICK CLICK CLICK

AN' FOR NO GOOD REASON AT ALL, HUMANS PREY ON EACH OTHER!

MISSING

HAVE YOU SEEN MELISSA -JONES

Lynn

15

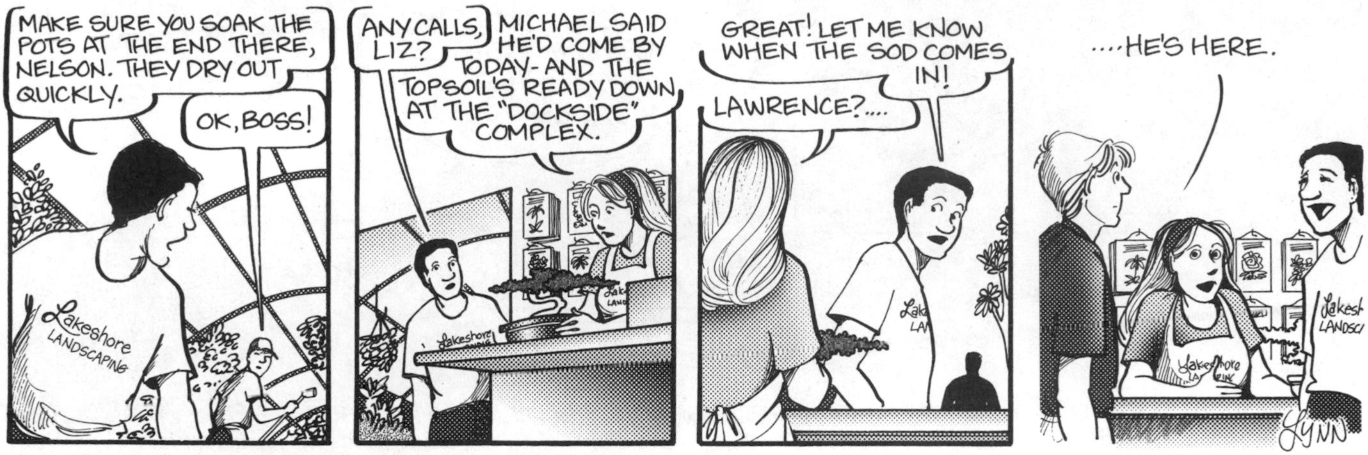
MAKE SURE YOU SOAK THE POTS AT THE END THERE, NELSON. THEY DRY OUT QUICKLY.
OK, BOSS!
ANY CALLS, LIZ?
MICHAEL SAID HE'D COME BY TODAY- AND THE TOPSOIL'S READY DOWN AT THE "DOCKSIDE" COMPLEX.
GREAT! LET ME KNOW WHEN THE SOD COMES IN!
LAWRENCE?....
....HE'S HERE.
Lakeshore LANDSCAPING
LYNN

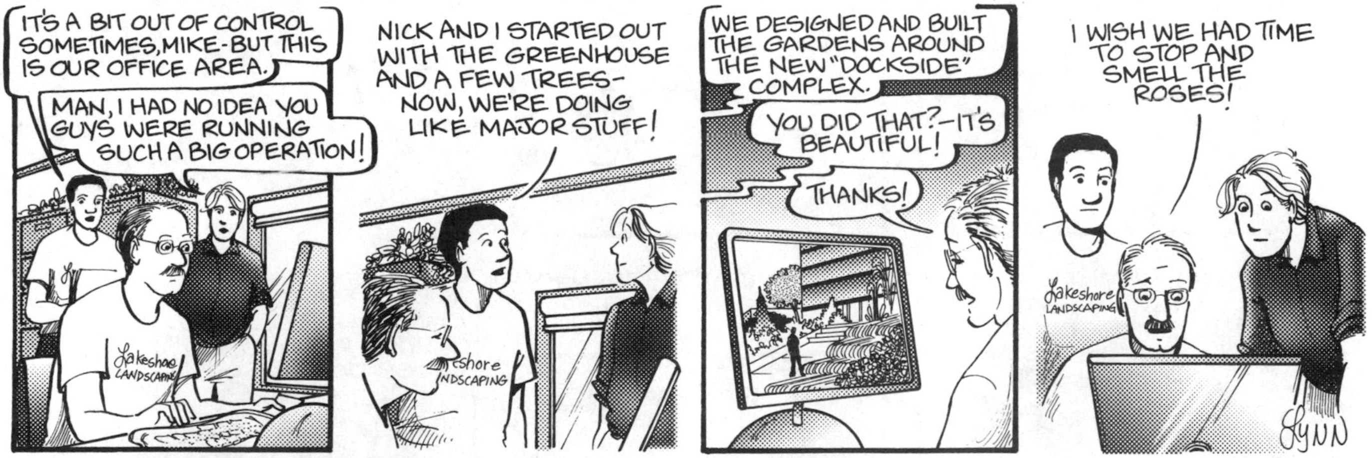
IT'S A BIT OUT OF CONTROL SOMETIMES, MIKE- BUT THIS IS OUR OFFICE AREA.
MAN, I HAD NO IDEA YOU GUYS WERE RUNNING SUCH A BIG OPERATION!
NICK AND I STARTED OUT WITH THE GREENHOUSE AND A FEW TREES- NOW, WE'RE DOING LIKE MAJOR STUFF!
WE DESIGNED AND BUILT THE GARDENS AROUND THE NEW "DOCKSIDE" COMPLEX.
YOU DID THAT?- IT'S BEAUTIFUL!
THANKS!
I WISH WE HAD TIME TO STOP AND SMELL THE ROSES!
Lakeshore LANDSCAPING
LYNN

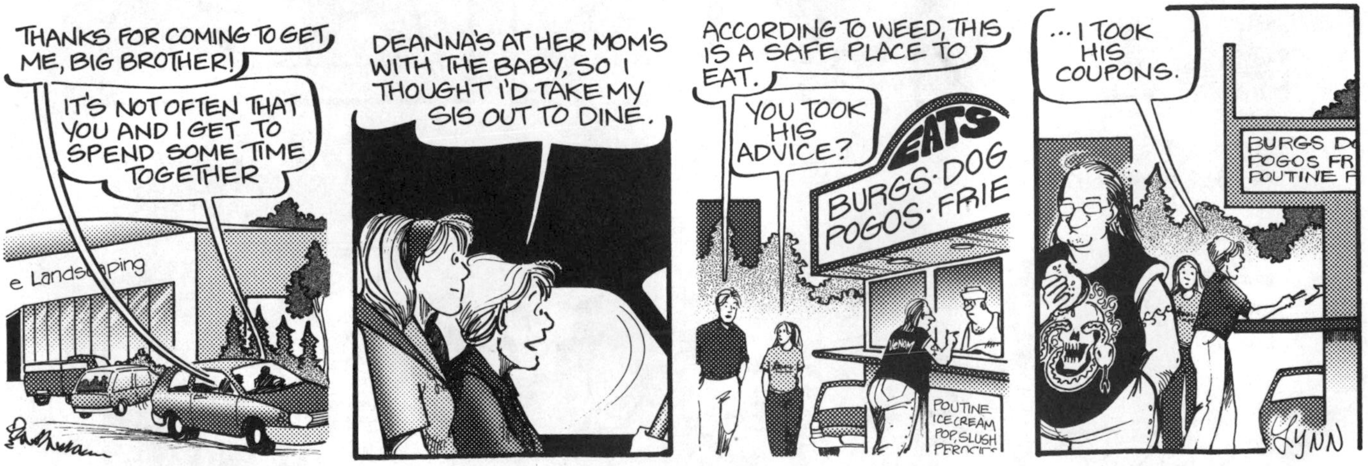
THANKS FOR COMING TO GET ME, BIG BROTHER!
IT'S NOT OFTEN THAT YOU AND I GET TO SPEND SOME TIME TOGETHER
e Landscaping
DEANNA'S AT HER MOM'S WITH THE BABY, SO I THOUGHT I'D TAKE MY SIS OUT TO DINE.
ACCORDING TO WEED, THIS IS A SAFE PLACE TO EAT.
YOU TOOK HIS ADVICE?
EATS
BURGS·DOG
POGOS·FRIE
POUTINE ICE CREAM POP, SLUSH
...I TOOK HIS COUPONS.
BURGS D
POGOS FR
POUTINE F
LYNN

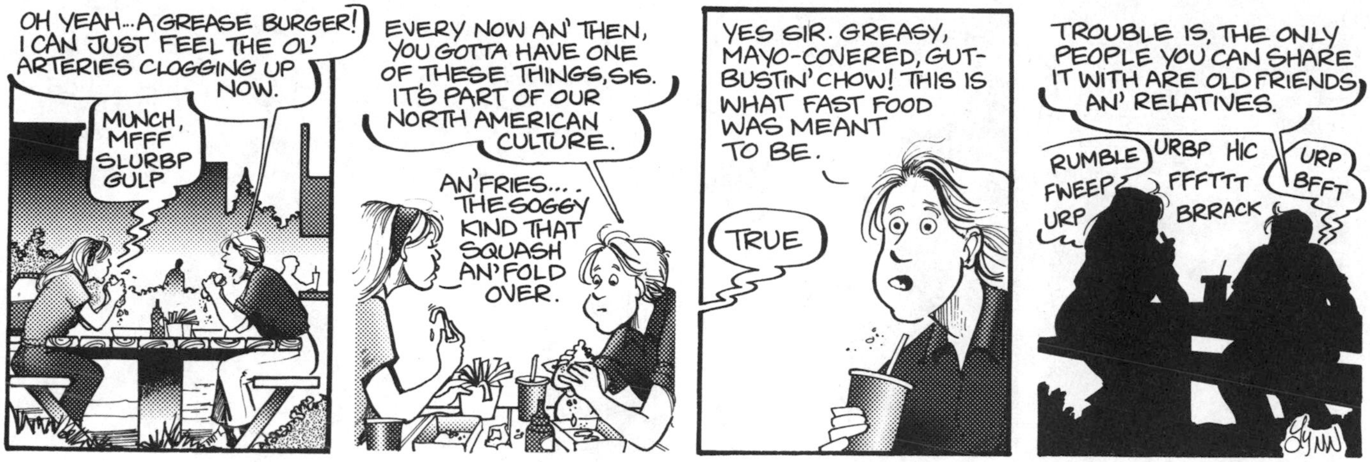
OH YEAH...A GREASE BURGER! I CAN JUST FEEL THE OL' ARTERIES CLOGGING UP NOW.
MUNCH, MFFF SLURBP GULP
EVERY NOW AN' THEN, YOU GOTTA HAVE ONE OF THESE THINGS, SIS. IT'S PART OF OUR NORTH AMERICAN CULTURE.
AN' FRIES.... THE SOGGY KIND THAT SQUASH AN' FOLD OVER.
YES SIR. GREASY, MAYO-COVERED, GUT-BUSTIN' CHOW! THIS IS WHAT FAST FOOD WAS MEANT TO BE.
TRUE
TROUBLE IS, THE ONLY PEOPLE YOU CAN SHARE IT WITH ARE OLD FRIENDS AN' RELATIVES.
RUMBLE URBP HIC
FWEEP FFFTTT
URP BRRACK
URP BFFT
Lynn

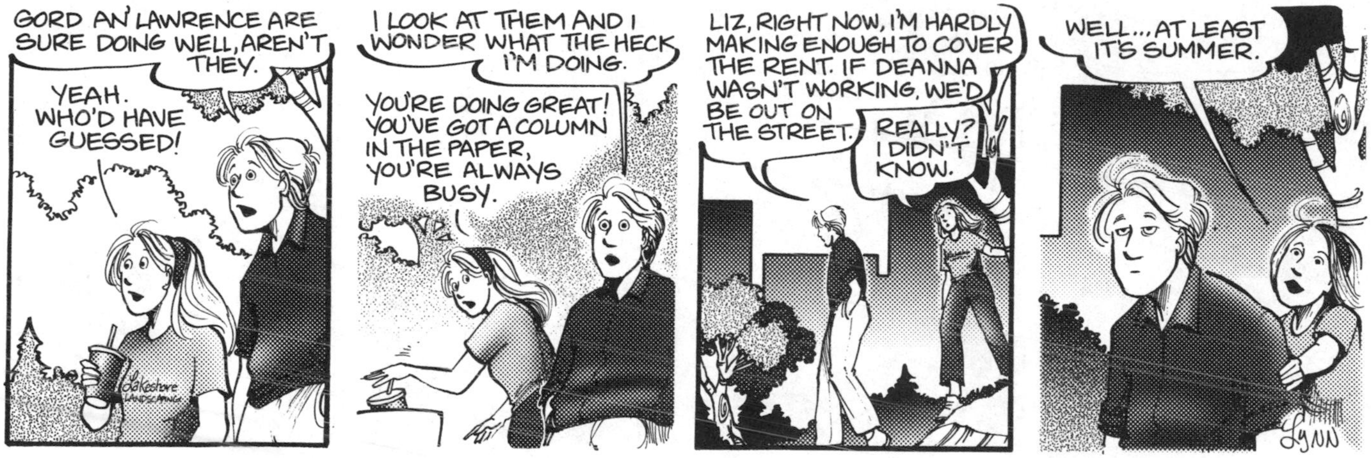
GORD AN' LAWRENCE ARE SURE DOING WELL, AREN'T THEY.
YEAH. WHO'D HAVE GUESSED!
Lakeshore LANDSCAPING
I LOOK AT THEM AND I WONDER WHAT THE HECK I'M DOING.
YOU'RE DOING GREAT! YOU'VE GOT A COLUMN IN THE PAPER, YOU'RE ALWAYS BUSY.
LIZ, RIGHT NOW, I'M HARDLY MAKING ENOUGH TO COVER THE RENT. IF DEANNA WASN'T WORKING, WE'D BE OUT ON THE STREET.
REALLY? I DIDN'T KNOW.
WELL... AT LEAST IT'S SUMMER.
Lynn

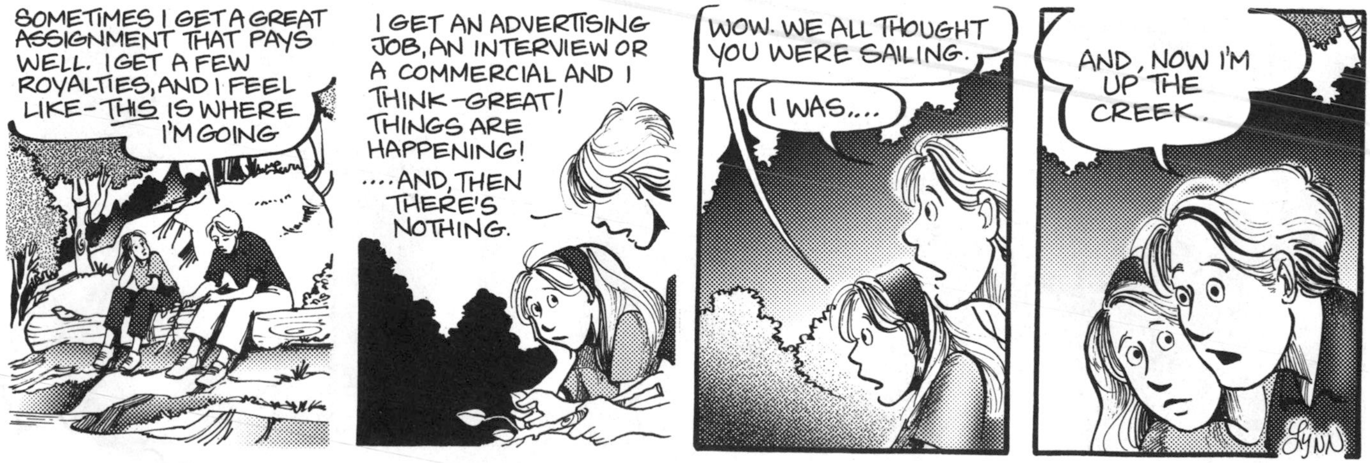
SOMETIMES I GET A GREAT ASSIGNMENT THAT PAYS WELL. I GET A FEW ROYALTIES, AND I FEEL LIKE- THIS IS WHERE I'M GOING
I GET AN ADVERTISING JOB, AN INTERVIEW OR A COMMERCIAL AND I THINK-GREAT! THINGS ARE HAPPENING!
....AND, THEN THERE'S NOTHING.
WOW. WE ALL THOUGHT YOU WERE SAILING.
I WAS,...
AND, NOW I'M UP THE CREEK.
Lynn

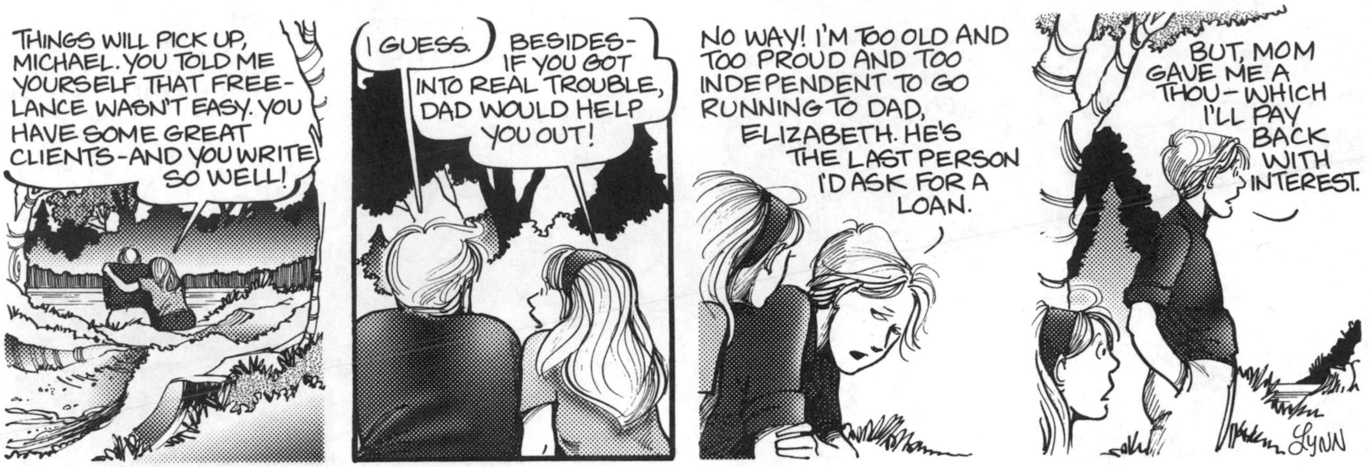
THINGS WILL PICK UP, MICHAEL. YOU TOLD ME YOURSELF THAT FREE-LANCE WASN'T EASY. YOU HAVE SOME GREAT CLIENTS-AND YOU WRITE SO WELL!
I GUESS.
BESIDES-IF YOU GOT INTO REAL TROUBLE, DAD WOULD HELP YOU OUT!
NO WAY! I'M TOO OLD AND TOO PROUD AND TOO INDEPENDENT TO GO RUNNING TO DAD, ELIZABETH. HE'S THE LAST PERSON I'D ASK FOR A LOAN.
BUT, MOM GAVE ME A THOU-WHICH I'LL PAY BACK WITH INTEREST.
LYNN

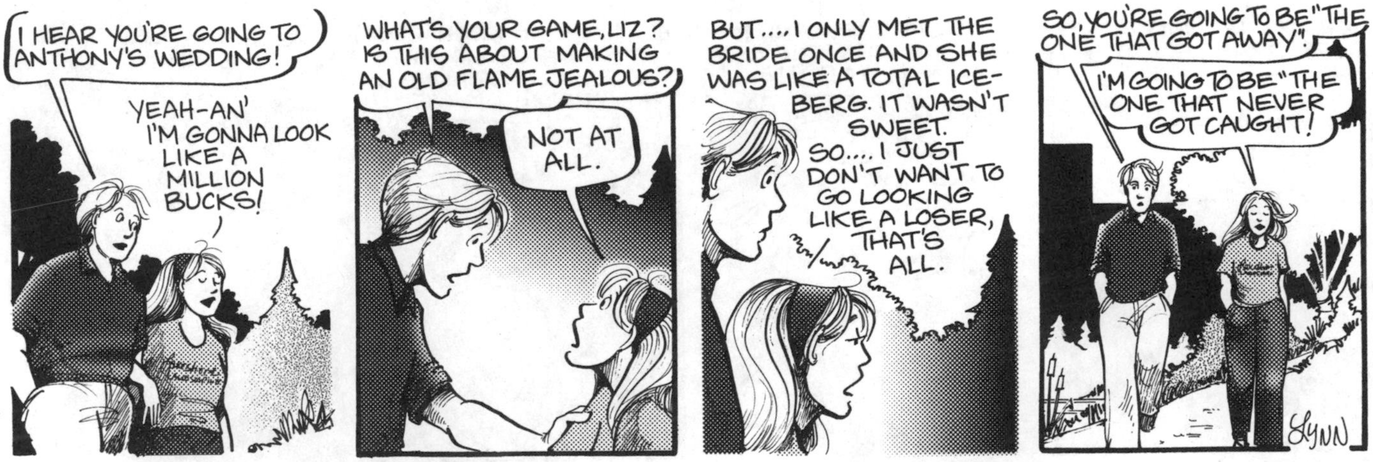
I HEAR YOU'RE GOING TO ANTHONY'S WEDDING!
YEAH-AN' I'M GONNA LOOK LIKE A MILLION BUCKS!
WHAT'S YOUR GAME, LIZ? IS THIS ABOUT MAKING AN OLD FLAME JEALOUS?
NOT AT ALL.
BUT...., I ONLY MET THE BRIDE ONCE AND SHE WAS LIKE A TOTAL ICE-BERG. IT WASN'T SWEET.
SO.... I JUST DON'T WANT TO GO LOOKING LIKE A LOSER, THAT'S ALL.
SO, YOU'RE GOING TO BE "THE ONE THAT GOT AWAY".
I'M GOING TO BE "THE ONE THAT NEVER GOT CAUGHT!
LYNN

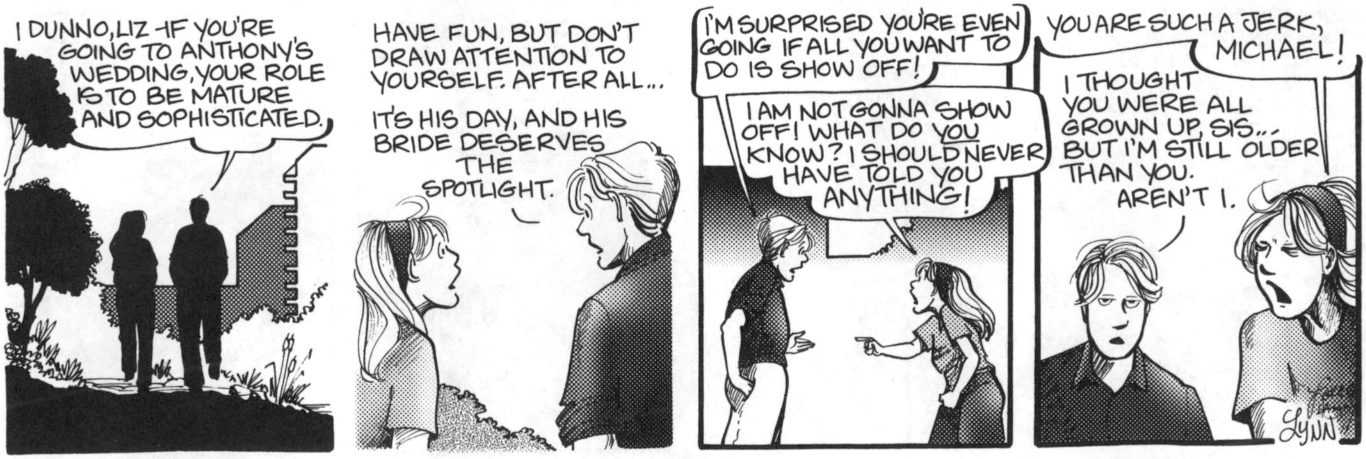
I DUNNO, LIZ-IF YOU'RE GOING TO ANTHONY'S WEDDING, YOUR ROLE IS TO BE MATURE AND SOPHISTICATED.
HAVE FUN, BUT DON'T DRAW ATTENTION TO YOURSELF. AFTER ALL...
IT'S HIS DAY, AND HIS BRIDE DESERVES THE SPOTLIGHT.
I'M SURPRISED YOU'RE EVEN GOING IF ALL YOU WANT TO DO IS SHOW OFF!
I AM NOT GONNA SHOW OFF! WHAT DO YOU KNOW? I SHOULD NEVER HAVE TOLD YOU ANYTHING!
YOU ARE SUCH A JERK, MICHAEL!
I THOUGHT YOU WERE ALL GROWN UP, SIS... BUT I'M STILL OLDER THAN YOU. AREN'T I.
LYNN

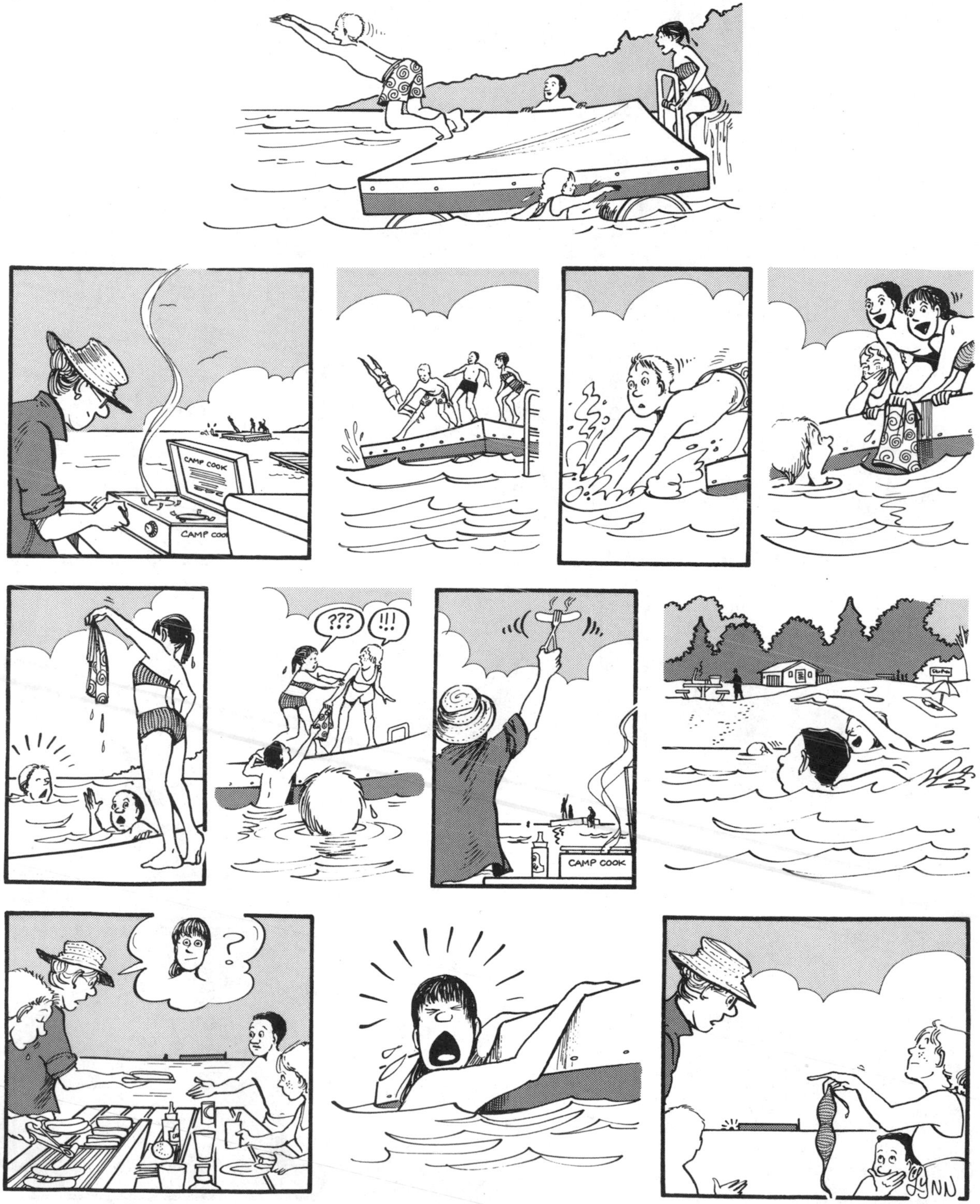
CAMP COOK
CAMP COOK
???
!!!
CAMP COOK
?
LYNN

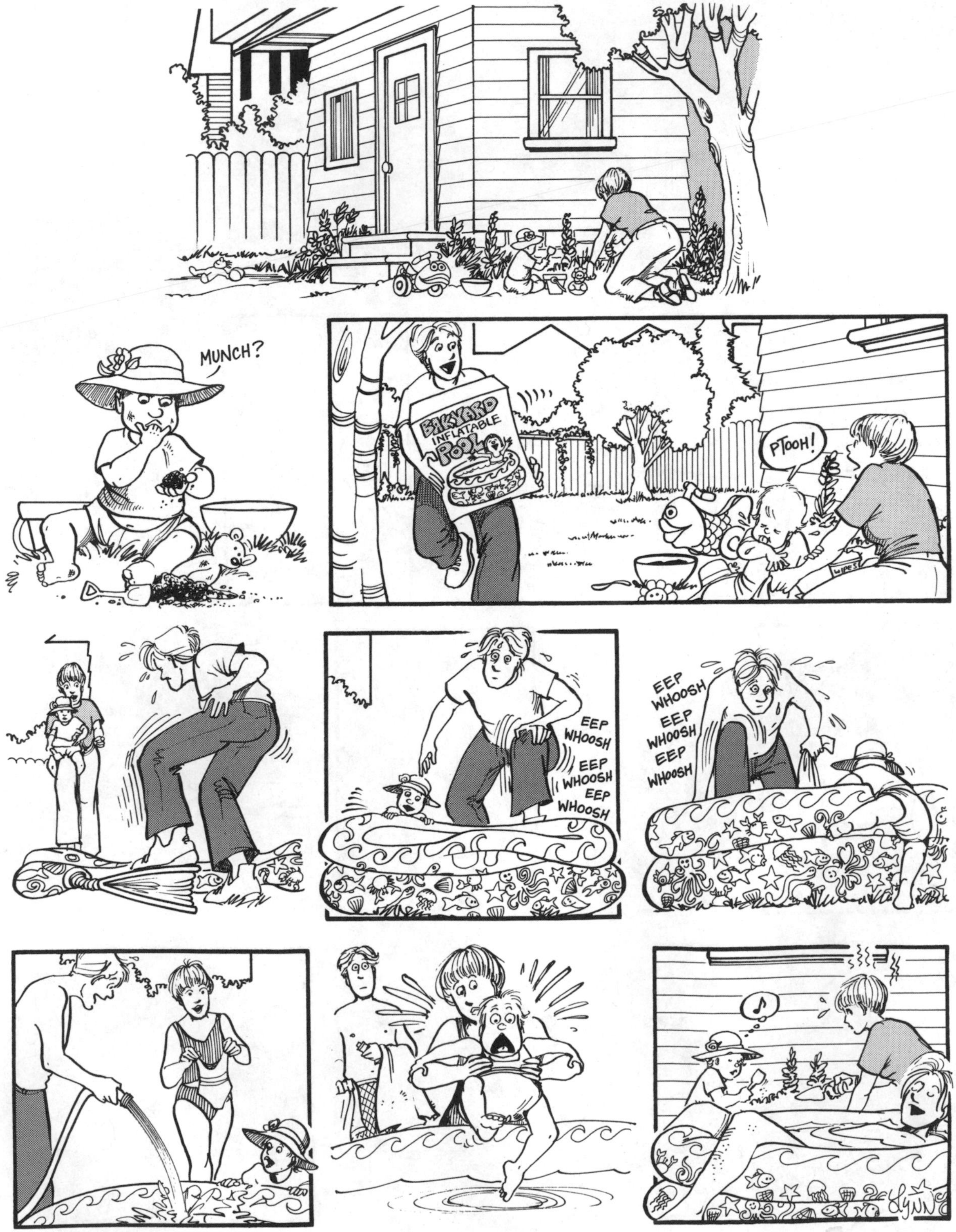
MUNCH?
BACKYARD INFLATABLE POOL
PTOOH!
EEP
WHOOSH
EEP
WHOOSH
EEP
WHOOSH
EEP
WHOOSH
EEP
WHOOSH
EEP
WHOOSH
♪
Lynn

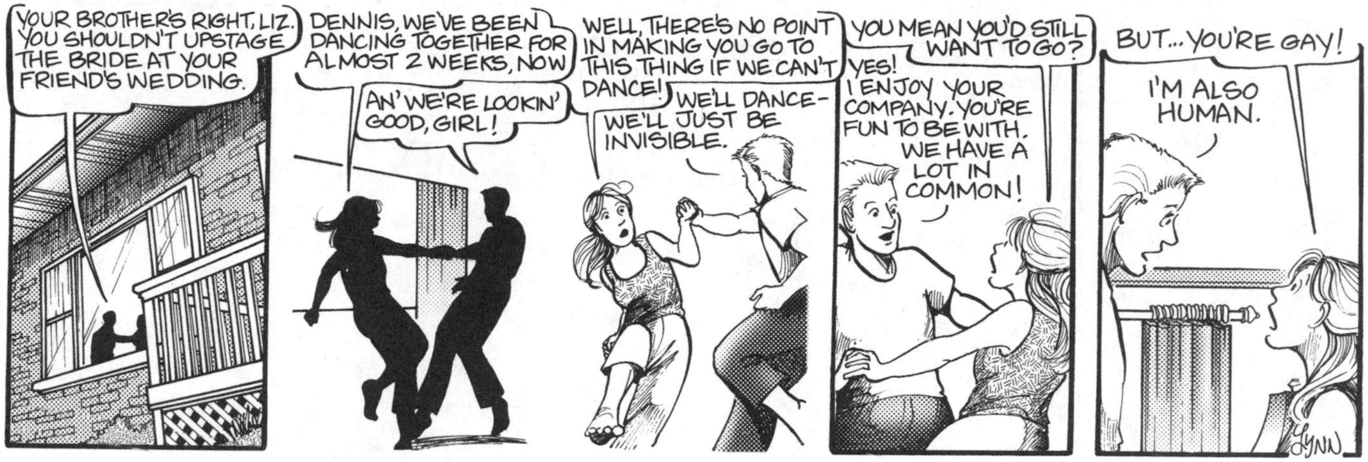
YOUR BROTHER'S RIGHT, LIZ. YOU SHOULDN'T UPSTAGE THE BRIDE AT YOUR FRIEND'S WEDDING.
DENNIS, WE'VE BEEN DANCING TOGETHER FOR ALMOST 2 WEEKS, NOW.
AN' WE'RE LOOKIN' GOOD, GIRL!
WELL, THERE'S NO POINT IN MAKING YOU GO TO THIS THING IF WE CAN'T DANCE!
WE'LL DANCE- WE'LL JUST BE INVISIBLE.
YOU MEAN YOU'D STILL WANT TO GO?
YES! I ENJOY YOUR COMPANY. YOU'RE FUN TO BE WITH. WE HAVE A LOT IN COMMON!
BUT... YOU'RE GAY!
I'M ALSO HUMAN.
LYNN

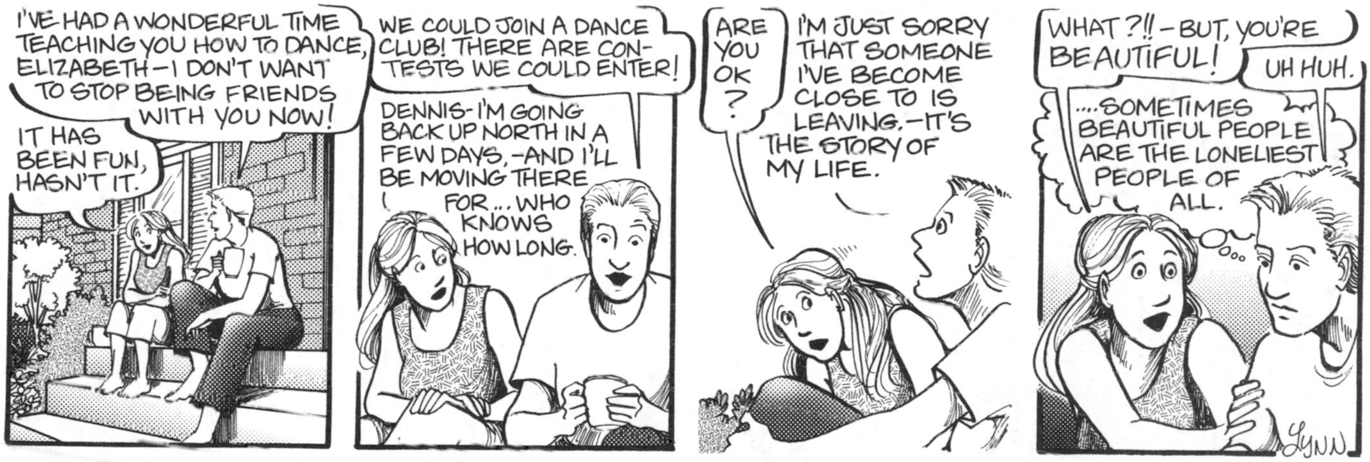
I'VE HAD A WONDERFUL TIME TEACHING YOU HOW TO DANCE, ELIZABETH — I DON'T WANT TO STOP BEING FRIENDS WITH YOU NOW!
IT HAS BEEN FUN, HASN'T IT.
WE COULD JOIN A DANCE CLUB! THERE ARE CONTESTS WE COULD ENTER!
DENNIS- I'M GOING BACK UP NORTH IN A FEW DAYS, — AND I'LL BE MOVING THERE FOR... WHO KNOWS HOW LONG.
ARE YOU OK?
I'M JUST SORRY THAT SOMEONE I'VE BECOME CLOSE TO IS LEAVING. — IT'S THE STORY OF MY LIFE.
WHAT?!! — BUT, YOU'RE BEAUTIFUL!
UH HUH.
....SOMETIMES BEAUTIFUL PEOPLE ARE THE LONELIEST PEOPLE OF ALL.
LYNN

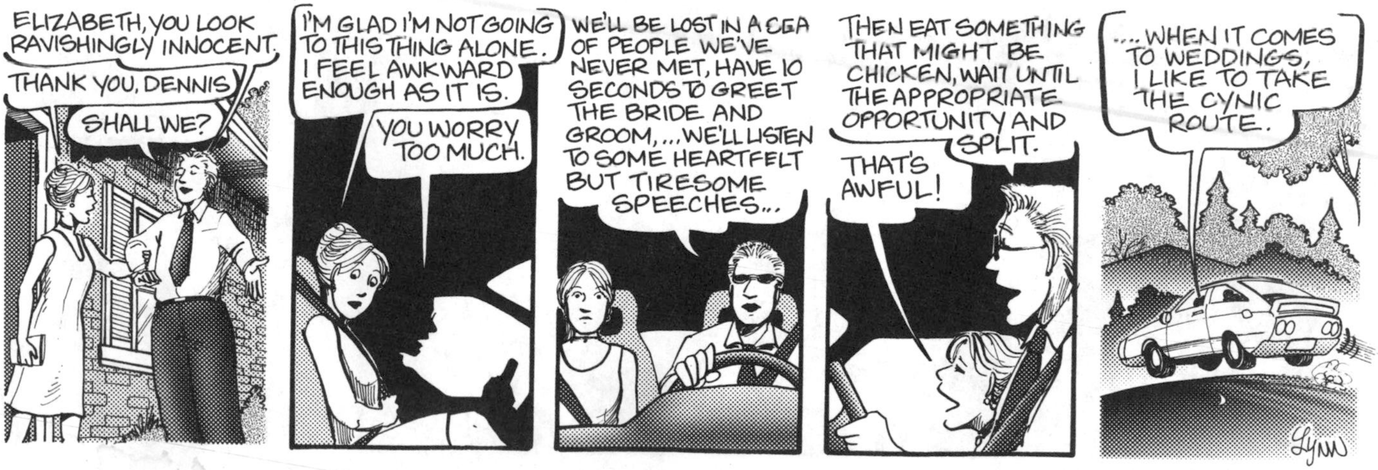
ELIZABETH, YOU LOOK RAVISHINGLY INNOCENT.
THANK YOU, DENNIS.
SHALL WE?
I'M GLAD I'M NOT GOING TO THIS THING ALONE. I FEEL AWKWARD ENOUGH AS IT IS.
YOU WORRY TOO MUCH.
WE'LL BE LOST IN A SEA OF PEOPLE WE'VE NEVER MET, HAVE 10 SECONDS TO GREET THE BRIDE AND GROOM, ... WE'LL LISTEN TO SOME HEARTFELT BUT TIRESOME SPEECHES...
THEN EAT SOMETHING THAT MIGHT BE CHICKEN, WAIT UNTIL THE APPROPRIATE OPPORTUNITY AND SPLIT.
THAT'S AWFUL!
... WHEN IT COMES TO WEDDINGS, I LIKE TO TAKE THE CYNIC ROUTE.
LYNN

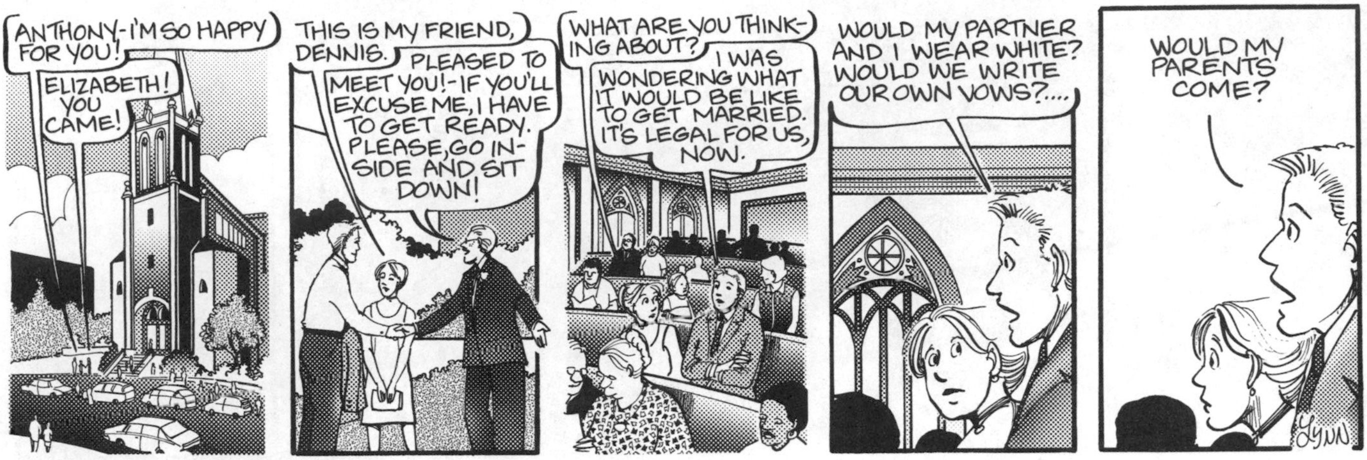
ANTHONY- I'M SO HAPPY FOR YOU!
ELIZABETH! YOU CAME!
THIS IS MY FRIEND, DENNIS.
PLEASED TO MEET YOU! - IF YOU'LL EXCUSE ME, I HAVE TO GET READY. PLEASE, GO INSIDE AND SIT DOWN!
WHAT ARE YOU THINKING ABOUT?
I WAS WONDERING WHAT IT WOULD BE LIKE TO GET MARRIED. IT'S LEGAL FOR US, NOW.
WOULD MY PARTNER AND I WEAR WHITE? WOULD WE WRITE OUR OWN VOWS?....
WOULD MY PARENTS COME?
LYNN

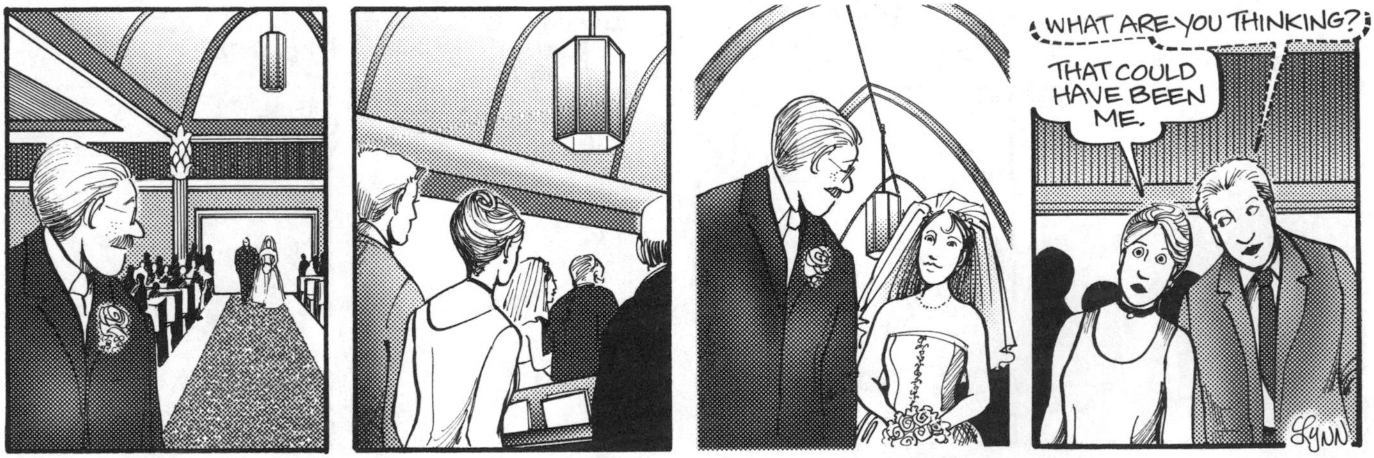
WHAT ARE YOU THINKING?
THAT COULD HAVE BEEN ME.
LYNN

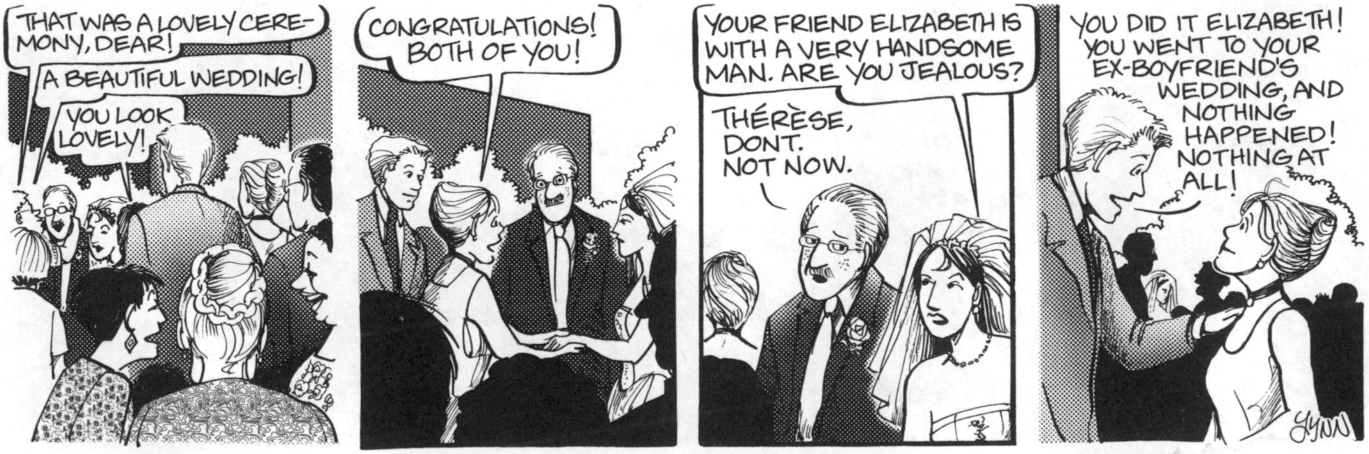
THAT WAS A LOVELY CEREMONY, DEAR!
A BEAUTIFUL WEDDING!
YOU LOOK LOVELY!
CONGRATULATIONS! BOTH OF YOU!
YOUR FRIEND ELIZABETH IS WITH A VERY HANDSOME MAN. ARE YOU JEALOUS?
THÉRÈSE, DONT. NOT NOW.
YOU DID IT ELIZABETH! YOU WENT TO YOUR EX-BOYFRIEND'S WEDDING, AND NOTHING HAPPENED! NOTHING AT ALL!
LYNN

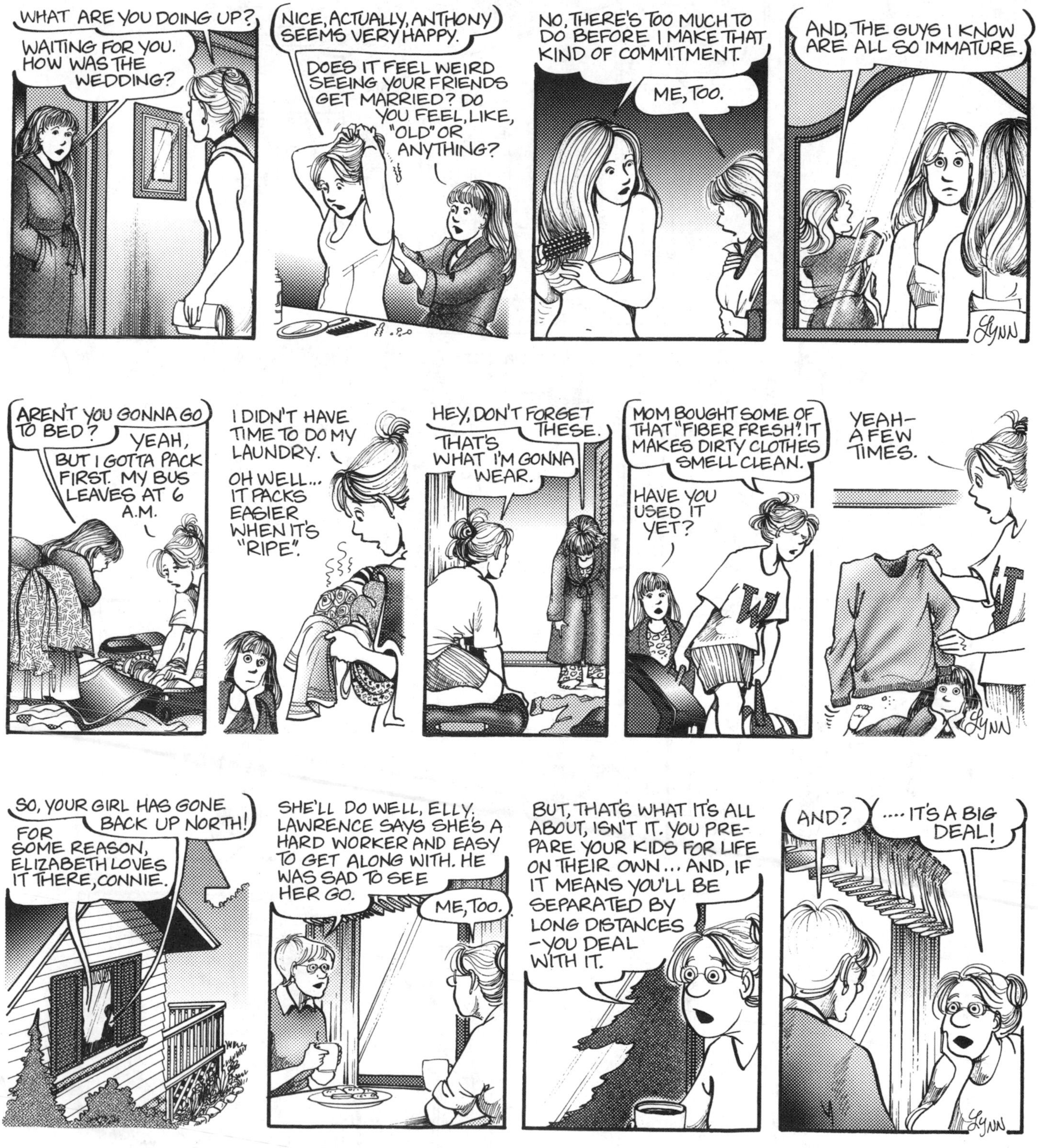
WHAT ARE YOU DOING UP?
WAITING FOR YOU. HOW WAS THE WEDDING?
NICE, ACTUALLY, ANTHONY SEEMS VERY HAPPY.
DOES IT FEEL WEIRD SEEING YOUR FRIENDS GET MARRIED? DO YOU FEEL, LIKE, "OLD" OR ANYTHING?
NO, THERE'S TOO MUCH TO DO BEFORE I MAKE THAT KIND OF COMMITMENT.
ME, TOO.
AND, THE GUYS I KNOW ARE ALL SO IMMATURE.
LYNN
AREN'T YOU GONNA GO TO BED?
YEAH, BUT I GOTTA PACK FIRST. MY BUS LEAVES AT 6 A.M.
I DIDN'T HAVE TIME TO DO MY LAUNDRY.
OH WELL... IT PACKS EASIER WHEN IT'S "RIPE".
HEY, DON'T FORGET THESE.
THAT'S WHAT I'M GONNA WEAR.
MOM BOUGHT SOME OF THAT "FIBER FRESH"! IT MAKES DIRTY CLOTHES SMELL CLEAN.
HAVE YOU USED IT YET?
YEAH– A FEW TIMES.
LYNN
SO, YOUR GIRL HAS GONE BACK UP NORTH!
FOR SOME REASON, ELIZABETH LOVES IT THERE, CONNIE.
SHE'LL DO WELL, ELLY. LAWRENCE SAYS SHE'S A HARD WORKER AND EASY TO GET ALONG WITH. HE WAS SAD TO SEE HER GO.
ME, TOO.
BUT, THAT'S WHAT IT'S ALL ABOUT, ISN'T IT. YOU PREPARE YOUR KIDS FOR LIFE ON THEIR OWN... AND, IF IT MEANS YOU'LL BE SEPARATED BY LONG DISTANCES –YOU DEAL WITH IT.
AND?
.... IT'S A BIG DEAL!
LYNN

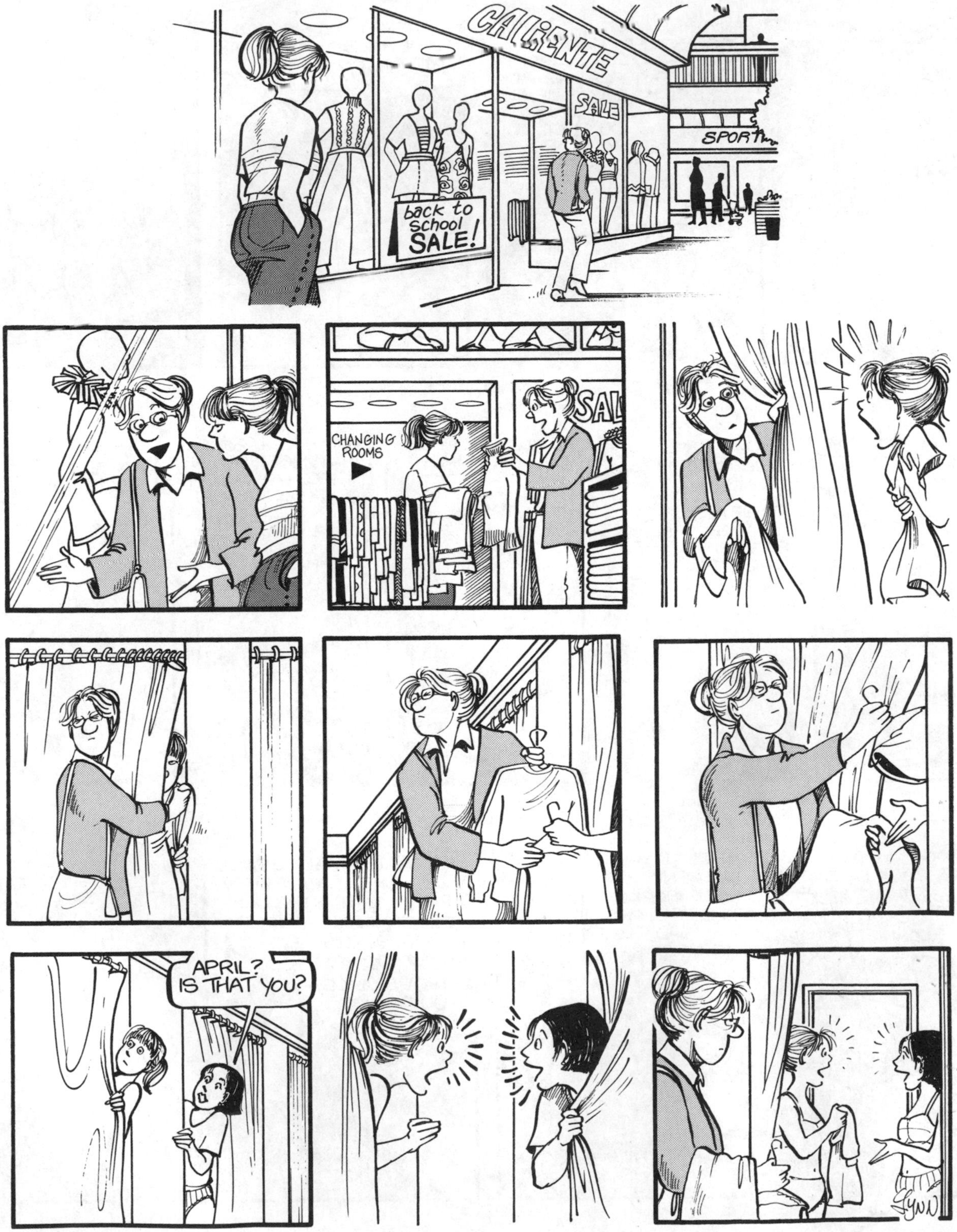
CALIENTE
SALE
SPORT
back to school SALE!
CHANGING ROOMS
SALE
APRIL? IS THAT YOU?
LYNN

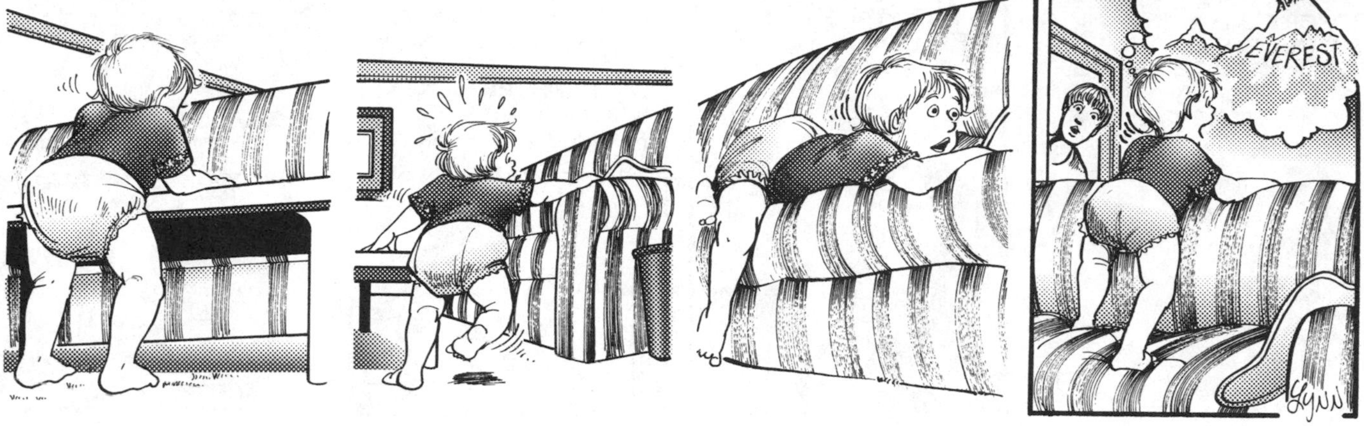
EVEREST

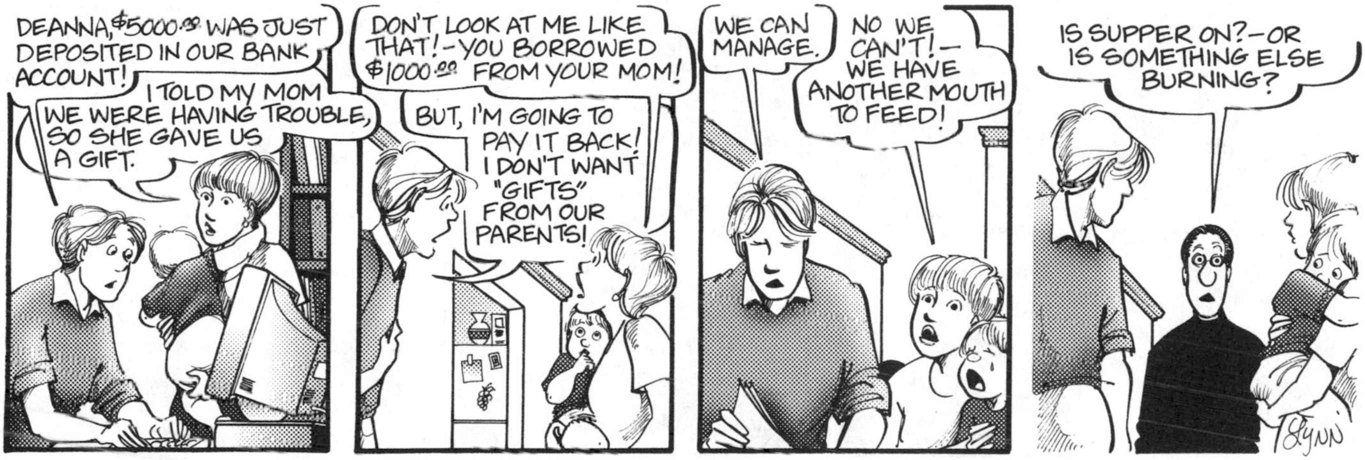
DEANNA, $5000.00 WAS JUST DEPOSITED IN OUR BANK ACCOUNT!
I TOLD MY MOM WE WERE HAVING TROUBLE, SO SHE GAVE US A GIFT.
DON'T LOOK AT ME LIKE THAT! - YOU BORROWED $1000.00 FROM YOUR MOM!
BUT, I'M GOING TO PAY IT BACK! I DON'T WANT "GIFTS" FROM OUR PARENTS!
WE CAN MANAGE.
NO WE CAN'T! - WE HAVE ANOTHER MOUTH TO FEED!
IS SUPPER ON? - OR IS SOMETHING ELSE BURNING?

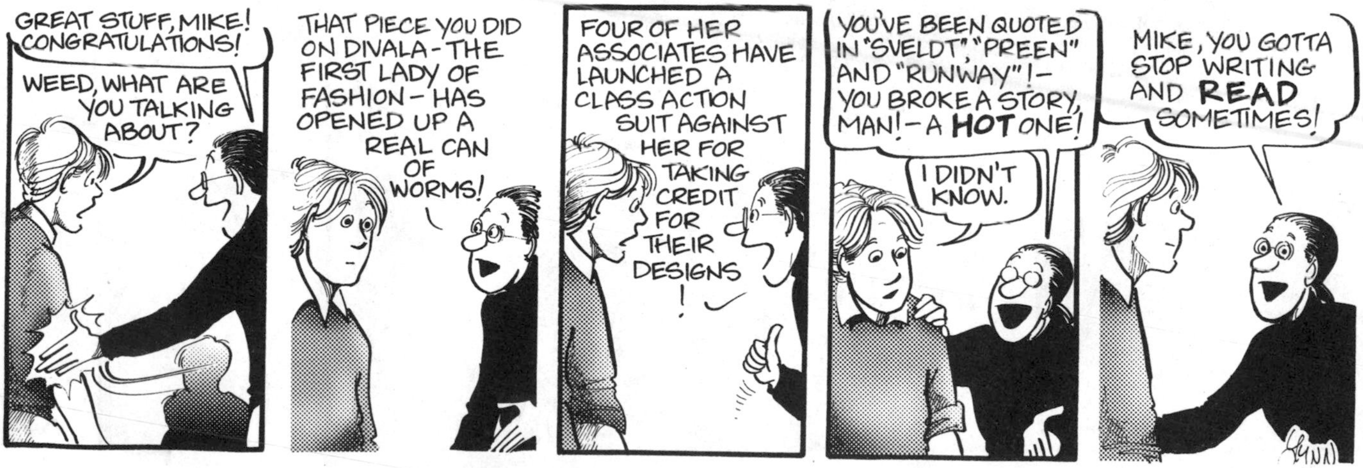
GREAT STUFF, MIKE! CONGRATULATIONS!
WEED, WHAT ARE YOU TALKING ABOUT?
THAT PIECE YOU DID ON DIVALA - THE FIRST LADY OF FASHION - HAS OPENED UP A REAL CAN OF WORMS!
FOUR OF HER ASSOCIATES HAVE LAUNCHED A CLASS ACTION SUIT AGAINST HER FOR TAKING CREDIT FOR THEIR DESIGNS!
YOU'VE BEEN QUOTED IN "SVELDT", "PREEN" AND "RUNWAY"! - YOU BROKE A STORY, MAN! - A HOT ONE!
I DIDN'T KNOW.
MIKE, YOU GOTTA STOP WRITING AND READ SOMETIMES!

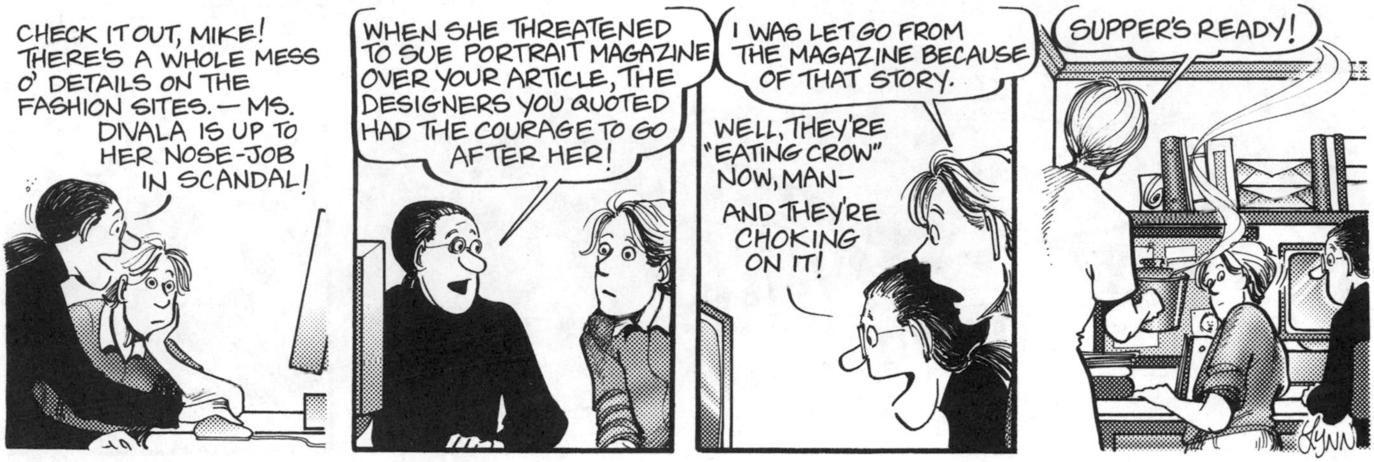
CHECK IT OUT, MIKE! THERE'S A WHOLE MESS O' DETAILS ON THE FASHION SITES. — MS. DIVALA IS UP TO HER NOSE-JOB IN SCANDAL!
WHEN SHE THREATENED TO SUE PORTRAIT MAGAZINE OVER YOUR ARTICLE, THE DESIGNERS YOU QUOTED HAD THE COURAGE TO GO AFTER HER!
I WAS LET GO FROM THE MAGAZINE BECAUSE OF THAT STORY.
WELL, THEY'RE "EATING CROW" NOW, MAN—
AND THEY'RE CHOKING ON IT!
SUPPER'S READY!
LYNN

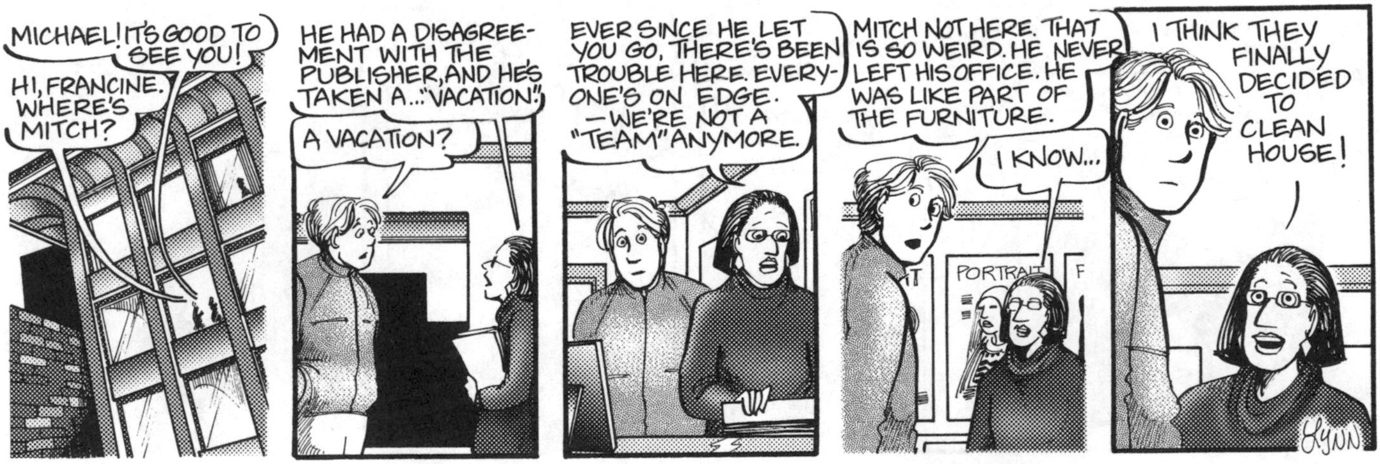
MICHAEL! IT'S GOOD TO SEE YOU!
HI, FRANCINE. WHERE'S MITCH?
HE HAD A DISAGREEMENT WITH THE PUBLISHER, AND HE'S TAKEN A..."VACATION".
A VACATION?
EVER SINCE HE LET YOU GO, THERE'S BEEN TROUBLE HERE. EVERYONE'S ON EDGE. —WE'RE NOT A "TEAM" ANYMORE.
MITCH NOT HERE. THAT IS SO WEIRD. HE NEVER LEFT HIS OFFICE. HE WAS LIKE PART OF THE FURNITURE.
I KNOW...
PORTRAIT
I THINK THEY FINALLY DECIDED TO CLEAN HOUSE!
LYNN

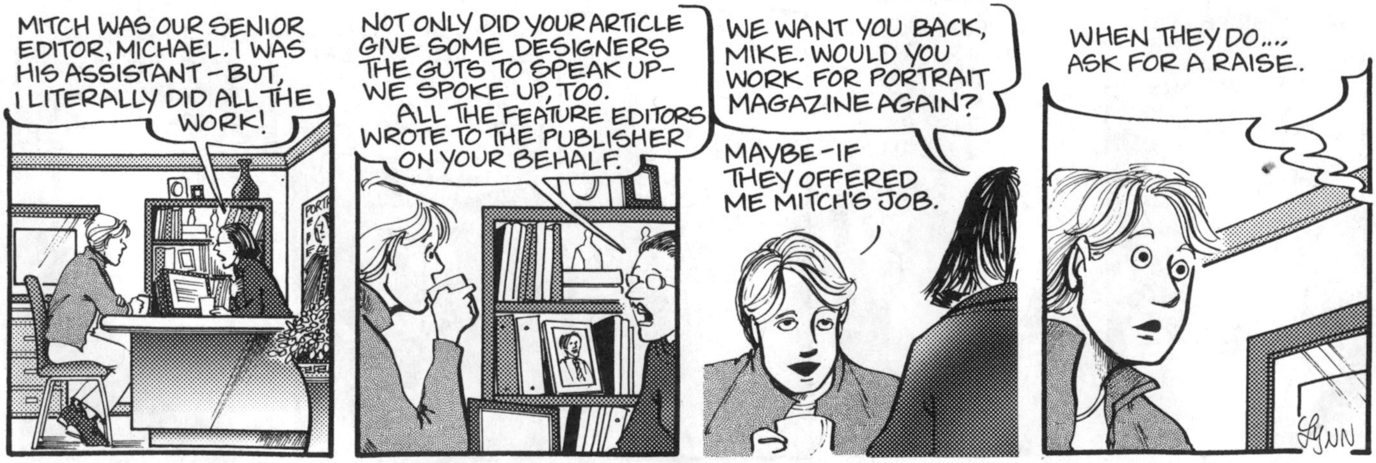
MITCH WAS OUR SENIOR EDITOR, MICHAEL. I WAS HIS ASSISTANT — BUT, I LITERALLY DID ALL THE WORK!
NOT ONLY DID YOUR ARTICLE GIVE SOME DESIGNERS THE GUTS TO SPEAK UP— WE SPOKE UP, TOO.
ALL THE FEATURE EDITORS WROTE TO THE PUBLISHER ON YOUR BEHALF.
WE WANT YOU BACK, MIKE. WOULD YOU WORK FOR PORTRAIT MAGAZINE AGAIN?
MAYBE—IF THEY OFFERED ME MITCH'S JOB.
WHEN THEY DO.... ASK FOR A RAISE.
LYNN

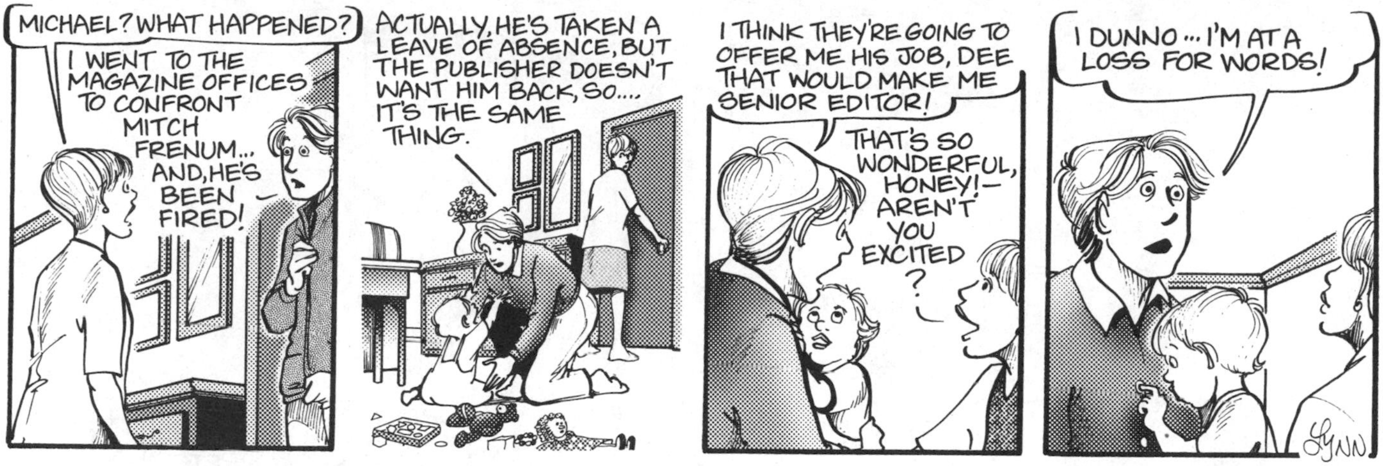
MICHAEL? WHAT HAPPENED?
I WENT TO THE MAGAZINE OFFICES TO CONFRONT MITCH FRENUM... AND, HE'S BEEN FIRED!
ACTUALLY, HE'S TAKEN A LEAVE OF ABSENCE, BUT THE PUBLISHER DOESN'T WANT HIM BACK, SO.... IT'S THE SAME THING.
I THINK THEY'RE GOING TO OFFER ME HIS JOB, DEE THAT WOULD MAKE ME SENIOR EDITOR!
THAT'S SO WONDERFUL, HONEY! — AREN'T YOU EXCITED ?
I DUNNO... I'M AT A LOSS FOR WORDS!
LYNN

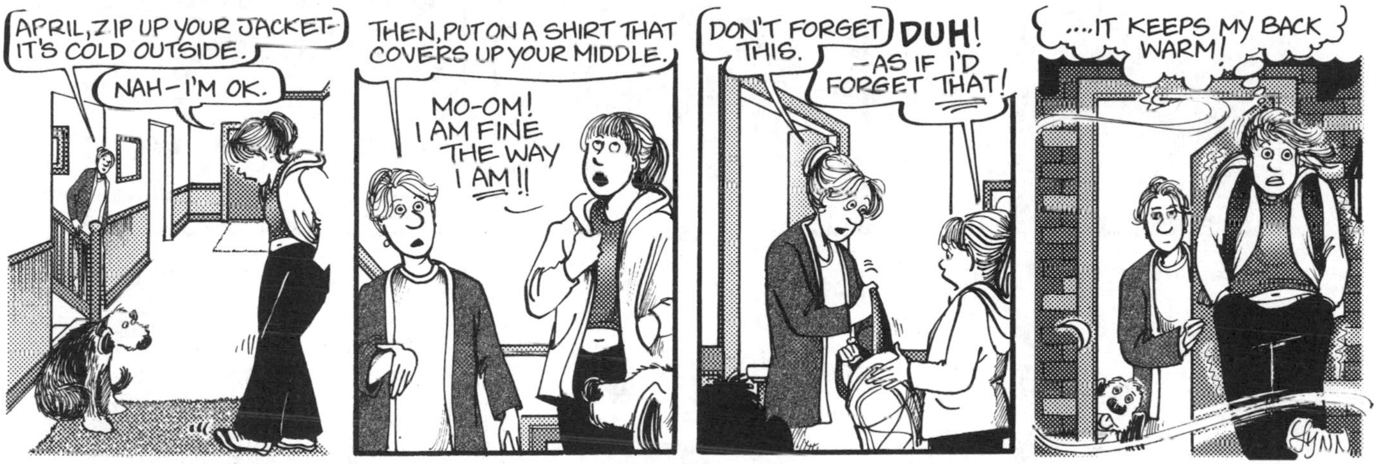
APRIL, ZIP UP YOUR JACKET - IT'S COLD OUTSIDE.
NAH - I'M OK.
THEN, PUT ON A SHIRT THAT COVERS UP YOUR MIDDLE.
MO-OM! I AM FINE THE WAY I AM!!
DON'T FORGET THIS.
DUH! - AS IF I'D FORGET THAT!
....IT KEEPS MY BACK WARM!
LYNN

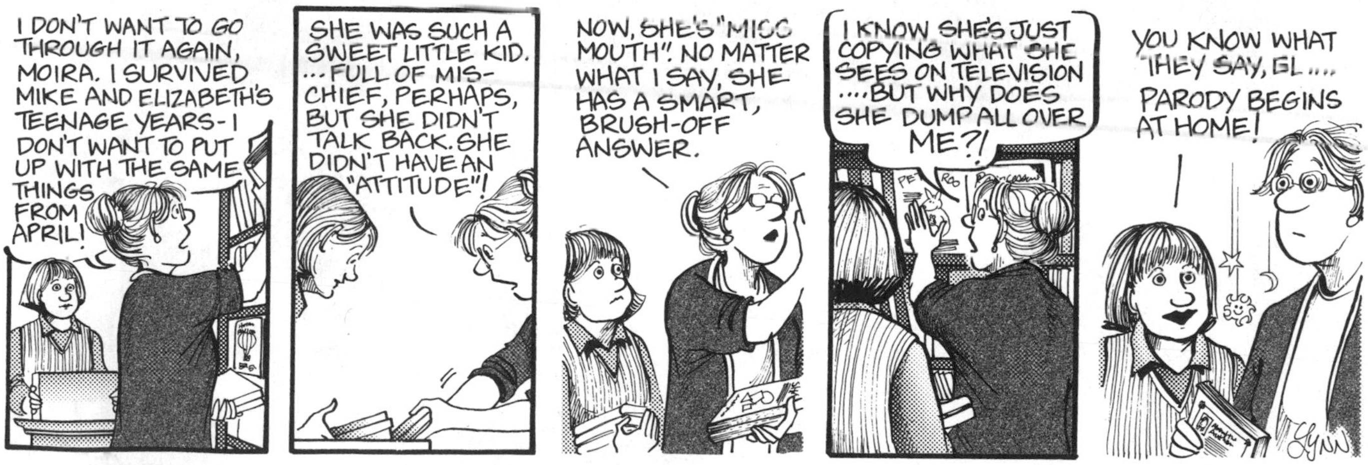
I DON'T WANT TO GO THROUGH IT AGAIN, MOIRA. I SURVIVED MIKE AND ELIZABETH'S TEENAGE YEARS - I DON'T WANT TO PUT UP WITH THE SAME THINGS FROM APRIL!
SHE WAS SUCH A SWEET LITTLE KID. ... FULL OF MIS-CHIEF, PERHAPS, BUT SHE DIDN'T TALK BACK. SHE DIDN'T HAVE AN "ATTITUDE"!
NOW, SHE'S "MISS MOUTH". NO MATTER WHAT I SAY, SHE HAS A SMART, BRUSH-OFF ANSWER.
I KNOW SHE'S JUST COPYING WHAT SHE SEES ON TELEVISION ....BUT WHY DOES SHE DUMP ALL OVER ME?!
YOU KNOW WHAT THEY SAY, EL .... PARODY BEGINS AT HOME!
LYNN

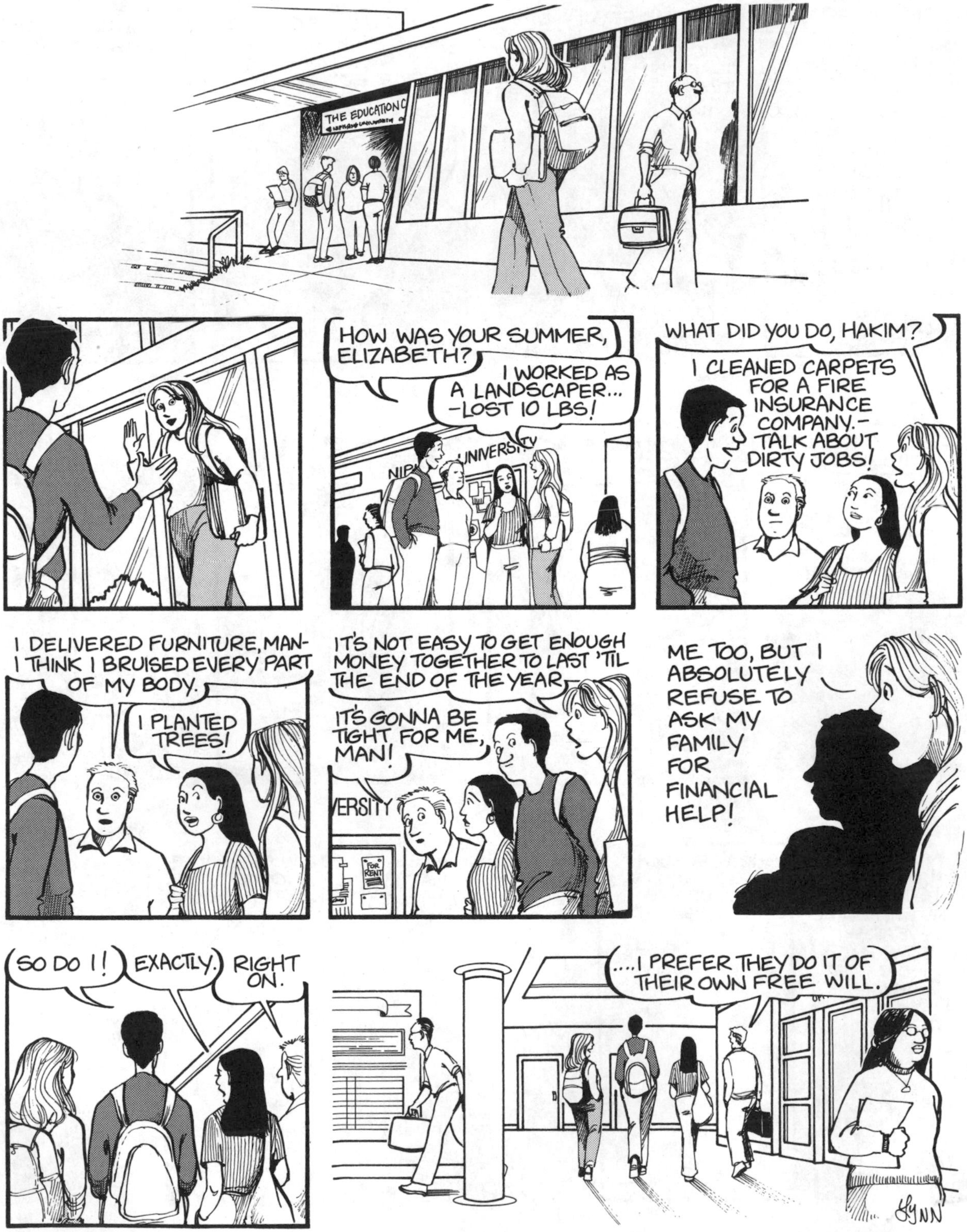
THE EDUCATION C
HOW WAS YOUR SUMMER, ELIZABETH?
I WORKED AS A LANDSCAPER... -LOST 10 LBS!
WHAT DID YOU DO, HAKIM?
I CLEANED CARPETS FOR A FIRE INSURANCE COMPANY.- TALK ABOUT DIRTY JOBS!
I DELIVERED FURNITURE, MAN- I THINK I BRUISED EVERY PART OF MY BODY.
I PLANTED TREES!
IT'S NOT EASY TO GET ENOUGH MONEY TOGETHER TO LAST 'TIL THE END OF THE YEAR.
IT'S GONNA BE TIGHT FOR ME, MAN!
FOR RENT
ME TOO, BUT I ABSOLUTELY REFUSE TO ASK MY FAMILY FOR FINANCIAL HELP!
SO DO I!
EXACTLY.
RIGHT ON.
....I PREFER THEY DO IT OF THEIR OWN FREE WILL.
LYNN

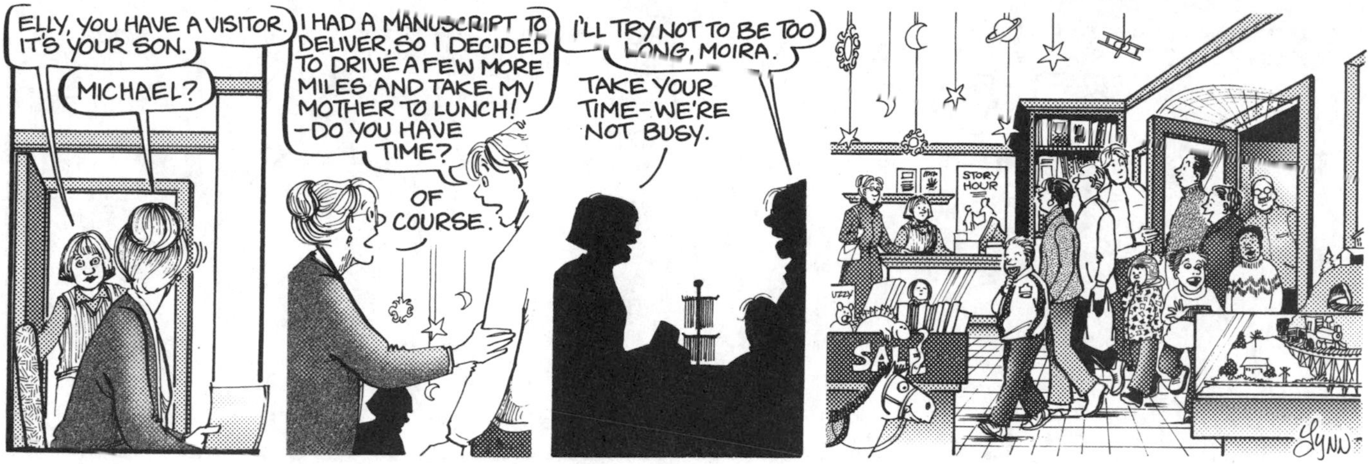
ELLY, YOU HAVE A VISITOR. IT'S YOUR SON.
MICHAEL?
I HAD A MANUSCRIPT TO DELIVER, SO I DECIDED TO DRIVE A FEW MORE MILES AND TAKE MY MOTHER TO LUNCH! —DO YOU HAVE TIME?
OF COURSE.
I'LL TRY NOT TO BE TOO LONG, MOIRA.
TAKE YOUR TIME—WE'RE NOT BUSY.
STORY HOUR
SALE
LYNN

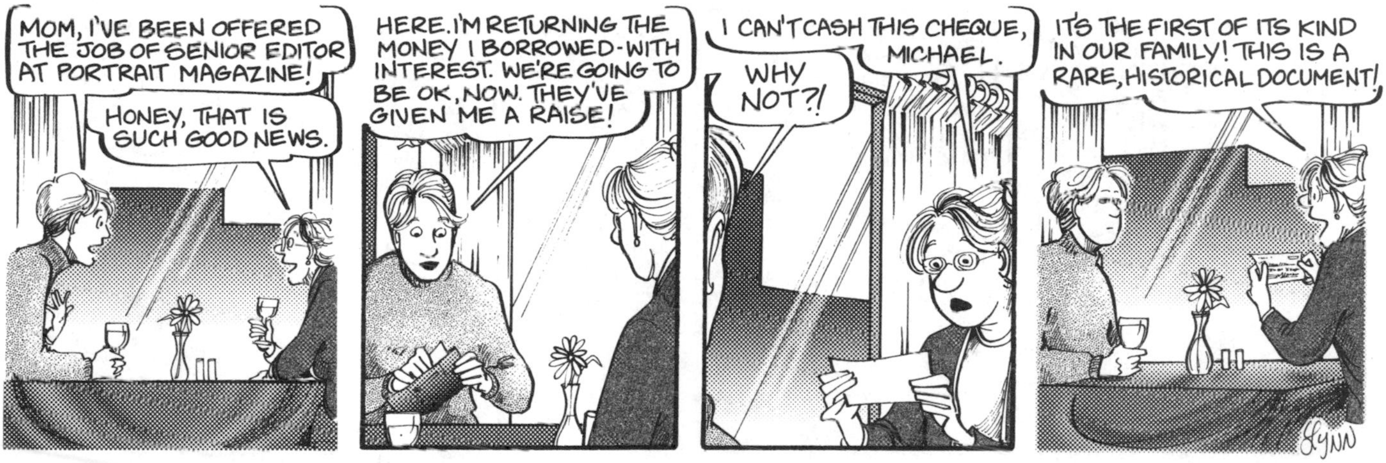
MOM, I'VE BEEN OFFERED THE JOB OF SENIOR EDITOR AT PORTRAIT MAGAZINE!
HONEY, THAT IS SUCH GOOD NEWS.
HERE. I'M RETURNING THE MONEY I BORROWED—WITH INTEREST. WE'RE GOING TO BE OK, NOW. THEY'VE GIVEN ME A RAISE!
I CAN'T CASH THIS CHEQUE, MICHAEL.
WHY NOT?!
IT'S THE FIRST OF ITS KIND IN OUR FAMILY! THIS IS A RARE, HISTORICAL DOCUMENT!
LYNN

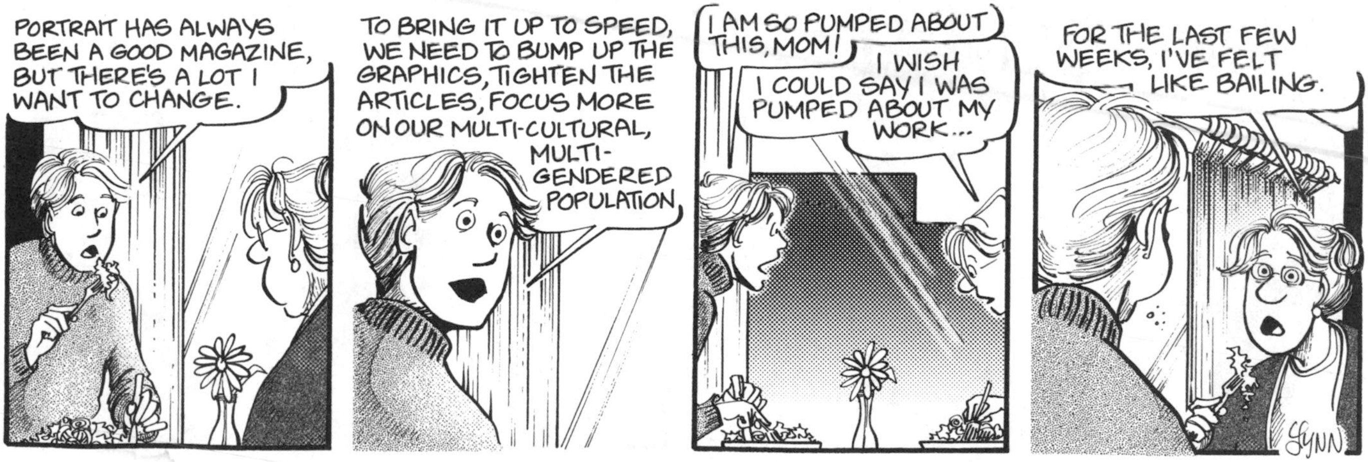
PORTRAIT HAS ALWAYS BEEN A GOOD MAGAZINE, BUT THERE'S A LOT I WANT TO CHANGE.
TO BRING IT UP TO SPEED, WE NEED TO BUMP UP THE GRAPHICS, TIGHTEN THE ARTICLES, FOCUS MORE ON OUR MULTI-CULTURAL, MULTI-GENDERED POPULATION
I AM SO PUMPED ABOUT THIS, MOM!
I WISH I COULD SAY I WAS PUMPED ABOUT MY WORK...
FOR THE LAST FEW WEEKS, I'VE FELT LIKE BAILING.
LYNN

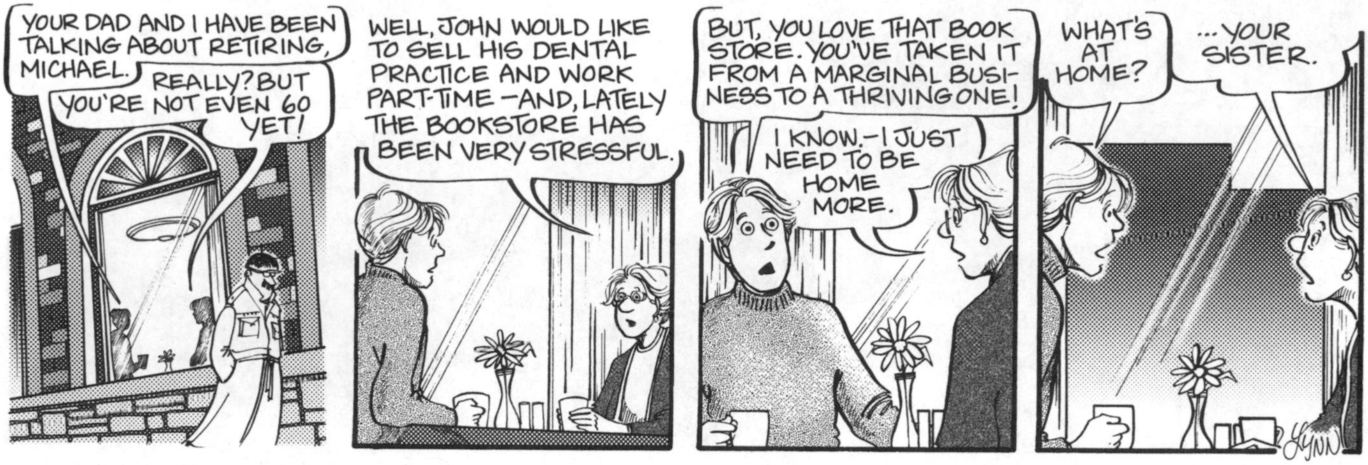
YOUR DAD AND I HAVE BEEN TALKING ABOUT RETIRING, MICHAEL.
REALLY? BUT YOU'RE NOT EVEN 60 YET!
WELL, JOHN WOULD LIKE TO SELL HIS DENTAL PRACTICE AND WORK PART-TIME —AND, LATELY THE BOOKSTORE HAS BEEN VERY STRESSFUL.
BUT, YOU LOVE THAT BOOK STORE. YOU'VE TAKEN IT FROM A MARGINAL BUSINESS TO A THRIVING ONE!
I KNOW.—I JUST NEED TO BE HOME MORE.
WHAT'S AT HOME?
...YOUR SISTER.
LYNN

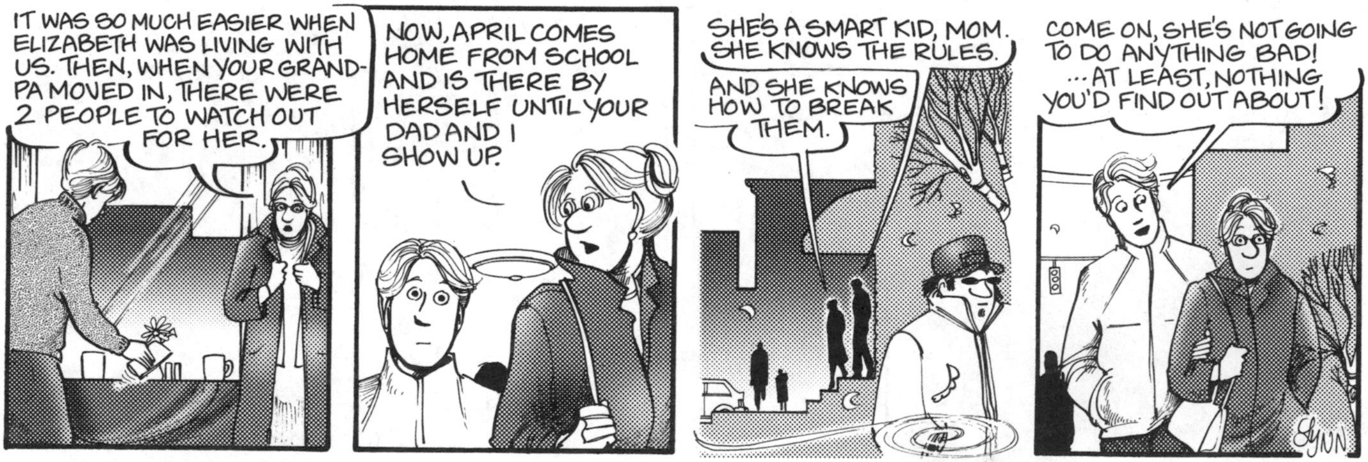
IT WAS SO MUCH EASIER WHEN ELIZABETH WAS LIVING WITH US. THEN, WHEN YOUR GRAND-PA MOVED IN, THERE WERE 2 PEOPLE TO WATCH OUT FOR HER.
NOW, APRIL COMES HOME FROM SCHOOL AND IS THERE BY HERSELF UNTIL YOUR DAD AND I SHOW UP.
SHE'S A SMART KID, MOM. SHE KNOWS THE RULES.
AND SHE KNOWS HOW TO BREAK THEM.
COME ON, SHE'S NOT GOING TO DO ANYTHING BAD! ...AT LEAST, NOTHING YOU'D FIND OUT ABOUT!
LYNN

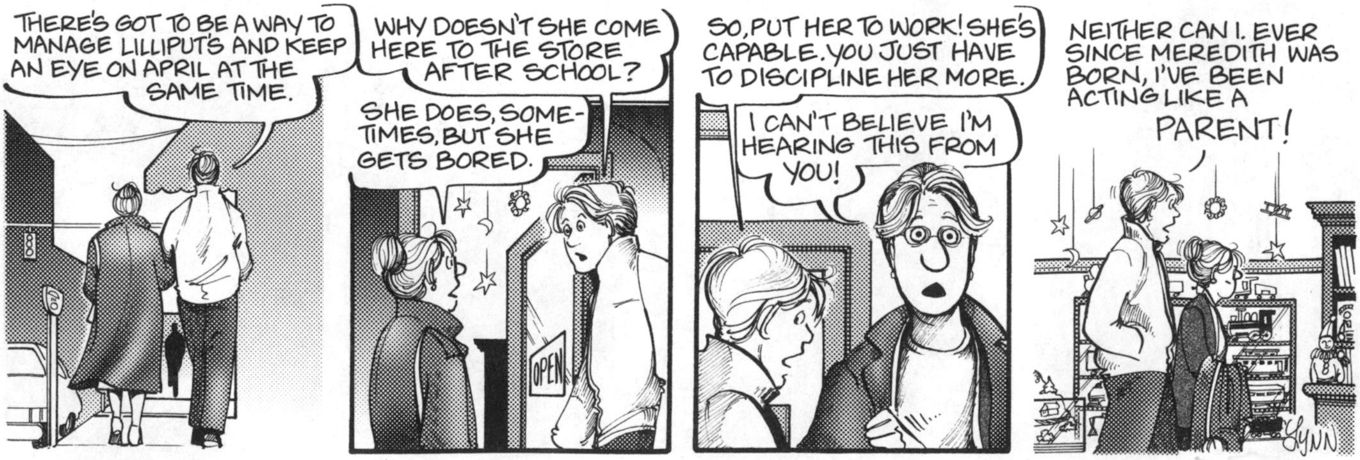
THERE'S GOT TO BE A WAY TO MANAGE LILLIPUT'S AND KEEP AN EYE ON APRIL AT THE SAME TIME.
WHY DOESN'T SHE COME HERE TO THE STORE AFTER SCHOOL?
SHE DOES, SOMETIMES, BUT SHE GETS BORED.
OPEN
SO, PUT HER TO WORK! SHE'S CAPABLE. YOU JUST HAVE TO DISCIPLINE HER MORE.
I CAN'T BELIEVE I'M HEARING THIS FROM YOU!
NEITHER CAN I. EVER SINCE MEREDITH WAS BORN, I'VE BEEN ACTING LIKE A PARENT!
LYNN

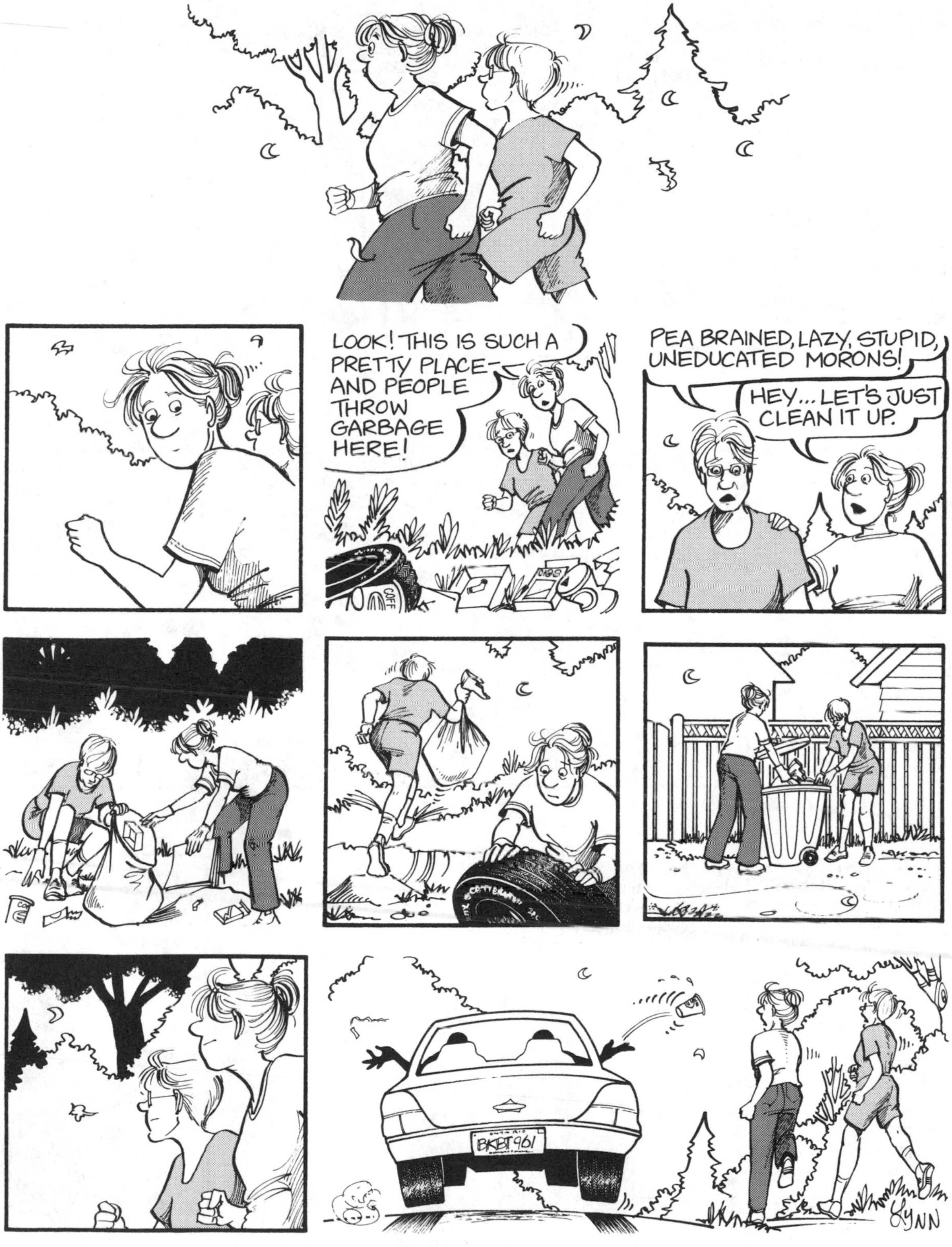
LOOK! THIS IS SUCH A PRETTY PLACE- AND PEOPLE THROW GARBAGE HERE!
PEA BRAINED, LAZY, STUPID, UNEDUCATED MORONS!
HEY... LET'S JUST CLEAN IT UP.
BKBT961
Lynn

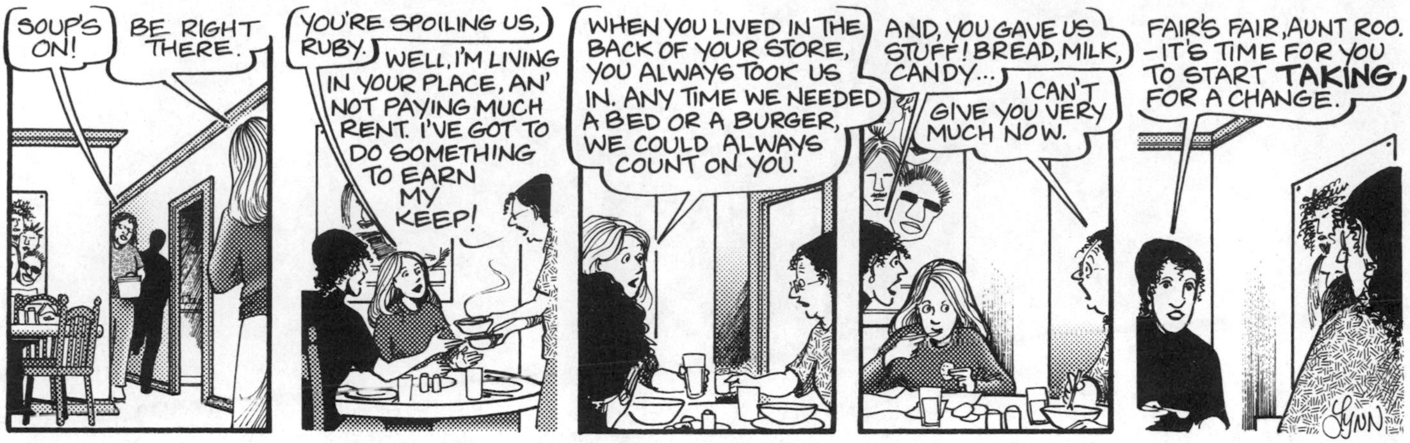
SOUP'S ON!
BE RIGHT THERE.
YOU'RE SPOILING US, RUBY.
WELL, I'M LIVING IN YOUR PLACE, AN' NOT PAYING MUCH RENT. I'VE GOT TO DO SOMETHING TO EARN MY KEEP!
WHEN YOU LIVED IN THE BACK OF YOUR STORE, YOU ALWAYS TOOK US IN. ANY TIME WE NEEDED A BED OR A BURGER, WE COULD ALWAYS COUNT ON YOU.
AND, YOU GAVE US STUFF! BREAD, MILK, CANDY...
I CAN'T GIVE YOU VERY MUCH NOW.
FAIR'S FAIR, AUNT ROO. -IT'S TIME FOR YOU TO START TAKING FOR A CHANGE.
LYNN

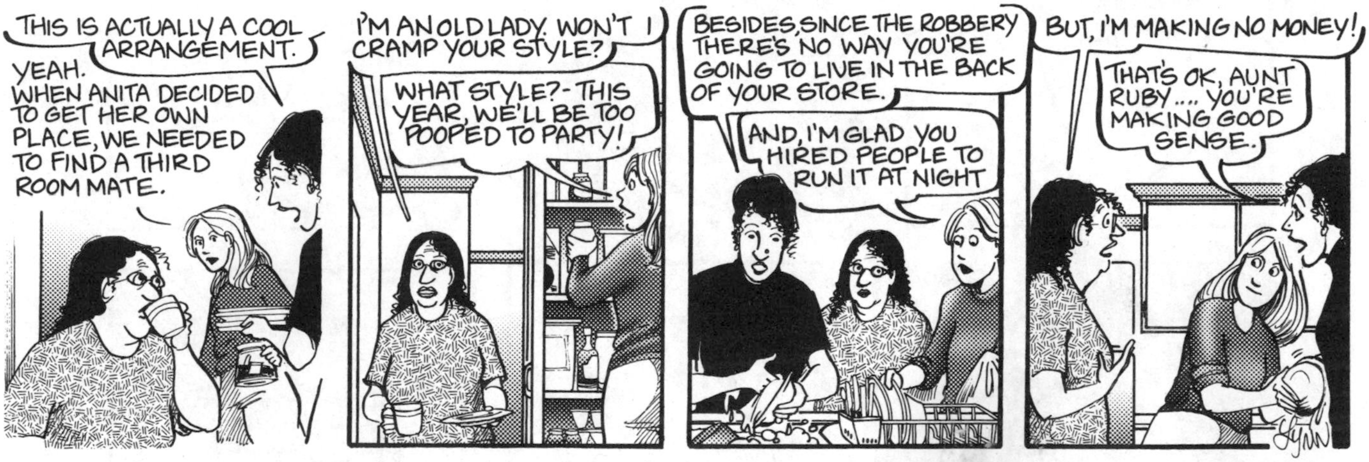
THIS IS ACTUALLY A COOL ARRANGEMENT.
YEAH. WHEN ANITA DECIDED TO GET HER OWN PLACE, WE NEEDED TO FIND A THIRD ROOM MATE.
I'M AN OLD LADY. WON'T I CRAMP YOUR STYLE?
WHAT STYLE?- THIS YEAR, WE'LL BE TOO POOPED TO PARTY!
BESIDES, SINCE THE ROBBERY THERE'S NO WAY YOU'RE GOING TO LIVE IN THE BACK OF YOUR STORE.
AND, I'M GLAD YOU HIRED PEOPLE TO RUN IT AT NIGHT
BUT, I'M MAKING NO MONEY!
THAT'S OK, AUNT RUBY.... YOU'RE MAKING GOOD SENSE.
LYNN

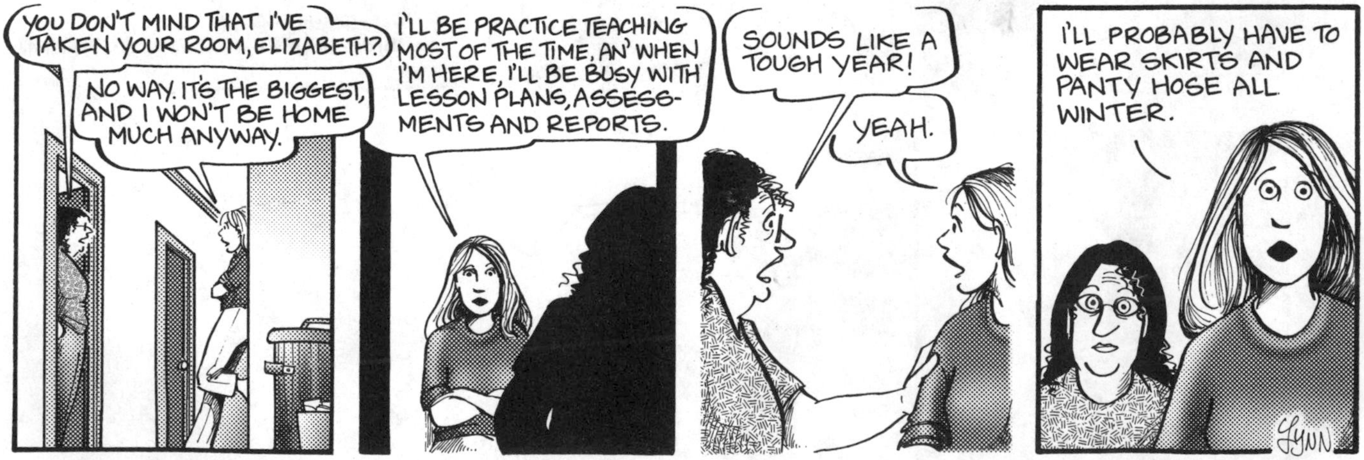
YOU DON'T MIND THAT I'VE TAKEN YOUR ROOM, ELIZABETH?
NO WAY. IT'S THE BIGGEST, AND I WON'T BE HOME MUCH ANYWAY.
I'LL BE PRACTICE TEACHING MOST OF THE TIME, AN' WHEN I'M HERE, I'LL BE BUSY WITH LESSON PLANS, ASSESS-MENTS AND REPORTS.
SOUNDS LIKE A TOUGH YEAR!
YEAH.
I'LL PROBABLY HAVE TO WEAR SKIRTS AND PANTY HOSE ALL WINTER.
LYNN

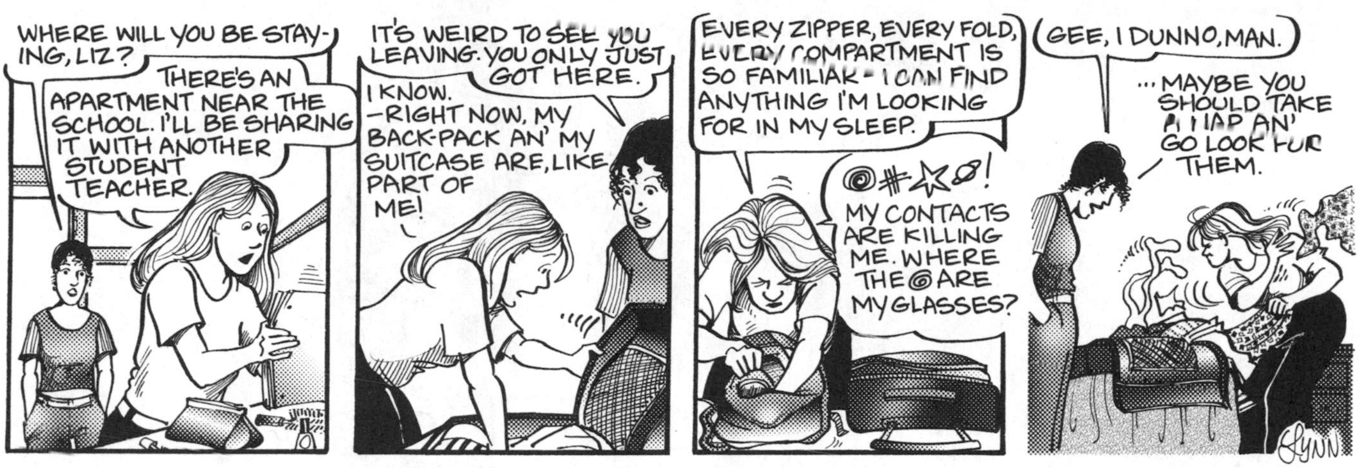
WHERE WILL YOU BE STAYING, LIZ?
THERE'S AN APARTMENT NEAR THE SCHOOL. I'LL BE SHARING IT WITH ANOTHER STUDENT TEACHER.
IT'S WEIRD TO SEE YOU LEAVING. YOU ONLY JUST GOT HERE.
I KNOW. –RIGHT NOW, MY BACK-PACK AN' MY SUITCASE ARE, LIKE PART OF ME!
EVERY ZIPPER, EVERY FOLD, EVERY COMPARTMENT IS SO FAMILIAR – I CAN FIND ANYTHING I'M LOOKING FOR IN MY SLEEP.
MY CONTACTS ARE KILLING ME. WHERE THE @ ARE MY GLASSES?
GEE, I DUNNO, MAN.
...MAYBE YOU SHOULD TAKE A MAP AN' GO LOOK FOR THEM.
LYNN

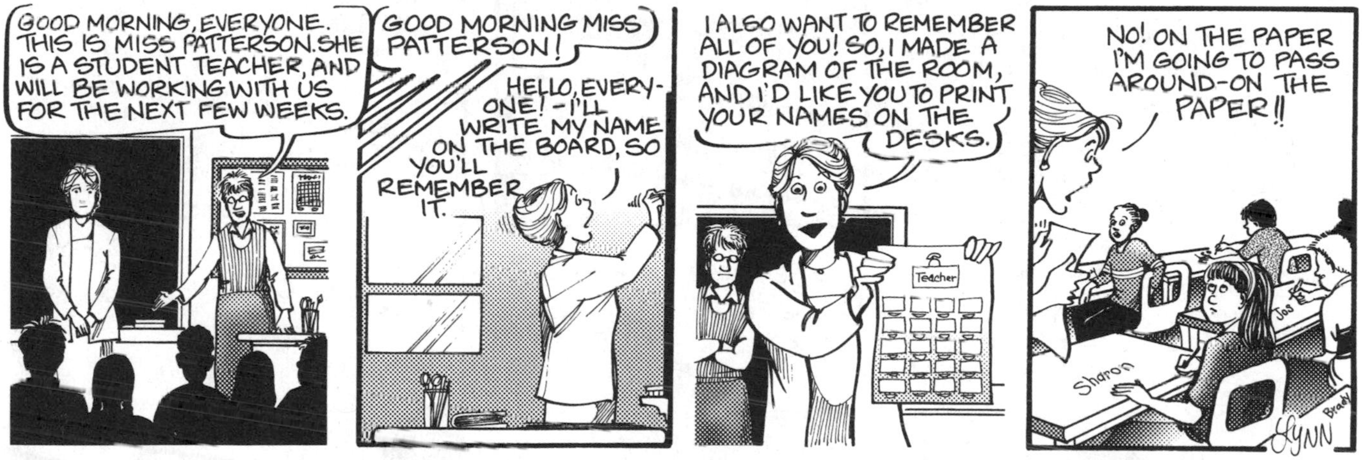
GOOD MORNING, EVERYONE. THIS IS MISS PATTERSON. SHE IS A STUDENT TEACHER, AND WILL BE WORKING WITH US FOR THE NEXT FEW WEEKS.
GOOD MORNING MISS PATTERSON!
HELLO, EVERYONE! – I'LL WRITE MY NAME ON THE BOARD, SO YOU'LL REMEMBER IT.
I ALSO WANT TO REMEMBER ALL OF YOU! SO, I MADE A DIAGRAM OF THE ROOM, AND I'D LIKE YOU TO PRINT YOUR NAMES ON THE DESKS.
Teacher
NO! ON THE PAPER I'M GOING TO PASS AROUND–ON THE PAPER!!
Joe
Sharon
LYNN

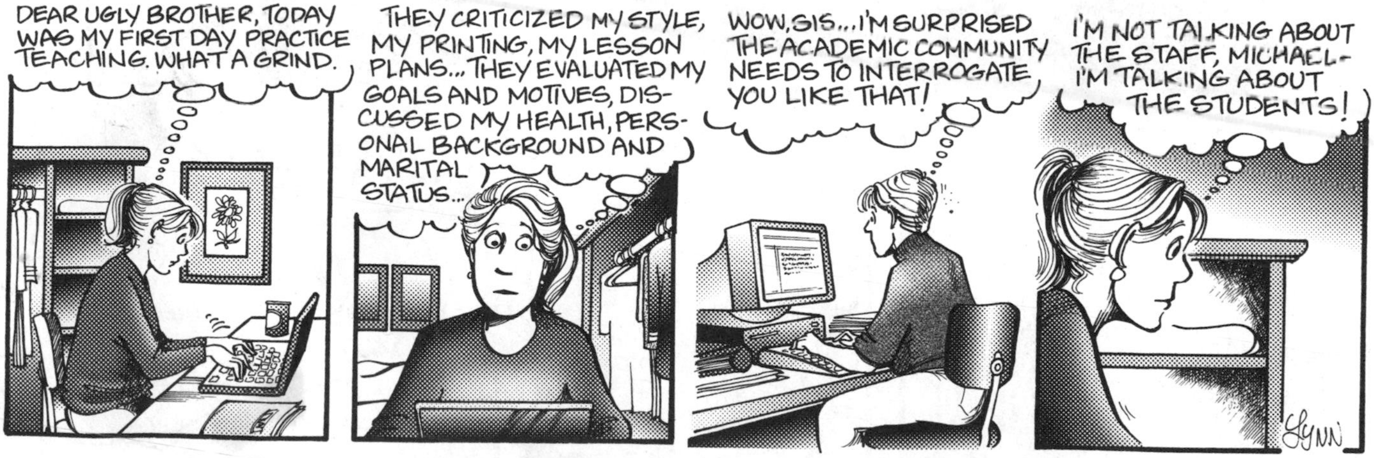
DEAR UGLY BROTHER, TODAY WAS MY FIRST DAY PRACTICE TEACHING. WHAT A GRIND.
THEY CRITICIZED MY STYLE, MY PRINTING, MY LESSON PLANS... THEY EVALUATED MY GOALS AND MOTIVES, DISCUSSED MY HEALTH, PERSONAL BACKGROUND AND MARITAL STATUS...
WOW, SIS... I'M SURPRISED THE ACADEMIC COMMUNITY NEEDS TO INTERROGATE YOU LIKE THAT!
I'M NOT TALKING ABOUT THE STAFF, MICHAEL – I'M TALKING ABOUT THE STUDENTS!
LYNN

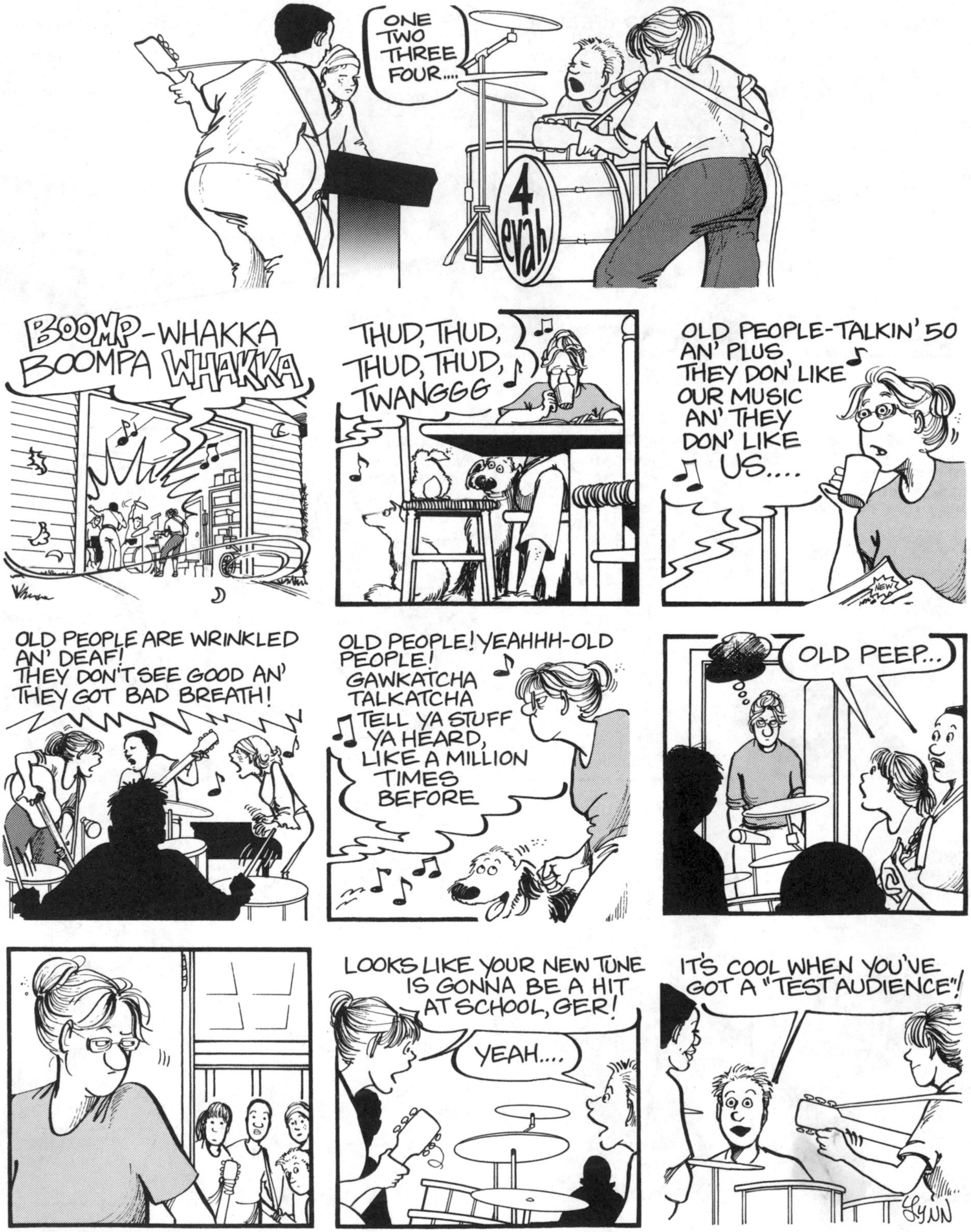
ONE TWO THREE FOUR....
4 evah
BOOMP-WHAKKA BOOMPA WHAKKA
THUD, THUD, THUD, THUD, TWANGGG
OLD PEOPLE-TALKIN' 50 AN' PLUS THEY DON' LIKE OUR MUSIC AN' THEY DON' LIKE US....
NEW
OLD PEOPLE ARE WRINKLED AN' DEAF! THEY DON'T SEE GOOD AN' THEY GOT BAD BREATH!
OLD PEOPLE! YEAHHH-OLD PEOPLE! GAWKATCHA TALKATCHA TELL YA STUFF YA HEARD, LIKE A MILLION TIMES BEFORE
OLD PEEP...
LOOKS LIKE YOUR NEW TUNE IS GONNA BE A HIT AT SCHOOL, GER!
YEAH....
IT'S COOL WHEN YOU'VE GOT A "TEST AUDIENCE"!
LYNN

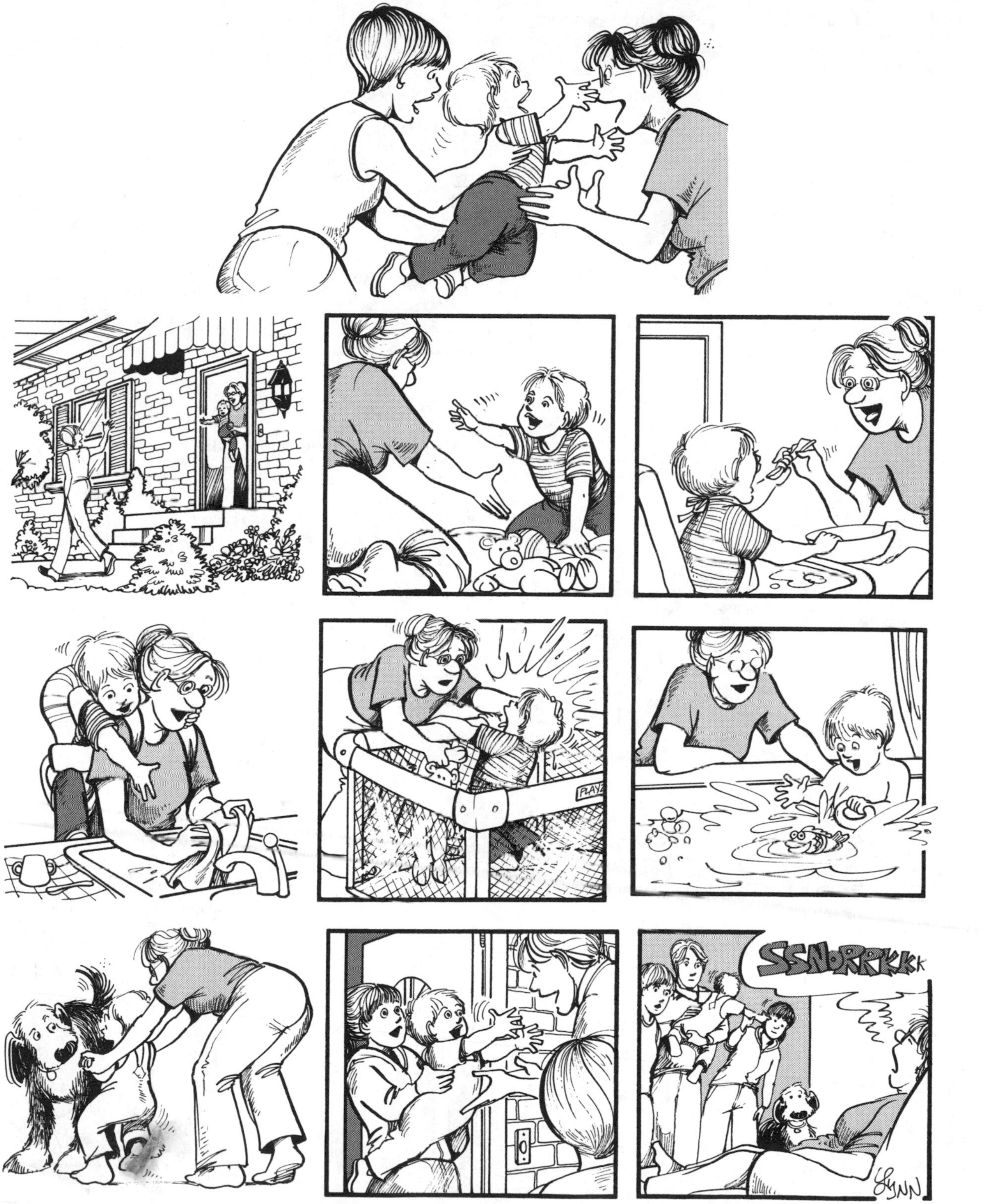
SSNORRKKK
LYNN

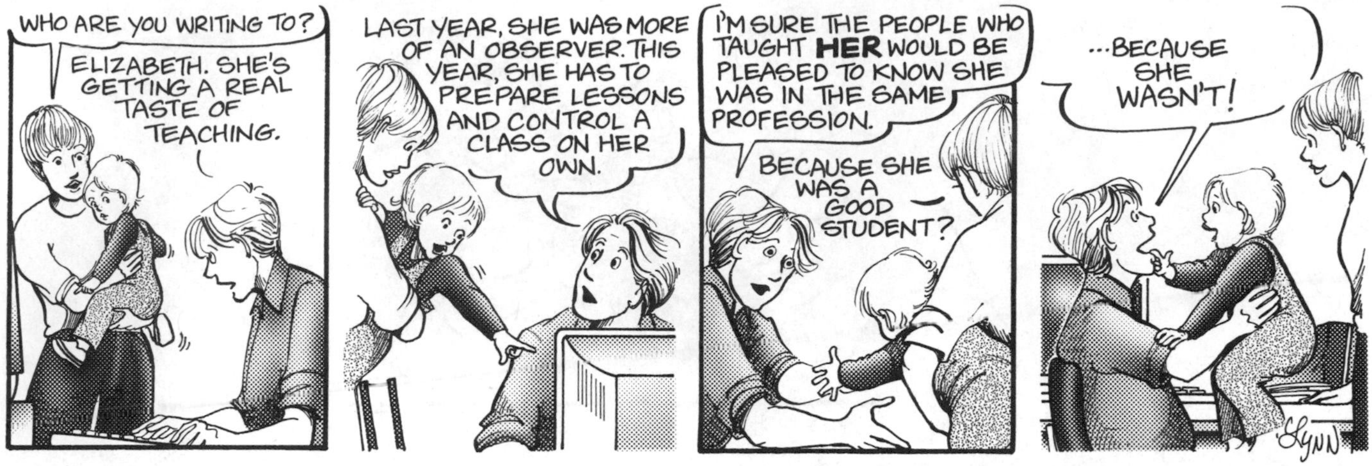
WHO ARE YOU WRITING TO?
ELIZABETH. SHE'S GETTING A REAL TASTE OF TEACHING.
LAST YEAR, SHE WAS MORE OF AN OBSERVER. THIS YEAR, SHE HAS TO PREPARE LESSONS AND CONTROL A CLASS ON HER OWN.
I'M SURE THE PEOPLE WHO TAUGHT HER WOULD BE PLEASED TO KNOW SHE WAS IN THE SAME PROFESSION.
BECAUSE SHE WAS A GOOD STUDENT?
...BECAUSE SHE WASN'T!
LYNN

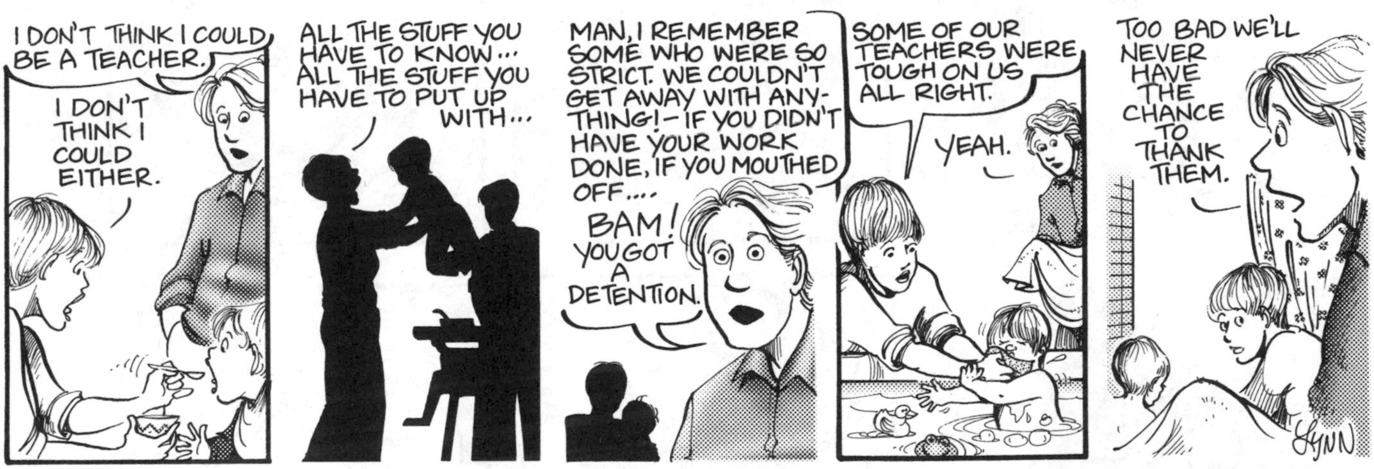
I DON'T THINK I COULD BE A TEACHER.
I DON'T THINK I COULD EITHER.
ALL THE STUFF YOU HAVE TO KNOW... ALL THE STUFF YOU HAVE TO PUT UP WITH...
MAN, I REMEMBER SOME WHO WERE SO STRICT. WE COULDN'T GET AWAY WITH ANY-THING! - IF YOU DIDN'T HAVE YOUR WORK DONE, IF YOU MOUTHED OFF....
BAM! YOU GOT A DETENTION.
SOME OF OUR TEACHERS WERE TOUGH ON US ALL RIGHT.
YEAH.
TOO BAD WE'LL NEVER HAVE THE CHANCE TO THANK THEM.
LYNN

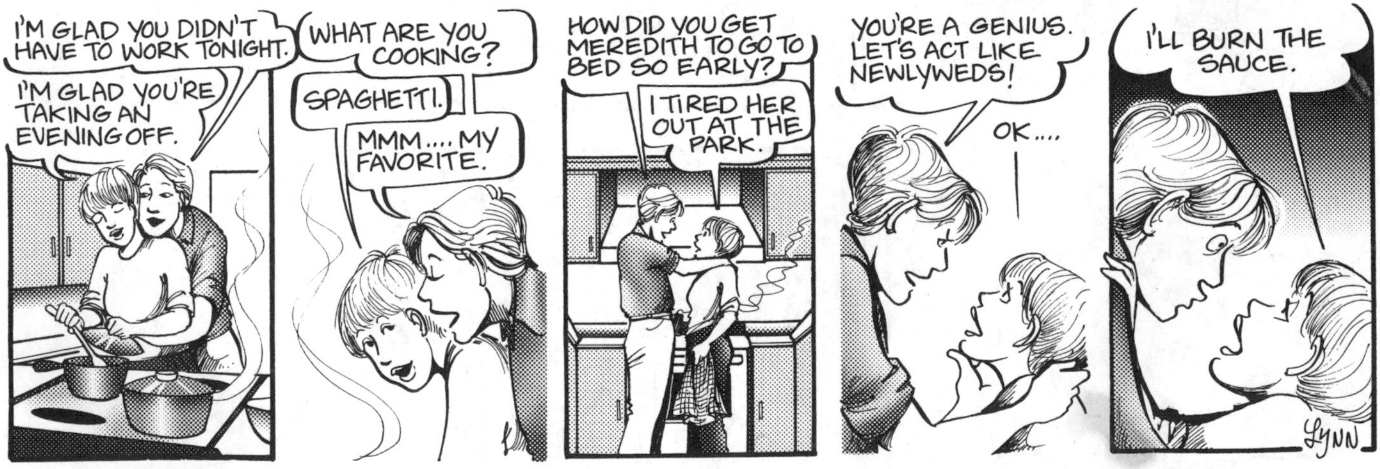
I'M GLAD YOU DIDN'T HAVE TO WORK TONIGHT.
I'M GLAD YOU'RE TAKING AN EVENING OFF.
WHAT ARE YOU COOKING?
SPAGHETTI.
MMM.... MY FAVORITE.
HOW DID YOU GET MEREDITH TO GO TO BED SO EARLY?
I TIRED HER OUT AT THE PARK.
YOU'RE A GENIUS. LET'S ACT LIKE NEWLYWEDS!
OK....
I'LL BURN THE SAUCE.
LYNN

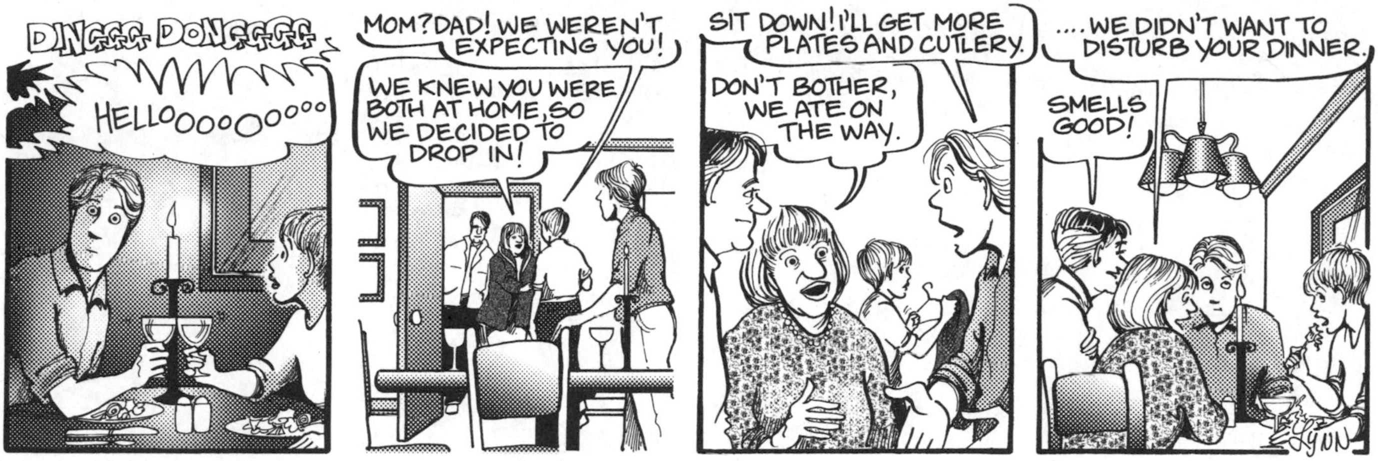
DINGGG DONGGGG
HELLOoooOoooo
MOM? DAD! WE WEREN'T EXPECTING YOU!
WE KNEW YOU WERE BOTH AT HOME, SO WE DECIDED TO DROP IN!
SIT DOWN! I'LL GET MORE PLATES AND CUTLERY.
DON'T BOTHER, WE ATE ON THE WAY.
....WE DIDN'T WANT TO DISTURB YOUR DINNER.
SMELLS GOOD!
LYNN

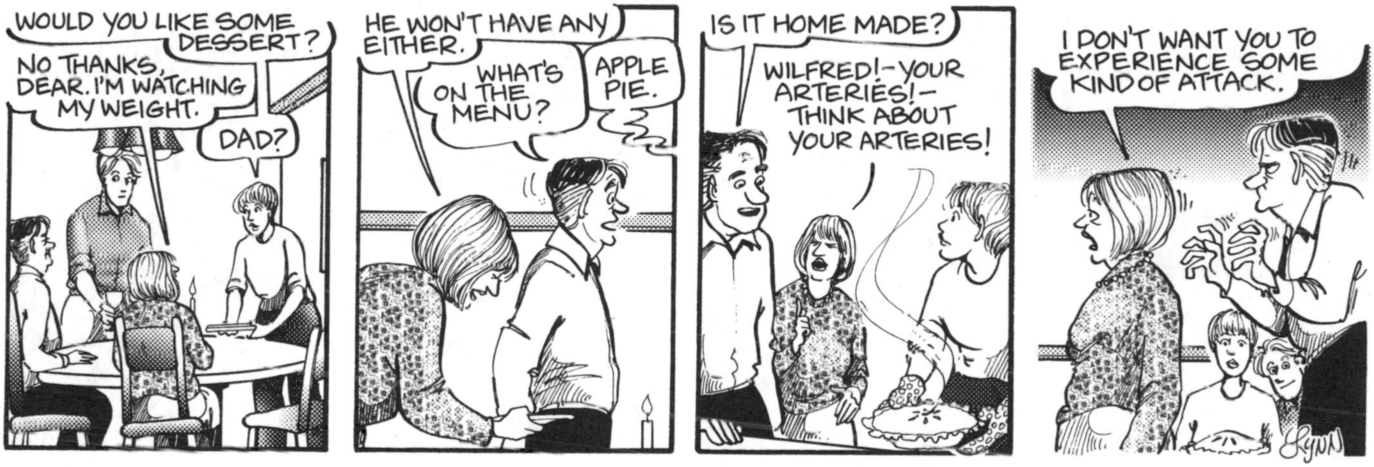
WOULD YOU LIKE SOME DESSERT?
NO THANKS, DEAR. I'M WATCHING MY WEIGHT.
DAD?
HE WON'T HAVE ANY EITHER.
WHAT'S ON THE MENU?
APPLE PIE.
IS IT HOME MADE?
WILFRED!-YOUR ARTERIES!-THINK ABOUT YOUR ARTERIES!
I DON'T WANT YOU TO EXPERIENCE SOME KIND OF ATTACK.
LYNN

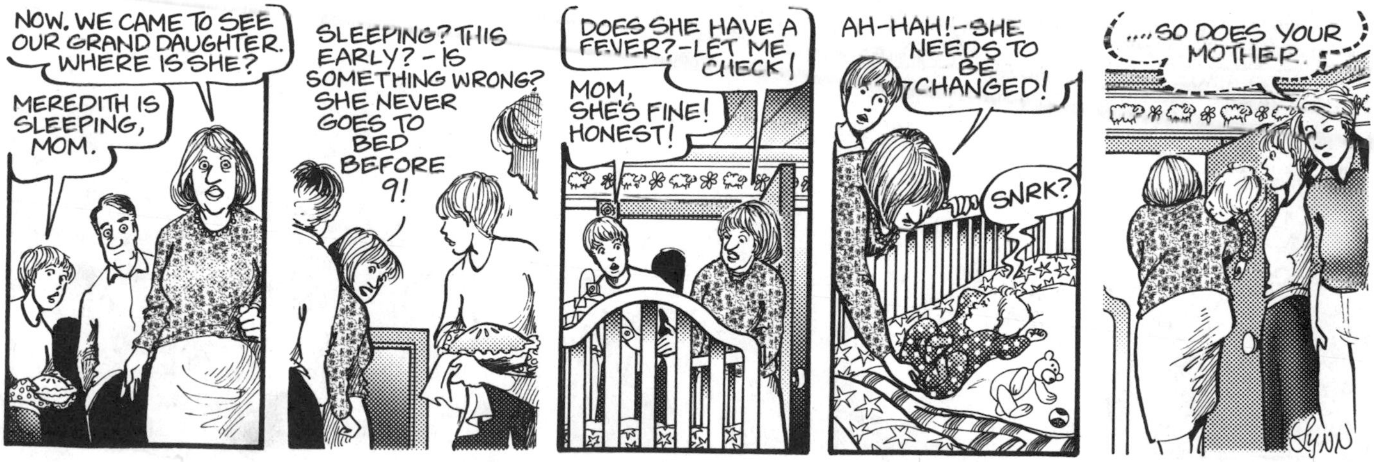
NOW. WE CAME TO SEE OUR GRAND DAUGHTER. WHERE IS SHE?
MEREDITH IS SLEEPING, MOM.
SLEEPING? THIS EARLY? - IS SOMETHING WRONG? SHE NEVER GOES TO BED BEFORE 9!
DOES SHE HAVE A FEVER?-LET ME CHECK!
MOM, SHE'S FINE! HONEST!
AH-HAH!-SHE NEEDS TO BE CHANGED!
SNRK?
....SO DOES YOUR MOTHER.
LYNN

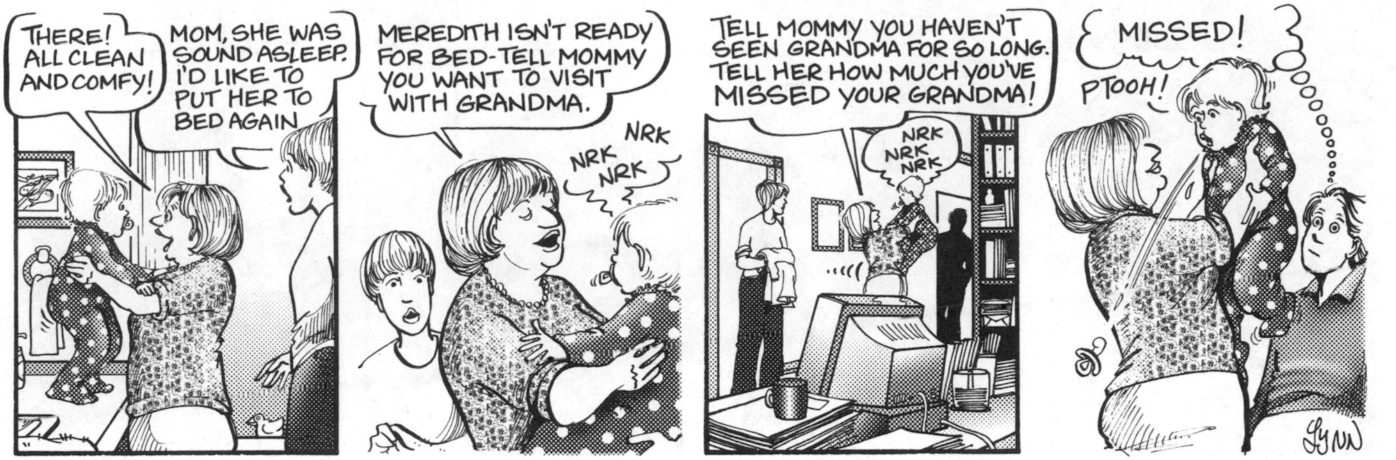
THERE! ALL CLEAN AND COMFY!
MOM, SHE WAS SOUND ASLEEP. I'D LIKE TO PUT HER TO BED AGAIN
MEREDITH ISN'T READY FOR BED-TELL MOMMY YOU WANT TO VISIT WITH GRANDMA.
NRK NRK NRK
TELL MOMMY YOU HAVEN'T SEEN GRANDMA FOR SO LONG. TELL HER HOW MUCH YOU'VE MISSED YOUR GRANDMA!
NRK NRK NRK
MISSED!
PTOOH!
LYNN

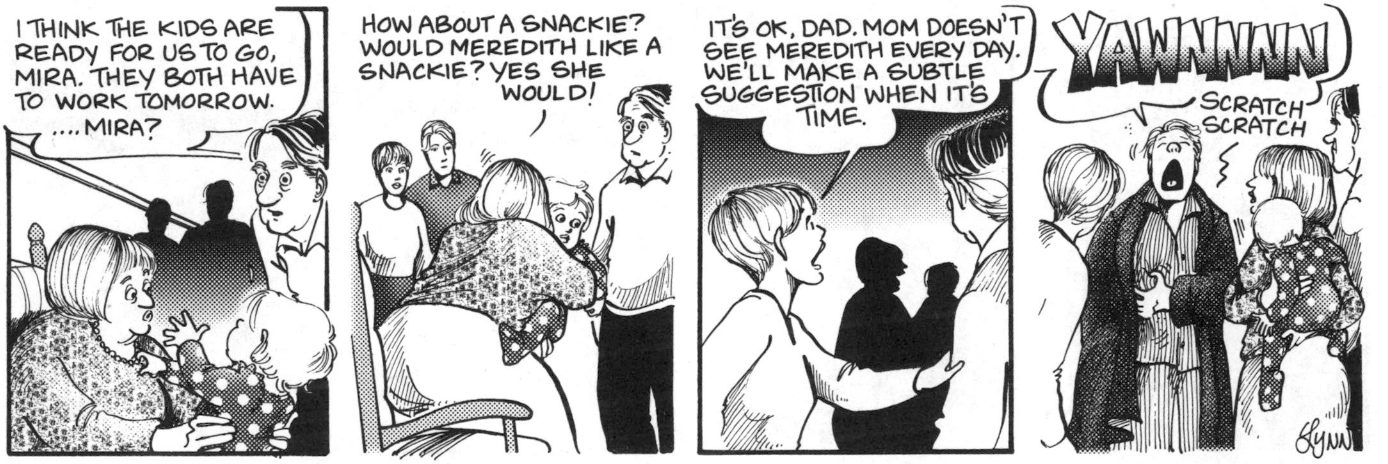
I THINK THE KIDS ARE READY FOR US TO GO, MIRA. THEY BOTH HAVE TO WORK TOMORROW. ....MIRA?
HOW ABOUT A SNACKIE? WOULD MEREDITH LIKE A SNACKIE? YES SHE WOULD!
IT'S OK, DAD. MOM DOESN'T SEE MEREDITH EVERY DAY. WE'LL MAKE A SUBTLE SUGGESTION WHEN IT'S TIME.
YAWNNNN
SCRATCH SCRATCH
LYNN

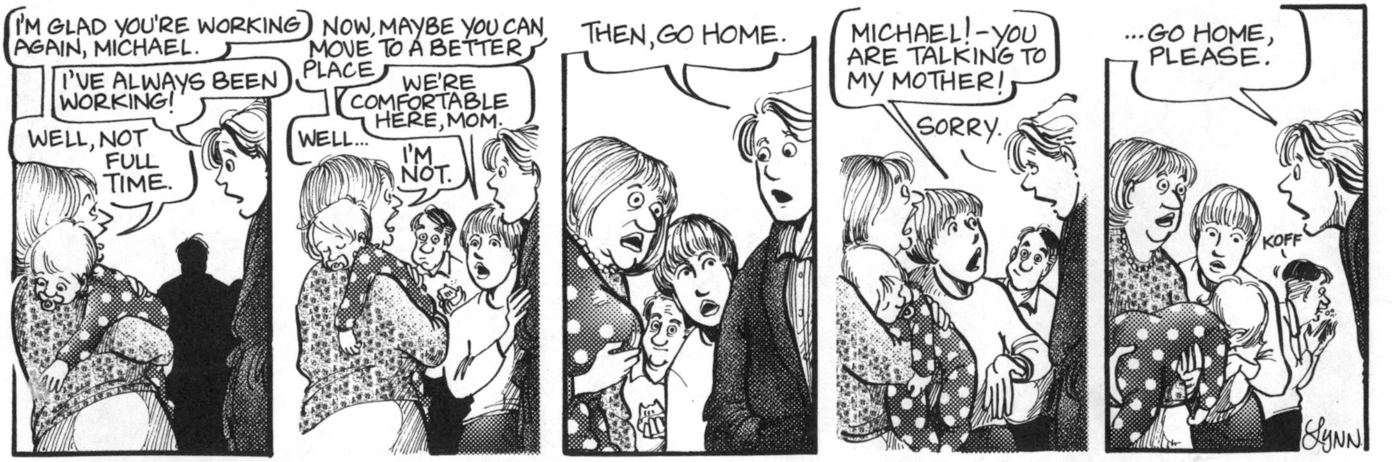
I'M GLAD YOU'RE WORKING AGAIN, MICHAEL.
I'VE ALWAYS BEEN WORKING!
WELL, NOT FULL TIME.
NOW, MAYBE YOU CAN MOVE TO A BETTER PLACE
WE'RE COMFORTABLE HERE, MOM.
WELL...
I'M NOT.
THEN, GO HOME.
MICHAEL!-YOU ARE TALKING TO MY MOTHER!
SORRY.
...GO HOME, PLEASE.
KOFF
LYNN

Panel 1: I AM SO OFFENDED!!! HE DIDN'T MEAN TO TELL YOU TO GO HOME, MOM!

Panel 2: YES I DID. EVERY TIME YOU SEE US, YOU HAVE SOMETHING NEGATIVE TO SAY.

Panel 3: OUR HOME ISN'T GOOD ENOUGH, MY JOB ISN'T GOOD ENOUGH, THE WAY WE PARENT OUR DAUGHTER ISN'T GOOD ENOUGH...

Panel 4: MOM... WAIT! MICHAEL'S NOT A MEAN PERSON! ...HE'LL APOLOGIZE!

Panel 5: THAT'S NOT GOOD ENOUGH.

Panel 6: WELL, I'LL SAY GOODNIGHT TO YOU, DEANNA, BUT I'M GOING TO IGNORE THE PERSON YOU CHOSE TO MARRY.

Panel 7: I'M NOT USED TO BEING SPOKEN TO THE WAY HE SPOKE TO ME THIS EVENING. AS HIS MOTHER-IN-LAW, I DESERVE MORE RESPECT.

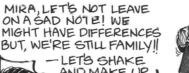

Panel 8: MIRA, LET'S NOT LEAVE ON A SAD NOTE! WE MIGHT HAVE DIFFERENCES BUT, WE'RE STILL FAMILY!! — LET'S SHAKE AND MAKE UP.

Panel 10: I'M SORRY MICHAEL. I WISH MY MOTHER WASN'T SO... ABRASIVE? SELF-CENTERED? CONTROLLING? — INTRUSIVE? INFLEXIBLE? YES

Panel 11: I CAN PUT UP WITH HER, DEANNA — AS LONG AS I HAVE YOU. YOU'RE SO DIFFERENT. THANKS. I NEED YOU, TOO.

Panel 12: SO, SHALL WE RETIRE AND FORGET WE WERE SO RUDELY INTERRUPTED?

Panel 13: WAAAAA AAAAAHHHH

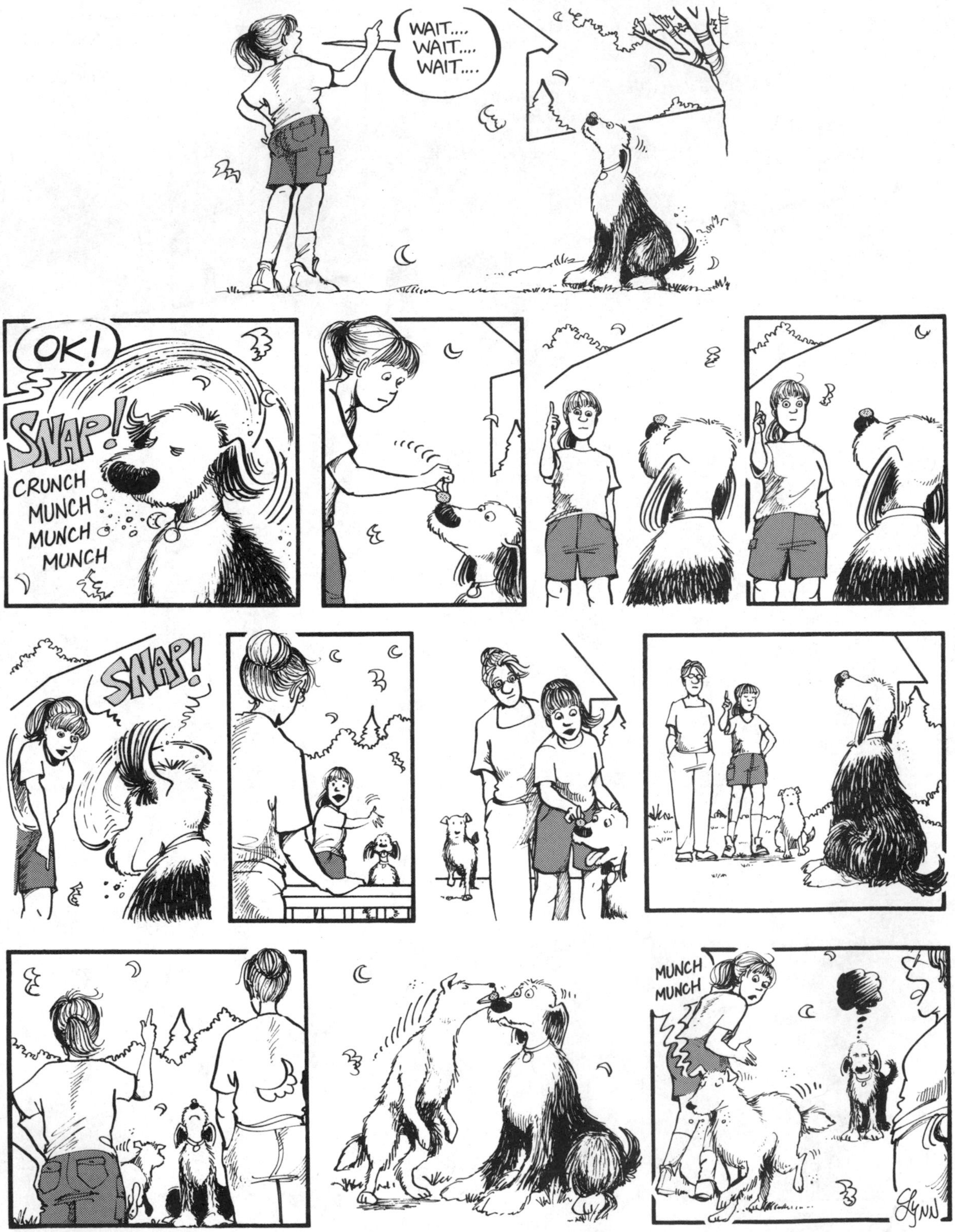
WAIT....
WAIT....
WAIT....
OK!
SNAP!
CRUNCH
MUNCH
MUNCH
MUNCH
SNAP!
MUNCH
MUNCH
LYNN

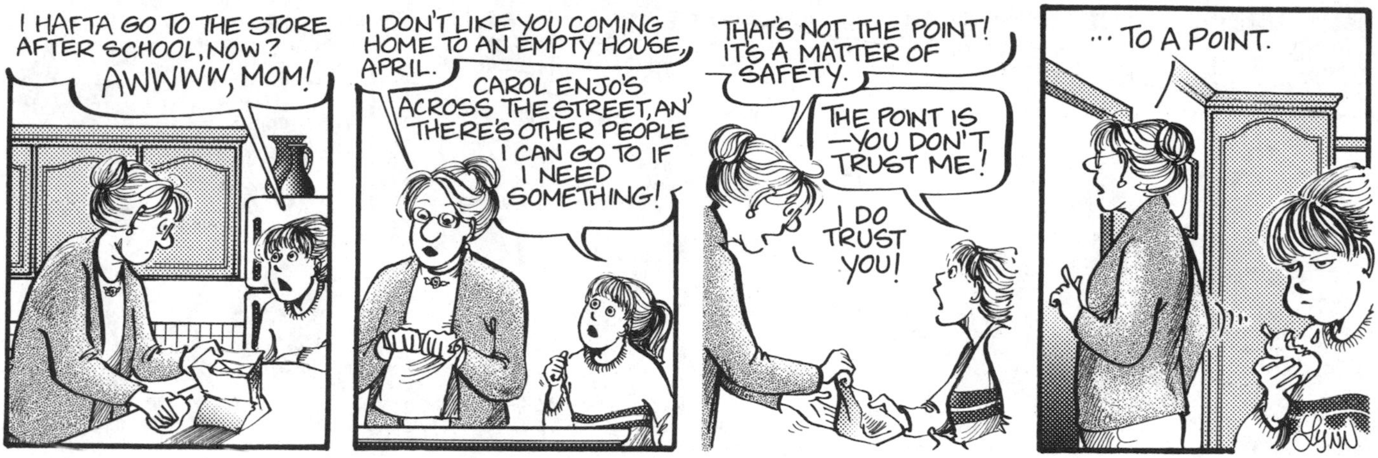
I HAFTA GO TO THE STORE AFTER SCHOOL, NOW? AWWWW, MOM!
I DON'T LIKE YOU COMING HOME TO AN EMPTY HOUSE, APRIL.
CAROL ENJO'S ACROSS THE STREET, AN' THERE'S OTHER PEOPLE I CAN GO TO IF I NEED SOMETHING!
THAT'S NOT THE POINT! IT'S A MATTER OF SAFETY.
THE POINT IS —YOU DON'T TRUST ME!
I DO TRUST YOU!
... TO A POINT.
LYNN

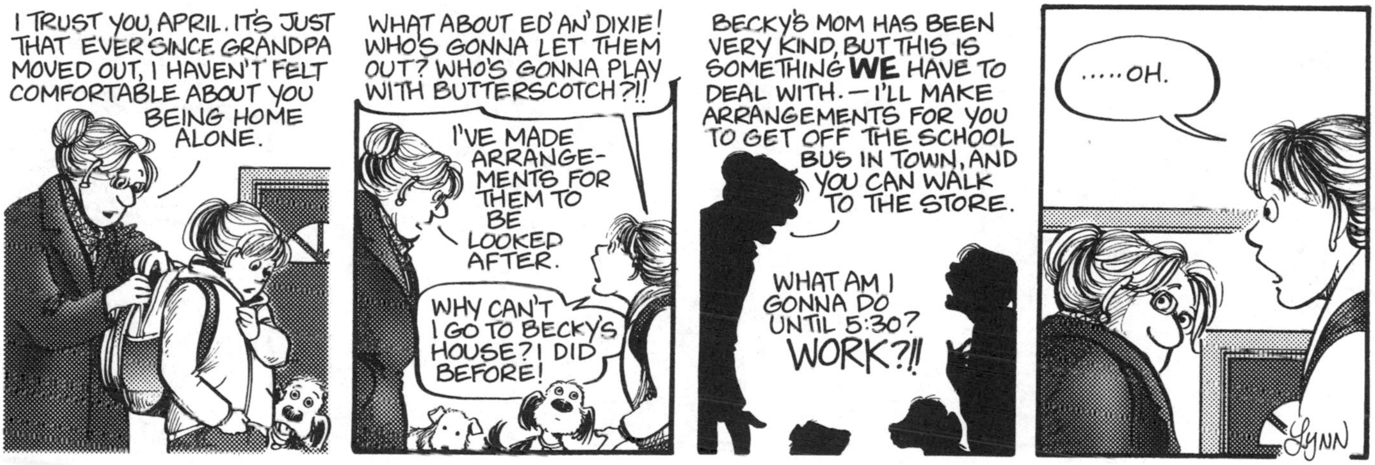
I TRUST YOU, APRIL. IT'S JUST THAT EVER SINCE GRANDPA MOVED OUT, I HAVEN'T FELT COMFORTABLE ABOUT YOU BEING HOME ALONE.
WHAT ABOUT ED AN' DIXIE! WHO'S GONNA LET THEM OUT? WHO'S GONNA PLAY WITH BUTTERSCOTCH?!!
I'VE MADE ARRANGEMENTS FOR THEM TO BE LOOKED AFTER.
WHY CAN'T I GO TO BECKY'S HOUSE?! I DID BEFORE!
BECKY'S MOM HAS BEEN VERY KIND, BUT THIS IS SOMETHING WE HAVE TO DEAL WITH. — I'LL MAKE ARRANGEMENTS FOR YOU TO GET OFF THE SCHOOL BUS IN TOWN, AND YOU CAN WALK TO THE STORE.
WHAT AM I GONNA DO UNTIL 5:30? WORK?!!
.....OH.
LYNN

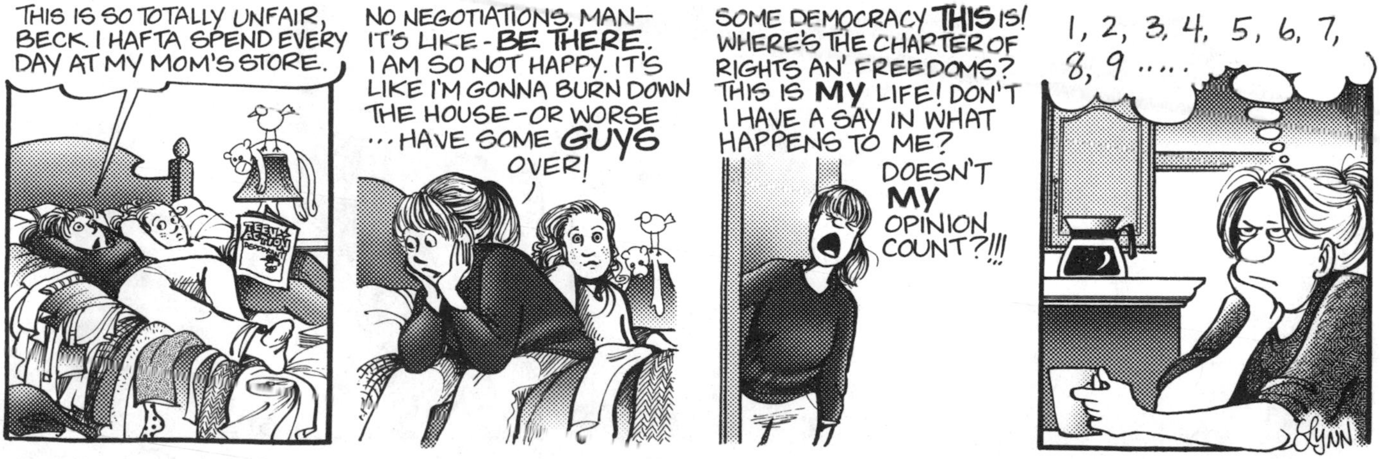
THIS IS SO TOTALLY UNFAIR, BECK. I HAFTA SPEND EVERY DAY AT MY MOM'S STORE.
NO NEGOTIATIONS, MAN— IT'S LIKE - BE THERE. I AM SO NOT HAPPY. IT'S LIKE I'M GONNA BURN DOWN THE HOUSE - OR WORSE ... HAVE SOME GUYS OVER!
SOME DEMOCRACY THIS IS! WHERE'S THE CHARTER OF RIGHTS AN' FREEDOMS? THIS IS MY LIFE! DON'T I HAVE A SAY IN WHAT HAPPENS TO ME?
DOESN'T MY OPINION COUNT?!!!
1, 2, 3, 4, 5, 6, 7, 8, 9 .....
LYNN

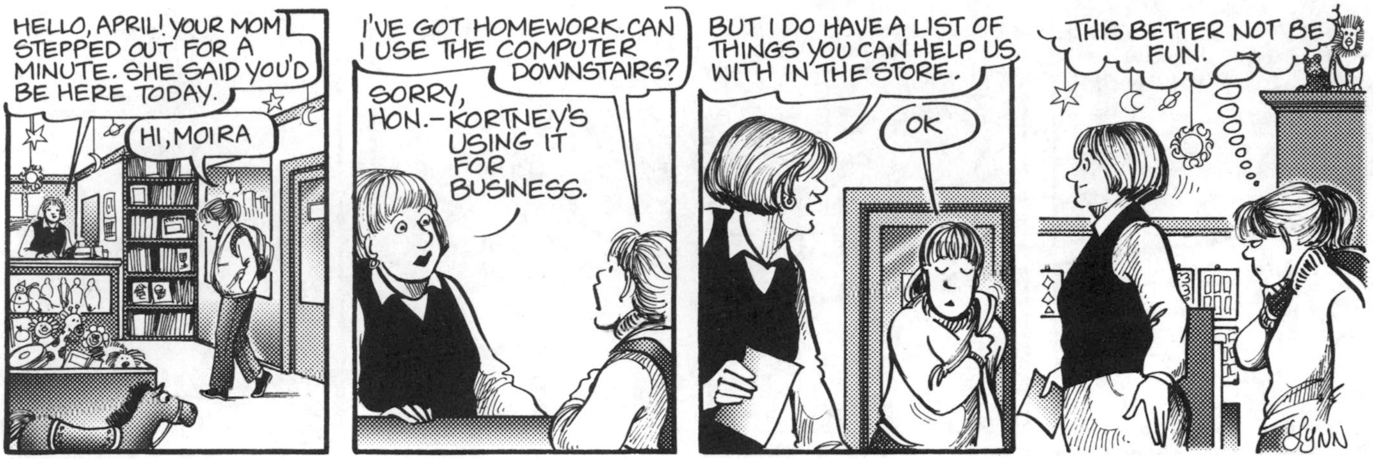
HELLO, APRIL! YOUR MOM STEPPED OUT FOR A MINUTE. SHE SAID YOU'D BE HERE TODAY.
HI, MOIRA
I'VE GOT HOMEWORK. CAN I USE THE COMPUTER DOWNSTAIRS?
SORRY, HON.– KORTNEY'S USING IT FOR BUSINESS.
BUT I DO HAVE A LIST OF THINGS YOU CAN HELP US WITH IN THE STORE.
OK
THIS BETTER NOT BE FUN.
LYNN

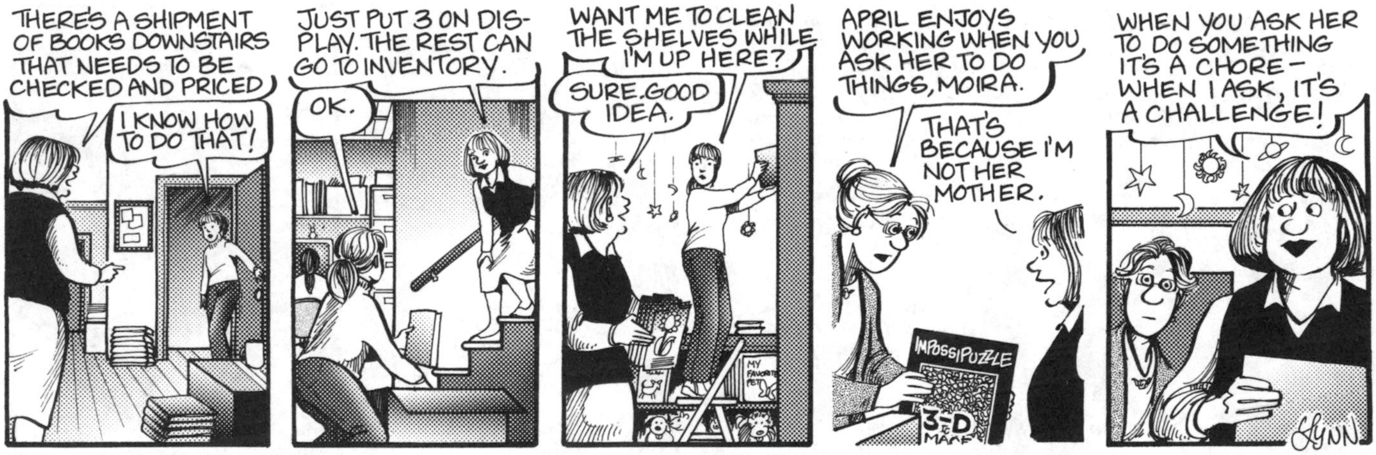
THERE'S A SHIPMENT OF BOOKS DOWNSTAIRS THAT NEEDS TO BE CHECKED AND PRICED
I KNOW HOW TO DO THAT!
JUST PUT 3 ON DISPLAY. THE REST CAN GO TO INVENTORY.
OK.
WANT ME TO CLEAN THE SHELVES WHILE I'M UP HERE?
SURE. GOOD IDEA.
MY FAVORITE PET
APRIL ENJOYS WORKING WHEN YOU ASK HER TO DO THINGS, MOIRA.
THAT'S BECAUSE I'M NOT HER MOTHER.
IMPOSSIPUZZLE
3-D
WHEN YOU ASK HER TO DO SOMETHING IT'S A CHORE– WHEN I ASK, IT'S A CHALLENGE!
LYNN

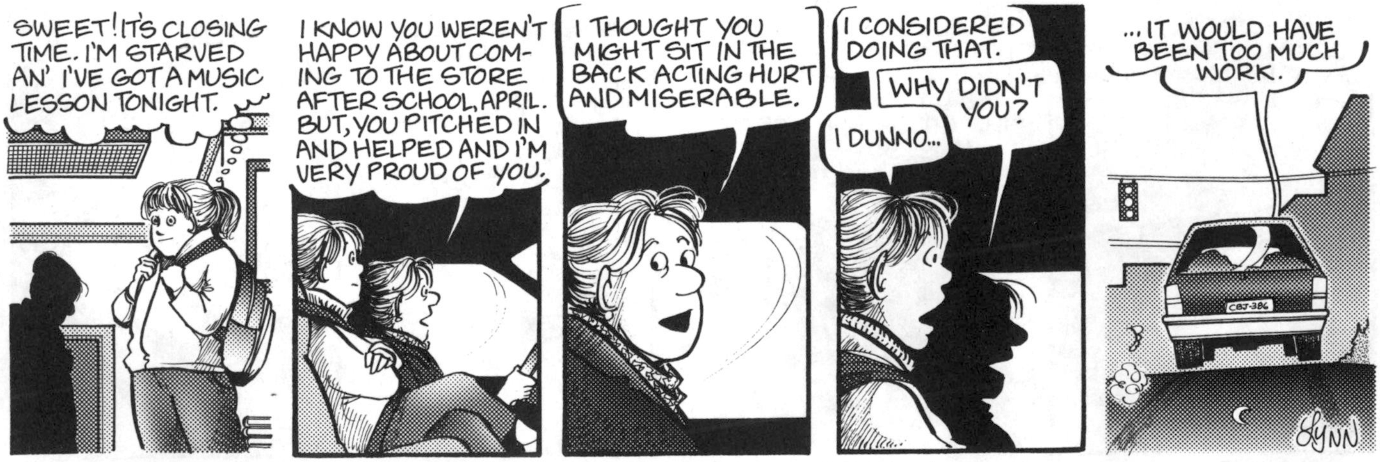
SWEET! IT'S CLOSING TIME. I'M STARVED AN' I'VE GOT A MUSIC LESSON TONIGHT.
I KNOW YOU WEREN'T HAPPY ABOUT COMING TO THE STORE AFTER SCHOOL, APRIL. BUT, YOU PITCHED IN AND HELPED AND I'M VERY PROUD OF YOU.
I THOUGHT YOU MIGHT SIT IN THE BACK ACTING HURT AND MISERABLE.
I CONSIDERED DOING THAT.
WHY DIDN'T YOU?
I DUNNO...
...IT WOULD HAVE BEEN TOO MUCH WORK.
CBJ-386
LYNN

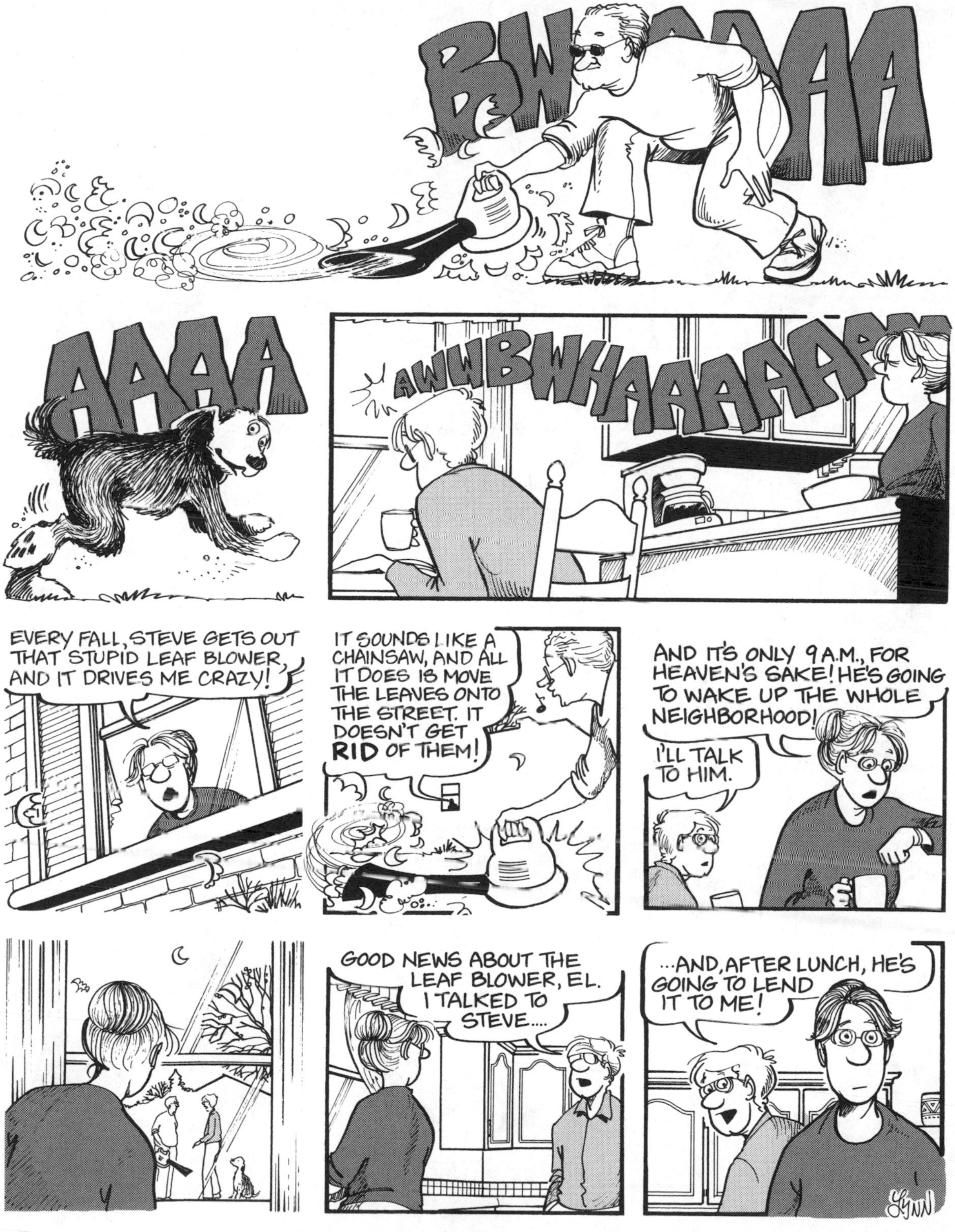
BWAAAAA
AAAA
AWWBWHAAAAAAAW
EVERY FALL, STEVE GETS OUT THAT STUPID LEAF BLOWER, AND IT DRIVES ME CRAZY!
IT SOUNDS LIKE A CHAINSAW, AND ALL IT DOES IS MOVE THE LEAVES ONTO THE STREET. IT DOESN'T GET **RID** OF THEM!
AND IT'S ONLY 9 A.M., FOR HEAVEN'S SAKE! HE'S GOING TO WAKE UP THE WHOLE NEIGHBORHOOD!
I'LL TALK TO HIM.
GOOD NEWS ABOUT THE LEAF BLOWER, EL. I TALKED TO STEVE....
...AND, AFTER LUNCH, HE'S GOING TO LEND IT TO ME!
LYNN

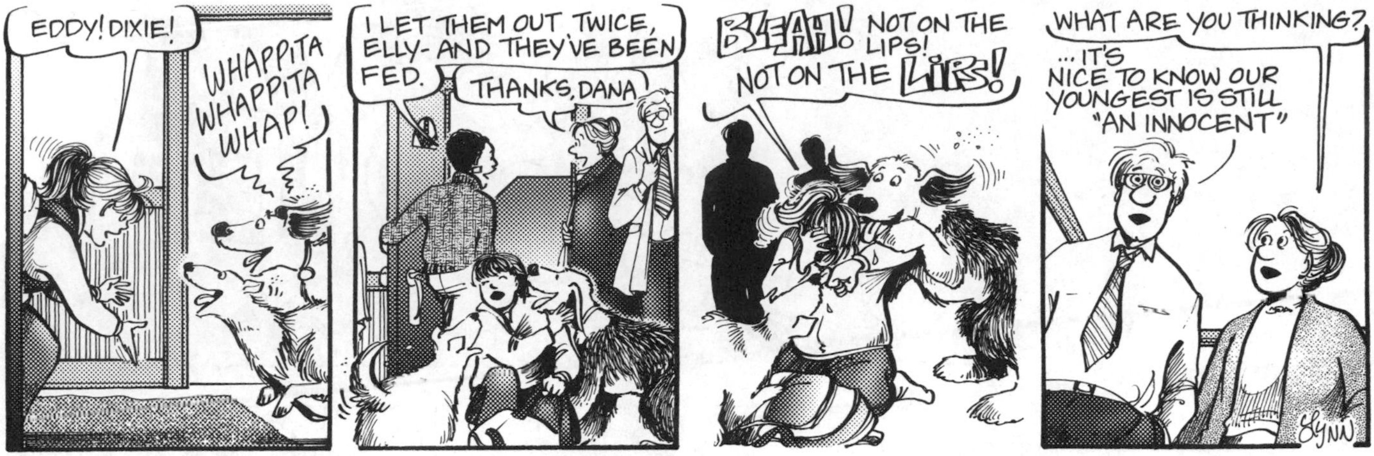
EDDY! DIXIE!
WHAPPITA WHAPPITA WHAP!
I LET THEM OUT TWICE, ELLY- AND THEY'VE BEEN FED.
THANKS, DANA
BLEAH! NOT ON THE LIPS! NOT ON THE LIPS!
WHAT ARE YOU THINKING?
... IT'S NICE TO KNOW OUR YOUNGEST IS STILL "AN INNOCENT"
LYNN

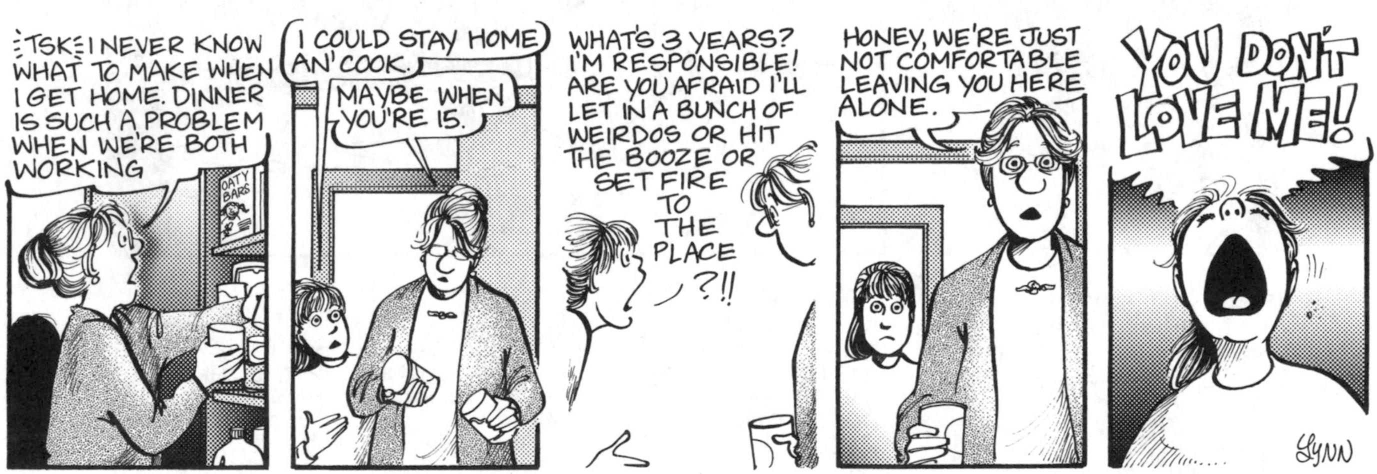
TSK I NEVER KNOW WHAT TO MAKE WHEN I GET HOME. DINNER IS SUCH A PROBLEM WHEN WE'RE BOTH WORKING
OATY BARS
I COULD STAY HOME AN' COOK.
MAYBE WHEN YOU'RE 15.
WHAT'S 3 YEARS? I'M RESPONSIBLE! ARE YOU AFRAID I'LL LET IN A BUNCH OF WEIRDOS OR HIT THE BOOZE OR SET FIRE TO THE PLACE
?!!
HONEY, WE'RE JUST NOT COMFORTABLE LEAVING YOU HERE ALONE.
YOU DON'T LOVE ME!
LYNN

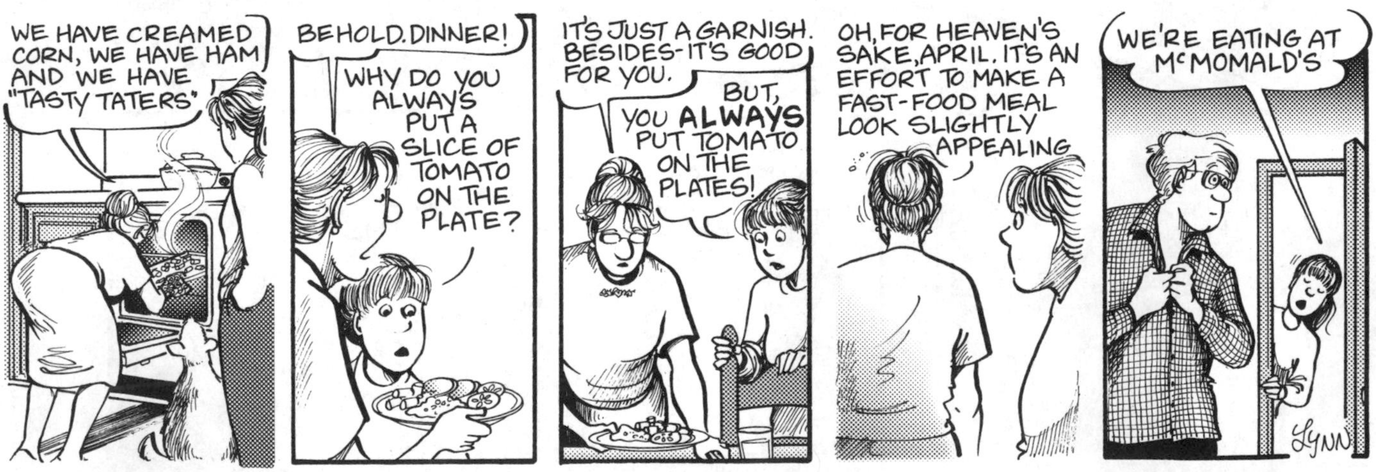
WE HAVE CREAMED CORN, WE HAVE HAM AND WE HAVE "TASTY TATERS"
BEHOLD. DINNER!
WHY DO YOU ALWAYS PUT A SLICE OF TOMATO ON THE PLATE?
IT'S JUST A GARNISH. BESIDES- IT'S GOOD FOR YOU.
BUT, YOU ALWAYS PUT TOMATO ON THE PLATES!
OH, FOR HEAVEN'S SAKE, APRIL. IT'S AN EFFORT TO MAKE A FAST-FOOD MEAL LOOK SLIGHTLY APPEALING
WE'RE EATING AT McMOMALD'S
LYNN

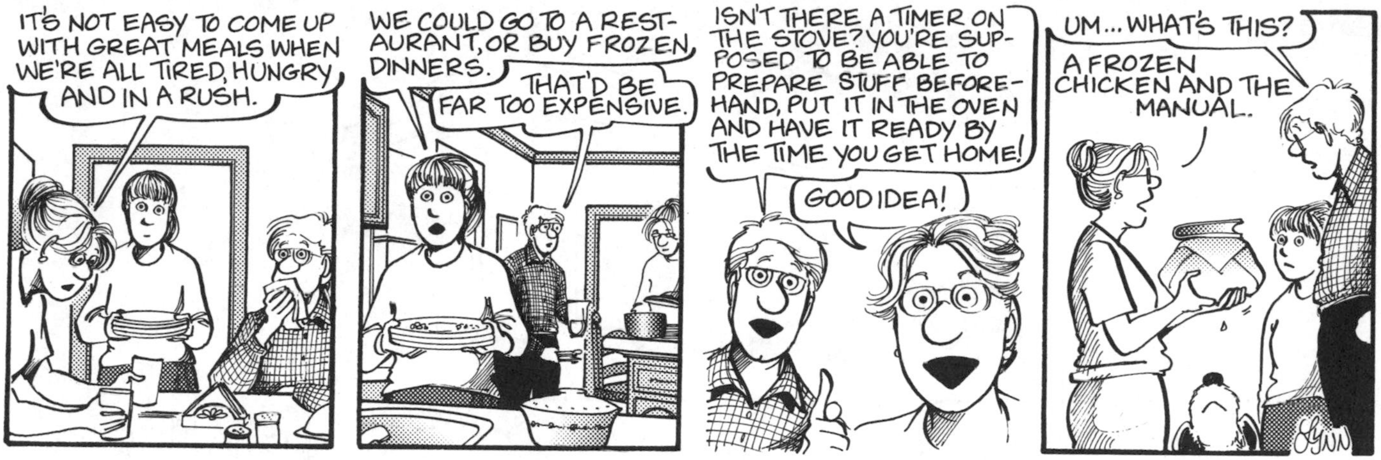
IT'S NOT EASY TO COME UP WITH GREAT MEALS WHEN WE'RE ALL TIRED, HUNGRY AND IN A RUSH.
WE COULD GO TO A RESTAURANT, OR BUY FROZEN DINNERS.
THAT'D BE FAR TOO EXPENSIVE.
ISN'T THERE A TIMER ON THE STOVE? YOU'RE SUPPOSED TO BE ABLE TO PREPARE STUFF BEFOREHAND, PUT IT IN THE OVEN AND HAVE IT READY BY THE TIME YOU GET HOME!
GOOD IDEA!
UM... WHAT'S THIS?
A FROZEN CHICKEN AND THE MANUAL.
LYNN

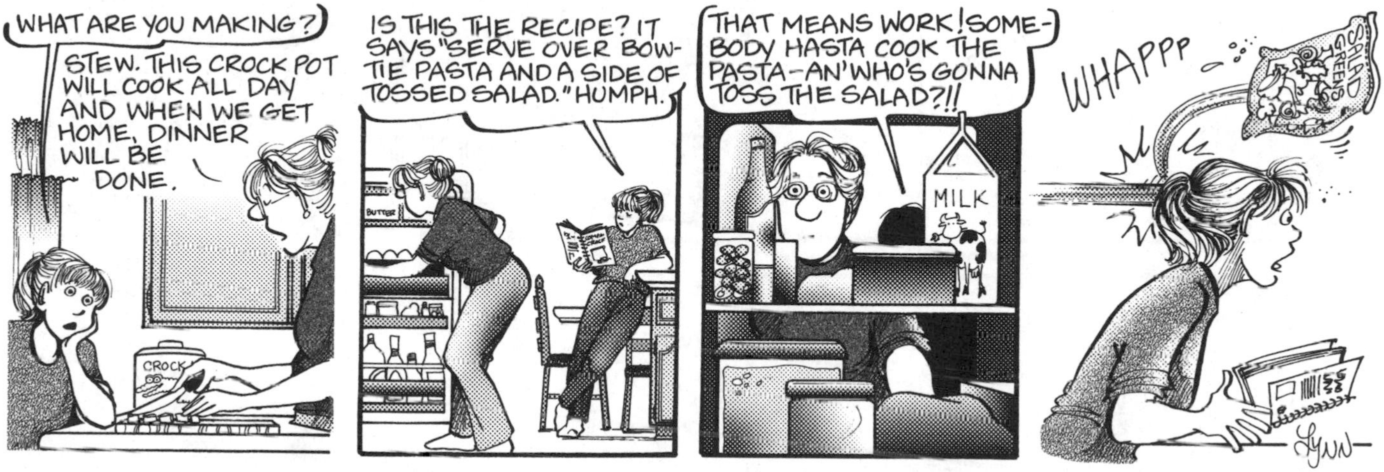
WHAT ARE YOU MAKING?
STEW. THIS CROCK POT WILL COOK ALL DAY AND WHEN WE GET HOME, DINNER WILL BE DONE.
CROCK
IS THIS THE RECIPE? IT SAYS "SERVE OVER BOWTIE PASTA AND A SIDE OF TOSSED SALAD." HUMPH.
THAT MEANS WORK! SOMEBODY HASTA COOK THE PASTA—AN' WHO'S GONNA TOSS THE SALAD?!!
MILK
WHAPPP
SALAD GREENS
LYNN

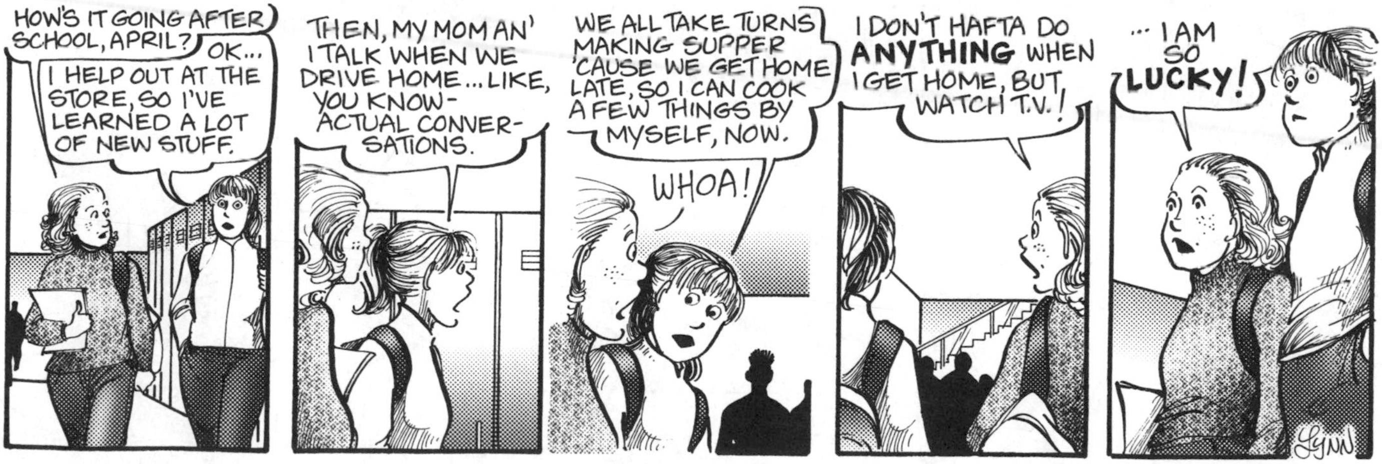
HOW'S IT GOING AFTER SCHOOL, APRIL?
OK... I HELP OUT AT THE STORE, SO I'VE LEARNED A LOT OF NEW STUFF.
THEN, MY MOM AN' I TALK WHEN WE DRIVE HOME... LIKE, YOU KNOW—ACTUAL CONVERSATIONS.
WE ALL TAKE TURNS MAKING SUPPER 'CAUSE WE GET HOME LATE, SO I CAN COOK A FEW THINGS BY MYSELF, NOW.
WHOA!
I DON'T HAFTA DO ANYTHING WHEN I GET HOME, BUT WATCH T.V.!
... I AM SO LUCKY!
LYNN

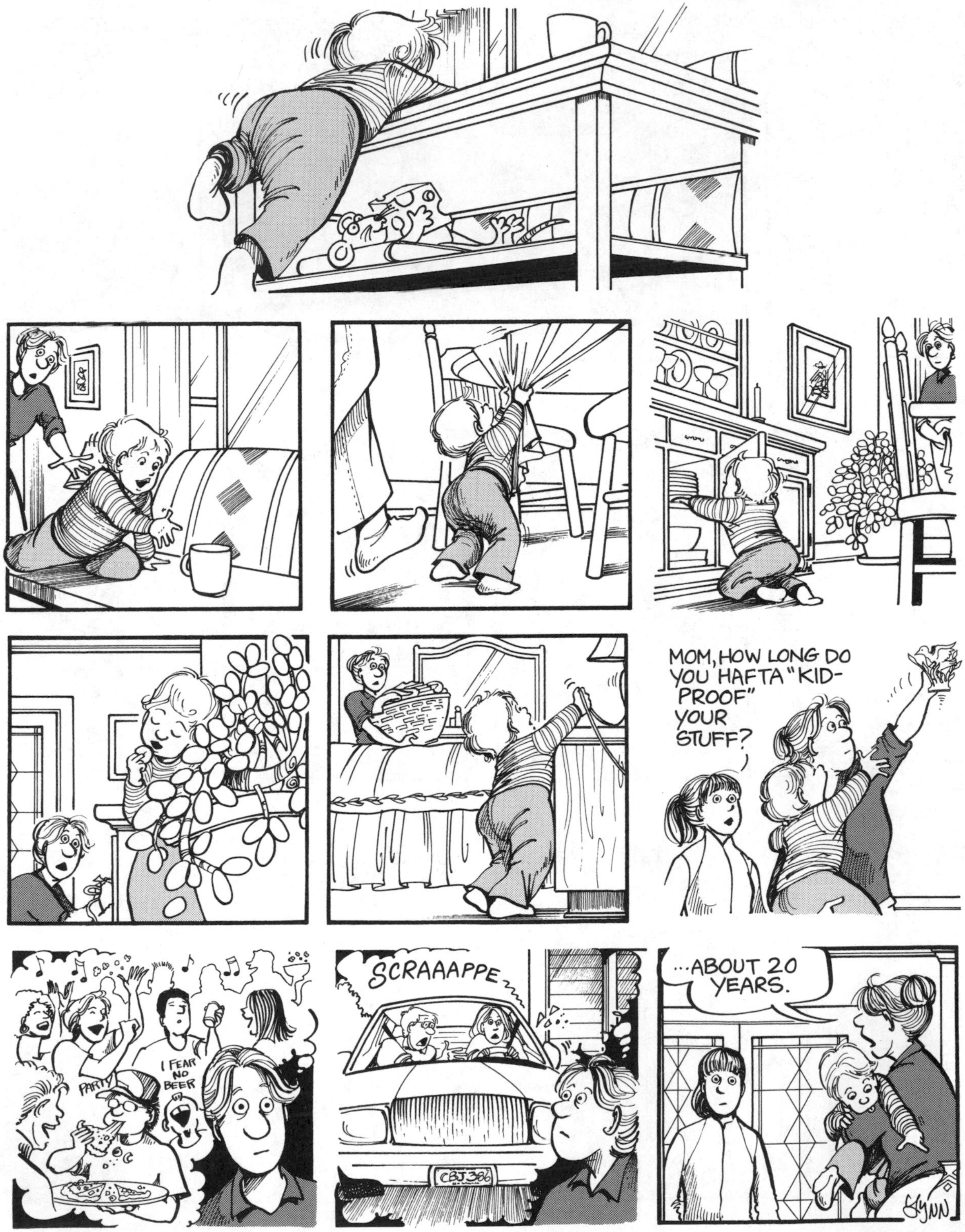
MOM, HOW LONG DO YOU HAFTA "KID-PROOF" YOUR STUFF?
PARTY
I FEAR NO BEER
SCRAAAPPE
CBJ 386
...ABOUT 20 YEARS.
LYNN

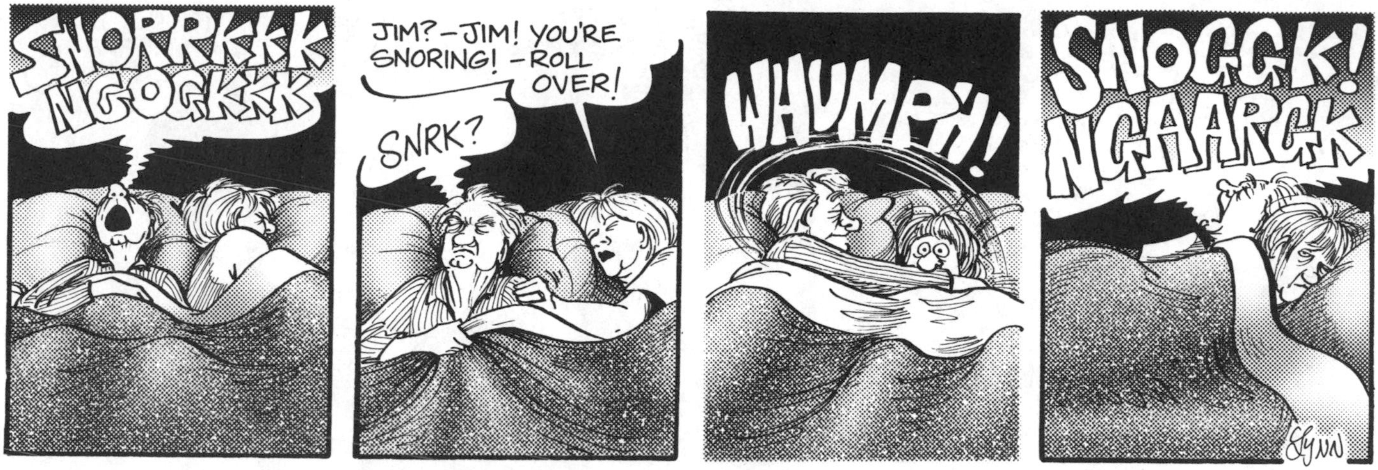
SNORRKKK NGOGKKK
JIM? –JIM! YOU'RE SNORING! –ROLL OVER!
SNRK?
WHUMPH!
SNOGGK! NGAARGK

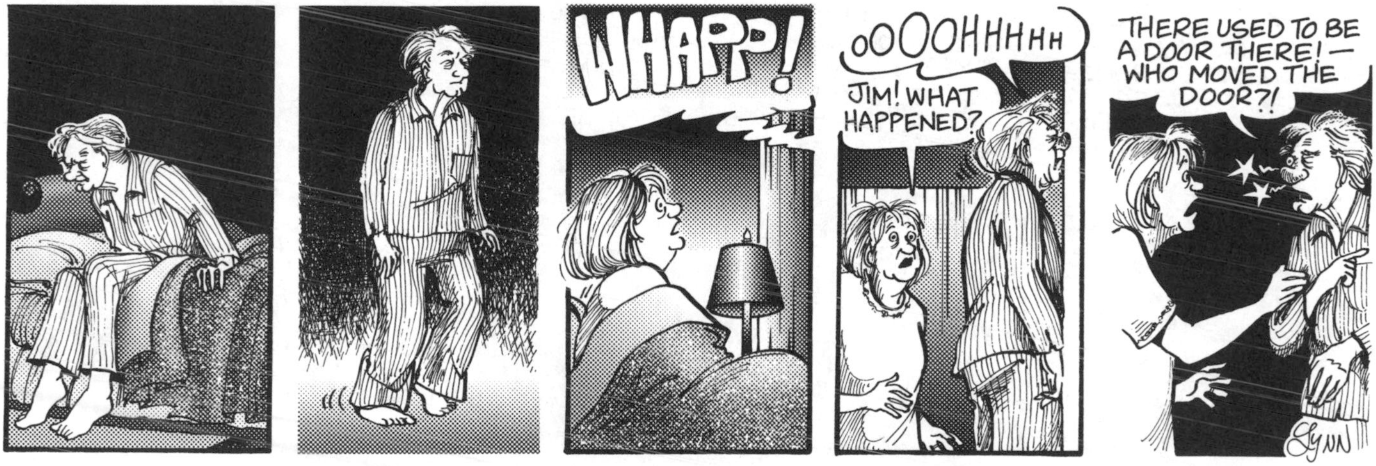
WHAPP!
oOOOHHHHH
JIM! WHAT HAPPENED?
THERE USED TO BE A DOOR THERE! – WHO MOVED THE DOOR?!

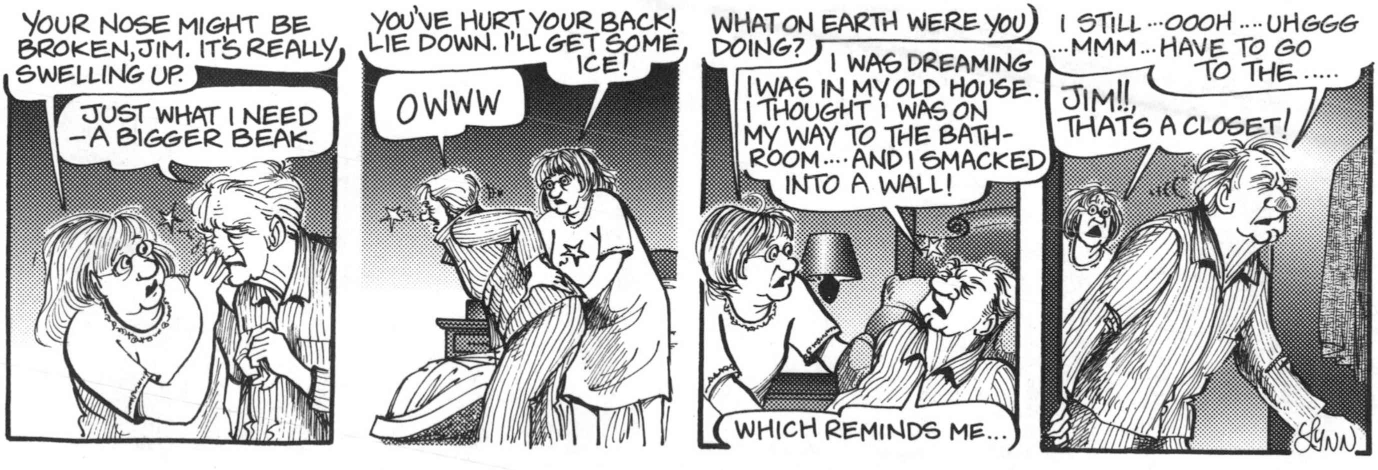
YOUR NOSE MIGHT BE BROKEN, JIM. IT'S REALLY SWELLING UP.
JUST WHAT I NEED –A BIGGER BEAK.
YOU'VE HURT YOUR BACK! LIE DOWN. I'LL GET SOME ICE!
OWWW
WHAT ON EARTH WERE YOU DOING?
I WAS DREAMING I WAS IN MY OLD HOUSE. I THOUGHT I WAS ON MY WAY TO THE BATHROOM.... AND I SMACKED INTO A WALL!
WHICH REMINDS ME...
I STILL ...OOOH .... UHGGG ...MMM... HAVE TO GO TO THE .....
JIM!! THATS A CLOSET!

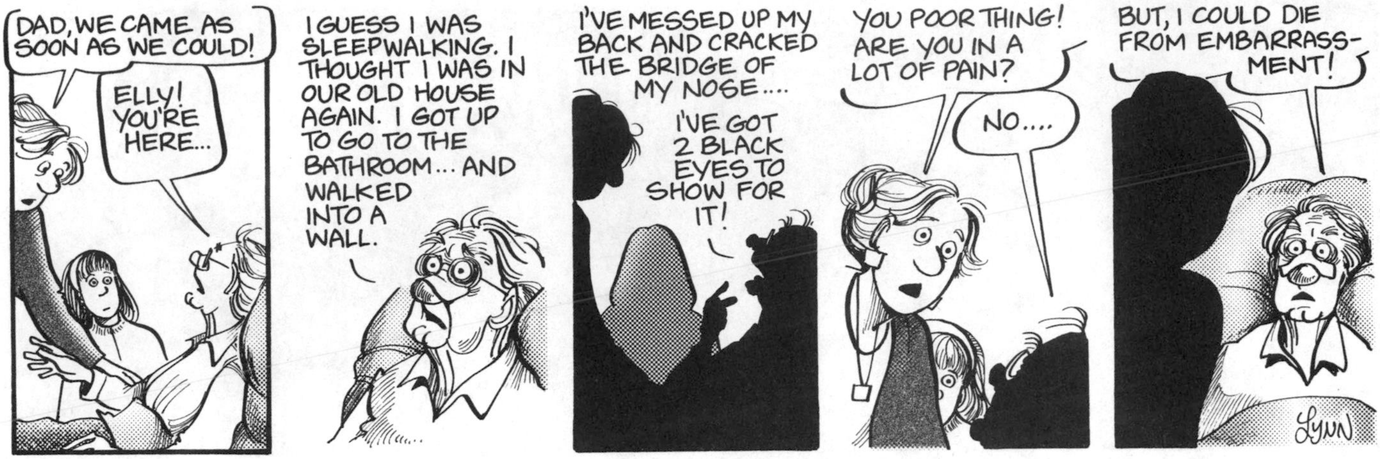
DAD, WE CAME AS SOON AS WE COULD!
ELLY! YOU'RE HERE...
I GUESS I WAS SLEEPWALKING. I THOUGHT I WAS IN OUR OLD HOUSE AGAIN. I GOT UP TO GO TO THE BATHROOM... AND WALKED INTO A WALL.
I'VE MESSED UP MY BACK AND CRACKED THE BRIDGE OF MY NOSE....
I'VE GOT 2 BLACK EYES TO SHOW FOR IT!
YOU POOR THING! ARE YOU IN A LOT OF PAIN?
NO....
BUT, I COULD DIE FROM EMBARRASS-MENT!
LYNN

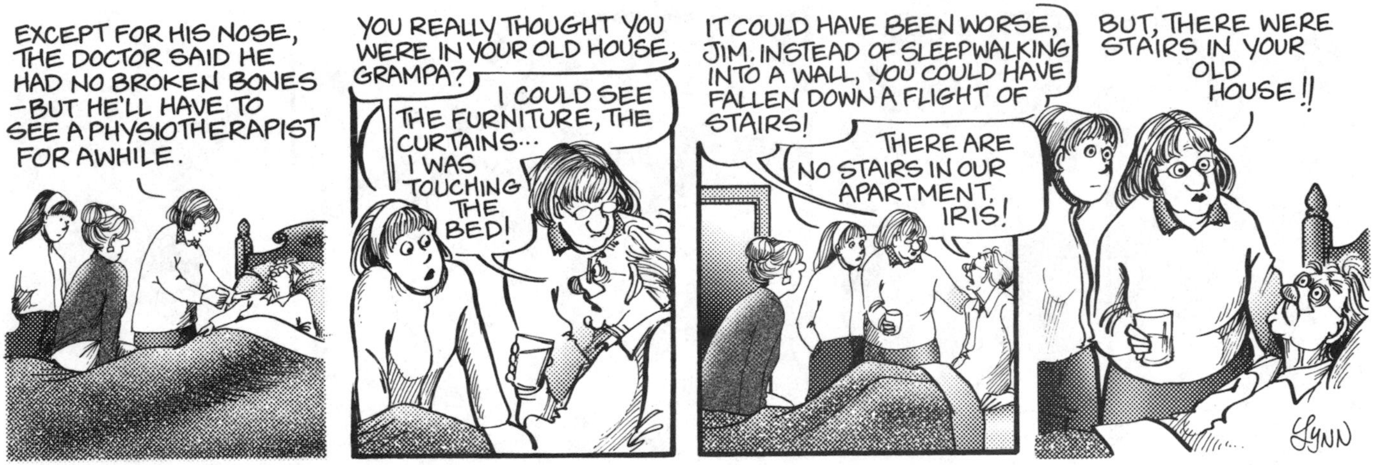
EXCEPT FOR HIS NOSE, THE DOCTOR SAID HE HAD NO BROKEN BONES - BUT HE'LL HAVE TO SEE A PHYSIOTHERAPIST FOR AWHILE.
YOU REALLY THOUGHT YOU WERE IN YOUR OLD HOUSE, GRAMPA?
I COULD SEE THE FURNITURE, THE CURTAINS... I WAS TOUCHING THE BED!
IT COULD HAVE BEEN WORSE, JIM. INSTEAD OF SLEEPWALKING INTO A WALL, YOU COULD HAVE FALLEN DOWN A FLIGHT OF STAIRS!
THERE ARE NO STAIRS IN OUR APARTMENT, IRIS!
BUT, THERE WERE STAIRS IN YOUR OLD HOUSE!!
LYNN

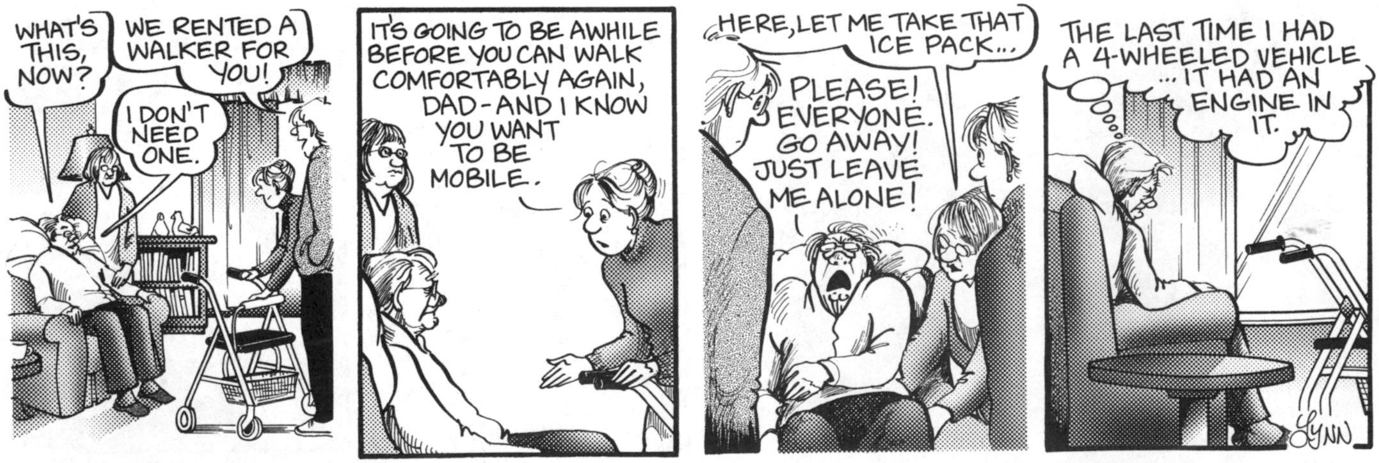
WHAT'S THIS, NOW?
WE RENTED A WALKER FOR YOU!
I DON'T NEED ONE.
IT'S GOING TO BE AWHILE BEFORE YOU CAN WALK COMFORTABLY AGAIN, DAD - AND I KNOW YOU WANT TO BE MOBILE.
HERE, LET ME TAKE THAT ICE PACK...
PLEASE! EVERYONE. GO AWAY! JUST LEAVE ME ALONE!
THE LAST TIME I HAD A 4-WHEELED VEHICLE ... IT HAD AN ENGINE IN IT.
LYNN

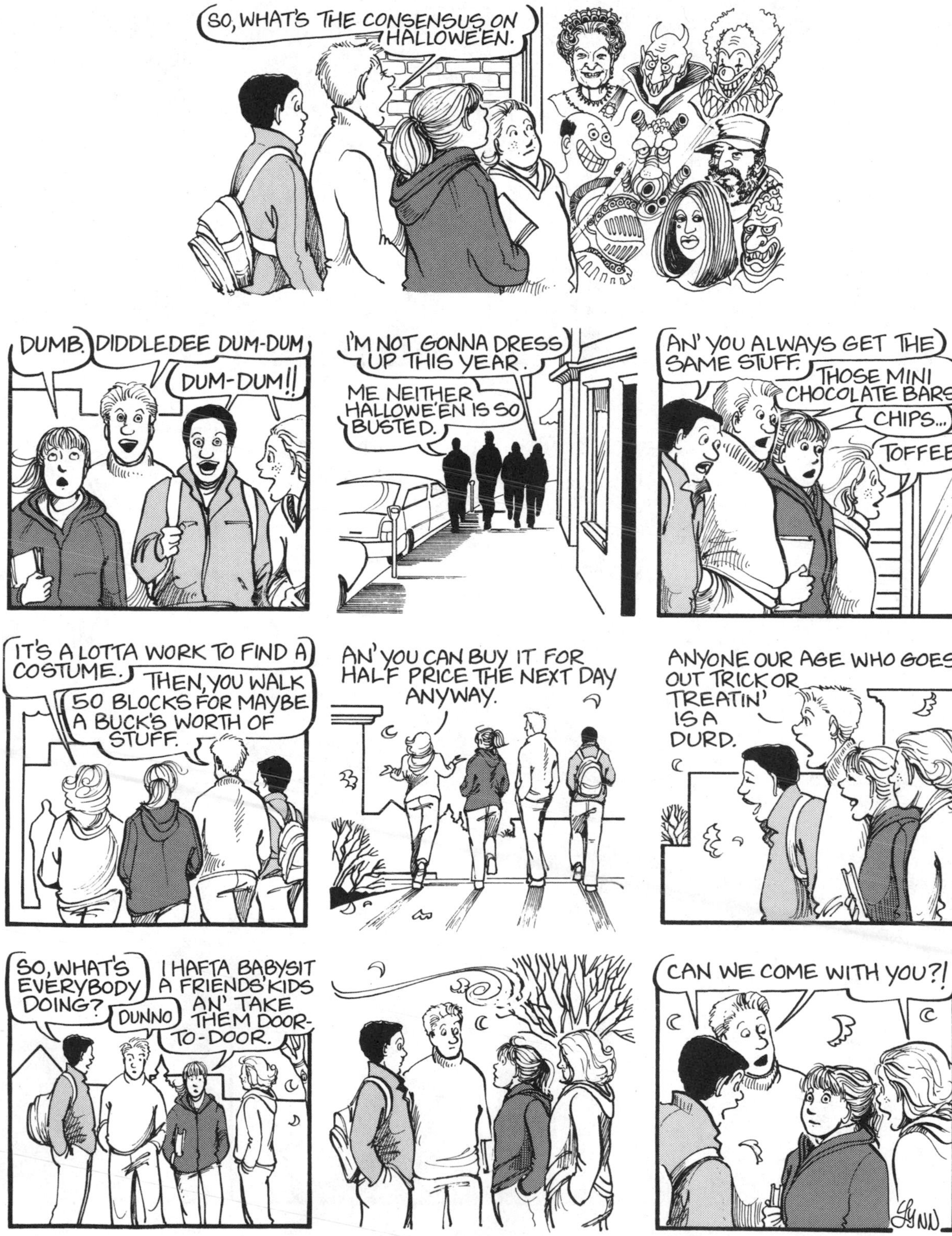
SO, WHAT'S THE CONSENSUS ON HALLOWE'EN.
DUMB.
DIDDLEDEE DUM-DUM
DUM-DUM!!
I'M NOT GONNA DRESS UP THIS YEAR.
ME NEITHER HALLOWE'EN IS SO BUSTED.
AN' YOU ALWAYS GET THE SAME STUFF.
THOSE MINI CHOCOLATE BARS
CHIPS...
TOFFEE
IT'S A LOTTA WORK TO FIND A COSTUME.
THEN, YOU WALK 50 BLOCKS FOR MAYBE A BUCK'S WORTH OF STUFF.
AN' YOU CAN BUY IT FOR HALF PRICE THE NEXT DAY ANYWAY.
ANYONE OUR AGE WHO GOES OUT TRICK OR TREATIN' IS A DURD.
SO, WHAT'S EVERYBODY DOING?
DUNNO
I HAFTA BABYSIT A FRIENDS' KIDS AN' TAKE THEM DOOR-TO-DOOR.
CAN WE COME WITH YOU?!
LYNN

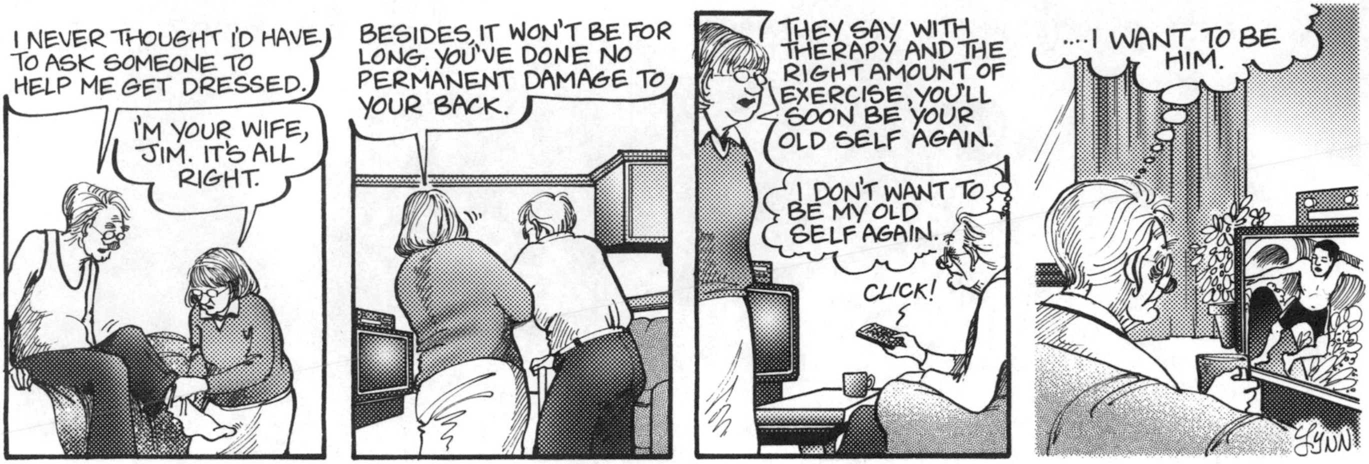
I NEVER THOUGHT I'D HAVE TO ASK SOMEONE TO HELP ME GET DRESSED.
I'M YOUR WIFE, JIM. IT'S ALL RIGHT.
BESIDES, IT WON'T BE FOR LONG. YOU'VE DONE NO PERMANENT DAMAGE TO YOUR BACK.
THEY SAY WITH THERAPY AND THE RIGHT AMOUNT OF EXERCISE, YOU'LL SOON BE YOUR OLD SELF AGAIN.
I DON'T WANT TO BE MY OLD SELF AGAIN.
CLICK!
....I WANT TO BE HIM.

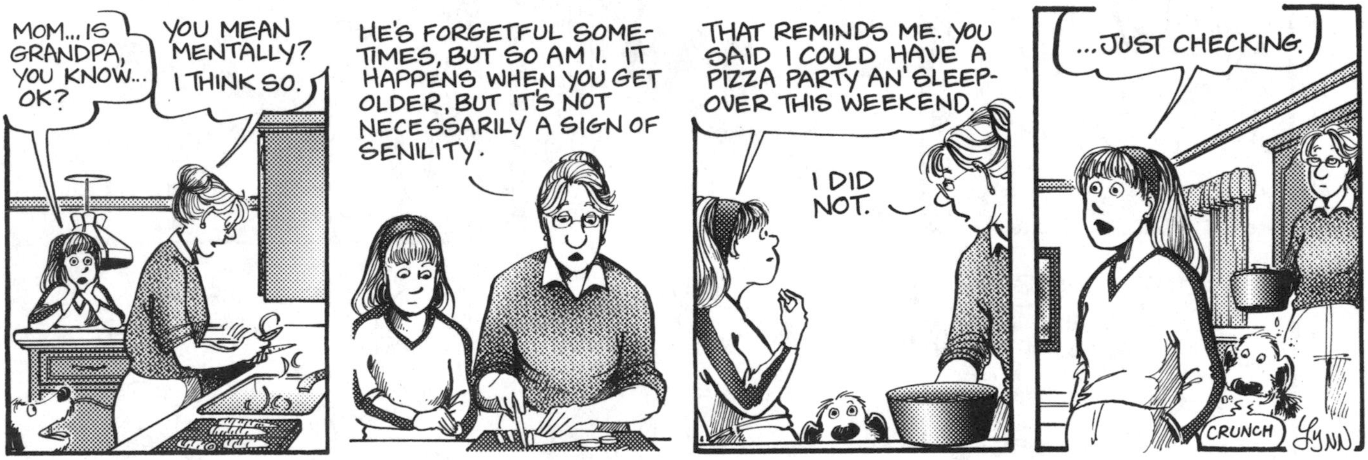
MOM... IS GRANDPA, YOU KNOW... OK?
YOU MEAN MENTALLY? I THINK SO.
HE'S FORGETFUL SOMETIMES, BUT SO AM I. IT HAPPENS WHEN YOU GET OLDER, BUT IT'S NOT NECESSARILY A SIGN OF SENILITY.
THAT REMINDS ME. YOU SAID I COULD HAVE A PIZZA PARTY AN' SLEEP-OVER THIS WEEKEND.
I DID NOT.
...JUST CHECKING.
CRUNCH

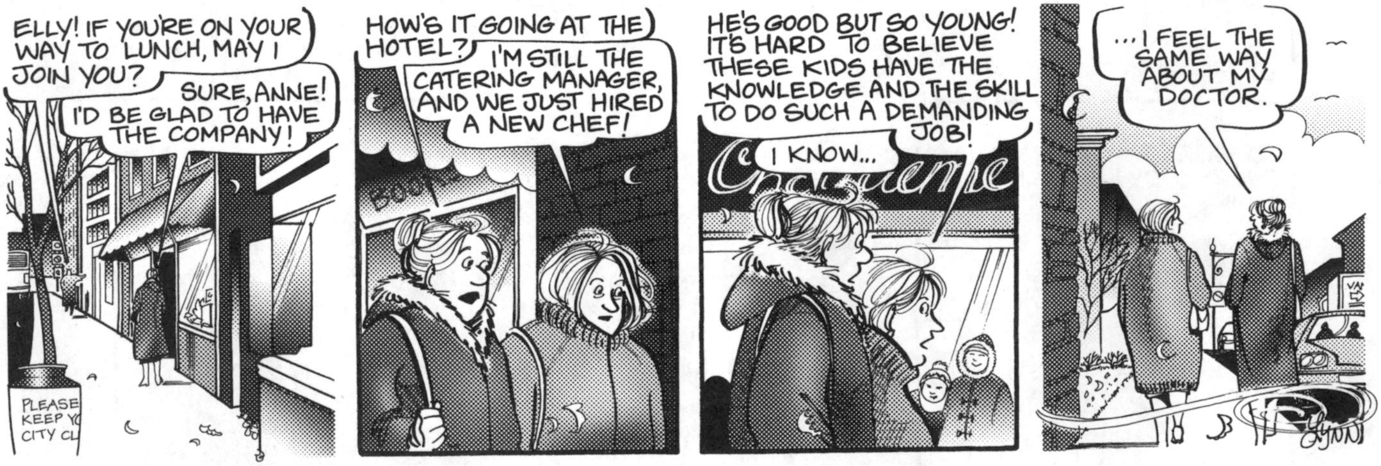
ELLY! IF YOU'RE ON YOUR WAY TO LUNCH, MAY I JOIN YOU?
SURE, ANNE! I'D BE GLAD TO HAVE THE COMPANY!
PLEASE
HOW'S IT GOING AT THE HOTEL?
I'M STILL THE CATERING MANAGER, AND WE JUST HIRED A NEW CHEF!
HE'S GOOD BUT SO YOUNG! IT'S HARD TO BELIEVE THESE KIDS HAVE THE KNOWLEDGE AND THE SKILL TO DO SUCH A DEMANDING JOB!
I KNOW...
...I FEEL THE SAME WAY ABOUT MY DOCTOR.

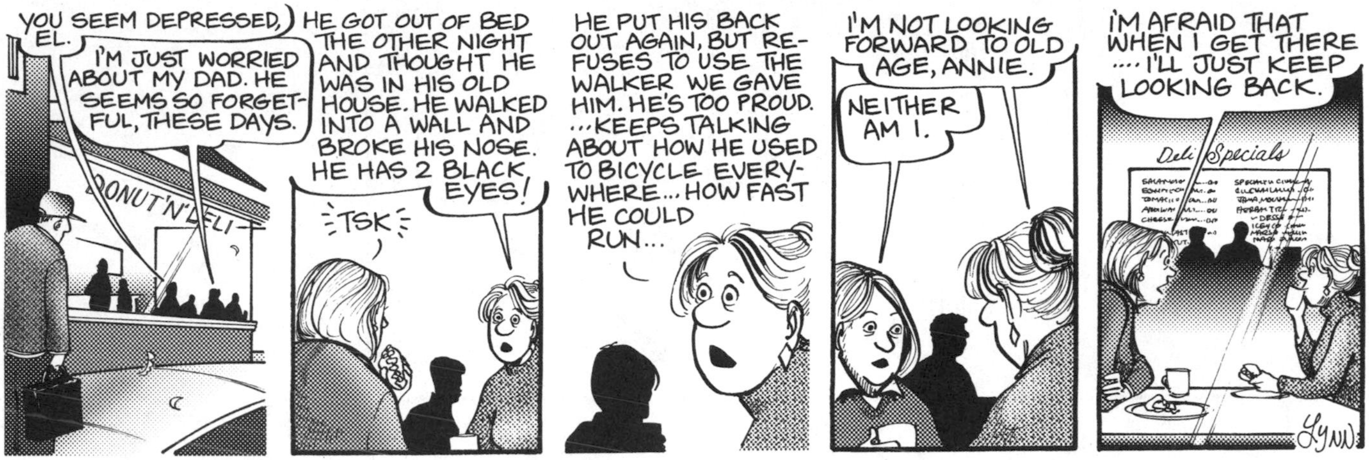
YOU SEEM DEPRESSED, EL.
I'M JUST WORRIED ABOUT MY DAD. HE SEEMS SO FORGETFUL, THESE DAYS.
DONUT'N'DELI
HE GOT OUT OF BED THE OTHER NIGHT AND THOUGHT HE WAS IN HIS OLD HOUSE. HE WALKED INTO A WALL AND BROKE HIS NOSE. HE HAS 2 BLACK EYES!
TSK
HE PUT HIS BACK OUT AGAIN, BUT REFUSES TO USE THE WALKER WE GAVE HIM. HE'S TOO PROUD. ...KEEPS TALKING ABOUT HOW HE USED TO BICYCLE EVERYWHERE... HOW FAST HE COULD RUN...
I'M NOT LOOKING FORWARD TO OLD AGE, ANNIE.
NEITHER AM I.
I'M AFRAID THAT WHEN I GET THERE .... I'LL JUST KEEP LOOKING BACK.
Deli Specials
LYNN

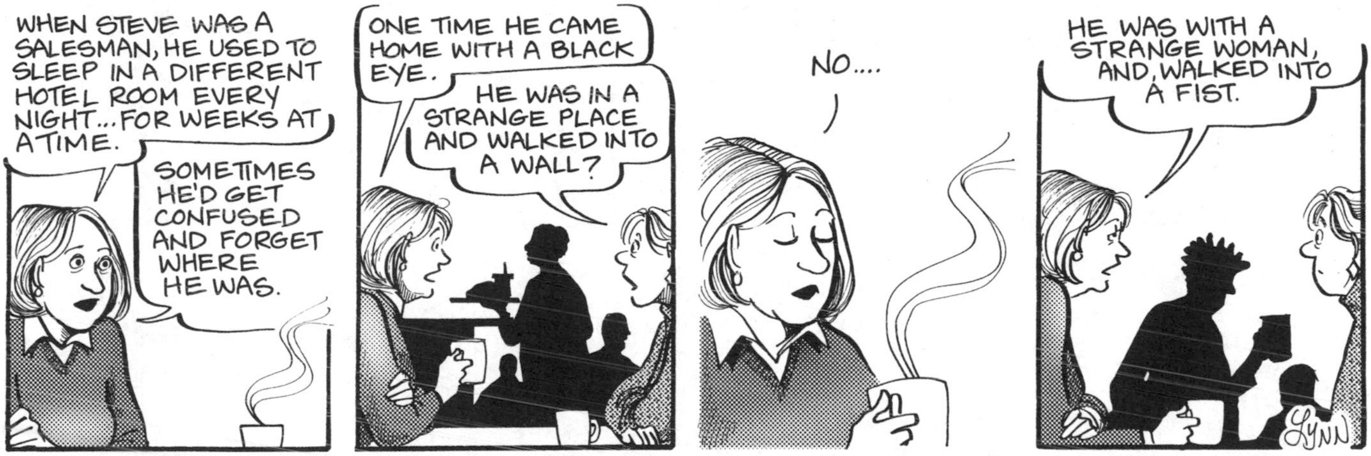
WHEN STEVE WAS A SALESMAN, HE USED TO SLEEP IN A DIFFERENT HOTEL ROOM EVERY NIGHT... FOR WEEKS AT A TIME.
SOMETIMES HE'D GET CONFUSED AND FORGET WHERE HE WAS.
ONE TIME HE CAME HOME WITH A BLACK EYE.
HE WAS IN A STRANGE PLACE AND WALKED INTO A WALL?
NO....
HE WAS WITH A STRANGE WOMAN, AND, WALKED INTO A FIST.
LYNN

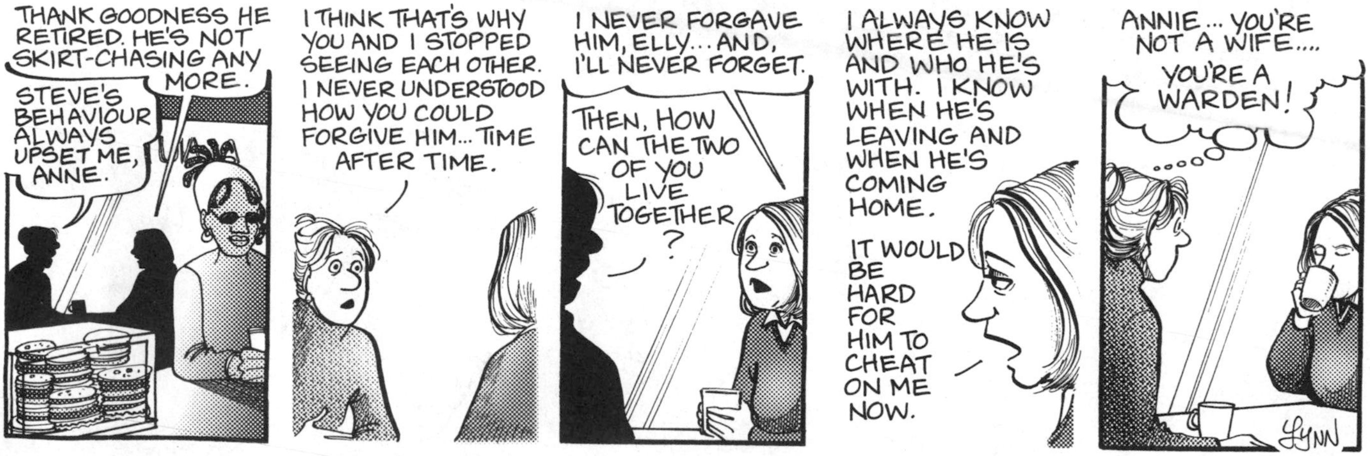
THANK GOODNESS HE RETIRED. HE'S NOT SKIRT-CHASING ANY MORE.
STEVE'S BEHAVIOUR ALWAYS UPSET ME, ANNE.
I THINK THAT'S WHY YOU AND I STOPPED SEEING EACH OTHER. I NEVER UNDERSTOOD HOW YOU COULD FORGIVE HIM... TIME AFTER TIME.
I NEVER FORGAVE HIM, ELLY... AND, I'LL NEVER FORGET.
THEN, HOW CAN THE TWO OF YOU LIVE TOGETHER?
I ALWAYS KNOW WHERE HE IS AND WHO HE'S WITH. I KNOW WHEN HE'S LEAVING AND WHEN HE'S COMING HOME.
IT WOULD BE HARD FOR HIM TO CHEAT ON ME NOW.
ANNIE... YOU'RE NOT A WIFE....
YOU'RE A WARDEN!
LYNN

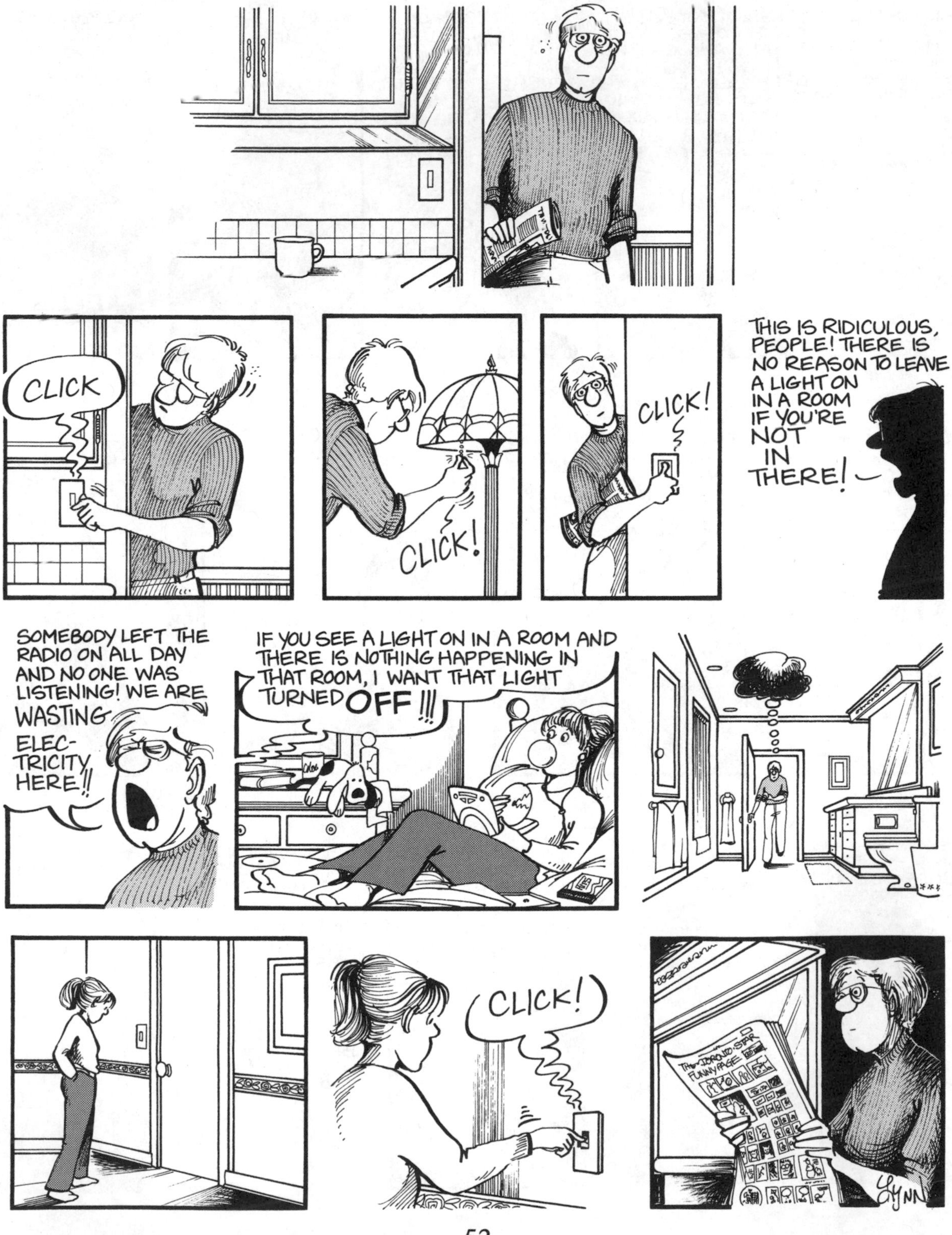
CLICK
CLICK!
CLICK!
THIS IS RIDICULOUS, PEOPLE! THERE IS NO REASON TO LEAVE A LIGHT ON IN A ROOM IF YOU'RE NOT IN THERE!
SOMEBODY LEFT THE RADIO ON ALL DAY AND NO ONE WAS LISTENING! WE ARE WASTING ELEC-TRICITY HERE!!
IF YOU SEE A LIGHT ON IN A ROOM AND THERE IS NOTHING HAPPENING IN THAT ROOM, I WANT THAT LIGHT TURNED OFF!!!
CLICK!
THE TORONTO STAR
FUNNY PAGE
LYNN

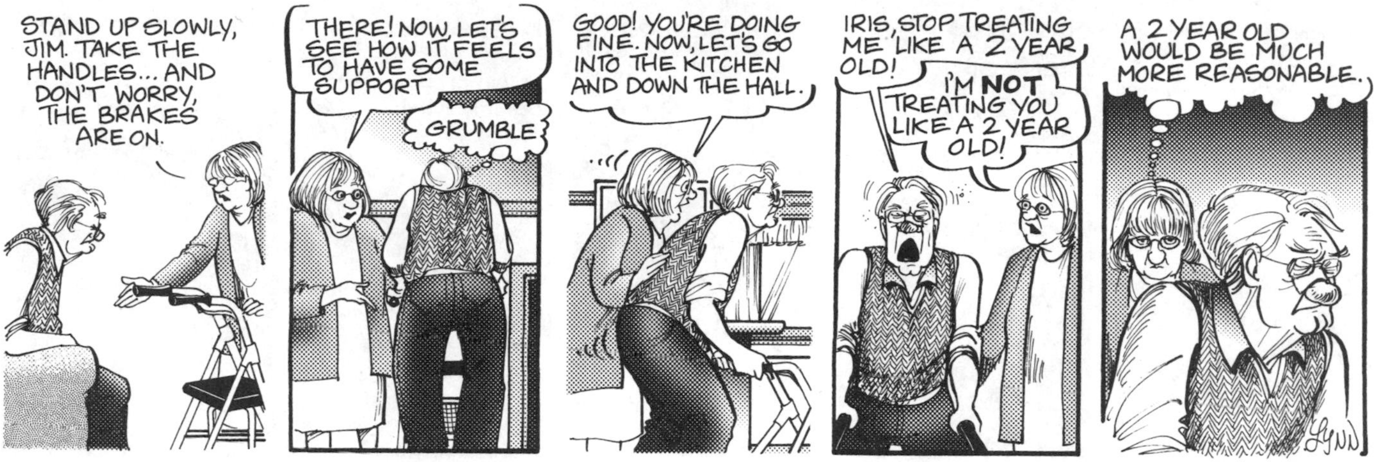
STAND UP SLOWLY, JIM. TAKE THE HANDLES... AND DON'T WORRY, THE BRAKES ARE ON.
THERE! NOW, LET'S SEE HOW IT FEELS TO HAVE SOME SUPPORT
GRUMBLE
GOOD! YOU'RE DOING FINE. NOW, LET'S GO INTO THE KITCHEN AND DOWN THE HALL.
IRIS, STOP TREATING ME LIKE A 2 YEAR OLD!
I'M **NOT** TREATING YOU LIKE A 2 YEAR OLD!
A 2 YEAR OLD WOULD BE MUCH MORE REASONABLE.
LYNN

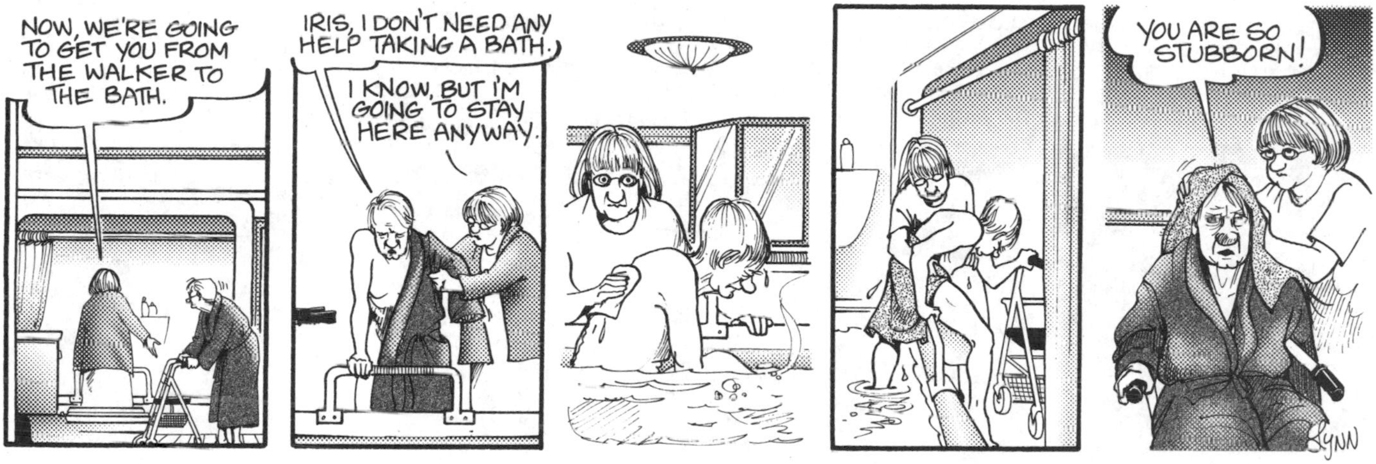
NOW, WE'RE GOING TO GET YOU FROM THE WALKER TO THE BATH.
IRIS, I DON'T NEED ANY HELP TAKING A BATH.
I KNOW, BUT I'M GOING TO STAY HERE ANYWAY.
YOU ARE SO STUBBORN!
LYNN

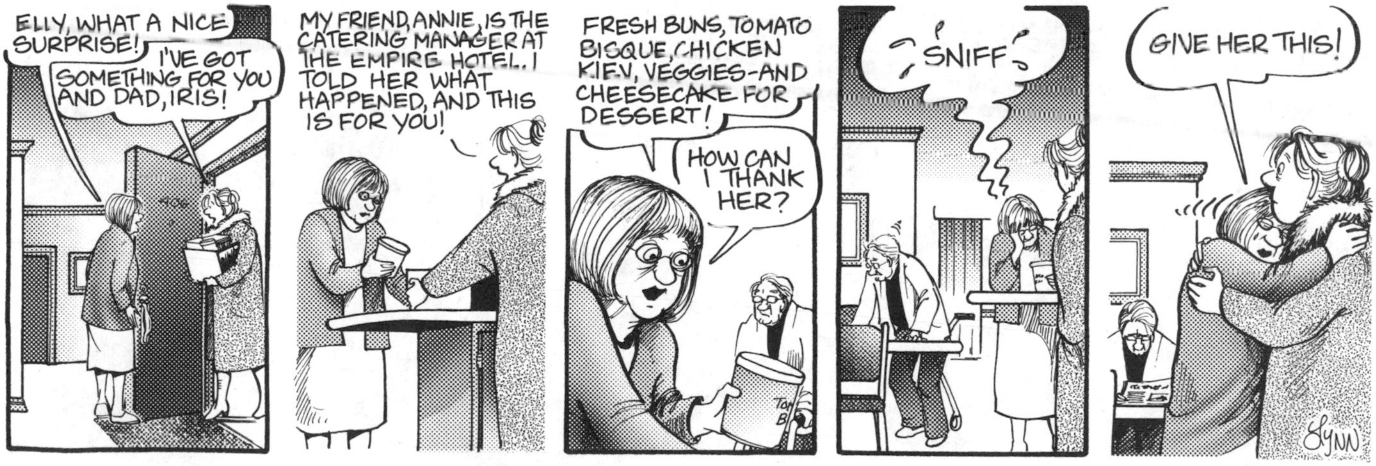
ELLY, WHAT A NICE SURPRISE!
I'VE GOT SOMETHING FOR YOU AND DAD, IRIS!
MY FRIEND, ANNIE, IS THE CATERING MANAGER AT THE EMPIRE HOTEL. I TOLD HER WHAT HAPPENED, AND THIS IS FOR YOU!
FRESH BUNS, TOMATO BISQUE, CHICKEN KIEV, VEGGIES-AND CHEESECAKE FOR DESSERT!
HOW CAN I THANK HER?
SNIFF
GIVE HER THIS!
LYNN

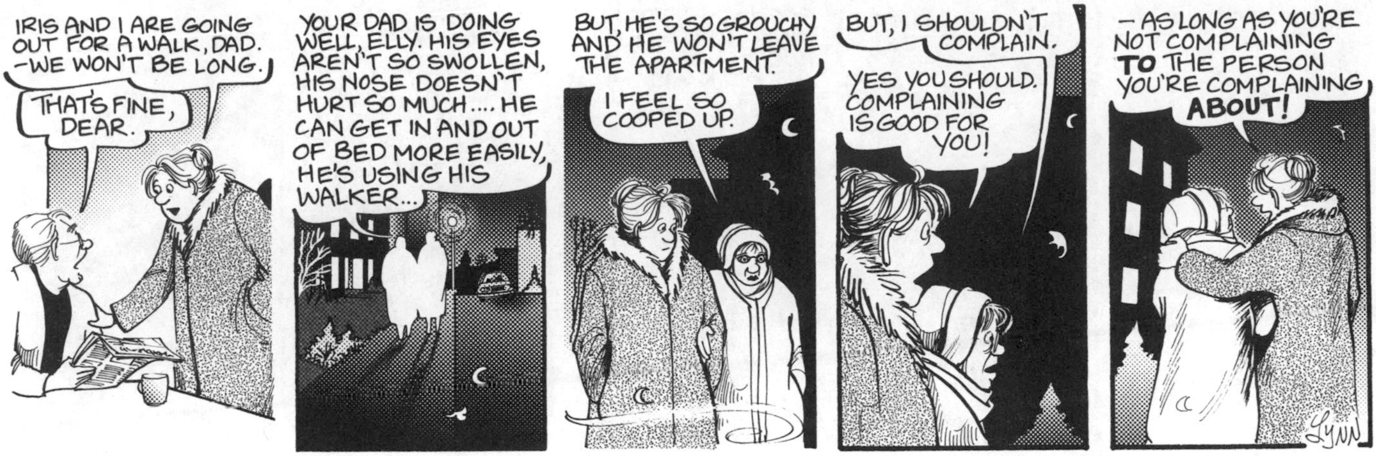
IRIS AND I ARE GOING OUT FOR A WALK, DAD. -WE WON'T BE LONG.
THAT'S FINE, DEAR.
YOUR DAD IS DOING WELL, ELLY. HIS EYES AREN'T SO SWOLLEN, HIS NOSE DOESN'T HURT SO MUCH.... HE CAN GET IN AND OUT OF BED MORE EASILY, HE'S USING HIS WALKER...
BUT, HE'S SO GROUCHY AND HE WON'T LEAVE THE APARTMENT.
I FEEL SO COOPED UP.
BUT, I SHOULDN'T COMPLAIN.
YES YOU SHOULD. COMPLAINING IS GOOD FOR YOU!
- AS LONG AS YOU'RE NOT COMPLAINING **TO** THE PERSON YOU'RE COMPLAINING **ABOUT**!
LYNN

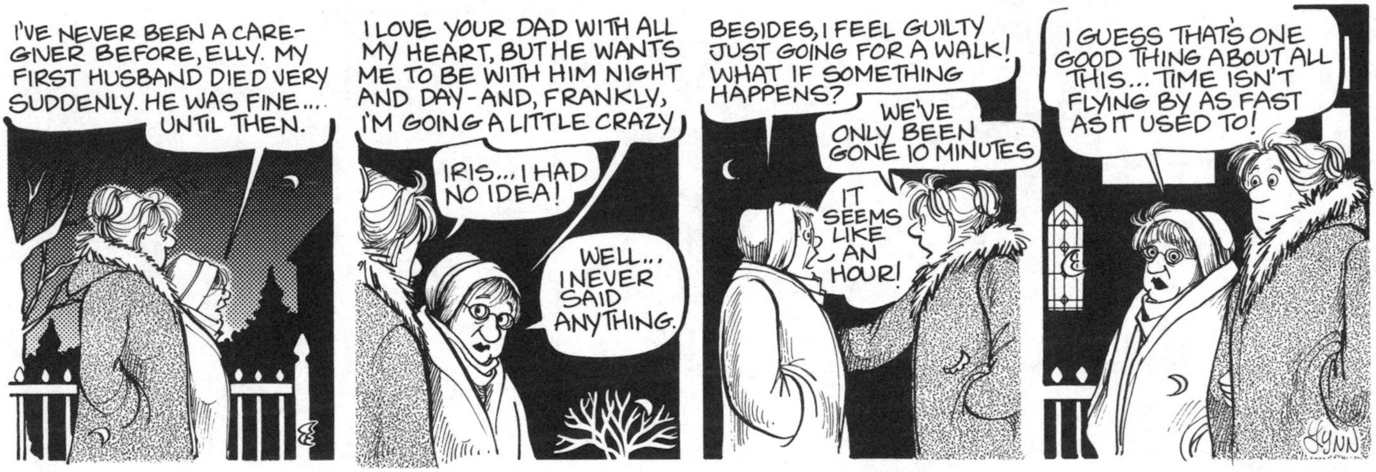
I'VE NEVER BEEN A CARE-GIVER BEFORE, ELLY. MY FIRST HUSBAND DIED VERY SUDDENLY. HE WAS FINE.... UNTIL THEN.
I LOVE YOUR DAD WITH ALL MY HEART, BUT HE WANTS ME TO BE WITH HIM NIGHT AND DAY - AND, FRANKLY, I'M GOING A LITTLE CRAZY
IRIS... I HAD NO IDEA!
WELL... I NEVER SAID ANYTHING.
BESIDES, I FEEL GUILTY JUST GOING FOR A WALK! WHAT IF SOMETHING HAPPENS?
WE'VE ONLY BEEN GONE 10 MINUTES
IT SEEMS LIKE AN HOUR!
I GUESS THAT'S ONE GOOD THING ABOUT ALL THIS... TIME ISN'T FLYING BY AS FAST AS IT USED TO!
LYNN

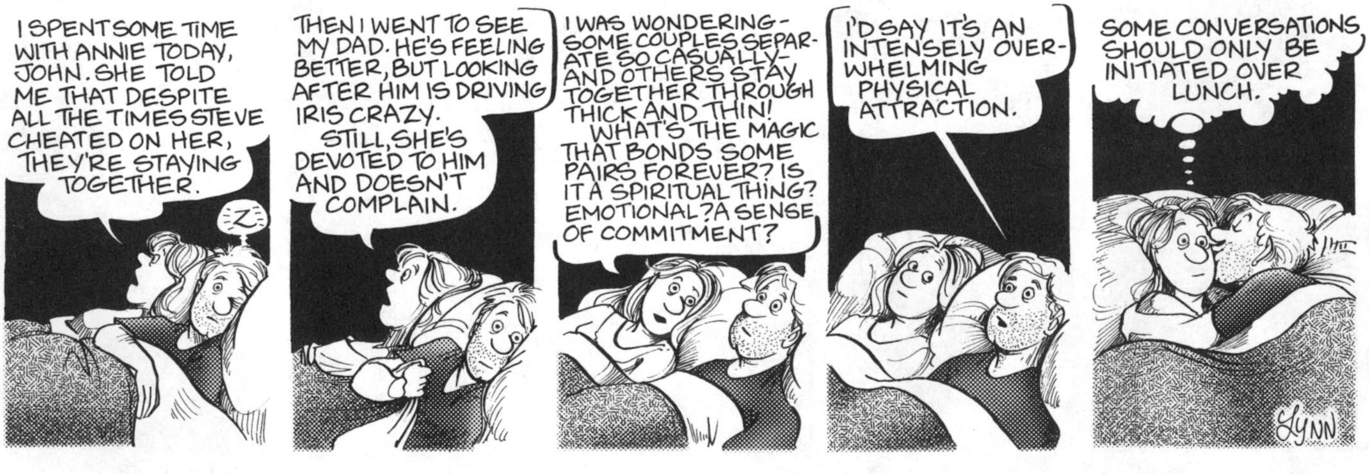
I SPENT SOME TIME WITH ANNIE TODAY, JOHN. SHE TOLD ME THAT DESPITE ALL THE TIMES STEVE CHEATED ON HER, THEY'RE STAYING TOGETHER.
Z
THEN I WENT TO SEE MY DAD. HE'S FEELING BETTER, BUT LOOKING AFTER HIM IS DRIVING IRIS CRAZY.
STILL, SHE'S DEVOTED TO HIM AND DOESN'T COMPLAIN.
I WAS WONDERING - SOME COUPLES SEPAR-ATE SO CASUALLY - AND OTHERS STAY TOGETHER THROUGH THICK AND THIN!
WHAT'S THE MAGIC THAT BONDS SOME PAIRS FOREVER? IS IT A SPIRITUAL THING? EMOTIONAL? A SENSE OF COMMITMENT?
I'D SAY IT'S AN INTENSELY OVER-WHELMING PHYSICAL ATTRACTION.
SOME CONVERSATIONS SHOULD ONLY BE INITIATED OVER LUNCH.
LYNN

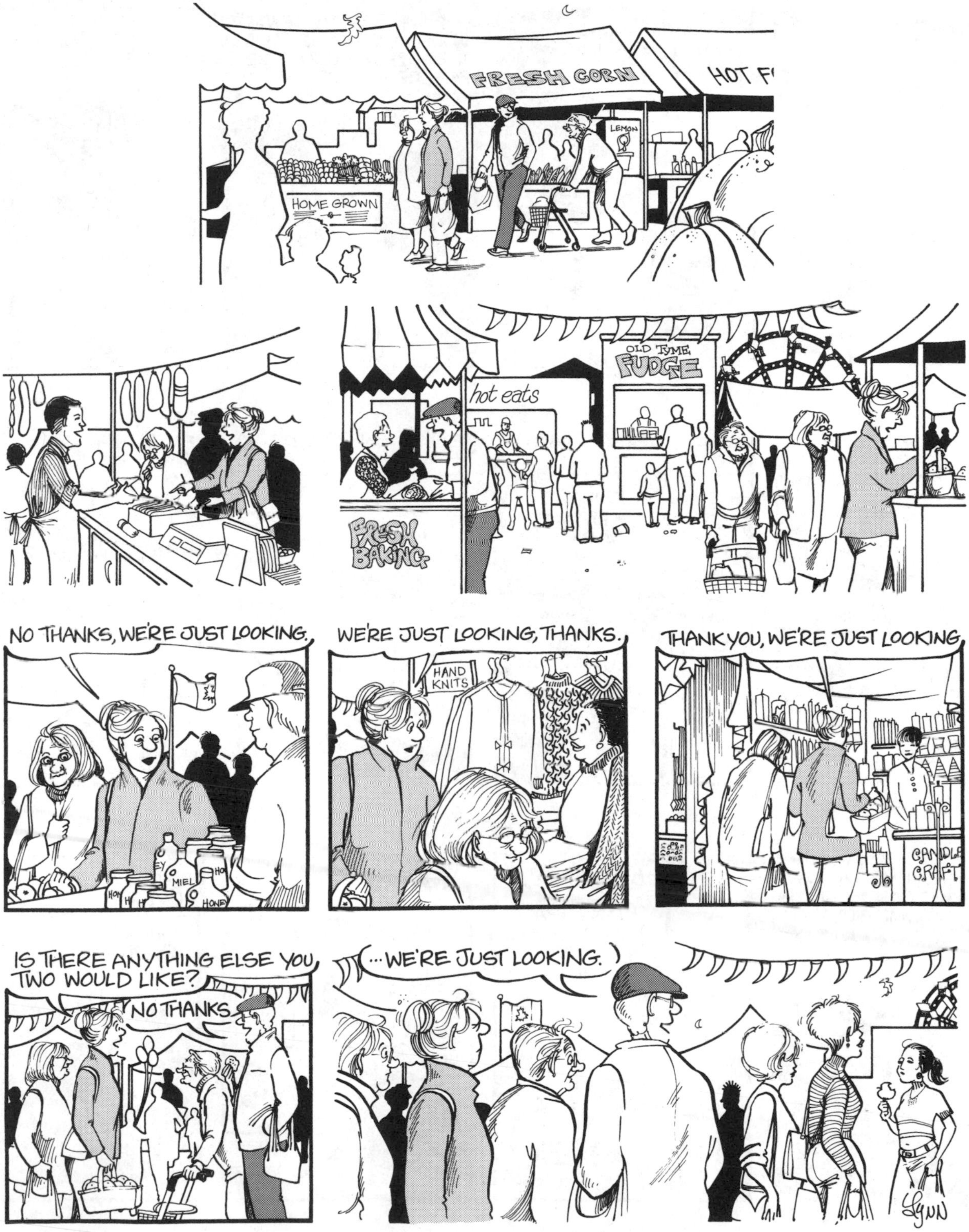
FRESH CORN
LEMON
HOME GROWN
OLD TYME FUDGE
hot eats
FRESH BAKING
NO THANKS, WE'RE JUST LOOKING.
MIEL
HONEY
WE'RE JUST LOOKING, THANKS.
HAND KNITS
THANK YOU, WE'RE JUST LOOKING.
IS THERE ANYTHING ELSE YOU TWO WOULD LIKE?
NO THANKS.
(... WE'RE JUST LOOKING.)
LYNN

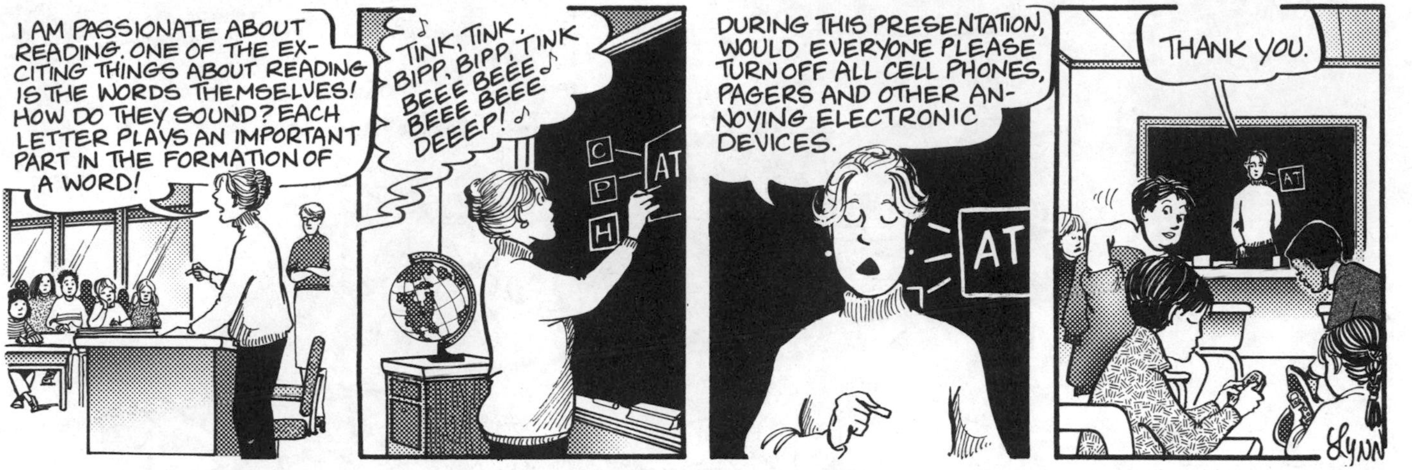
I AM PASSIONATE ABOUT READING. ONE OF THE EXCITING THINGS ABOUT READING IS THE WORDS THEMSELVES! HOW DO THEY SOUND? EACH LETTER PLAYS AN IMPORTANT PART IN THE FORMATION OF A WORD!
TINK, TINK, BIPP, BIPP, TINK BEEE BEEE BEEE BEEE DEEEP!
C
P
H
AT
DURING THIS PRESENTATION, WOULD EVERYONE PLEASE TURN OFF ALL CELL PHONES, PAGERS AND OTHER ANNOYING ELECTRONIC DEVICES.
AT
THANK YOU.
AT

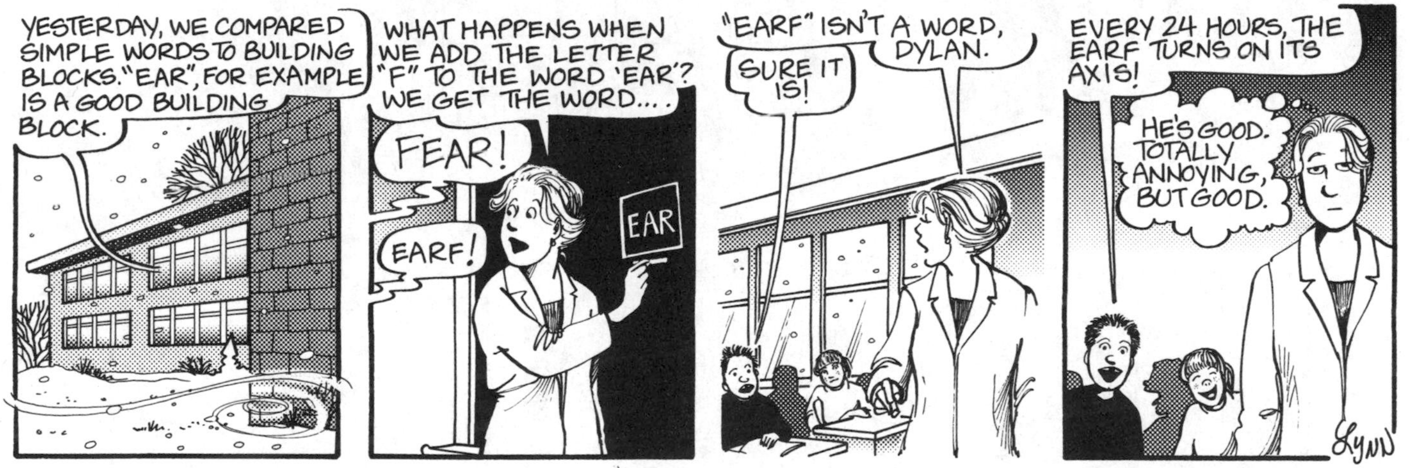
YESTERDAY, WE COMPARED SIMPLE WORDS TO BUILDING BLOCKS. "EAR", FOR EXAMPLE IS A GOOD BUILDING BLOCK.
WHAT HAPPENS WHEN WE ADD THE LETTER "F" TO THE WORD 'EAR'? WE GET THE WORD....
FEAR!
EARF!
EAR
"EARF" ISN'T A WORD, DYLAN.
SURE IT IS!
EVERY 24 HOURS, THE EARF TURNS ON ITS AXIS!
HE'S GOOD. TOTALLY ANNOYING, BUT GOOD.

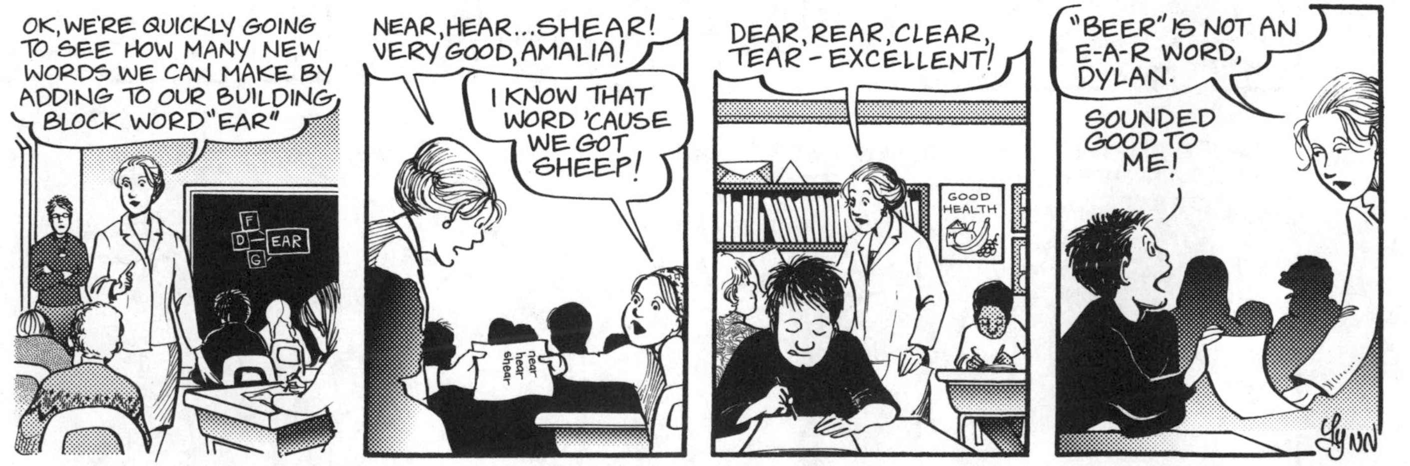
OK, WE'RE QUICKLY GOING TO SEE HOW MANY NEW WORDS WE CAN MAKE BY ADDING TO OUR BUILDING BLOCK WORD "EAR"
F
D
G
EAR
NEAR, HEAR...SHEAR! VERY GOOD, AMALIA!
I KNOW THAT WORD 'CAUSE WE GOT SHEEP!
near
hear
shear
DEAR, REAR, CLEAR, TEAR - EXCELLENT!
GOOD HEALTH
"BEER" IS NOT AN E-A-R WORD, DYLAN.
SOUNDED GOOD TO ME!

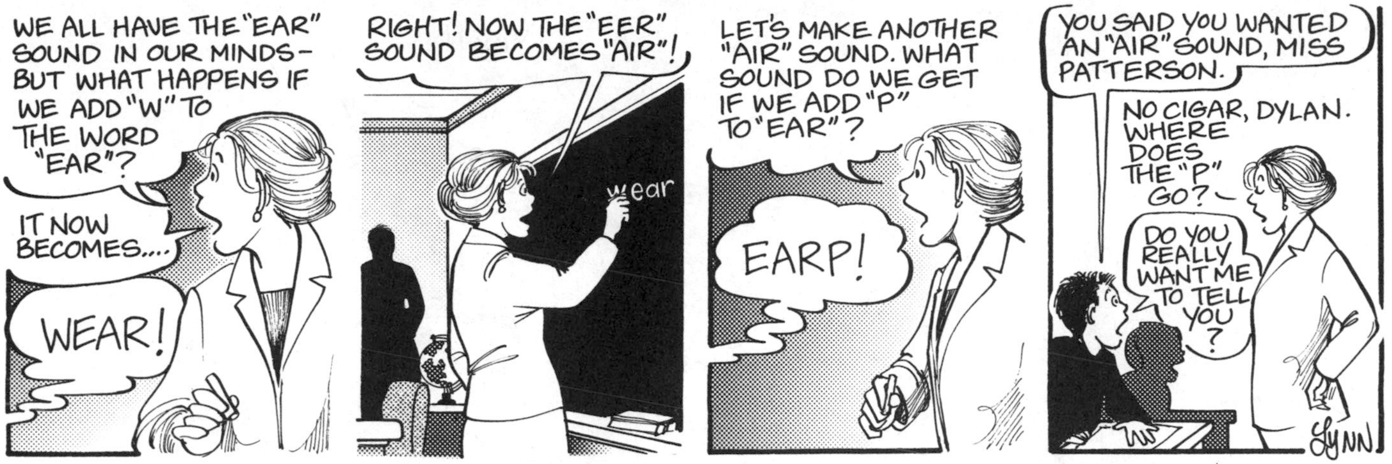
WE ALL HAVE THE "EAR" SOUND IN OUR MINDS- BUT WHAT HAPPENS IF WE ADD "W" TO THE WORD "EAR"?
IT NOW BECOMES....
WEAR!
RIGHT! NOW THE "EER" SOUND BECOMES "AIR"!
wear
LET'S MAKE ANOTHER "AIR" SOUND. WHAT SOUND DO WE GET IF WE ADD "P" TO "EAR"?
EARP!
YOU SAID YOU WANTED AN "AIR" SOUND, MISS PATTERSON.
NO CIGAR, DYLAN. WHERE DOES THE "P" GO?
DO YOU REALLY WANT ME TO TELL YOU?
LYNN

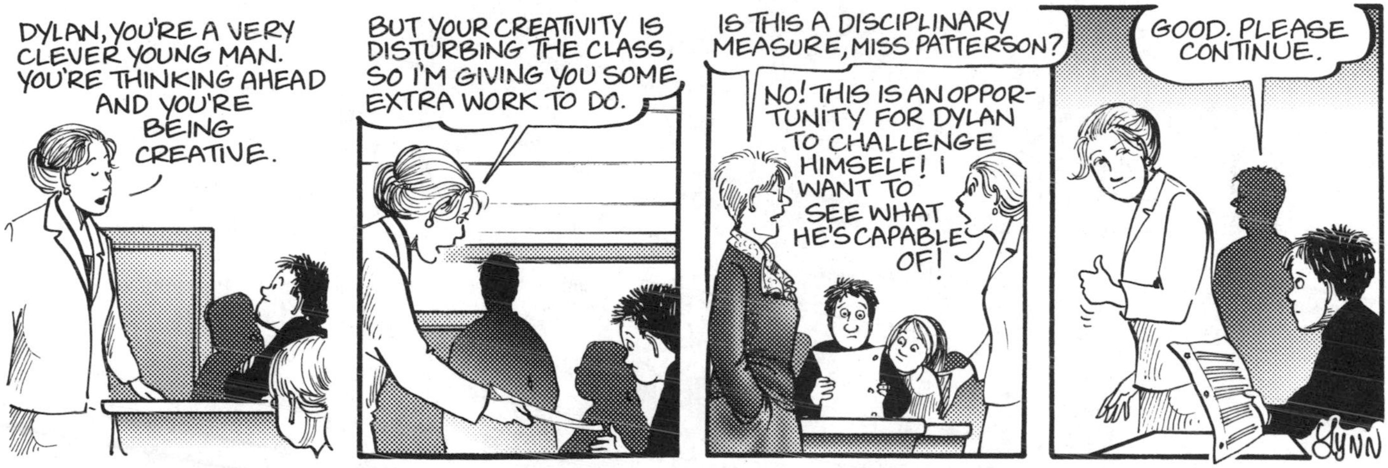
DYLAN, YOU'RE A VERY CLEVER YOUNG MAN. YOU'RE THINKING AHEAD AND YOU'RE BEING CREATIVE.
BUT YOUR CREATIVITY IS DISTURBING THE CLASS, SO I'M GIVING YOU SOME EXTRA WORK TO DO.
IS THIS A DISCIPLINARY MEASURE, MISS PATTERSON?
NO! THIS IS AN OPPORTUNITY FOR DYLAN TO CHALLENGE HIMSELF! I WANT TO SEE WHAT HE'S CAPABLE OF!
GOOD. PLEASE CONTINUE.
LYNN

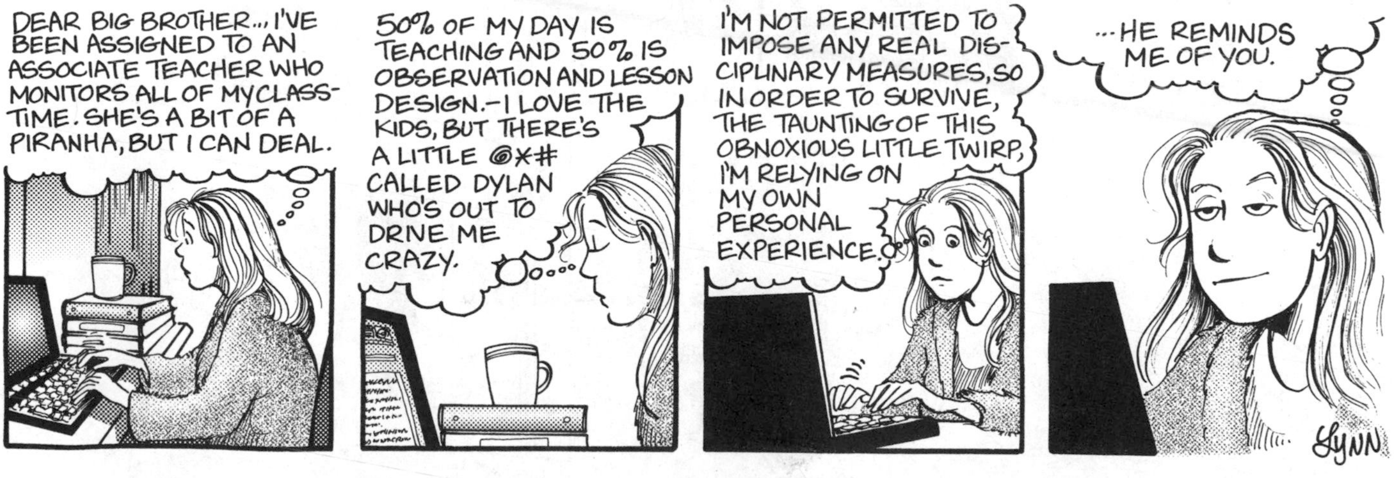
DEAR BIG BROTHER... I'VE BEEN ASSIGNED TO AN ASSOCIATE TEACHER WHO MONITORS ALL OF MY CLASS-TIME. SHE'S A BIT OF A PIRANHA, BUT I CAN DEAL.
50% OF MY DAY IS TEACHING AND 50% IS OBSERVATION AND LESSON DESIGN.-I LOVE THE KIDS, BUT THERE'S A LITTLE @*# CALLED DYLAN WHO'S OUT TO DRIVE ME CRAZY.
I'M NOT PERMITTED TO IMPOSE ANY REAL DISCIPLINARY MEASURES, SO IN ORDER TO SURVIVE, THE TAUNTING OF THIS OBNOXIOUS LITTLE TWIRP, I'M RELYING ON MY OWN PERSONAL EXPERIENCE.
...HE REMINDS ME OF YOU.
LYNN

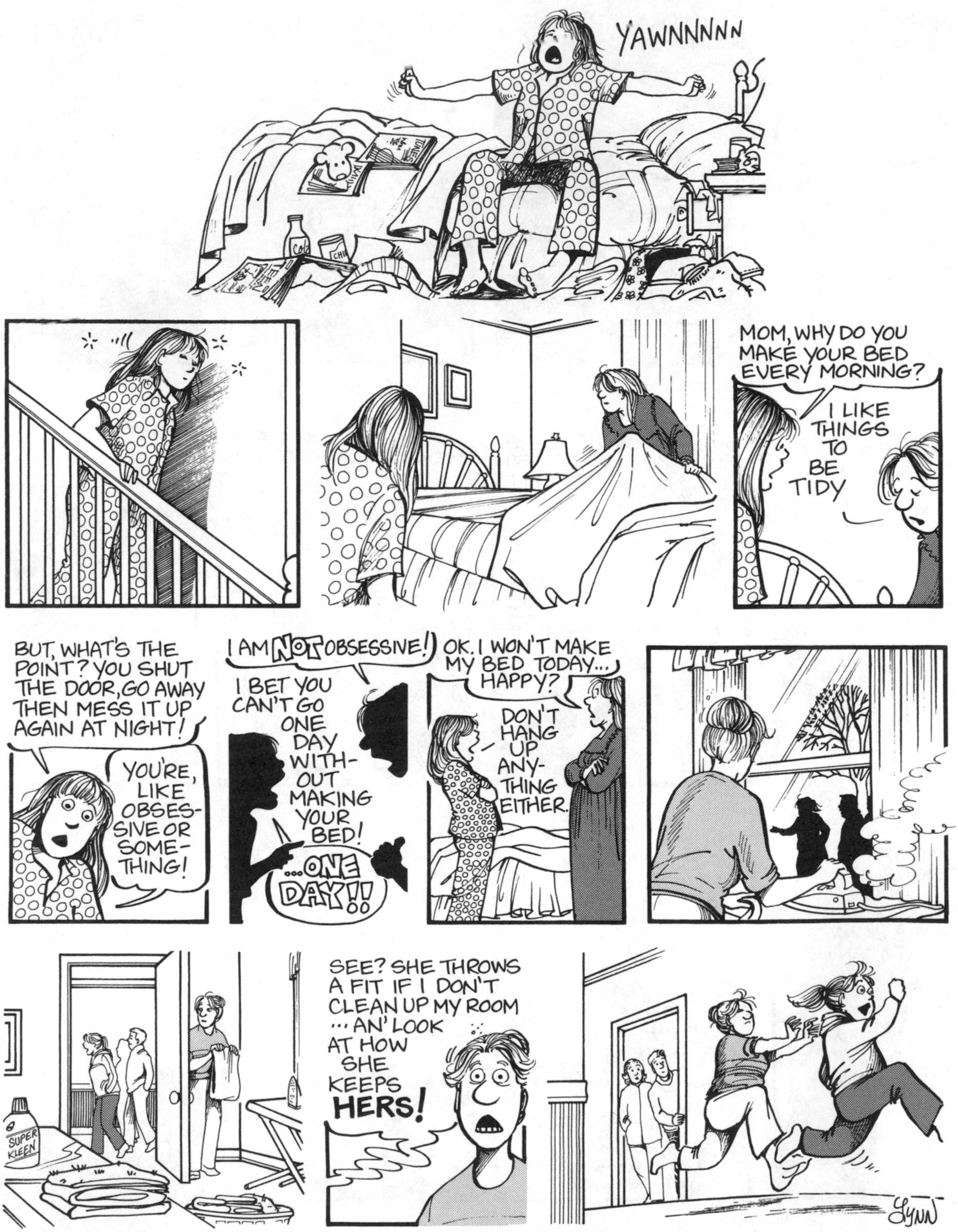
YAWNNNNN
MOM, WHY DO YOU MAKE YOUR BED EVERY MORNING?
I LIKE THINGS TO BE TIDY
BUT, WHAT'S THE POINT? YOU SHUT THE DOOR, GO AWAY THEN MESS IT UP AGAIN AT NIGHT!
YOU'RE, LIKE OBSESSIVE OR SOMETHING!
I AM NOT OBSESSIVE!
I BET YOU CAN'T GO ONE DAY WITHOUT MAKING YOUR BED!
...ONE DAY!!
OK. I WON'T MAKE MY BED TODAY... HAPPY?
DON'T HANG UP ANYTHING EITHER.
SUPER KLEEN
SEE? SHE THROWS A FIT IF I DON'T CLEAN UP MY ROOM ...AN' LOOK AT HOW SHE KEEPS HERS!
LYNN

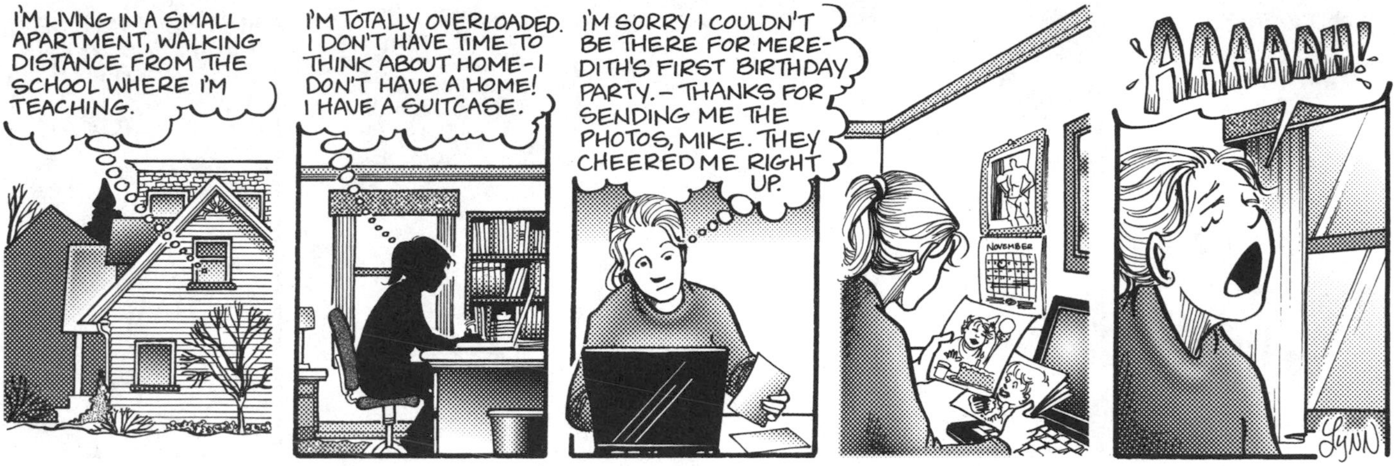
I'M LIVING IN A SMALL APARTMENT, WALKING DISTANCE FROM THE SCHOOL WHERE I'M TEACHING.
I'M TOTALLY OVERLOADED. I DON'T HAVE TIME TO THINK ABOUT HOME - I DON'T HAVE A HOME! I HAVE A SUITCASE.
I'M SORRY I COULDN'T BE THERE FOR MEREDITH'S FIRST BIRTHDAY PARTY. – THANKS FOR SENDING ME THE PHOTOS, MIKE. THEY CHEERED ME RIGHT UP.
NOVEMBER
AAAAAH!
LYNN

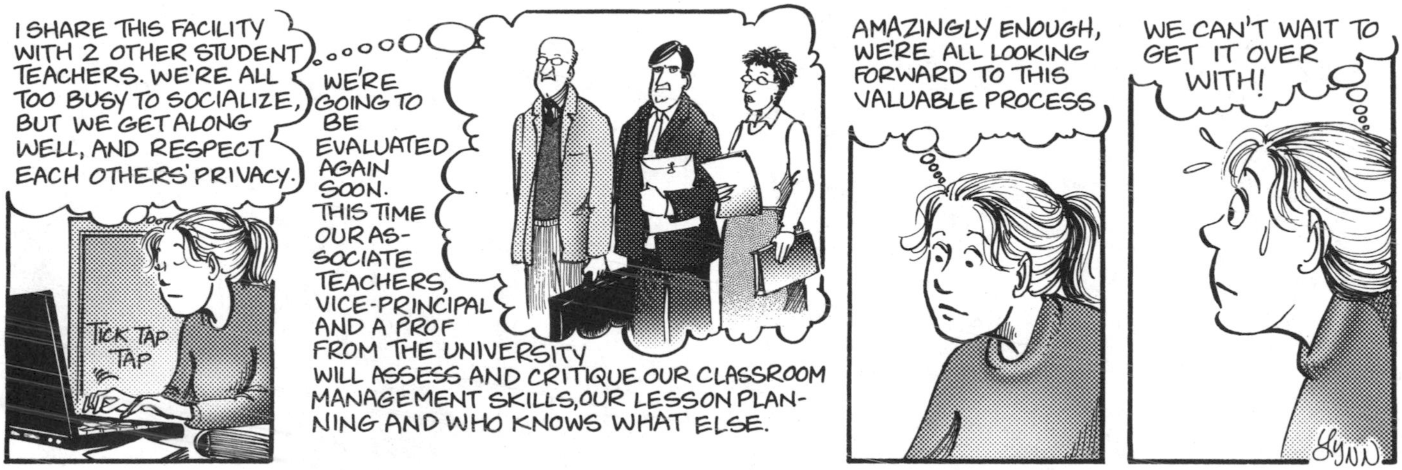
I SHARE THIS FACILITY WITH 2 OTHER STUDENT TEACHERS. WE'RE ALL TOO BUSY TO SOCIALIZE, BUT WE GET ALONG WELL, AND RESPECT EACH OTHERS' PRIVACY.
TICK TAP TAP
WE'RE GOING TO BE EVALUATED AGAIN SOON. THIS TIME OUR ASSOCIATE TEACHERS, VICE-PRINCIPAL AND A PROF FROM THE UNIVERSITY WILL ASSESS AND CRITIQUE OUR CLASSROOM MANAGEMENT SKILLS, OUR LESSON PLANNING AND WHO KNOWS WHAT ELSE.
AMAZINGLY ENOUGH, WE'RE ALL LOOKING FORWARD TO THIS VALUABLE PROCESS
WE CAN'T WAIT TO GET IT OVER WITH!
LYNN

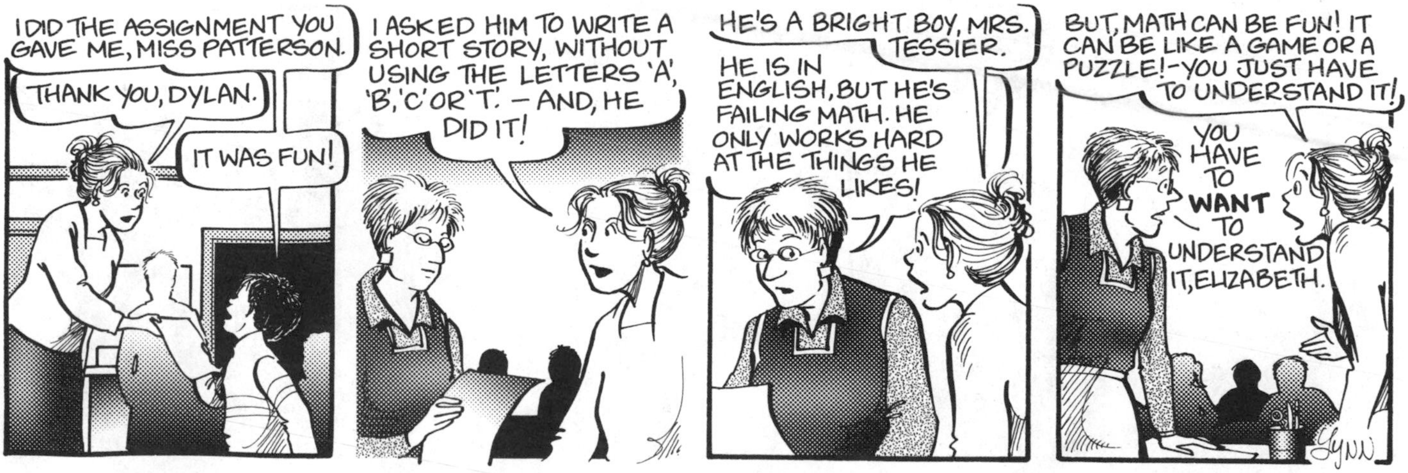
I DID THE ASSIGNMENT YOU GAVE ME, MISS PATTERSON.
THANK YOU, DYLAN.
IT WAS FUN!
I ASKED HIM TO WRITE A SHORT STORY, WITHOUT USING THE LETTERS 'A', 'B', 'C' OR 'T'. – AND, HE DID IT!
HE'S A BRIGHT BOY, MRS. TESSIER.
HE IS IN ENGLISH, BUT HE'S FAILING MATH. HE ONLY WORKS HARD AT THE THINGS HE LIKES!
BUT, MATH CAN BE FUN! IT CAN BE LIKE A GAME OR A PUZZLE! – YOU JUST HAVE TO UNDERSTAND IT!
YOU HAVE TO WANT TO UNDERSTAND IT, ELIZABETH.
LYNN

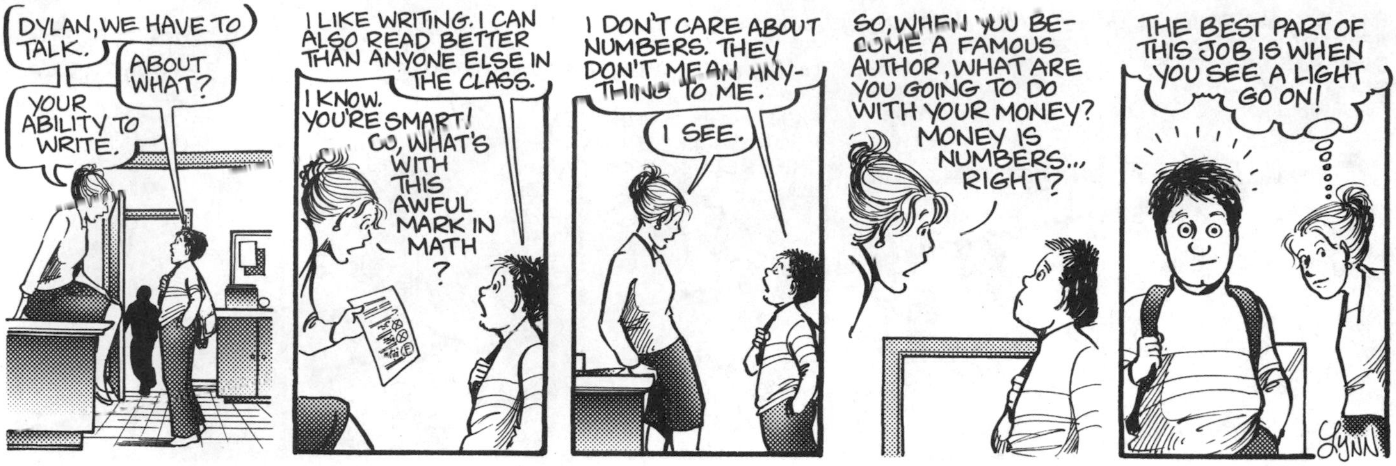
DYLAN, WE HAVE TO TALK.
ABOUT WHAT?
YOUR ABILITY TO WRITE.
I LIKE WRITING. I CAN ALSO READ BETTER THAN ANYONE ELSE IN THE CLASS.
I KNOW. YOU'RE SMART! SO, WHAT'S WITH THIS AWFUL MARK IN MATH?
I DON'T CARE ABOUT NUMBERS. THEY DON'T MEAN ANYTHING TO ME.
I SEE.
SO, WHEN YOU BECOME A FAMOUS AUTHOR, WHAT ARE YOU GOING TO DO WITH YOUR MONEY?
MONEY IS NUMBERS... RIGHT?
THE BEST PART OF THIS JOB IS WHEN YOU SEE A LIGHT GO ON!
LYNN

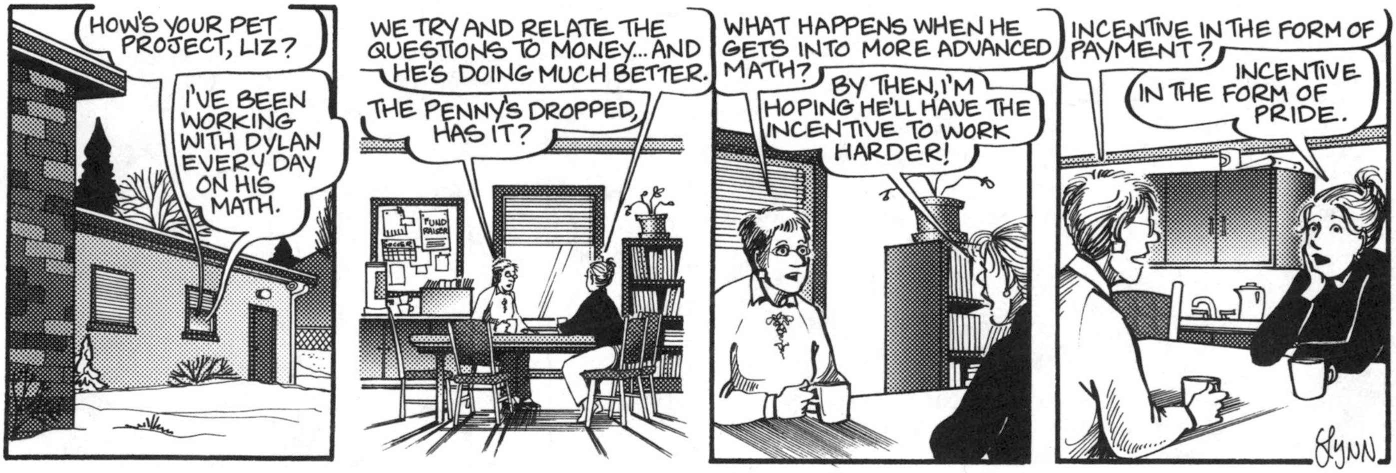
HOW'S YOUR PET PROJECT, LIZ?
I'VE BEEN WORKING WITH DYLAN EVERY DAY ON HIS MATH.
WE TRY AND RELATE THE QUESTIONS TO MONEY... AND HE'S DOING MUCH BETTER.
THE PENNY'S DROPPED, HAS IT?
WHAT HAPPENS WHEN HE GETS INTO MORE ADVANCED MATH?
BY THEN, I'M HOPING HE'LL HAVE THE INCENTIVE TO WORK HARDER!
INCENTIVE IN THE FORM OF PAYMENT?
INCENTIVE IN THE FORM OF PRIDE.
LYNN

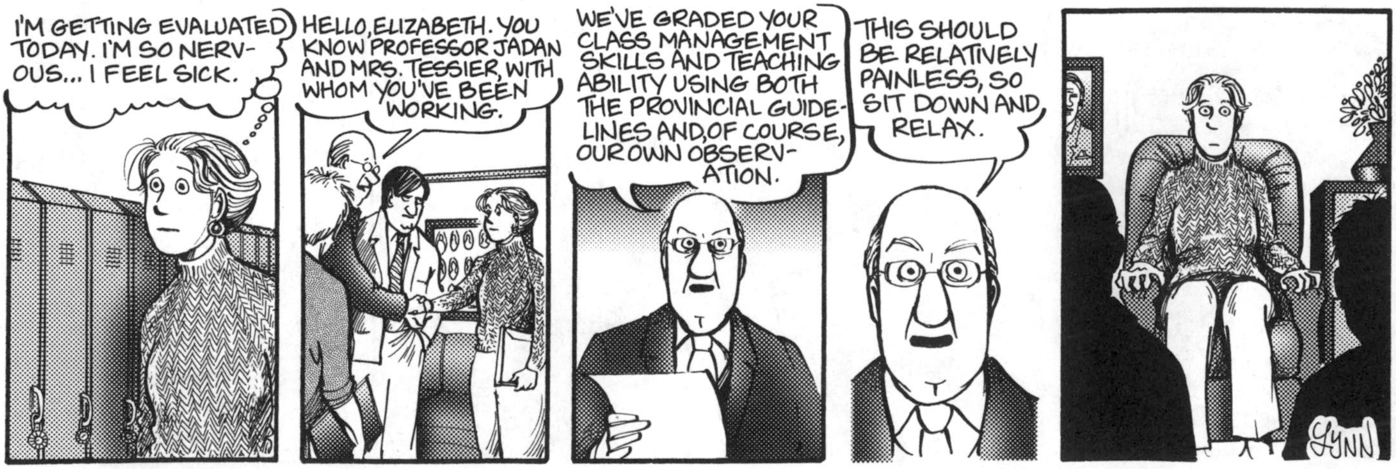
I'M GETTING EVALUATED TODAY. I'M SO NERVOUS... I FEEL SICK.
HELLO, ELIZABETH. YOU KNOW PROFESSOR JADAN AND MRS. TESSIER, WITH WHOM YOU'VE BEEN WORKING.
WE'VE GRADED YOUR CLASS MANAGEMENT SKILLS AND TEACHING ABILITY USING BOTH THE PROVINCIAL GUIDELINES AND, OF COURSE, OUR OWN OBSERVATION.
THIS SHOULD BE RELATIVELY PAINLESS, SO SIT DOWN AND RELAX.
LYNN

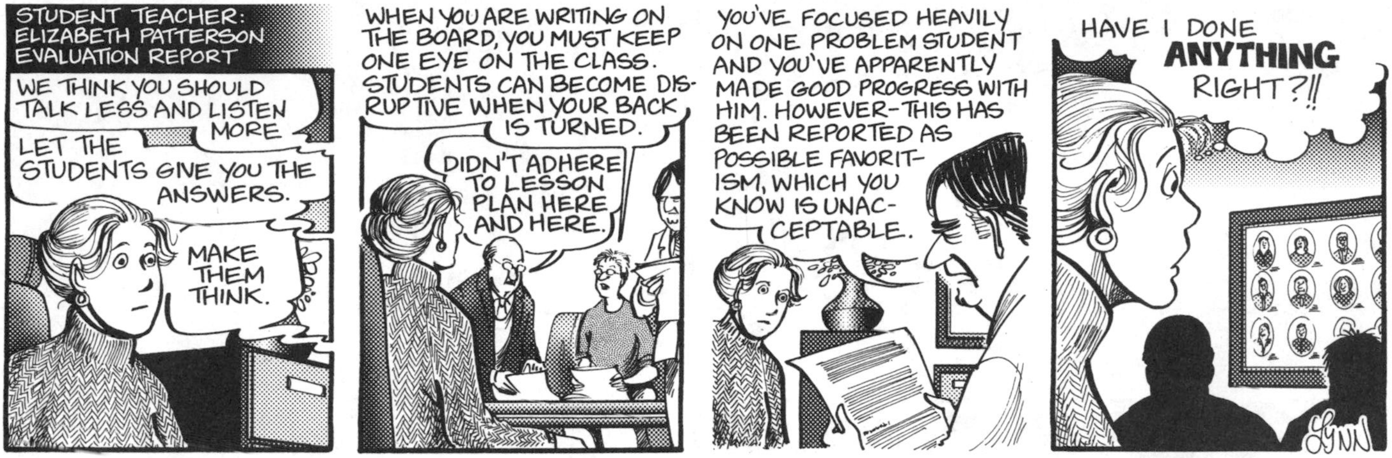
STUDENT TEACHER: ELIZABETH PATTERSON EVALUATION REPORT
WE THINK YOU SHOULD TALK LESS AND LISTEN MORE
LET THE STUDENTS GIVE YOU THE ANSWERS.
MAKE THEM THINK.
WHEN YOU ARE WRITING ON THE BOARD, YOU MUST KEEP ONE EYE ON THE CLASS. STUDENTS CAN BECOME DISRUPTIVE WHEN YOUR BACK IS TURNED.
DIDN'T ADHERE TO LESSON PLAN HERE AND HERE.
YOU'VE FOCUSED HEAVILY ON ONE PROBLEM STUDENT AND YOU'VE APPARENTLY MADE GOOD PROGRESS WITH HIM. HOWEVER-THIS HAS BEEN REPORTED AS POSSIBLE FAVORITISM, WHICH YOU KNOW IS UNACCEPTABLE.
HAVE I DONE **ANYTHING** RIGHT?!!
LYNN

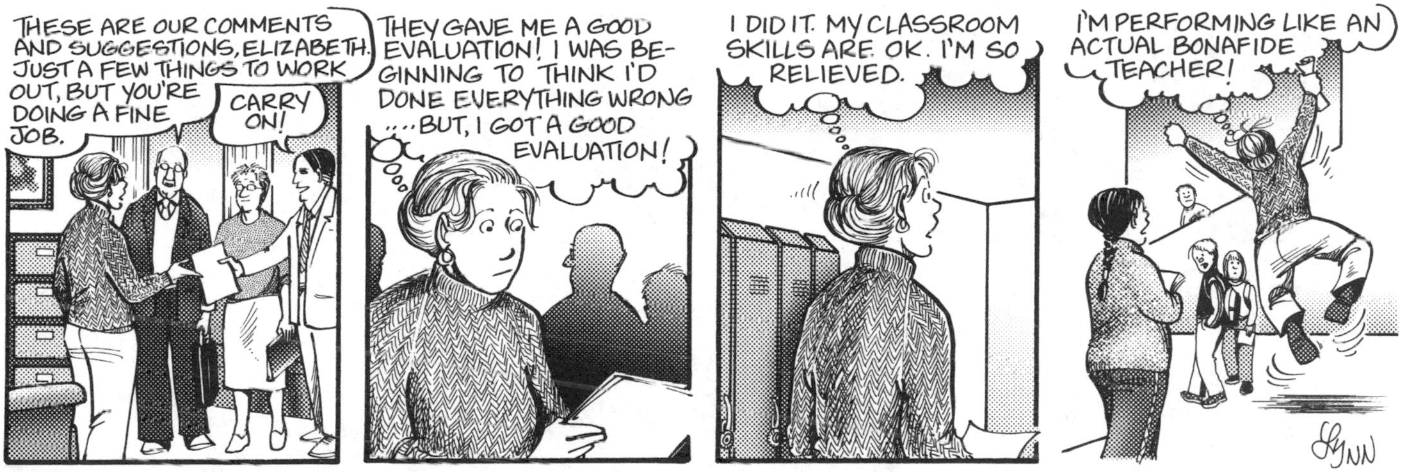
THESE ARE OUR COMMENTS AND SUGGESTIONS, ELIZABETH. JUST A FEW THINGS TO WORK OUT, BUT YOU'RE DOING A FINE JOB.
CARRY ON!
THEY GAVE ME A GOOD EVALUATION! I WAS BEGINNING TO THINK I'D DONE EVERYTHING WRONG ....BUT, I GOT A GOOD EVALUATION!
I DID IT. MY CLASSROOM SKILLS ARE OK. I'M SO RELIEVED.
I'M PERFORMING LIKE AN ACTUAL BONAFIDE TEACHER!
LYNN

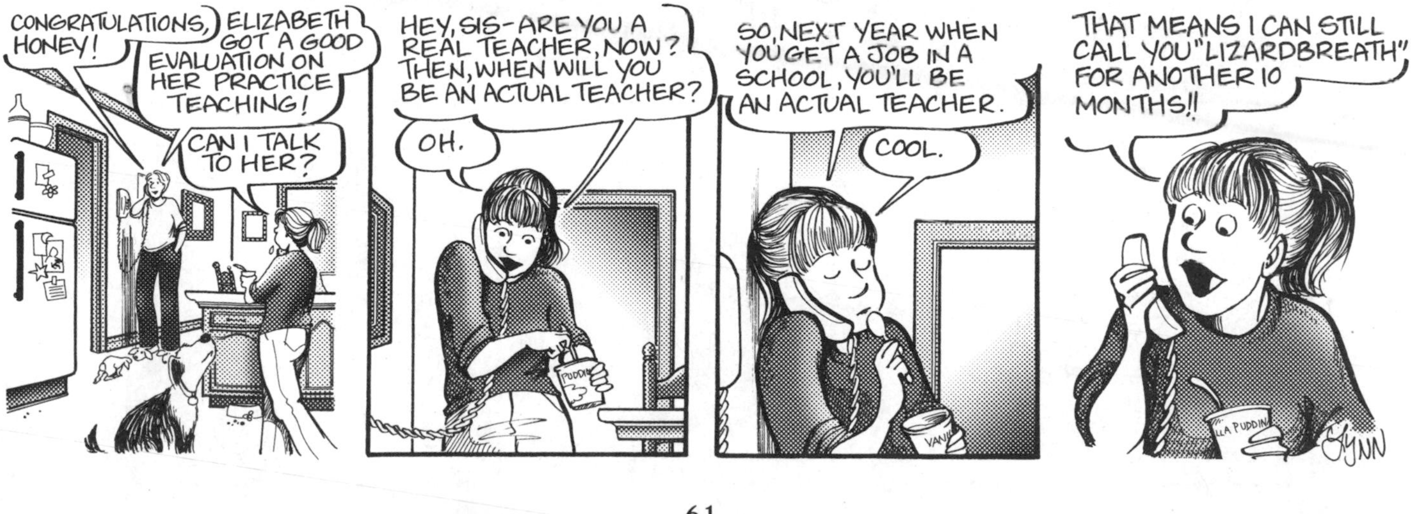
CONGRATULATIONS, HONEY!
ELIZABETH GOT A GOOD EVALUATION ON HER PRACTICE TEACHING!
CAN I TALK TO HER?
HEY, SIS-ARE YOU A REAL TEACHER, NOW? THEN, WHEN WILL YOU BE AN ACTUAL TEACHER?
OH.
SO, NEXT YEAR WHEN YOU GET A JOB IN A SCHOOL, YOU'LL BE AN ACTUAL TEACHER.
COOL.
THAT MEANS I CAN STILL CALL YOU "LIZARDBREATH" FOR ANOTHER 10 MONTHS!!
LYNN

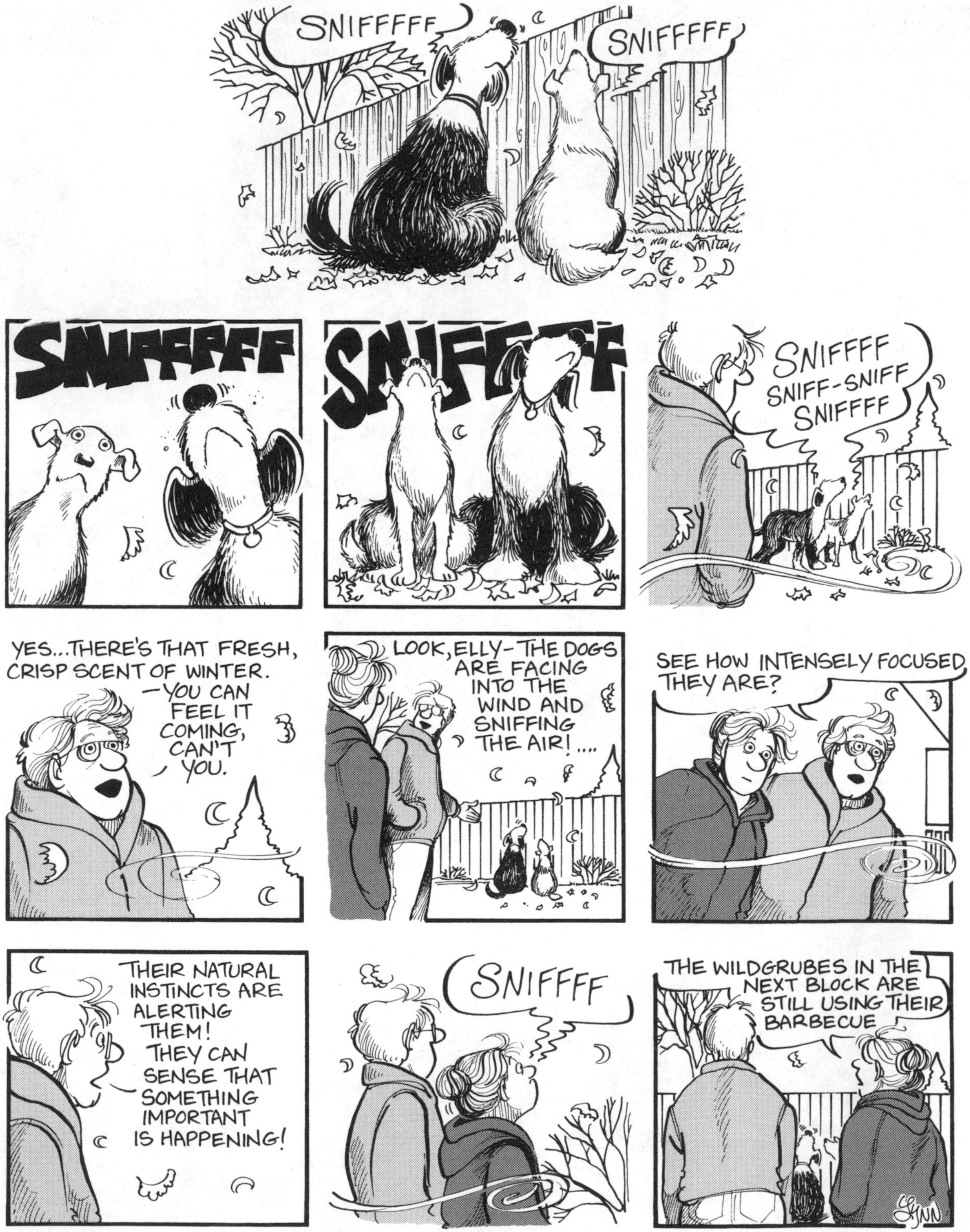
SNIFFFFF
SNIFFFFF
SNIFFFFF
SNIFFFFF
SNIFFFF
SNIFF-SNIFF
SNIFFFF
YES... THERE'S THAT FRESH, CRISP SCENT OF WINTER.
—YOU CAN FEEL IT COMING, CAN'T YOU.
LOOK, ELLY- THE DOGS ARE FACING INTO THE WIND AND SNIFFING THE AIR! ....
SEE HOW INTENSELY FOCUSED THEY ARE?
THEIR NATURAL INSTINCTS ARE ALERTING THEM! THEY CAN SENSE THAT SOMETHING IMPORTANT IS HAPPENING!
SNIFFFF
THE WILDGRUBES IN THE NEXT BLOCK ARE STILL USING THEIR BARBECUE
LYNN

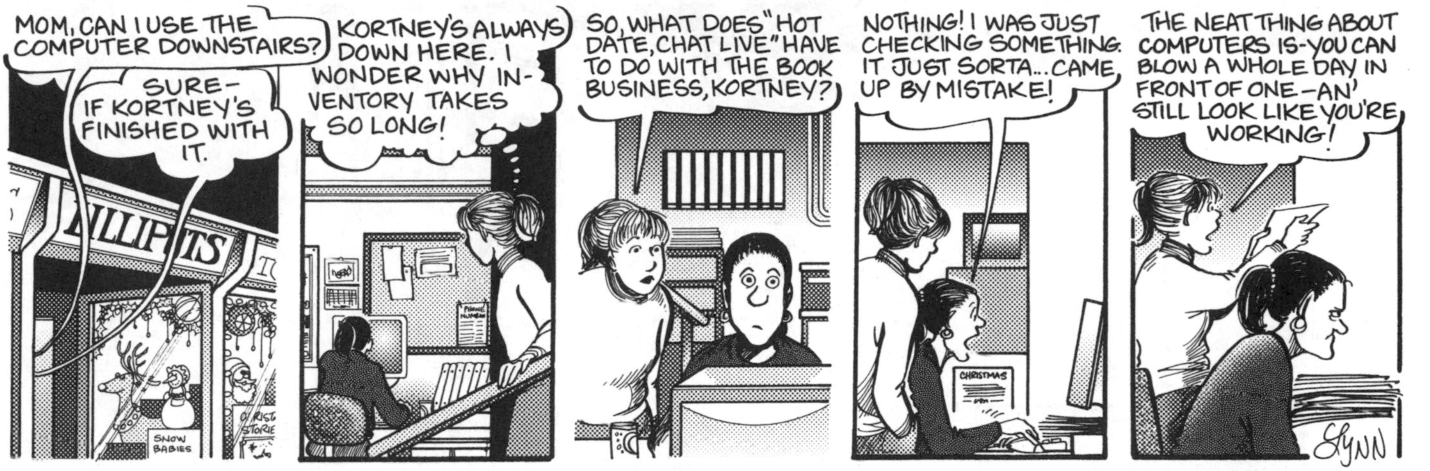
MOM, CAN I USE THE COMPUTER DOWNSTAIRS?
SURE- IF KORTNEY'S FINISHED WITH IT.
LILLIPUTS
SNOW BABIES
KORTNEY'S ALWAYS DOWN HERE. I WONDER WHY IN-VENTORY TAKES SO LONG!
SO, WHAT DOES "HOT DATE, CHAT LIVE" HAVE TO DO WITH THE BOOK BUSINESS, KORTNEY?
NOTHING! I WAS JUST CHECKING SOMETHING. IT JUST SORTA... CAME UP BY MISTAKE!
CHRISTMAS
THE NEAT THING ABOUT COMPUTERS IS-YOU CAN BLOW A WHOLE DAY IN FRONT OF ONE-AN' STILL LOOK LIKE YOU'RE WORKING!
LYNN

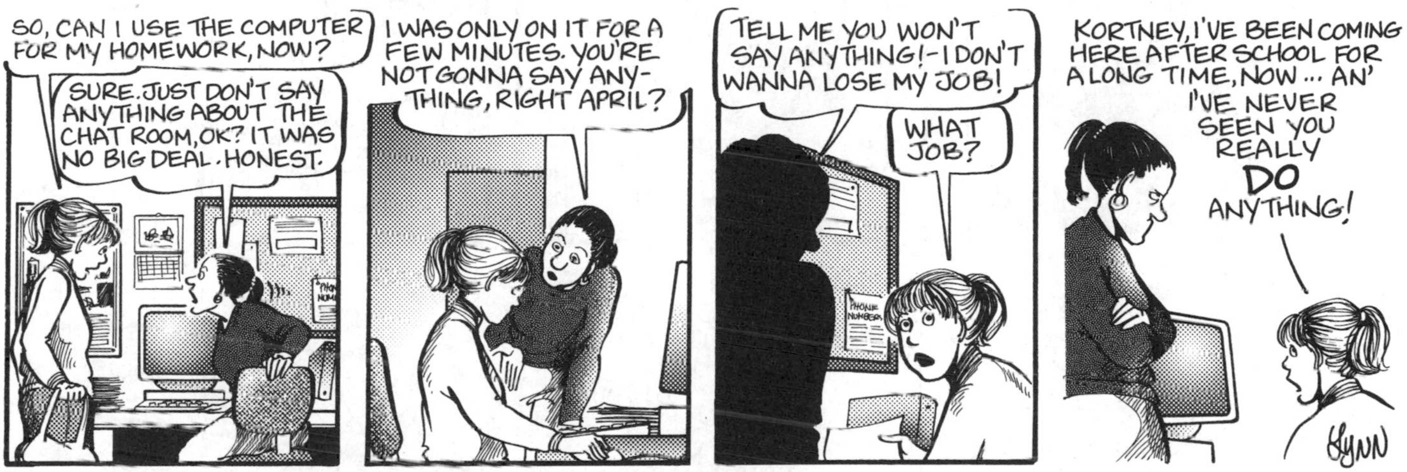
SO, CAN I USE THE COMPUTER FOR MY HOMEWORK, NOW?
SURE. JUST DON'T SAY ANYTHING ABOUT THE CHAT ROOM, OK? IT WAS NO BIG DEAL. HONEST.
I WAS ONLY ON IT FOR A FEW MINUTES. YOU'RE NOT GONNA SAY ANY-THING, RIGHT APRIL?
TELL ME YOU WON'T SAY ANYTHING!-I DON'T WANNA LOSE MY JOB!
WHAT JOB?
PHONE NUMBERS
KORTNEY, I'VE BEEN COMING HERE AFTER SCHOOL FOR A LONG TIME, NOW ... AN' I'VE NEVER SEEN YOU REALLY DO ANYTHING!
LYNN

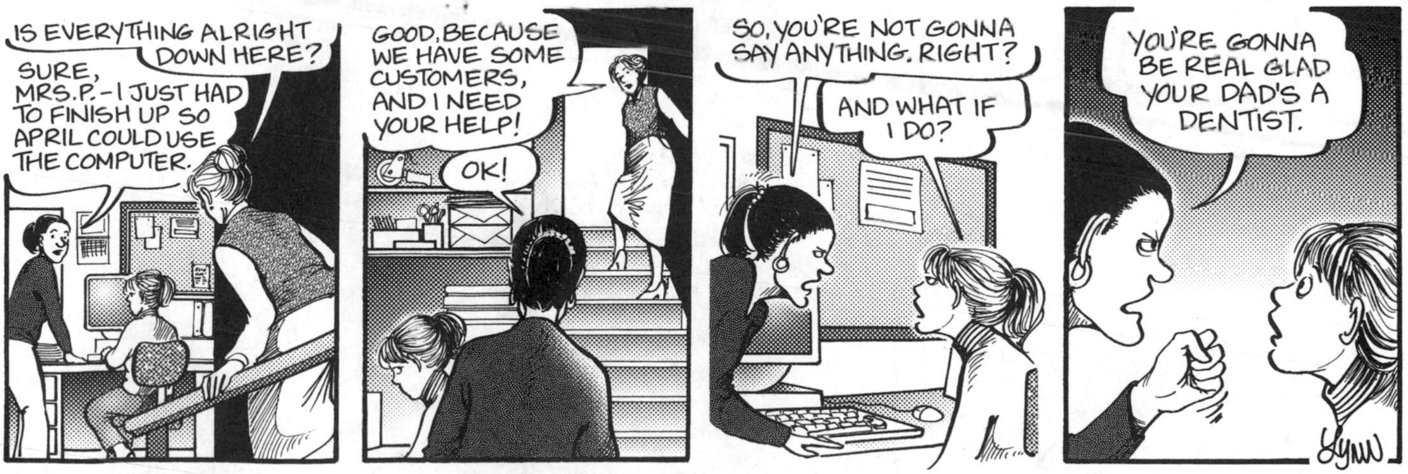
IS EVERYTHING ALRIGHT DOWN HERE?
SURE, MRS. P.-I JUST HAD TO FINISH UP SO APRIL COULD USE THE COMPUTER.
GOOD, BECAUSE WE HAVE SOME CUSTOMERS, AND I NEED YOUR HELP!
OK!
SO, YOU'RE NOT GONNA SAY ANYTHING. RIGHT?
AND WHAT IF I DO?
YOU'RE GONNA BE REAL GLAD YOUR DAD'S A DENTIST.
LYNN

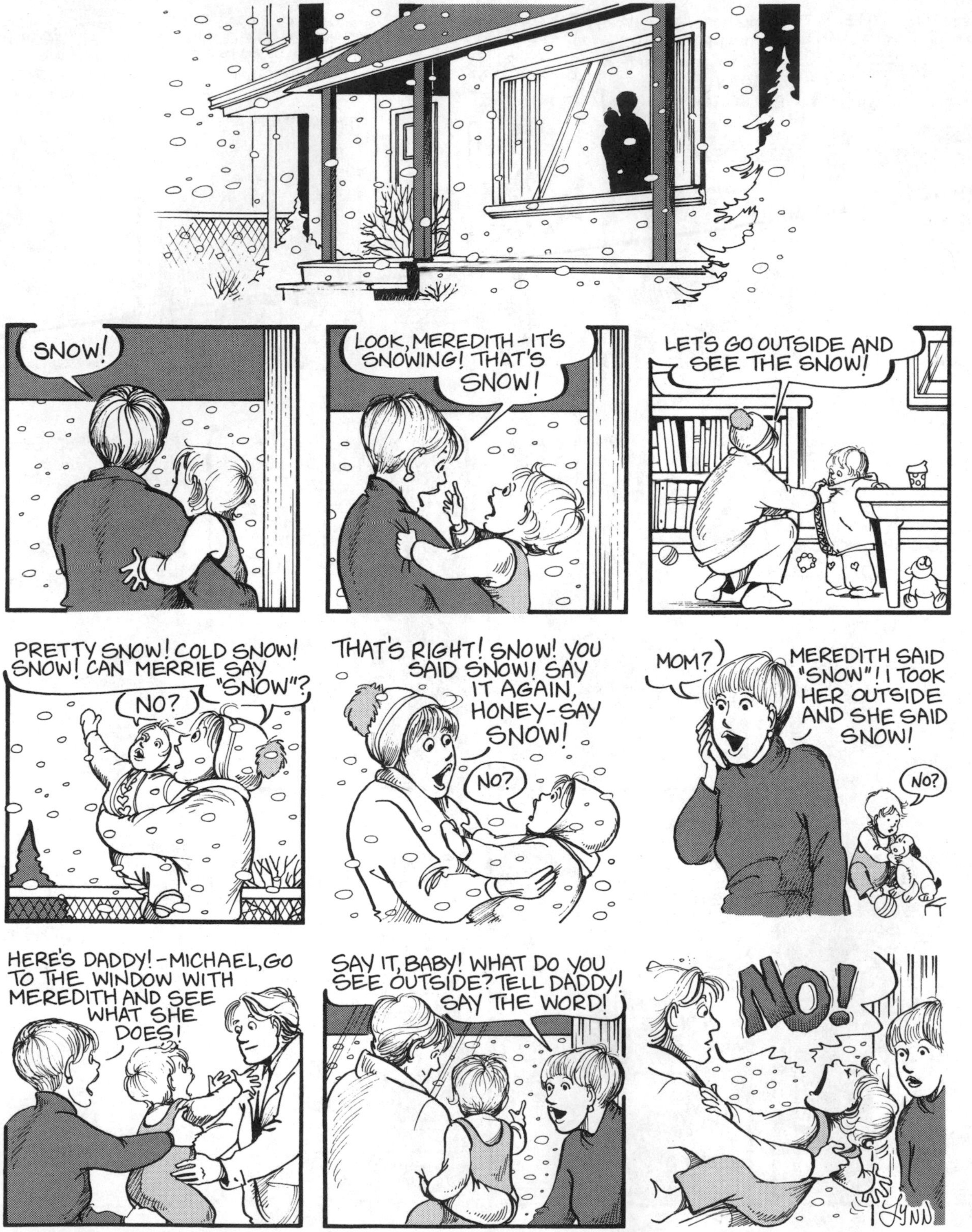
SNOW!
LOOK, MEREDITH - IT'S SNOWING! THAT'S SNOW!
LET'S GO OUTSIDE AND SEE THE SNOW!
PRETTY SNOW! COLD SNOW! SNOW! CAN MERRIE SAY "SNOW"?
NO?
THAT'S RIGHT! SNOW! YOU SAID SNOW! SAY IT AGAIN, HONEY-SAY SNOW!
NO?
MOM?
MEREDITH SAID "SNOW"! I TOOK HER OUTSIDE AND SHE SAID SNOW!
NO?
HERE'S DADDY! - MICHAEL, GO TO THE WINDOW WITH MEREDITH AND SEE WHAT SHE DOES!
SAY IT, BABY! WHAT DO YOU SEE OUTSIDE? TELL DADDY! SAY THE WORD!
NO!
LYNN

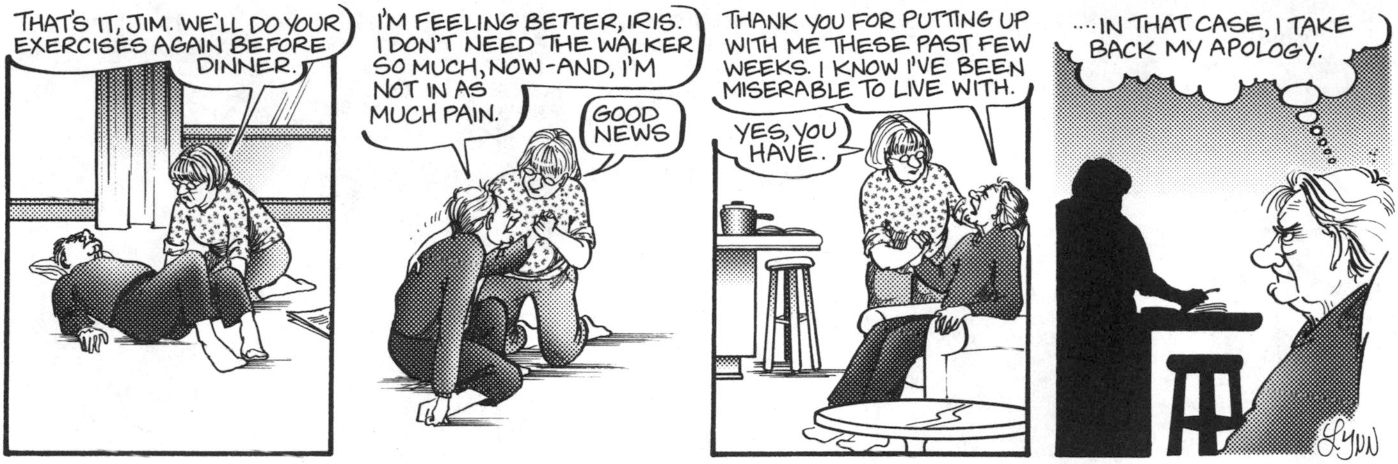
THAT'S IT, JIM. WE'LL DO YOUR EXERCISES AGAIN BEFORE DINNER.
I'M FEELING BETTER, IRIS. I DON'T NEED THE WALKER SO MUCH, NOW-AND, I'M NOT IN AS MUCH PAIN.
GOOD NEWS
THANK YOU FOR PUTTING UP WITH ME THESE PAST FEW WEEKS. I KNOW I'VE BEEN MISERABLE TO LIVE WITH.
YES, YOU HAVE.
....IN THAT CASE, I TAKE BACK MY APOLOGY.
LYNN

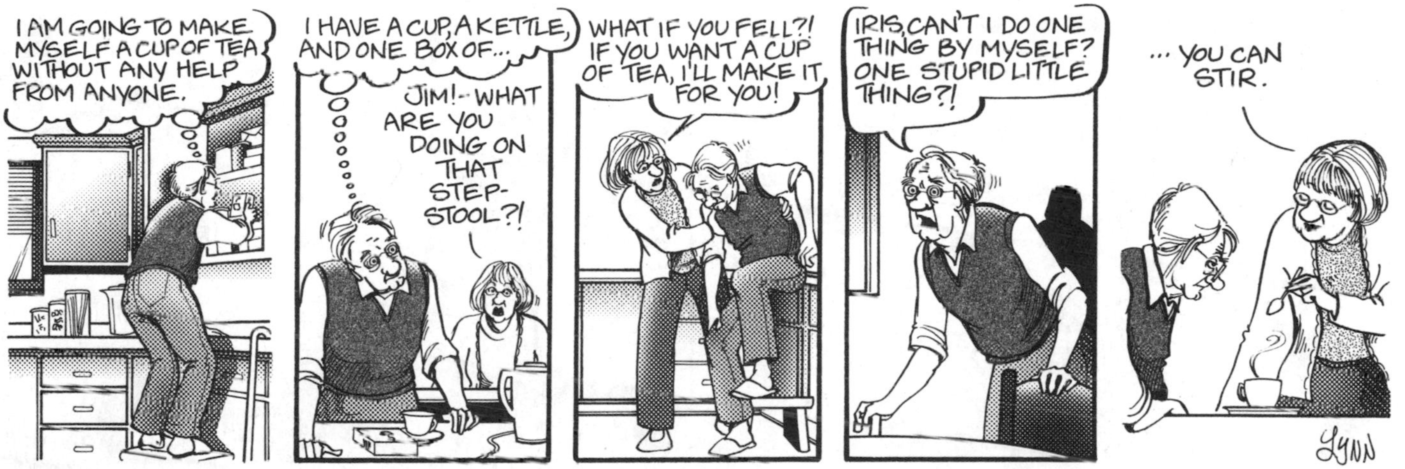
I AM GOING TO MAKE MYSELF A CUP OF TEA WITHOUT ANY HELP FROM ANYONE.
I HAVE A CUP, A KETTLE, AND ONE BOX OF...
JIM! - WHAT ARE YOU DOING ON THAT STEP-STOOL?!
WHAT IF YOU FELL?! IF YOU WANT A CUP OF TEA, I'LL MAKE IT FOR YOU!
IRIS, CAN'T I DO ONE THING BY MYSELF? ONE STUPID LITTLE THING?!
... YOU CAN STIR.
LYNN

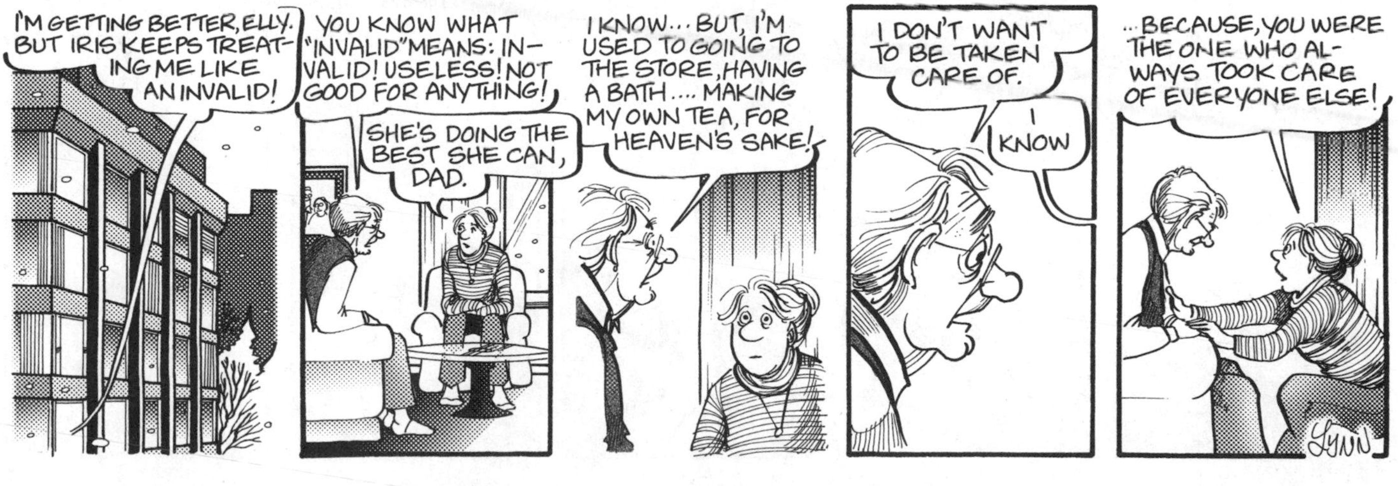
I'M GETTING BETTER, ELLY. BUT IRIS KEEPS TREAT-ING ME LIKE AN INVALID!
YOU KNOW WHAT "INVALID" MEANS: IN-VALID! USELESS! NOT GOOD FOR ANYTHING!
SHE'S DOING THE BEST SHE CAN, DAD.
I KNOW... BUT, I'M USED TO GOING TO THE STORE, HAVING A BATH.... MAKING MY OWN TEA, FOR HEAVEN'S SAKE!
I DON'T WANT TO BE TAKEN CARE OF.
I KNOW
...BECAUSE, YOU WERE THE ONE WHO AL-WAYS TOOK CARE OF EVERYONE ELSE!
LYNN

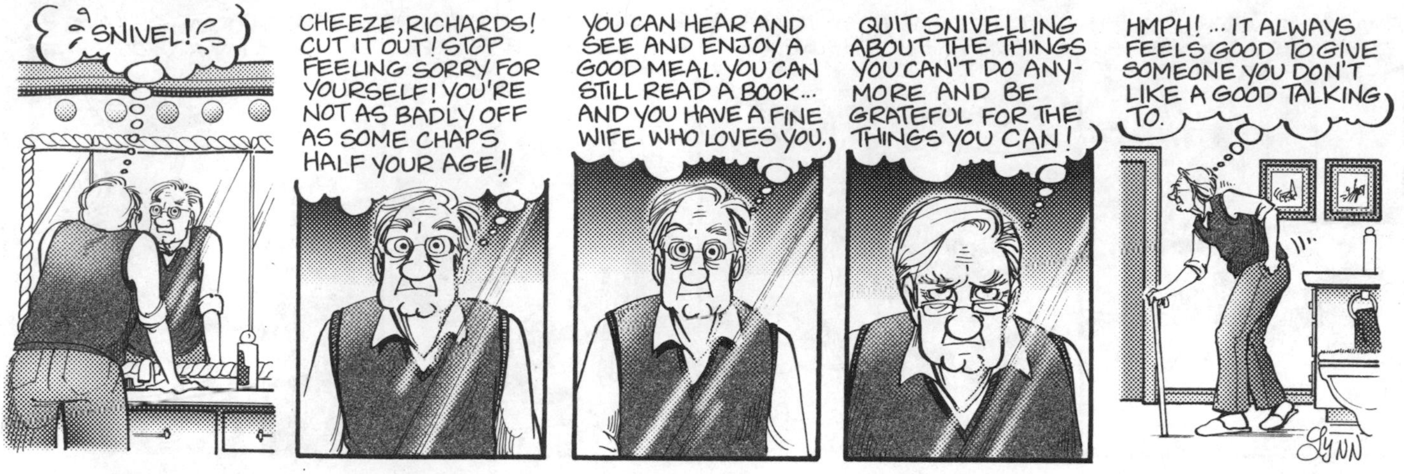
SNIVEL!
CHEEZE, RICHARDS! CUT IT OUT! STOP FEELING SORRY FOR YOURSELF! YOU'RE NOT AS BADLY OFF AS SOME CHAPS HALF YOUR AGE!!
YOU CAN HEAR AND SEE AND ENJOY A GOOD MEAL. YOU CAN STILL READ A BOOK... AND YOU HAVE A FINE WIFE WHO LOVES YOU.
QUIT SNIVELLING ABOUT THE THINGS YOU CAN'T DO ANYMORE AND BE GRATEFUL FOR THE THINGS YOU CAN!
HMPH! ... IT ALWAYS FEELS GOOD TO GIVE SOMEONE YOU DON'T LIKE A GOOD TALKING TO.
LYNN

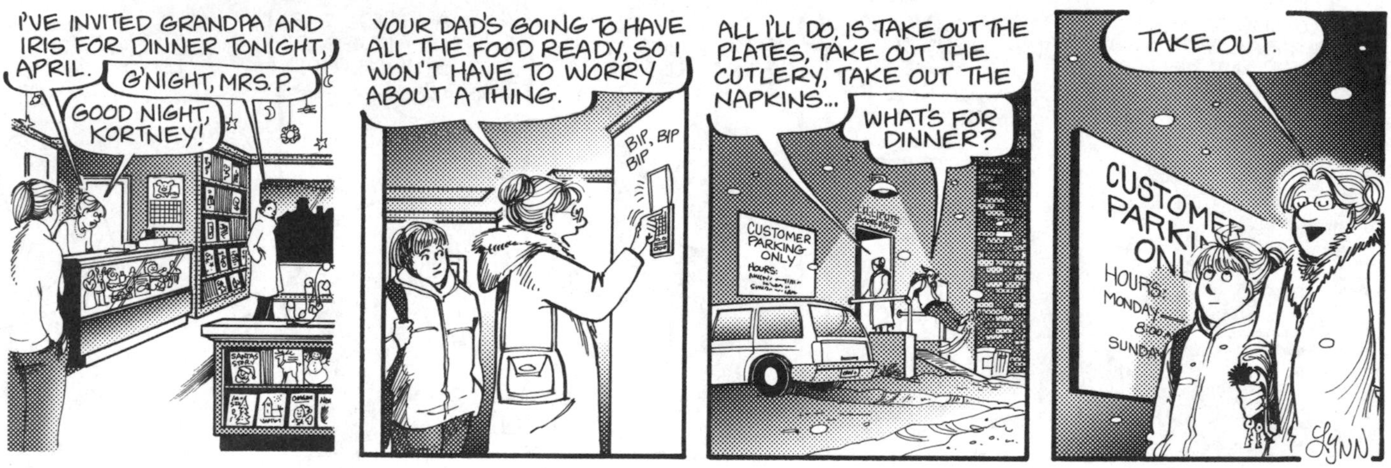
I'VE INVITED GRANDPA AND IRIS FOR DINNER TONIGHT, APRIL.
G'NIGHT, MRS. P.
GOOD NIGHT, KORTNEY!
YOUR DAD'S GOING TO HAVE ALL THE FOOD READY, SO I WON'T HAVE TO WORRY ABOUT A THING.
BIP, BIP BIP
ALL I'LL DO, IS TAKE OUT THE PLATES, TAKE OUT THE CUTLERY, TAKE OUT THE NAPKINS...
WHAT'S FOR DINNER?
CUSTOMER PARKING ONLY
TAKE OUT.
LYNN

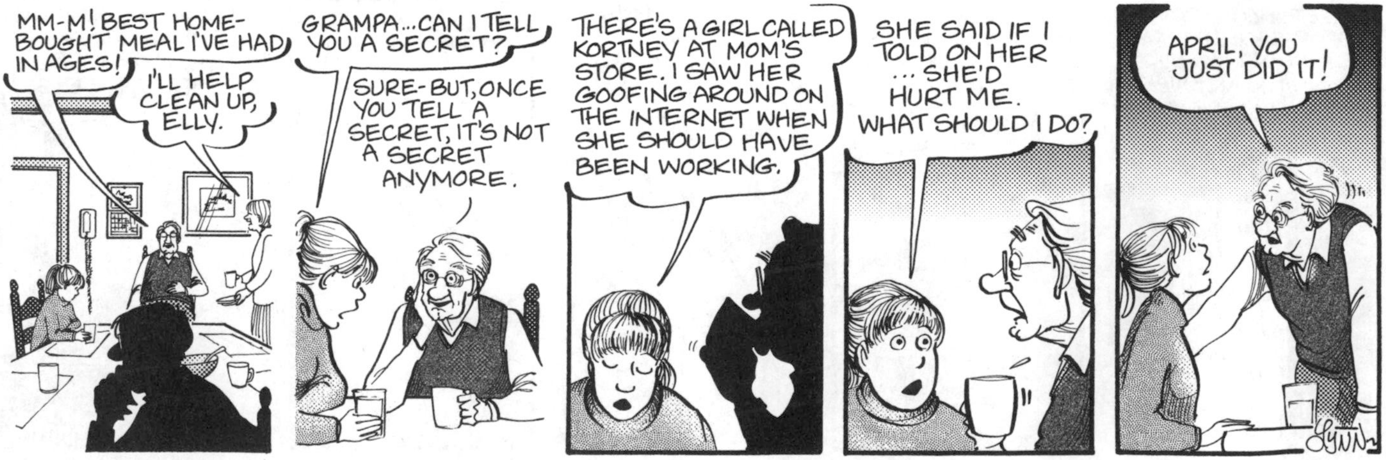
MM-M! BEST HOME-BOUGHT MEAL I'VE HAD IN AGES!
I'LL HELP CLEAN UP, ELLY.
GRAMPA...CAN I TELL YOU A SECRET?
SURE-BUT, ONCE YOU TELL A SECRET, IT'S NOT A SECRET ANYMORE.
THERE'S A GIRL CALLED KORTNEY AT MOM'S STORE. I SAW HER GOOFING AROUND ON THE INTERNET WHEN SHE SHOULD HAVE BEEN WORKING.
SHE SAID IF I TOLD ON HER ... SHE'D HURT ME. WHAT SHOULD I DO?
APRIL, YOU JUST DID IT!
LYNN

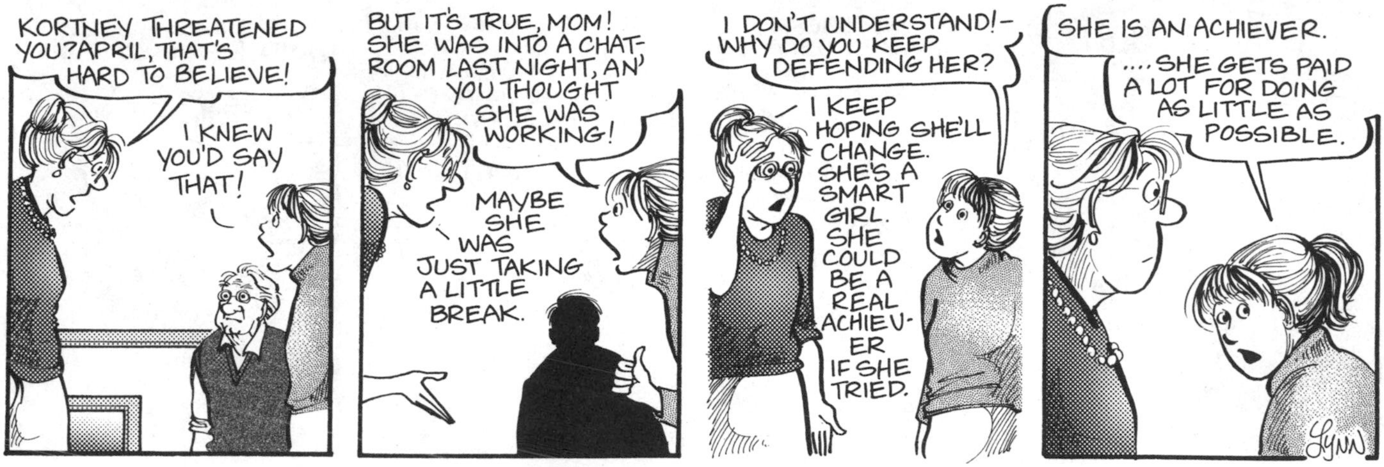
KORTNEY THREATENED YOU? APRIL, THAT'S HARD TO BELIEVE!
I KNEW YOU'D SAY THAT!
BUT IT'S TRUE, MOM! SHE WAS INTO A CHAT-ROOM LAST NIGHT, AN' YOU THOUGHT SHE WAS WORKING!
MAYBE SHE WAS JUST TAKING A LITTLE BREAK.
I DON'T UNDERSTAND! – WHY DO YOU KEEP DEFENDING HER?
I KEEP HOPING SHE'LL CHANGE. SHE'S A SMART GIRL. SHE COULD BE A REAL ACHIEVU-ER IF SHE TRIED.
SHE IS AN ACHIEVER.
....SHE GETS PAID A LOT FOR DOING AS LITTLE AS POSSIBLE.
LYNN

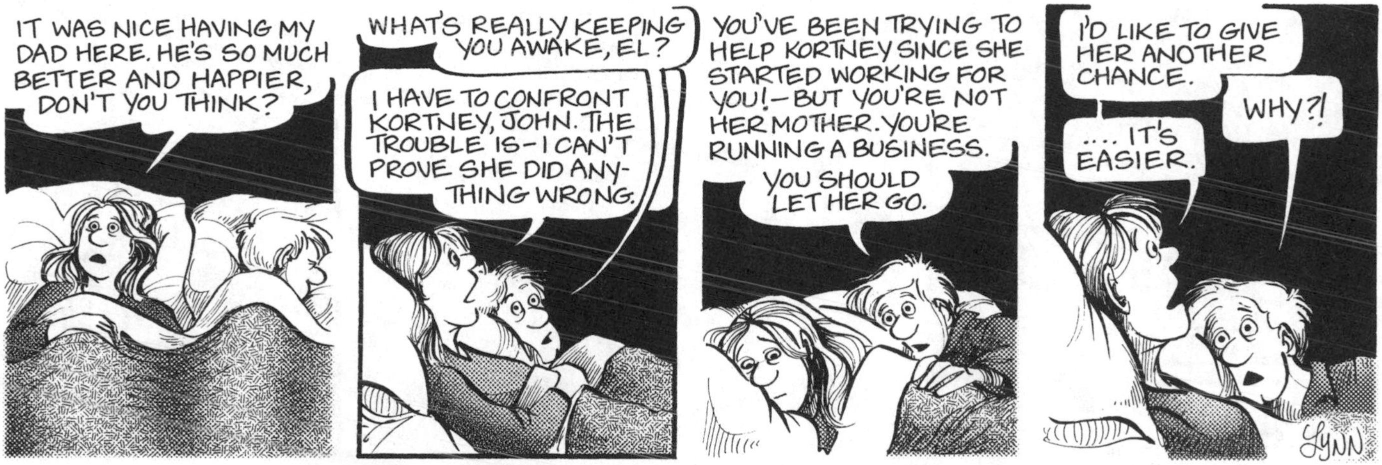
IT WAS NICE HAVING MY DAD HERE. HE'S SO MUCH BETTER AND HAPPIER, DON'T YOU THINK?
WHAT'S REALLY KEEPING YOU AWAKE, EL?
I HAVE TO CONFRONT KORTNEY, JOHN. THE TROUBLE IS – I CAN'T PROVE SHE DID ANY-THING WRONG.
YOU'VE BEEN TRYING TO HELP KORTNEY SINCE SHE STARTED WORKING FOR YOU! – BUT YOU'RE NOT HER MOTHER. YOU'RE RUNNING A BUSINESS.
YOU SHOULD LET HER GO.
I'D LIKE TO GIVE HER ANOTHER CHANCE.
WHY?!
.... IT'S EASIER.
LYNN

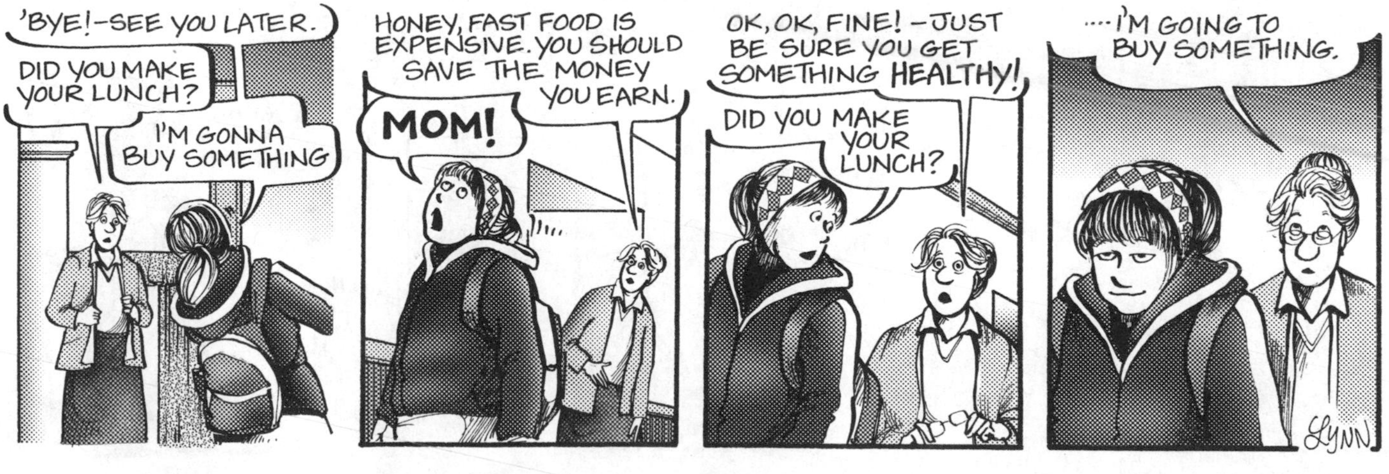
'BYE! – SEE YOU LATER.
DID YOU MAKE YOUR LUNCH?
I'M GONNA BUY SOMETHING
HONEY, FAST FOOD IS EXPENSIVE. YOU SHOULD SAVE THE MONEY YOU EARN.
MOM!
OK, OK, FINE! – JUST BE SURE YOU GET SOMETHING HEALTHY!
DID YOU MAKE YOUR LUNCH?
....I'M GOING TO BUY SOMETHING.
LYNN

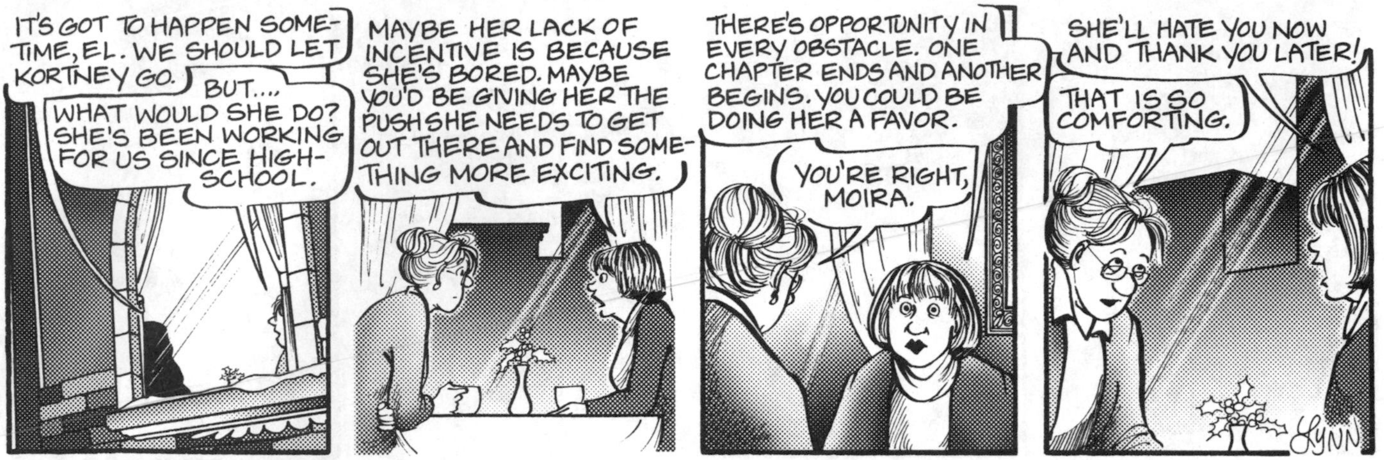
IT'S GOT TO HAPPEN SOME-TIME, EL. WE SHOULD LET KORTNEY GO.
BUT...., WHAT WOULD SHE DO? SHE'S BEEN WORKING FOR US SINCE HIGH-SCHOOL.
MAYBE HER LACK OF INCENTIVE IS BECAUSE SHE'S BORED. MAYBE YOU'D BE GIVING HER THE PUSH SHE NEEDS TO GET OUT THERE AND FIND SOME-THING MORE EXCITING.
THERE'S OPPORTUNITY IN EVERY OBSTACLE. ONE CHAPTER ENDS AND ANOTHER BEGINS. YOU COULD BE DOING HER A FAVOR.
YOU'RE RIGHT, MOIRA.
SHE'LL HATE YOU NOW AND THANK YOU LATER!
THAT IS SO COMFORTING.
LYNN

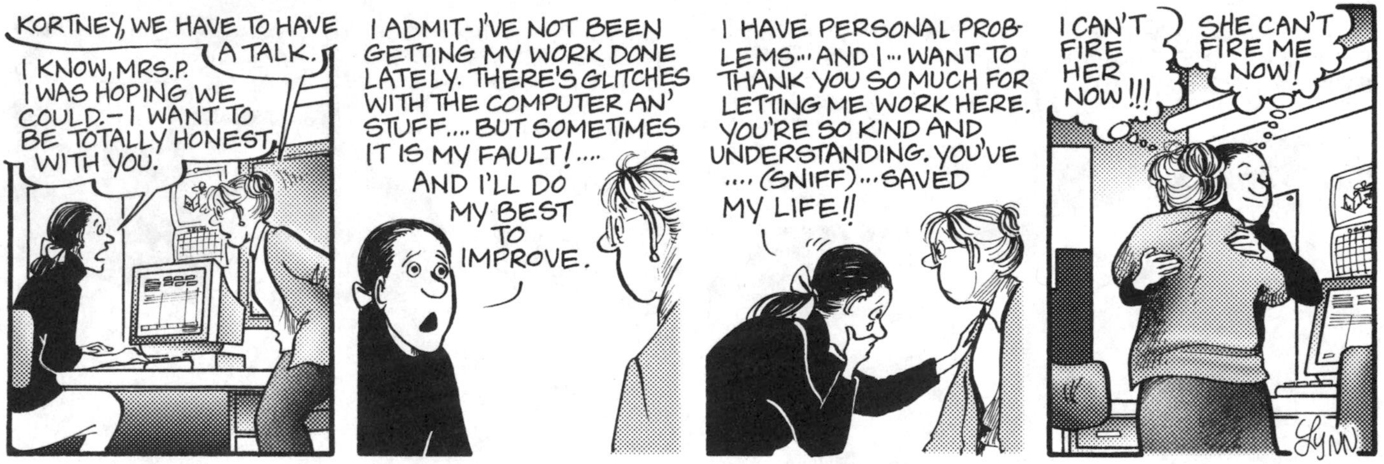
KORTNEY, WE HAVE TO HAVE A TALK.
I KNOW, MRS. P. I WAS HOPING WE COULD. – I WANT TO BE TOTALLY HONEST WITH YOU.
I ADMIT - I'VE NOT BEEN GETTING MY WORK DONE LATELY. THERE'S GLITCHES WITH THE COMPUTER AN' STUFF.... BUT SOMETIMES IT IS MY FAULT!....
AND I'LL DO MY BEST TO IMPROVE.
I HAVE PERSONAL PROB-LEMS... AND I ... WANT TO THANK YOU SO MUCH FOR LETTING ME WORK HERE. YOU'RE SO KIND AND UNDERSTANDING. YOU'VE .... (SNIFF) ... SAVED MY LIFE!!
I CAN'T FIRE HER NOW!!!
SHE CAN'T FIRE ME NOW!
LYNN

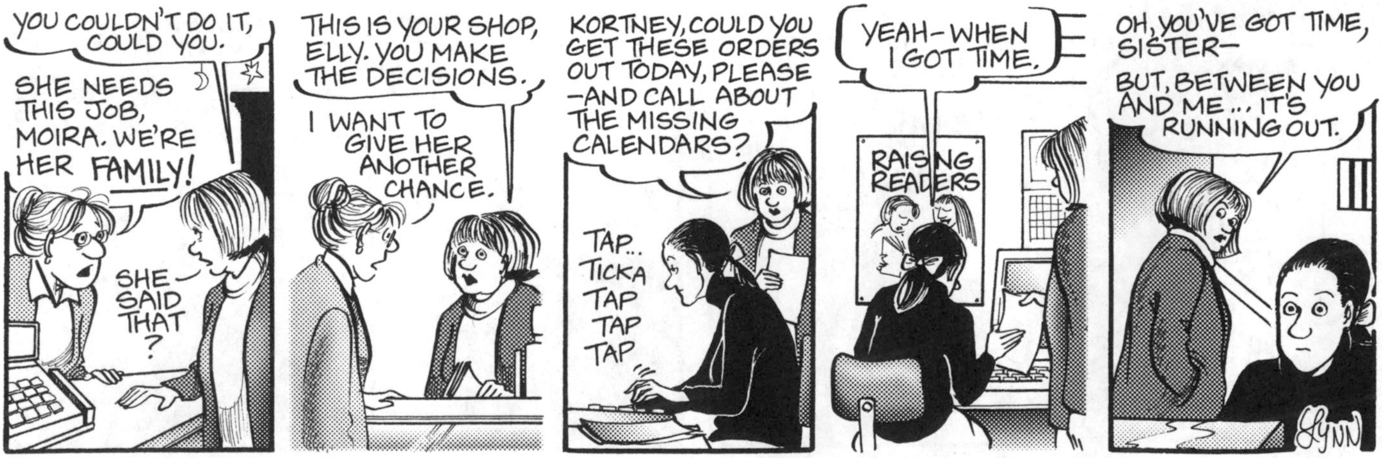
YOU COULDN'T DO IT, COULD YOU.
SHE NEEDS THIS JOB, MOIRA. WE'RE HER FAMILY!
SHE SAID THAT?
THIS IS YOUR SHOP, ELLY. YOU MAKE THE DECISIONS.
I WANT TO GIVE HER ANOTHER CHANCE.
KORTNEY, COULD YOU GET THESE ORDERS OUT TODAY, PLEASE —AND CALL ABOUT THE MISSING CALENDARS?
TAP... TICKA TAP TAP TAP
YEAH – WHEN I GOT TIME.
RAISING READERS
OH, YOU'VE GOT TIME, SISTER—
BUT, BETWEEN YOU AND ME ..., IT'S RUNNING OUT.
LYNN

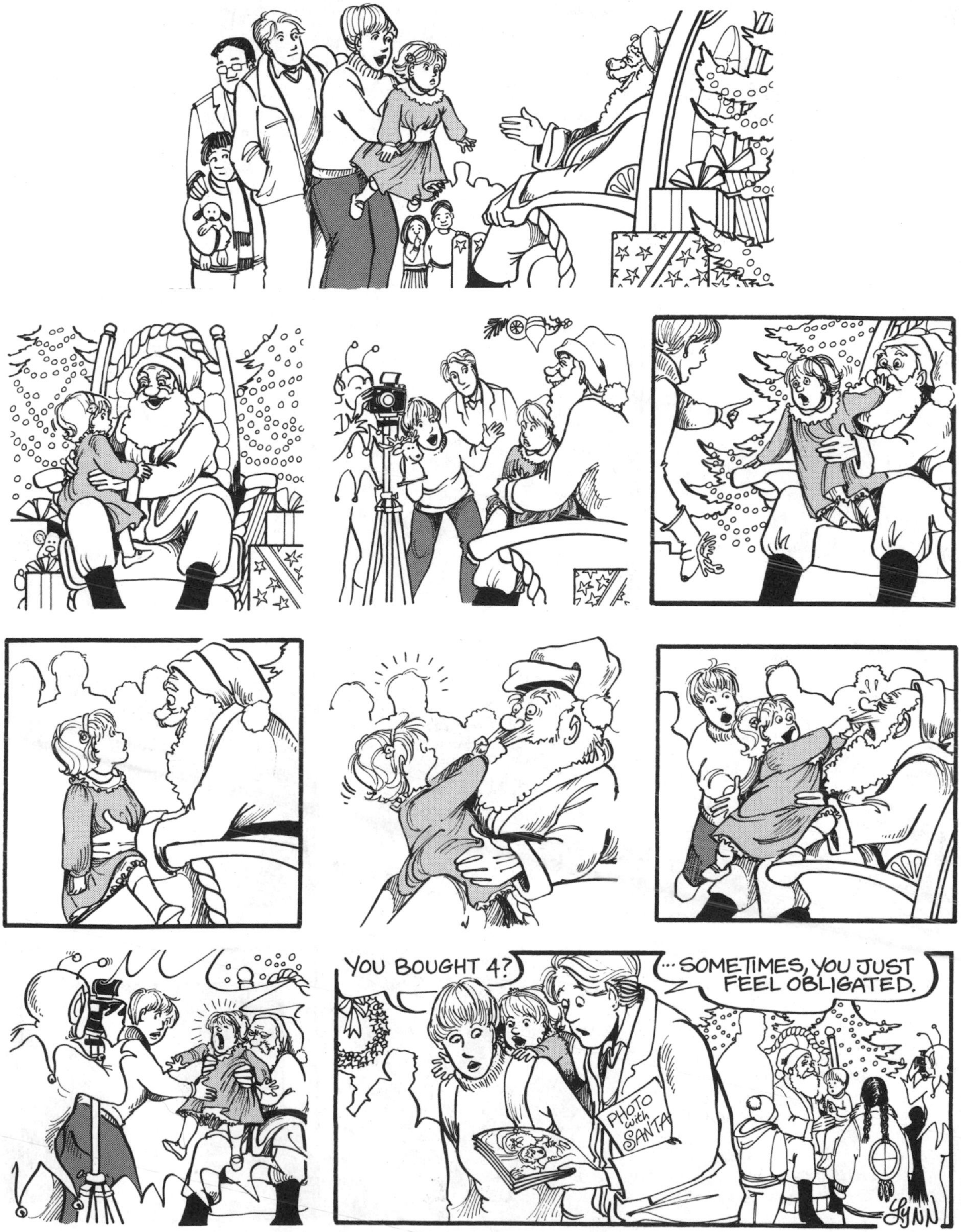
YOU BOUGHT 4?
...SOMETIMES, YOU JUST FEEL OBLIGATED.
PHOTO with SANTA
LYNN

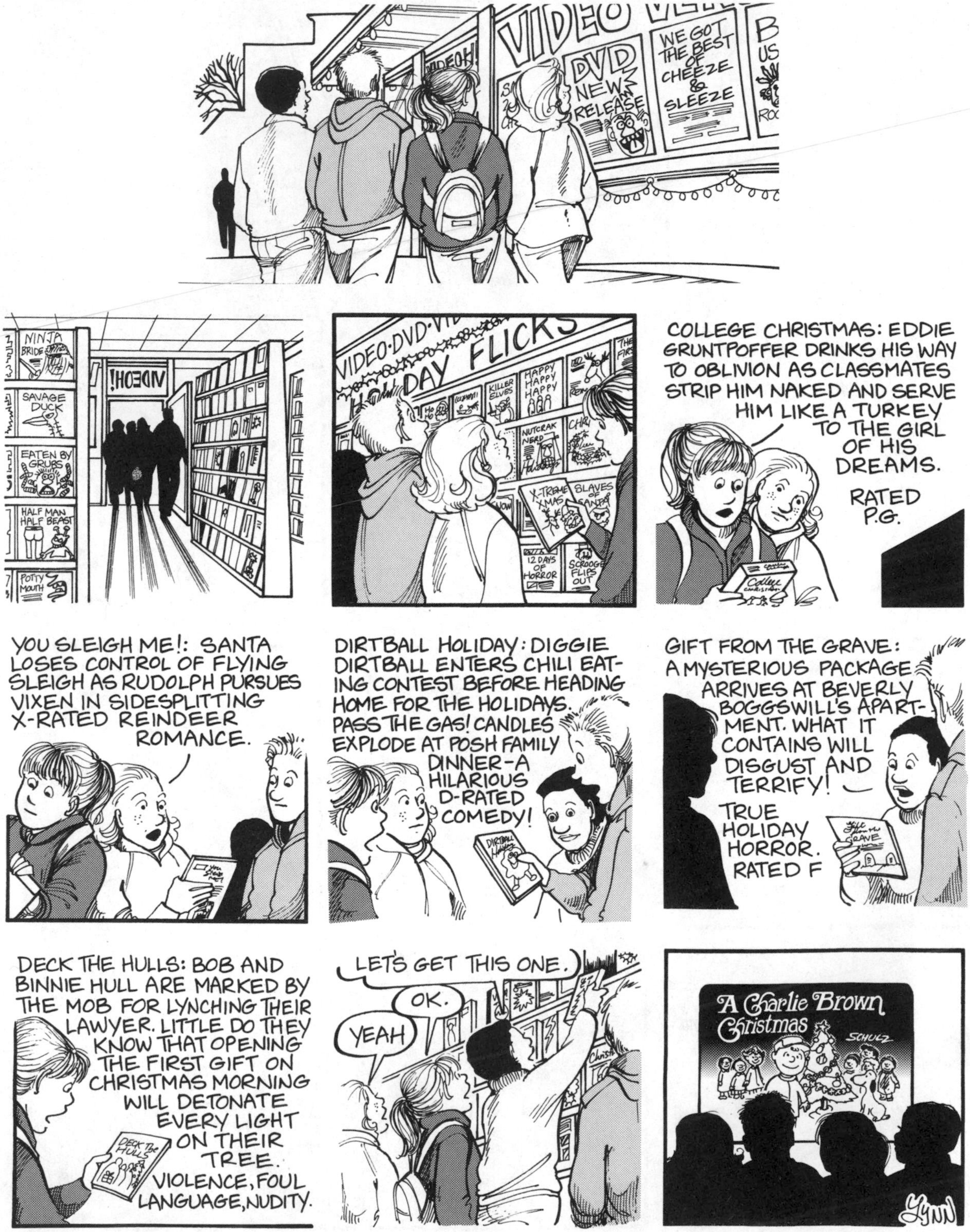
VIDEO
DVD NEW RELEASE
WE GOT THE BEST OF CHEEZE & SLEEZE
VIDEOH!
NINJA BRIDE
SAVAGE DUCK
EATEN BY GRUBS
HALF MAN HALF BEAST
POTTY MOUTH
VIDEO·DVD·
HOLIDAY FLICKS
KILLER ELVES
HAPPY HAPPY HAPPY
NUTCRAK NERD
X-TREME XMAS
SLAVES OF SANTA
12 DAYS OF HORROR
SCROOGE FLIPS OUT
COLLEGE CHRISTMAS: EDDIE GRUNTPOFFER DRINKS HIS WAY TO OBLIVION AS CLASSMATES STRIP HIM NAKED AND SERVE HIM LIKE A TURKEY TO THE GIRL OF HIS DREAMS.
RATED P.G.
YOU SLEIGH ME!: SANTA LOSES CONTROL OF FLYING SLEIGH AS RUDOLPH PURSUES VIXEN IN SIDESPLITTING X-RATED REINDEER ROMANCE.
DIRTBALL HOLIDAY: DIGGIE DIRTBALL ENTERS CHILI EATING CONTEST BEFORE HEADING HOME FOR THE HOLIDAYS.
PASS THE GAS! CANDLES EXPLODE AT POSH FAMILY DINNER-A HILARIOUS D-RATED COMEDY!
GIFT FROM THE GRAVE: A MYSTERIOUS PACKAGE ARRIVES AT BEVERLY BOGGSWILL'S APARTMENT. WHAT IT CONTAINS WILL DISGUST AND TERRIFY!
TRUE HOLIDAY HORROR. RATED F
DECK THE HULLS: BOB AND BINNIE HULL ARE MARKED BY THE MOB FOR LYNCHING THEIR LAWYER. LITTLE DO THEY KNOW THAT OPENING THE FIRST GIFT ON CHRISTMAS MORNING WILL DETONATE EVERY LIGHT ON THEIR TREE.
VIOLENCE, FOUL LANGUAGE, NUDITY.
DECK THE HULLS
LET'S GET THIS ONE.
OK.
YEAH
A Charlie Brown Christmas
SCHULZ
LYNN

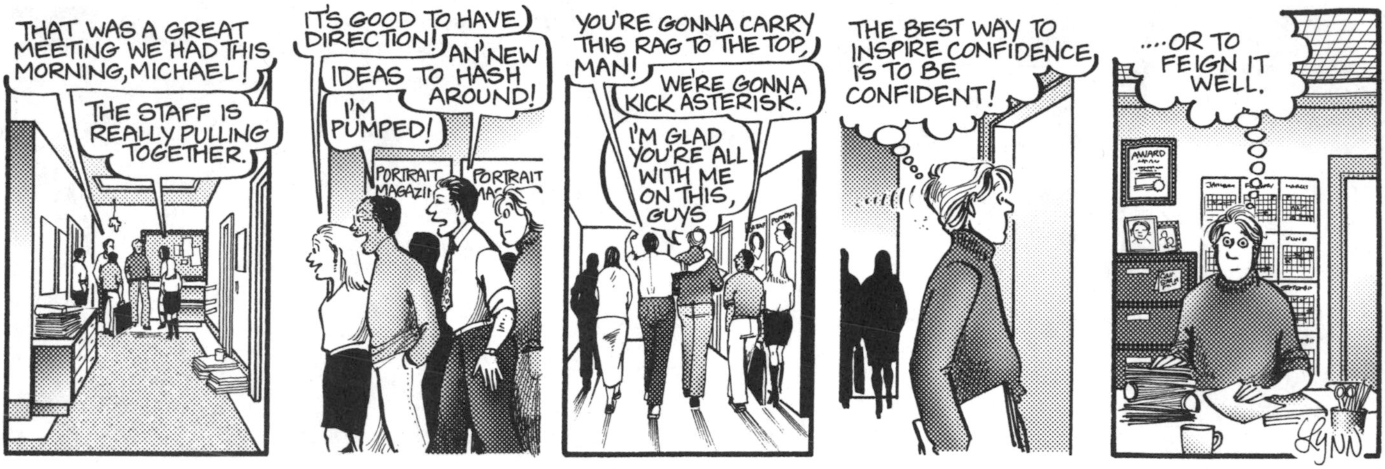
THAT WAS A GREAT MEETING WE HAD THIS MORNING, MICHAEL!
THE STAFF IS REALLY PULLING TOGETHER.
IT'S GOOD TO HAVE DIRECTION!
AN' NEW IDEAS TO HASH AROUND!
I'M PUMPED!
PORTRAIT MAGAZIN
PORTRAIT
YOU'RE GONNA CARRY THIS RAG TO THE TOP, MAN!
WE'RE GONNA KICK ASTERISK.
I'M GLAD YOU'RE ALL WITH ME ON THIS, GUYS
THE BEST WAY TO INSPIRE CONFIDENCE IS TO BE CONFIDENT!
....OR TO FEIGN IT WELL.
AWARD
LYNN

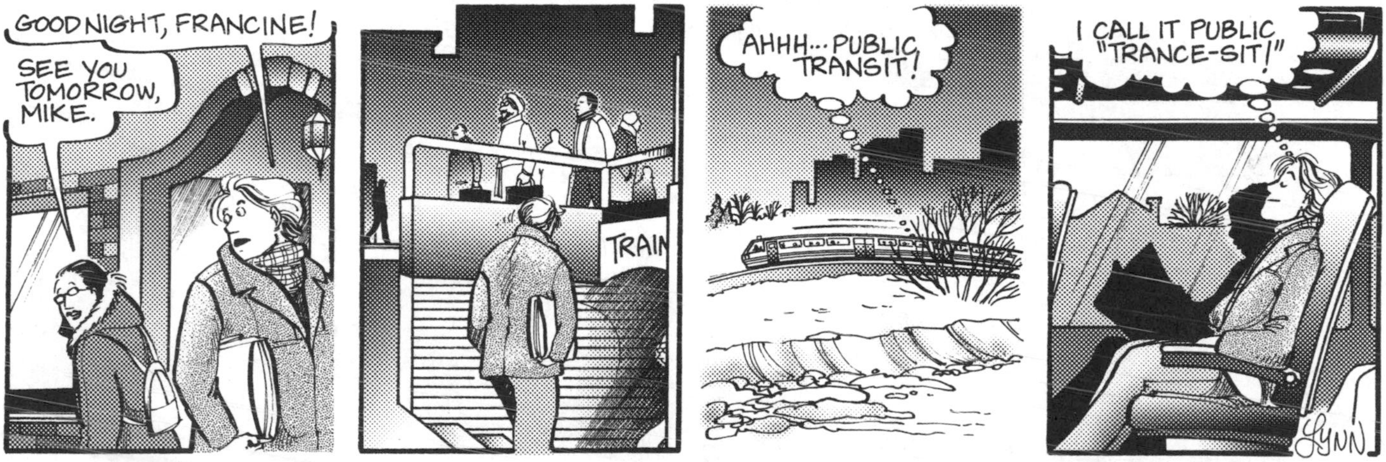
GOOD NIGHT, FRANCINE!
SEE YOU TOMORROW, MIKE.
TRAIN
AHHH... PUBLIC TRANSIT!
I CALL IT PUBLIC "TRANCE-SIT!"
LYNN

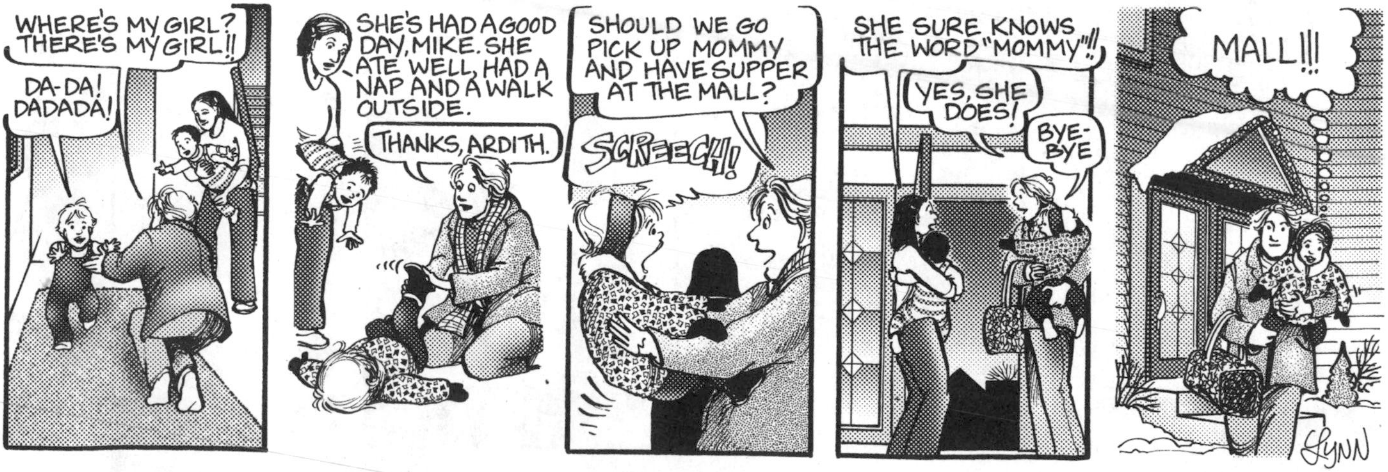
WHERE'S MY GIRL? THERE'S MY GIRL!!
DA-DA! DADADA!
SHE'S HAD A GOOD DAY, MIKE. SHE ATE WELL, HAD A NAP AND A WALK OUTSIDE.
THANKS, ARDITH.
SHOULD WE GO PICK UP MOMMY AND HAVE SUPPER AT THE MALL?
SCREECH!
SHE SURE KNOWS THE WORD "MOMMY"!!
YES, SHE DOES!
BYE-BYE
MALL!!!
LYNN

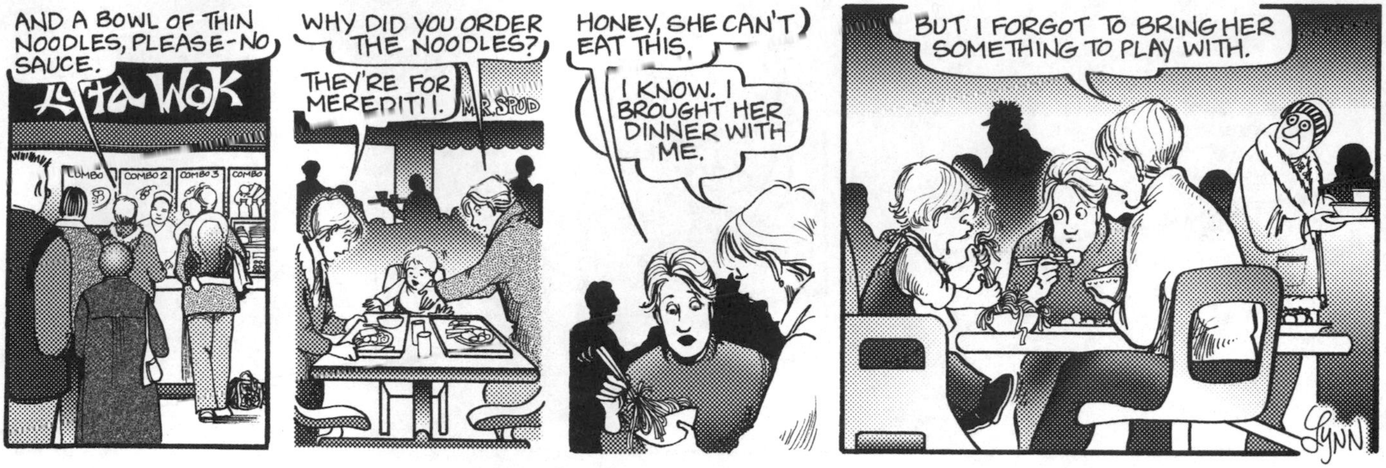
AND A BOWL OF THIN NOODLES, PLEASE-NO SAUCE.
COMBO 2
COMBO 3
WHY DID YOU ORDER THE NOODLES?
THEY'RE FOR MEREDITH!
MR. SPUD
HONEY, SHE CAN'T EAT THIS.
I KNOW. I BROUGHT HER DINNER WITH ME.
BUT I FORGOT TO BRING HER SOMETHING TO PLAY WITH.
LYNN

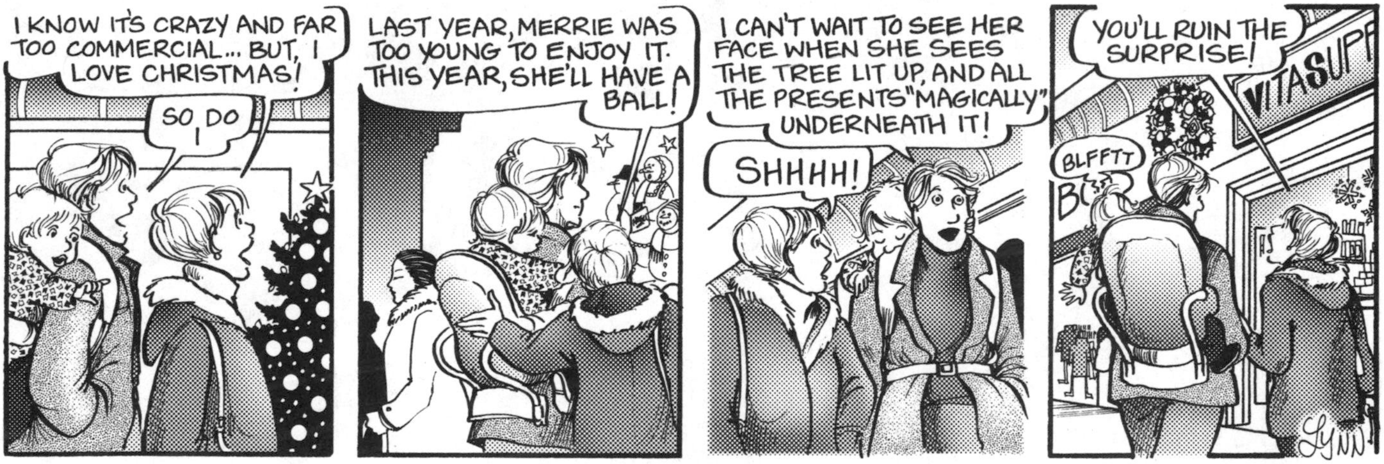
I KNOW IT'S CRAZY AND FAR TOO COMMERCIAL... BUT, I LOVE CHRISTMAS!
SO DO I
LAST YEAR, MERRIE WAS TOO YOUNG TO ENJOY IT. THIS YEAR, SHE'LL HAVE A BALL!
I CAN'T WAIT TO SEE HER FACE WHEN SHE SEES THE TREE LIT UP, AND ALL THE PRESENTS "MAGICALLY" UNDERNEATH IT!
SHHHH!
YOU'LL RUIN THE SURPRISE!
VITASUPP
BLFFTT
LYNN

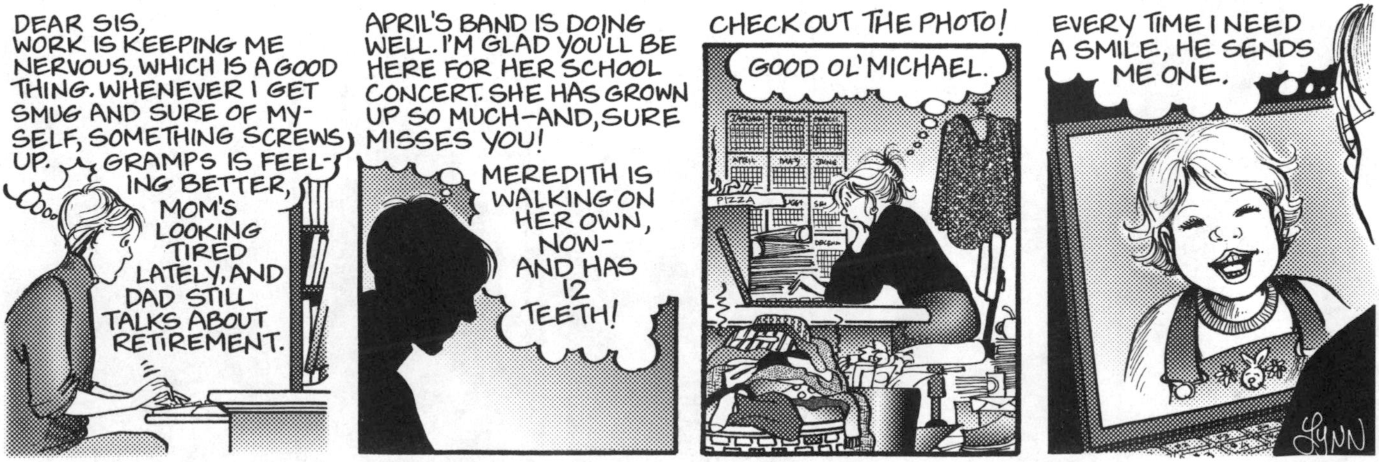
DEAR SIS, WORK IS KEEPING ME NERVOUS, WHICH IS A GOOD THING. WHENEVER I GET SMUG AND SURE OF MYSELF, SOMETHING SCREWS UP.
GRAMPS IS FEELING BETTER, MOM'S LOOKING TIRED LATELY, AND DAD STILL TALKS ABOUT RETIREMENT.
APRIL'S BAND IS DOING WELL. I'M GLAD YOU'LL BE HERE FOR HER SCHOOL CONCERT. SHE HAS GROWN UP SO MUCH-AND, SURE MISSES YOU!
MEREDITH IS WALKING ON HER OWN, NOW- AND HAS 12 TEETH!
CHECK OUT THE PHOTO!
GOOD OL' MICHAEL.
EVERY TIME I NEED A SMILE, HE SENDS ME ONE.
LYNN

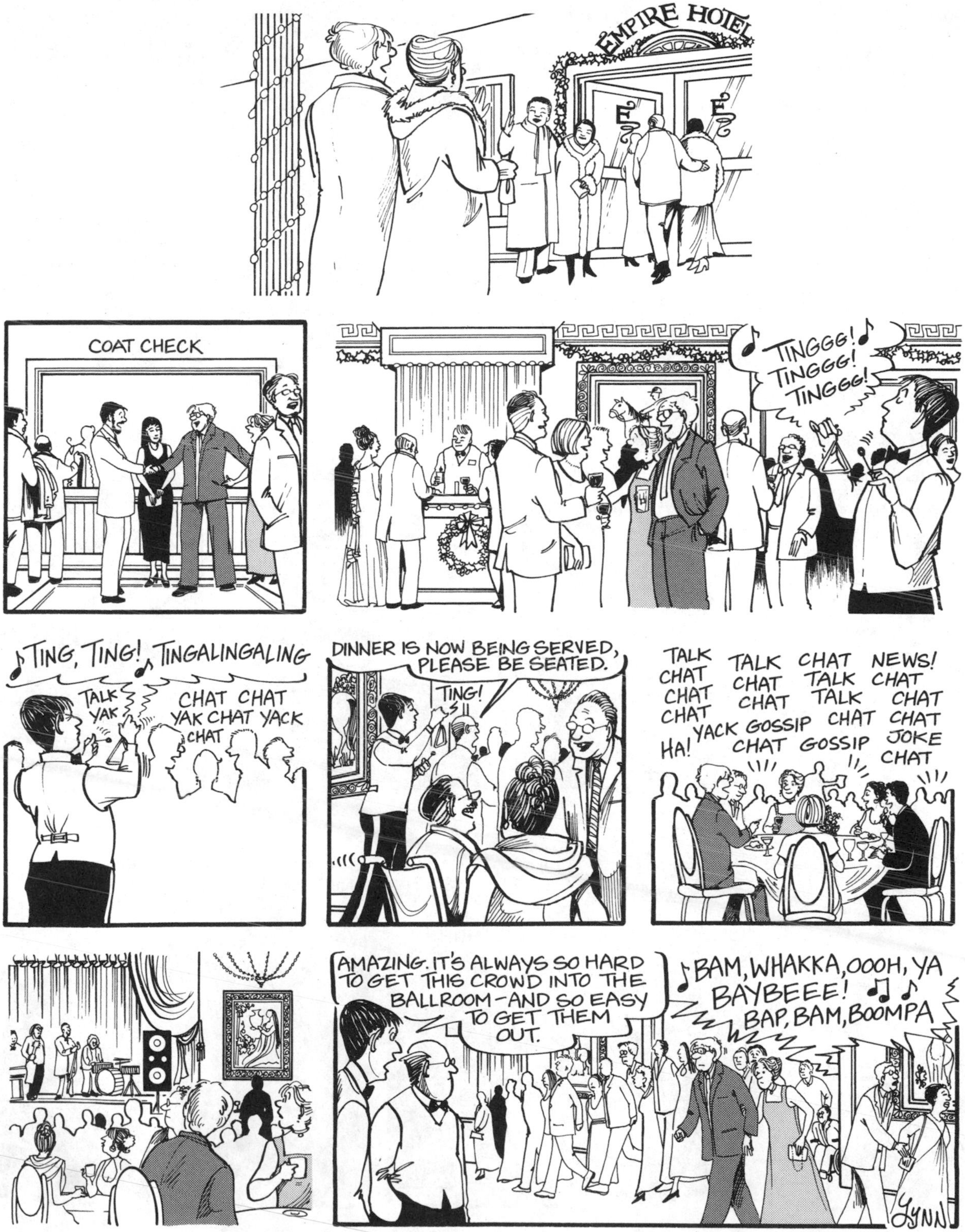
EMPIRE HOTEL
COAT CHECK
TINGGG! TINGGG! TINGGG!
TING, TING! TINGALINGALING
TALK YAK
CHAT CHAT YAK CHAT YACK CHAT
DINNER IS NOW BEING SERVED, PLEASE BE SEATED.
TING!
TALK CHAT CHAT CHAT
TALK CHAT CHAT
CHAT TALK TALK
NEWS! CHAT CHAT
YACK GOSSIP CHAT CHAT
CHAT GOSSIP JOKE CHAT
HA!
AMAZING. IT'S ALWAYS SO HARD TO GET THIS CROWD INTO THE BALLROOM – AND SO EASY TO GET THEM OUT.
BAM, WHAKKA, OOOH, YA BAYBEEE!
BAP, BAM, BOOMPA
LYNN

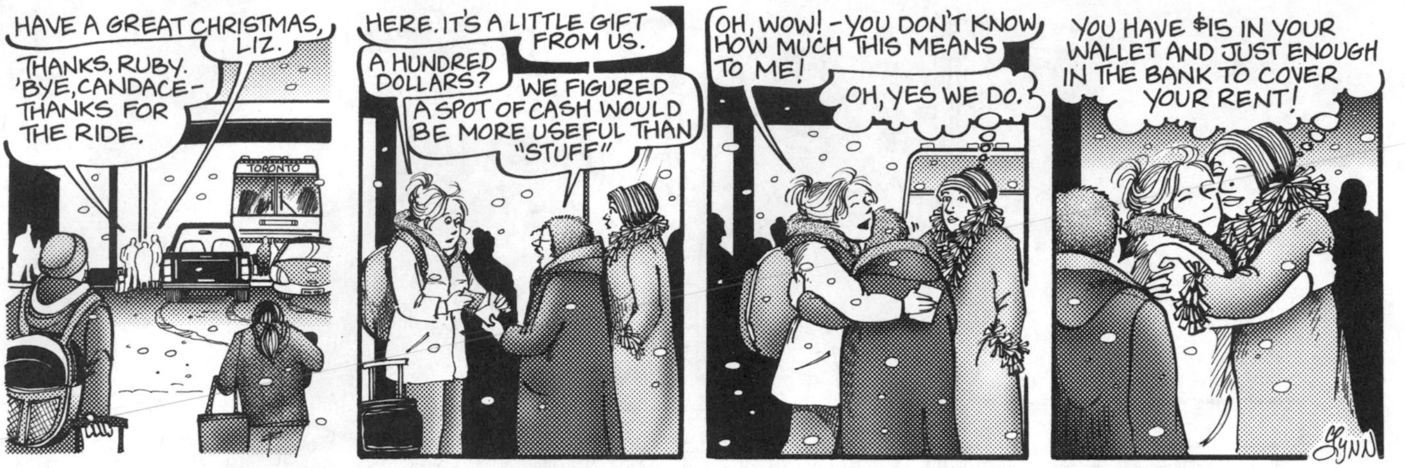
HAVE A GREAT CHRISTMAS, LIZ.
THANKS, RUBY. 'BYE, CANDACE- THANKS FOR THE RIDE.
TORONTO
HERE. IT'S A LITTLE GIFT FROM US.
A HUNDRED DOLLARS?
WE FIGURED A SPOT OF CASH WOULD BE MORE USEFUL THAN "STUFF"
OH, WOW! - YOU DON'T KNOW HOW MUCH THIS MEANS TO ME!
OH, YES WE DO.
YOU HAVE $15 IN YOUR WALLET AND JUST ENOUGH IN THE BANK TO COVER YOUR RENT!
LYNN

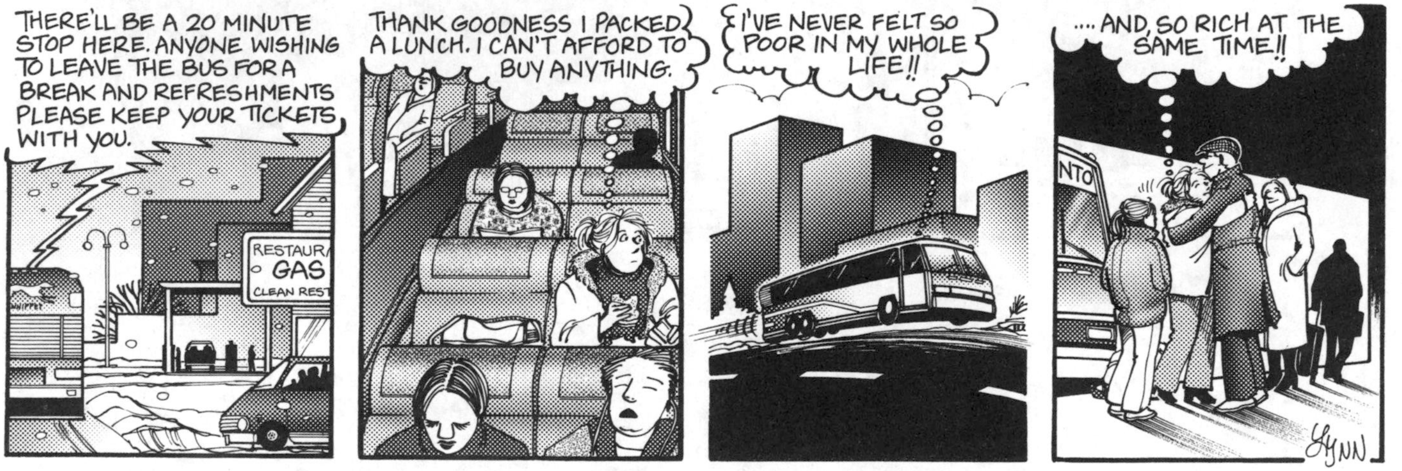
THERE'LL BE A 20 MINUTE STOP HERE. ANYONE WISHING TO LEAVE THE BUS FOR A BREAK AND REFRESHMENTS PLEASE KEEP YOUR TICKETS WITH YOU.
RESTAUR
GAS
CLEAN REST
THANK GOODNESS I PACKED A LUNCH. I CAN'T AFFORD TO BUY ANYTHING.
I'VE NEVER FELT SO POOR IN MY WHOLE LIFE!!
....AND, SO RICH AT THE SAME TIME!!
NTO
LYNN

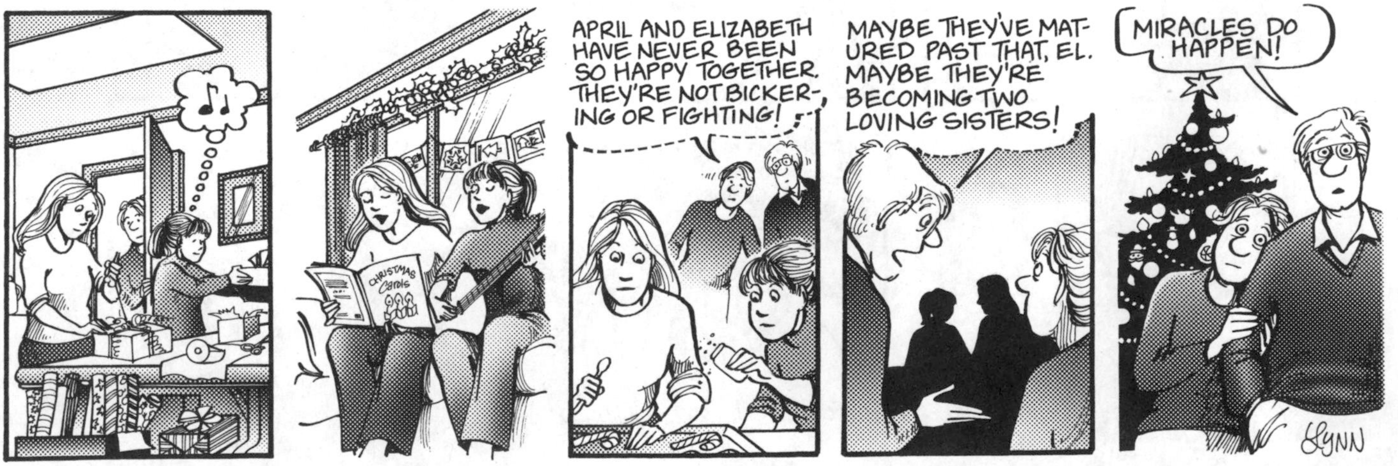
CHRISTMAS Carols
APRIL AND ELIZABETH HAVE NEVER BEEN SO HAPPY TOGETHER. THEY'RE NOT BICKERING OR FIGHTING!
MAYBE THEY'VE MATURED PAST THAT, EL. MAYBE THEY'RE BECOMING TWO LOVING SISTERS!
MIRACLES DO HAPPEN!
LYNN

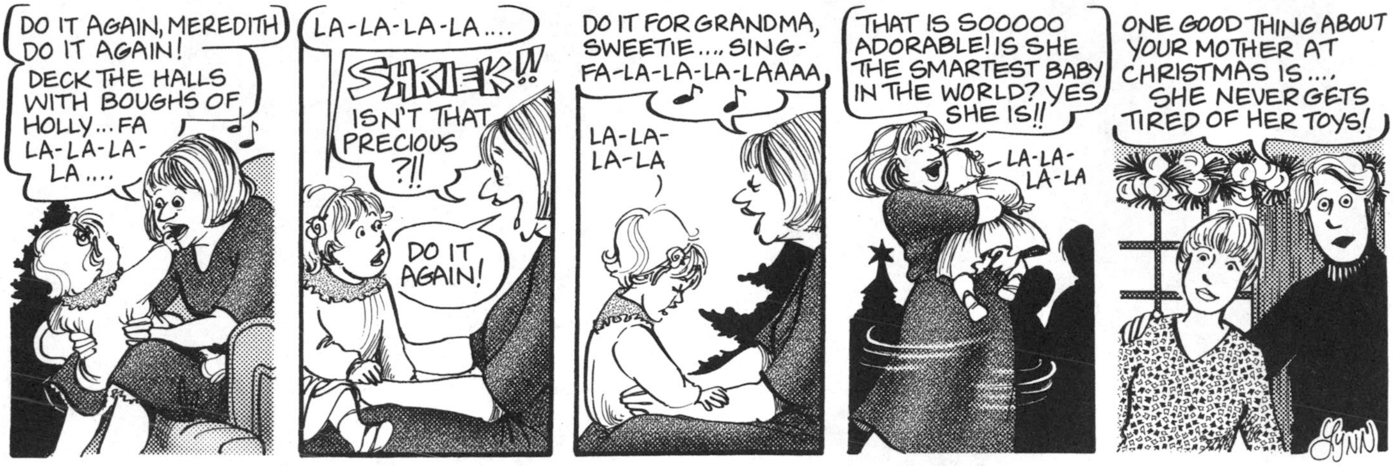
DO IT AGAIN, MEREDITH DO IT AGAIN!
DECK THE HALLS WITH BOUGHS OF HOLLY... FA LA-LA-LA-LA-LA....
LA-LA-LA-LA....
SHRIEK!!
ISN'T THAT PRECIOUS ?!!
DO IT AGAIN!
DO IT FOR GRANDMA, SWEETIE.... SING- FA-LA-LA-LA-LAAAA
LA-LA-LA-LA
THAT IS SOOOOO ADORABLE! IS SHE THE SMARTEST BABY IN THE WORLD? YES SHE IS!!
LA-LA-LA-LA
ONE GOOD THING ABOUT YOUR MOTHER AT CHRISTMAS IS....
SHE NEVER GETS TIRED OF HER TOYS!
LYNN

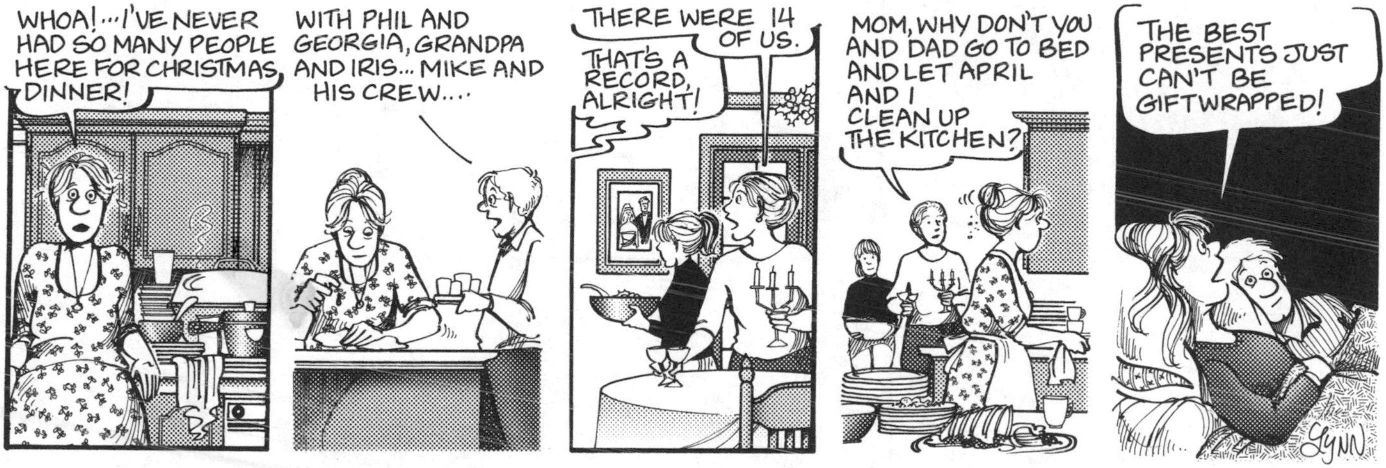
WHOA!...I'VE NEVER HAD SO MANY PEOPLE HERE FOR CHRISTMAS DINNER!
WITH PHIL AND GEORGIA, GRANDPA AND IRIS... MIKE AND HIS CREW....
THERE WERE 14 OF US.
THAT'S A RECORD, ALRIGHT!
MOM, WHY DON'T YOU AND DAD GO TO BED AND LET APRIL AND I CLEAN UP THE KITCHEN?
THE BEST PRESENTS JUST CAN'T BE GIFTWRAPPED!
LYNN

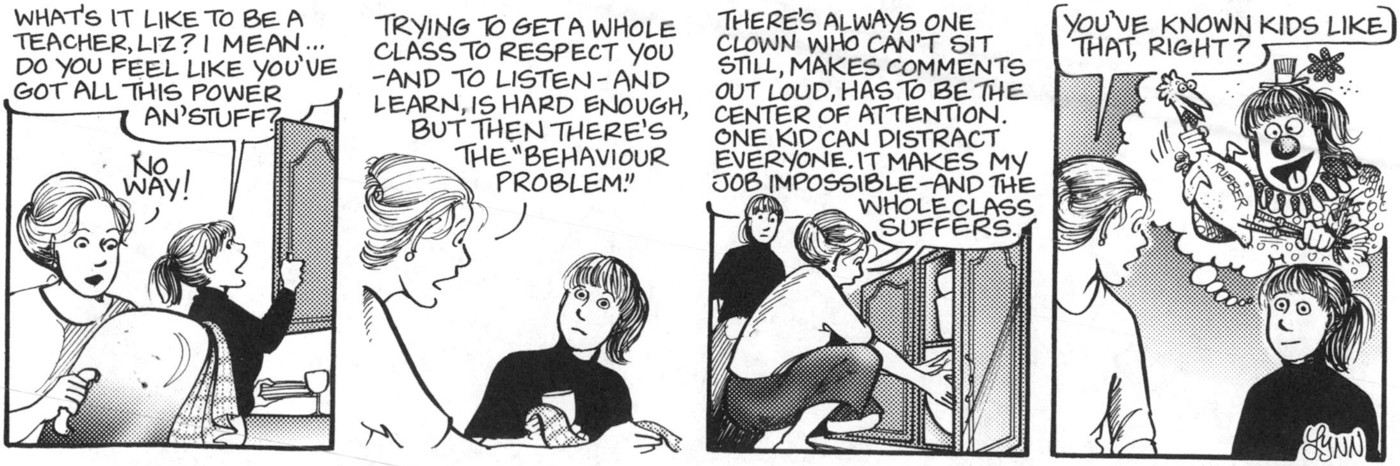
WHAT'S IT LIKE TO BE A TEACHER, LIZ? I MEAN... DO YOU FEEL LIKE YOU'VE GOT ALL THIS POWER AN'STUFF?
NO WAY!
TRYING TO GET A WHOLE CLASS TO RESPECT YOU -AND TO LISTEN- AND LEARN, IS HARD ENOUGH, BUT THEN THERE'S THE "BEHAVIOUR PROBLEM."
THERE'S ALWAYS ONE CLOWN WHO CAN'T SIT STILL, MAKES COMMENTS OUT LOUD, HAS TO BE THE CENTER OF ATTENTION. ONE KID CAN DISTRACT EVERYONE. IT MAKES MY JOB IMPOSSIBLE-AND THE WHOLE CLASS SUFFERS.
YOU'VE KNOWN KIDS LIKE THAT, RIGHT?
RUBBER
LYNN

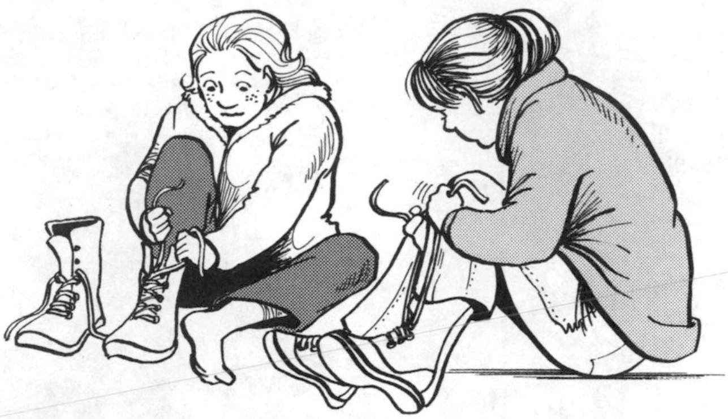

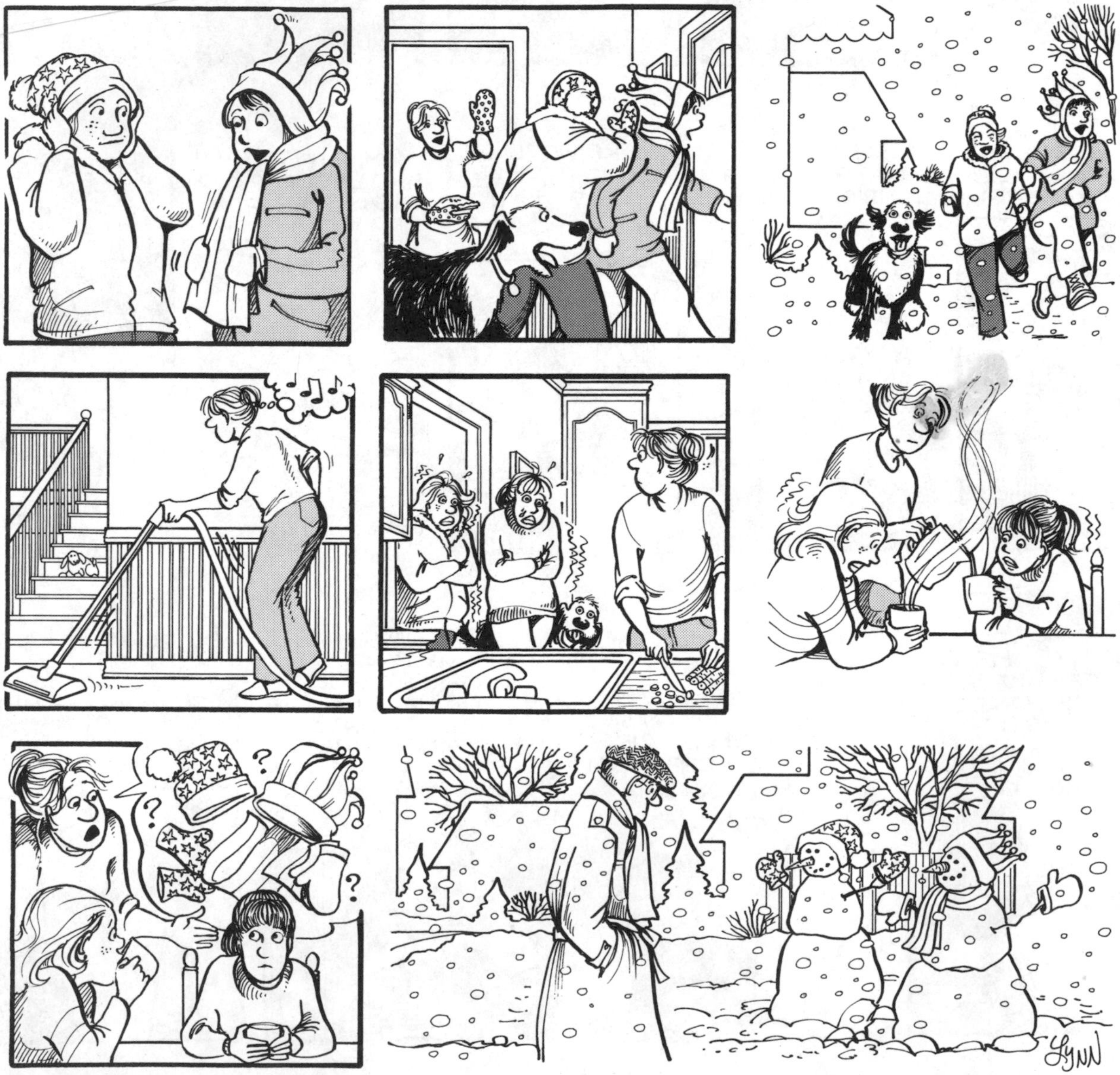
LYNN

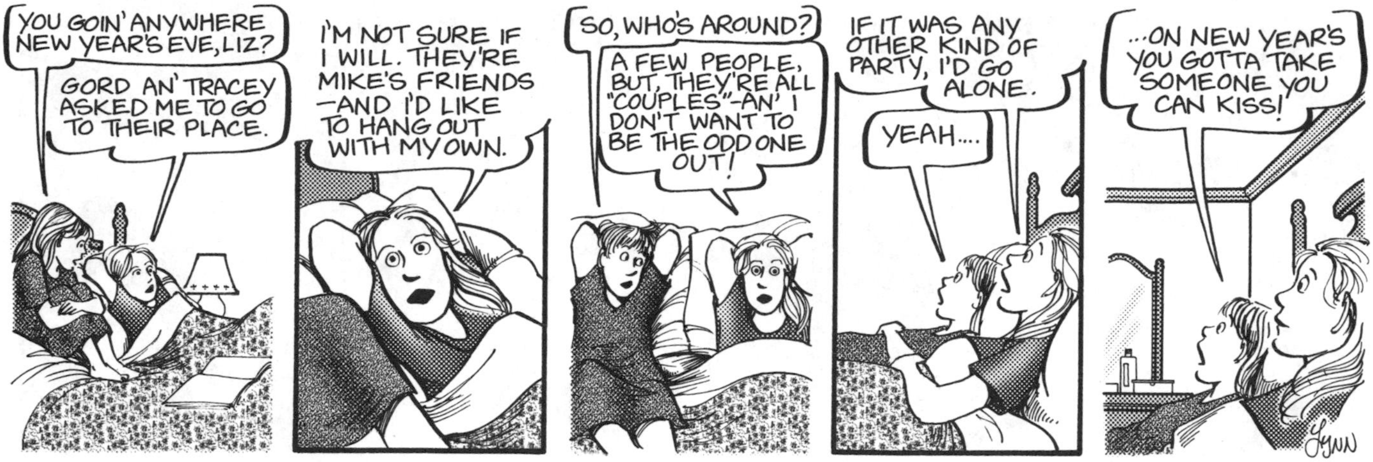
YOU GOIN' ANYWHERE NEW YEAR'S EVE, LIZ?
GORD AN' TRACEY ASKED ME TO GO TO THEIR PLACE.
I'M NOT SURE IF I WILL. THEY'RE MIKE'S FRIENDS —AND I'D LIKE TO HANG OUT WITH MY OWN.
SO, WHO'S AROUND?
A FEW PEOPLE, BUT, THEY'RE ALL "COUPLES"—AN' I DON'T WANT TO BE THE ODD ONE OUT!
IF IT WAS ANY OTHER KIND OF PARTY, I'D GO ALONE.
YEAH....
...ON NEW YEAR'S YOU GOTTA TAKE SOMEONE YOU CAN KISS!
LYNN

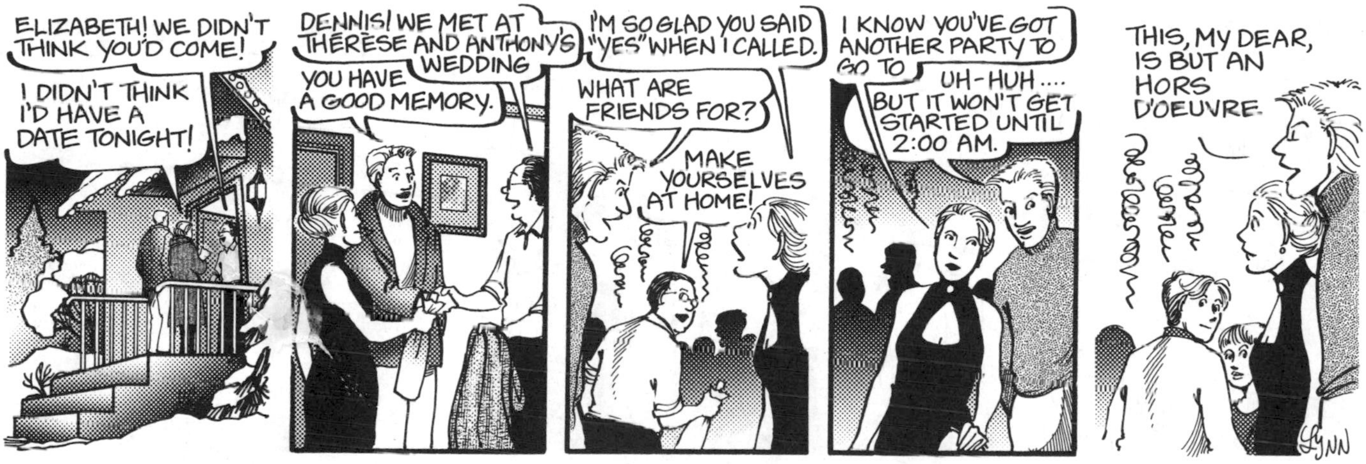
ELIZABETH! WE DIDN'T THINK YOU'D COME!
I DIDN'T THINK I'D HAVE A DATE TONIGHT!
DENNIS! WE MET AT THÉRÈSE AND ANTHONY'S WEDDING
YOU HAVE A GOOD MEMORY.
I'M SO GLAD YOU SAID "YES" WHEN I CALLED.
WHAT ARE FRIENDS FOR?
MAKE YOURSELVES AT HOME!
I KNOW YOU'VE GOT ANOTHER PARTY TO GO TO
UH-HUH.... BUT IT WON'T GET STARTED UNTIL 2:00 AM.
THIS, MY DEAR, IS BUT AN HORS D'OEUVRE.
LYNN

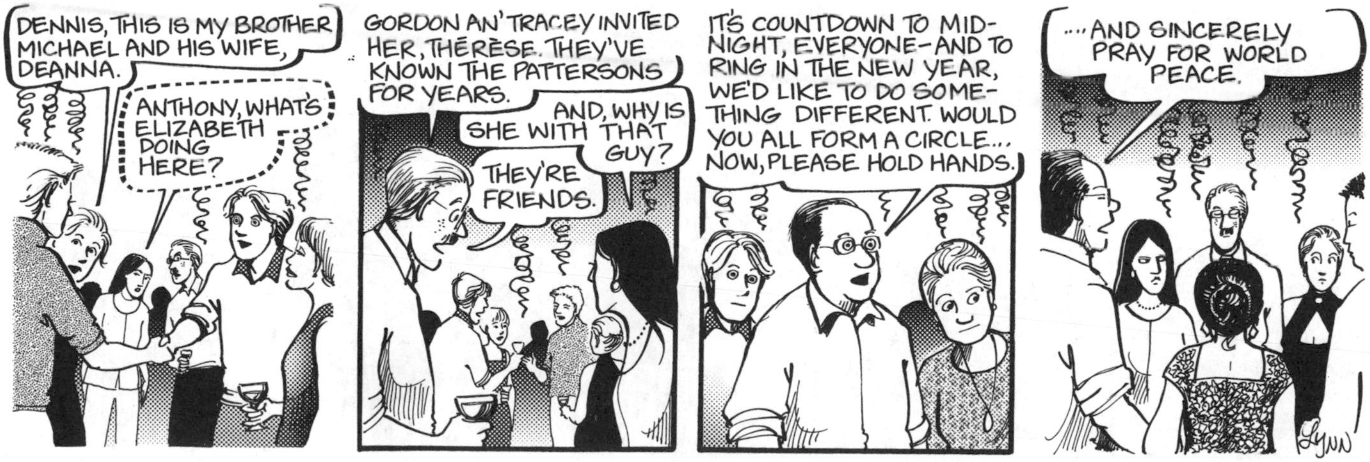
DENNIS, THIS IS MY BROTHER MICHAEL AND HIS WIFE, DEANNA.
ANTHONY, WHAT'S ELIZABETH DOING HERE?
GORDON AN' TRACEY INVITED HER, THÉRÈSE. THEY'VE KNOWN THE PATTERSONS FOR YEARS.
AND, WHY IS SHE WITH THAT GUY?
THEY'RE FRIENDS.
IT'S COUNTDOWN TO MID-NIGHT, EVERYONE—AND TO RING IN THE NEW YEAR, WE'D LIKE TO DO SOME-THING DIFFERENT. WOULD YOU ALL FORM A CIRCLE... NOW, PLEASE HOLD HANDS.
...AND SINCERELY PRAY FOR WORLD PEACE.
LYNN

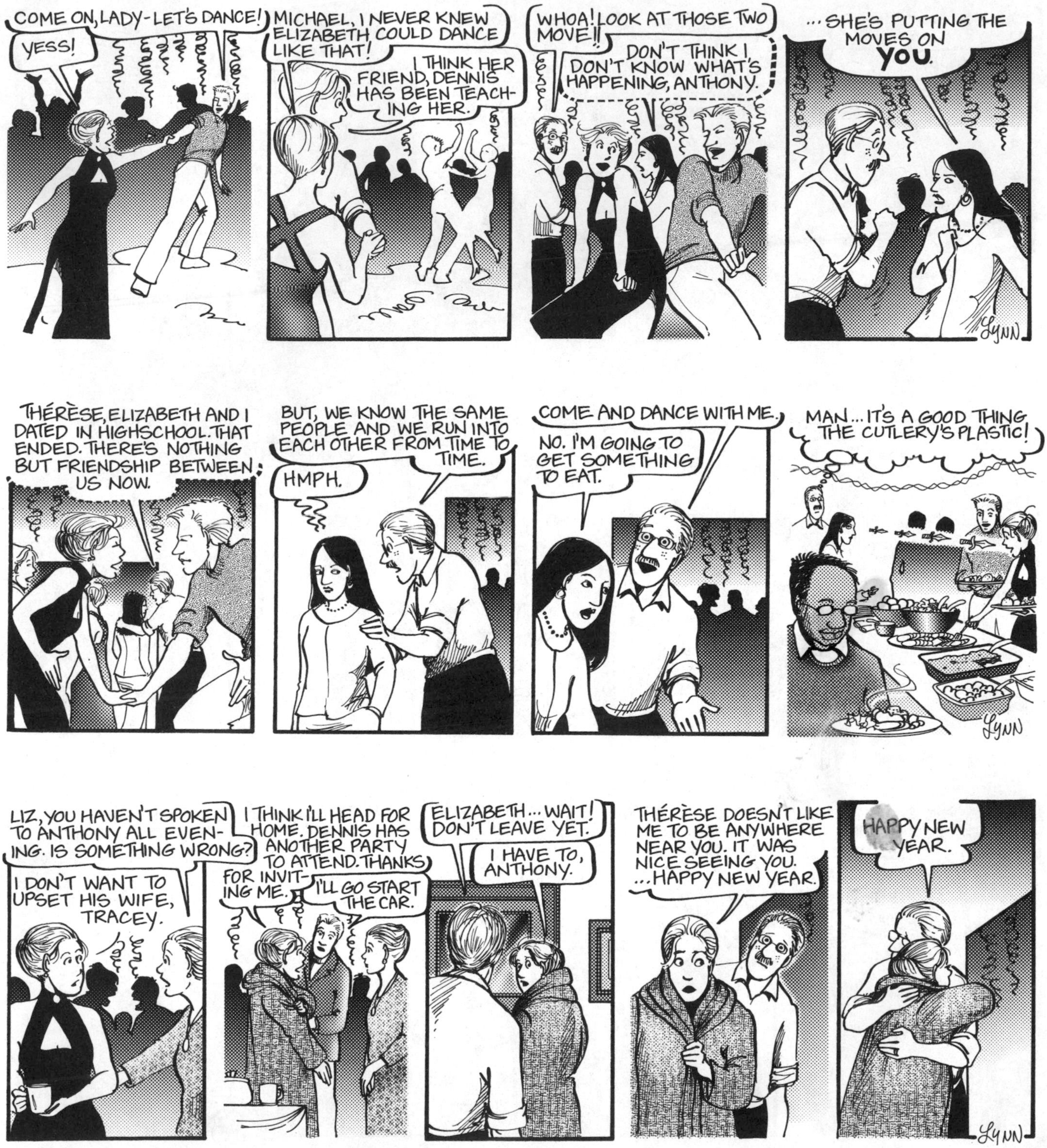
COME ON, LADY - LET'S DANCE!
YESS!
MICHAEL, I NEVER KNEW ELIZABETH COULD DANCE LIKE THAT!
I THINK HER FRIEND, DENNIS HAS BEEN TEACHING HER.
WHOA! LOOK AT THOSE TWO MOVE!!
DON'T THINK I DON'T KNOW WHAT'S HAPPENING, ANTHONY.
... SHE'S PUTTING THE MOVES ON YOU.
LYNN
THÉRÈSE, ELIZABETH AND I DATED IN HIGHSCHOOL. THAT ENDED. THERE'S NOTHING BUT FRIENDSHIP BETWEEN US NOW.
BUT, WE KNOW THE SAME PEOPLE AND WE RUN INTO EACH OTHER FROM TIME TO TIME.
HMPH.
COME AND DANCE WITH ME.
NO. I'M GOING TO GET SOMETHING TO EAT.
MAN... IT'S A GOOD THING THE CUTLERY'S PLASTIC!
LYNN
LIZ, YOU HAVEN'T SPOKEN TO ANTHONY ALL EVENING. IS SOMETHING WRONG?
I DON'T WANT TO UPSET HIS WIFE, TRACEY.
I THINK I'LL HEAD FOR HOME. DENNIS HAS ANOTHER PARTY TO ATTEND. THANKS FOR INVITING ME.
I'LL GO START THE CAR.
ELIZABETH... WAIT! DON'T LEAVE YET.
I HAVE TO, ANTHONY.
THÉRÈSE DOESN'T LIKE ME TO BE ANYWHERE NEAR YOU. IT WAS NICE SEEING YOU. ...HAPPY NEW YEAR.
HAPPY NEW YEAR.
LYNN

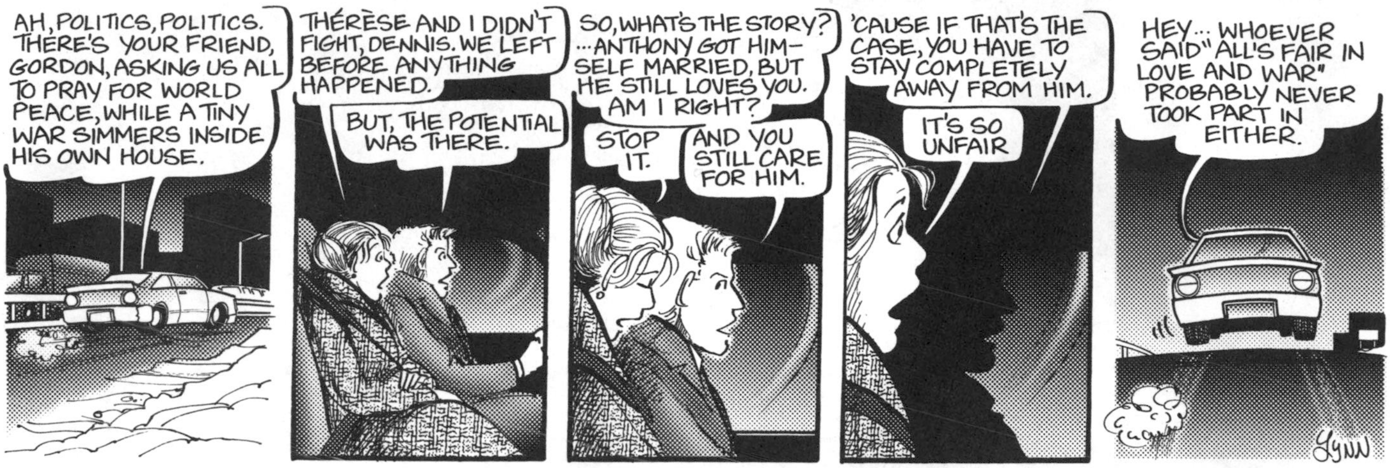
AH, POLITICS, POLITICS. THERE'S YOUR FRIEND, GORDON, ASKING US ALL TO PRAY FOR WORLD PEACE, WHILE A TINY WAR SIMMERS INSIDE HIS OWN HOUSE.
THÉRÈSE AND I DIDN'T FIGHT, DENNIS. WE LEFT BEFORE ANYTHING HAPPENED.
BUT, THE POTENTIAL WAS THERE.
SO, WHAT'S THE STORY? ...ANTHONY GOT HIMSELF MARRIED, BUT HE STILL LOVES YOU. AM I RIGHT?
STOP IT.
AND YOU STILL CARE FOR HIM.
'CAUSE IF THAT'S THE CASE, YOU HAVE TO STAY COMPLETELY AWAY FROM HIM.
IT'S SO UNFAIR
HEY... WHOEVER SAID "ALL'S FAIR IN LOVE AND WAR" PROBABLY NEVER TOOK PART IN EITHER.
LYNN

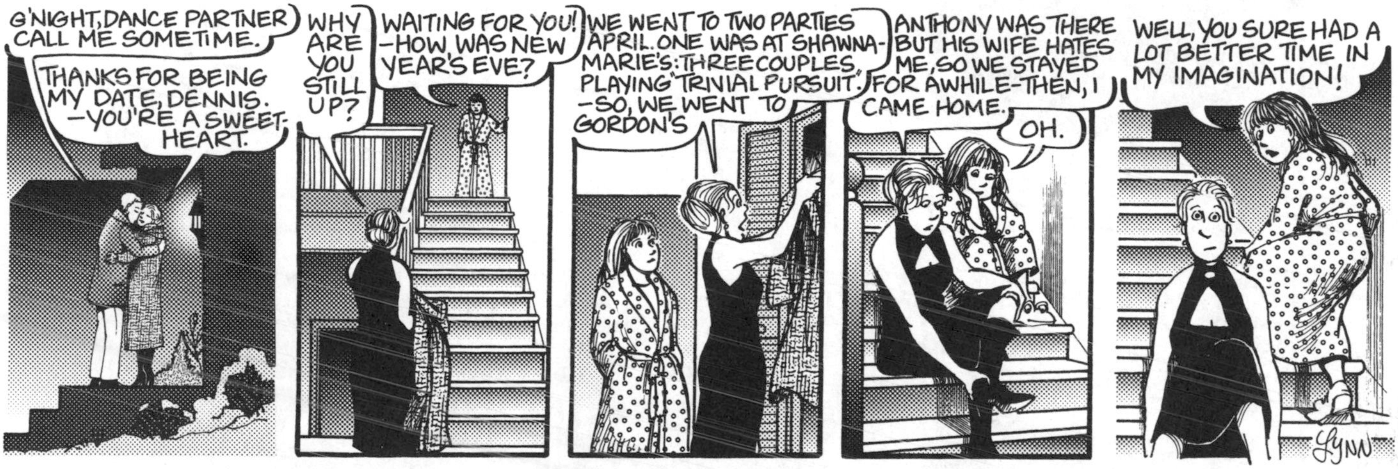
G'NIGHT, DANCE PARTNER CALL ME SOMETIME.
THANKS FOR BEING MY DATE, DENNIS. —YOU'RE A SWEETHEART.
WHY ARE YOU STILL UP?
WAITING FOR YOU! -HOW WAS NEW YEAR'S EVE?
WE WENT TO TWO PARTIES APRIL. ONE WAS AT SHAWNA-MARIE'S: THREE COUPLES, PLAYING "TRIVIAL PURSUIT." —SO, WE WENT TO GORDON'S
ANTHONY WAS THERE BUT HIS WIFE HATES ME, SO WE STAYED FOR AWHILE—THEN, I CAME HOME.
OH.
WELL, YOU SURE HAD A LOT BETTER TIME IN MY IMAGINATION!
LYNN

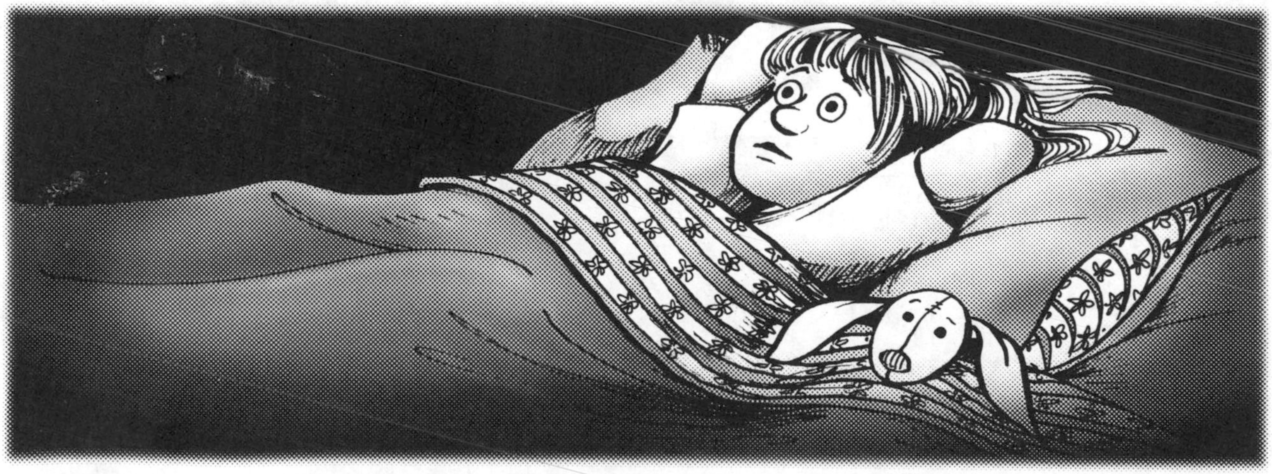

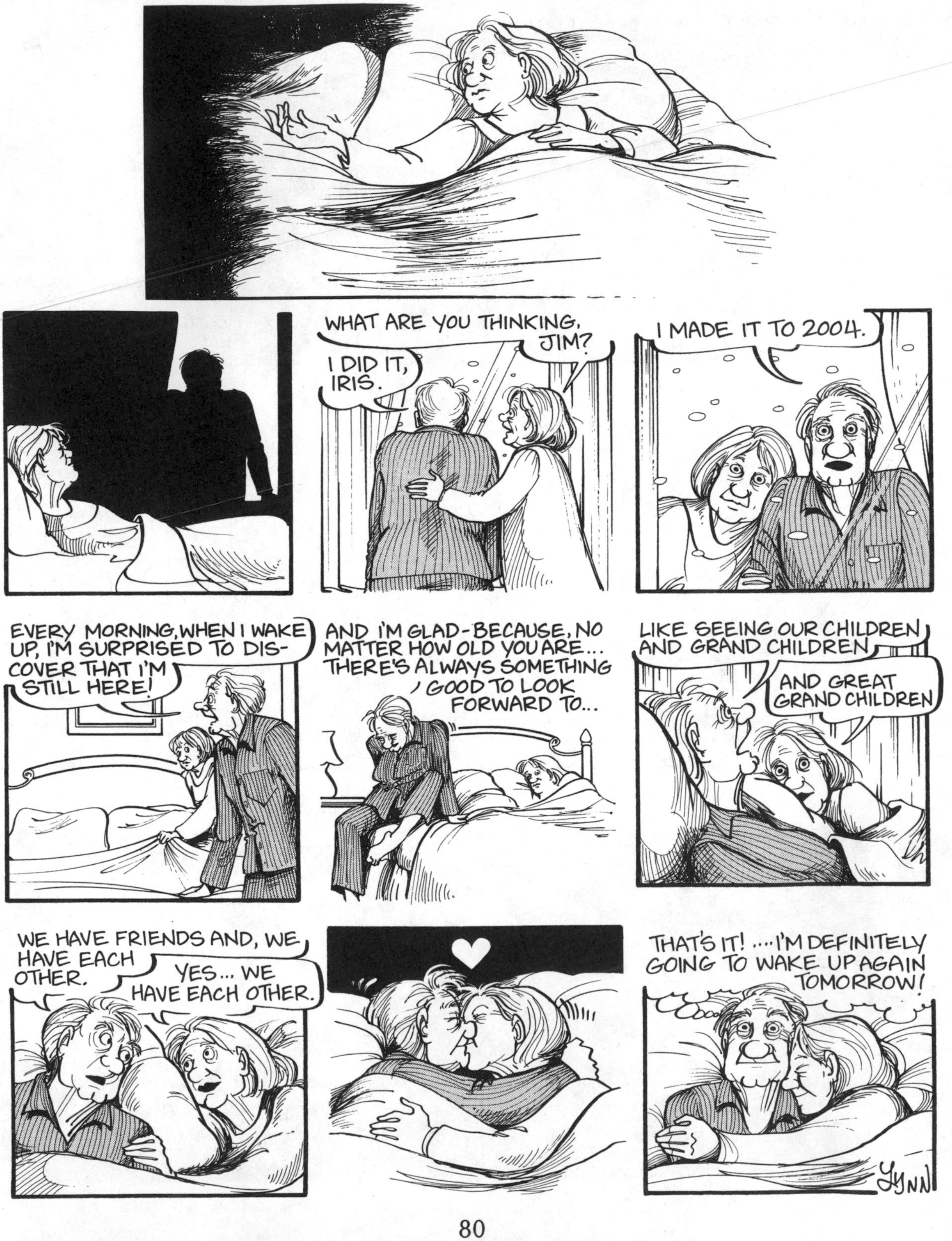

WHAT ARE YOU THINKING, JIM?
I DID IT, IRIS.
I MADE IT TO 2004.
EVERY MORNING, WHEN I WAKE UP, I'M SURPRISED TO DISCOVER THAT I'M STILL HERE!
AND I'M GLAD - BECAUSE, NO MATTER HOW OLD YOU ARE... THERE'S ALWAYS SOMETHING GOOD TO LOOK FORWARD TO...
LIKE SEEING OUR CHILDREN AND GRAND CHILDREN
AND GREAT GRAND CHILDREN
WE HAVE FRIENDS AND, WE HAVE EACH OTHER.
YES... WE HAVE EACH OTHER.
THAT'S IT! ....I'M DEFINITELY GOING TO WAKE UP AGAIN TOMORROW!
LYNN

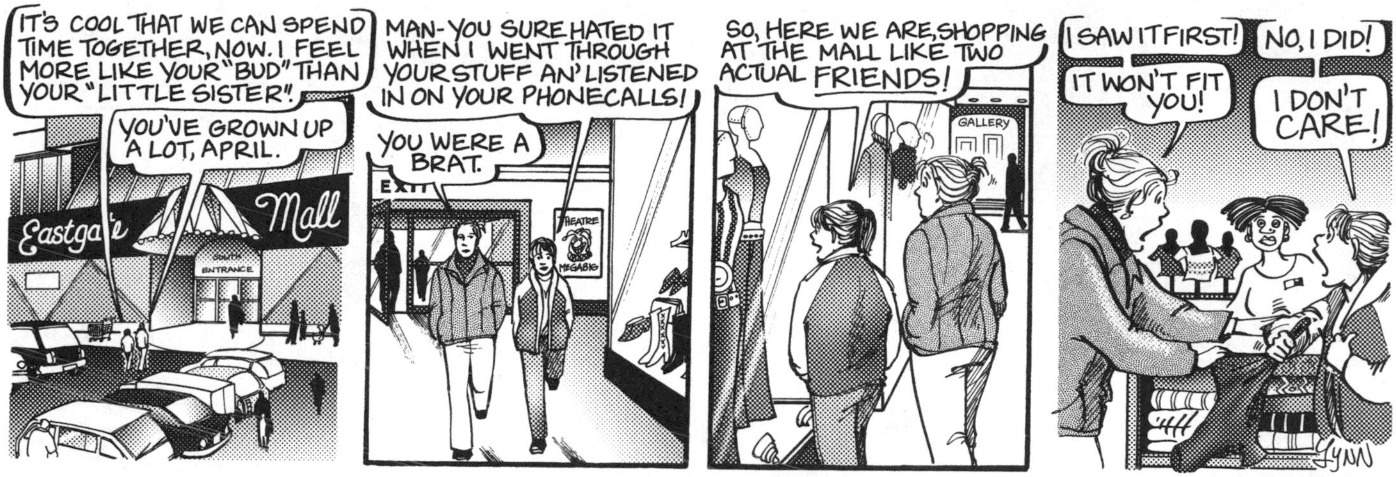
IT'S COOL THAT WE CAN SPEND TIME TOGETHER, NOW. I FEEL MORE LIKE YOUR "BUD" THAN YOUR "LITTLE SISTER".
YOU'VE GROWN UP A LOT, APRIL.
Eastgate Mall
SOUTH ENTRANCE
MAN- YOU SURE HATED IT WHEN I WENT THROUGH YOUR STUFF AN' LISTENED IN ON YOUR PHONECALLS!
YOU WERE A BRAT.
EXIT
THEATRE
MEGABIE
SO, HERE WE ARE, SHOPPING AT THE MALL LIKE TWO ACTUAL FRIENDS!
GALLERY
I SAW IT FIRST!
NO, I DID!
IT WON'T FIT YOU!
I DON'T CARE!
LYNN

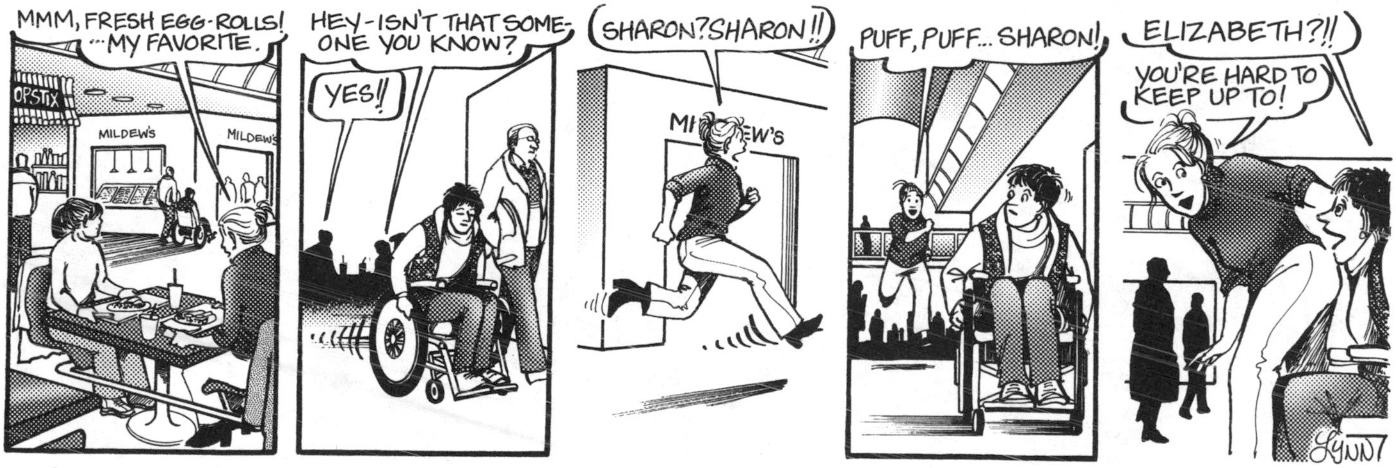
MMM, FRESH EGG-ROLLS! ...MY FAVORITE.
OPSTIX
MILDEW'S
MILDEW'S
HEY- ISN'T THAT SOME-ONE YOU KNOW?
YES!!
SHARON? SHARON!!
PUFF, PUFF... SHARON!
ELIZABETH?!!
YOU'RE HARD TO KEEP UP TO!
LYNN

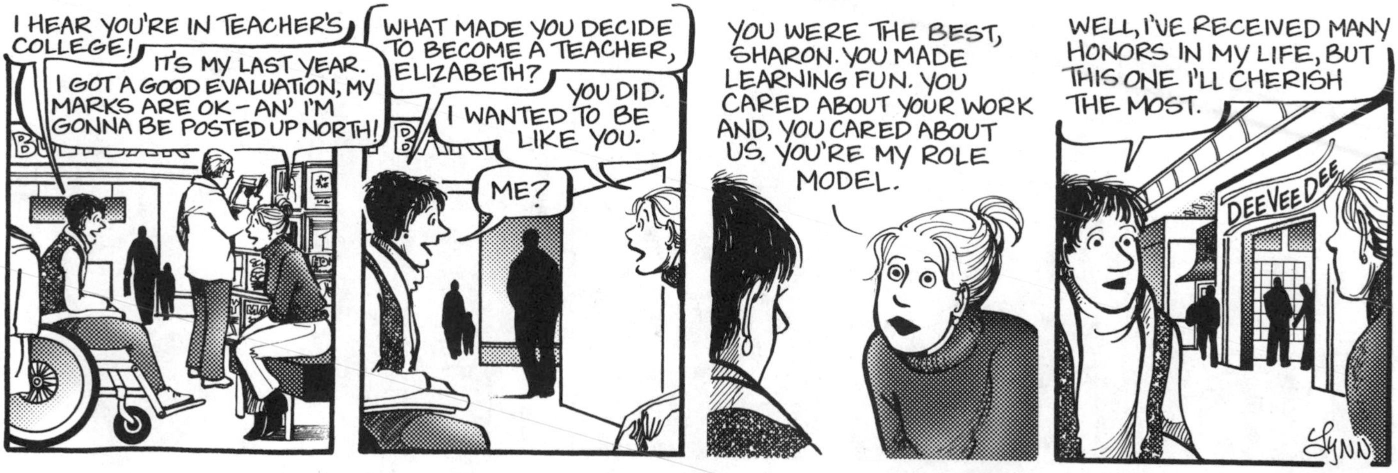
I HEAR YOU'RE IN TEACHER'S COLLEGE!
IT'S MY LAST YEAR. I GOT A GOOD EVALUATION, MY MARKS ARE OK – AN' I'M GONNA BE POSTED UP NORTH!
WHAT MADE YOU DECIDE TO BECOME A TEACHER, ELIZABETH?
YOU DID. I WANTED TO BE LIKE YOU.
ME?
YOU WERE THE BEST, SHARON. YOU MADE LEARNING FUN. YOU CARED ABOUT YOUR WORK AND, YOU CARED ABOUT US. YOU'RE MY ROLE MODEL.
WELL, I'VE RECEIVED MANY HONORS IN MY LIFE, BUT THIS ONE I'LL CHERISH THE MOST.
DEEVEEDEE
LYNN

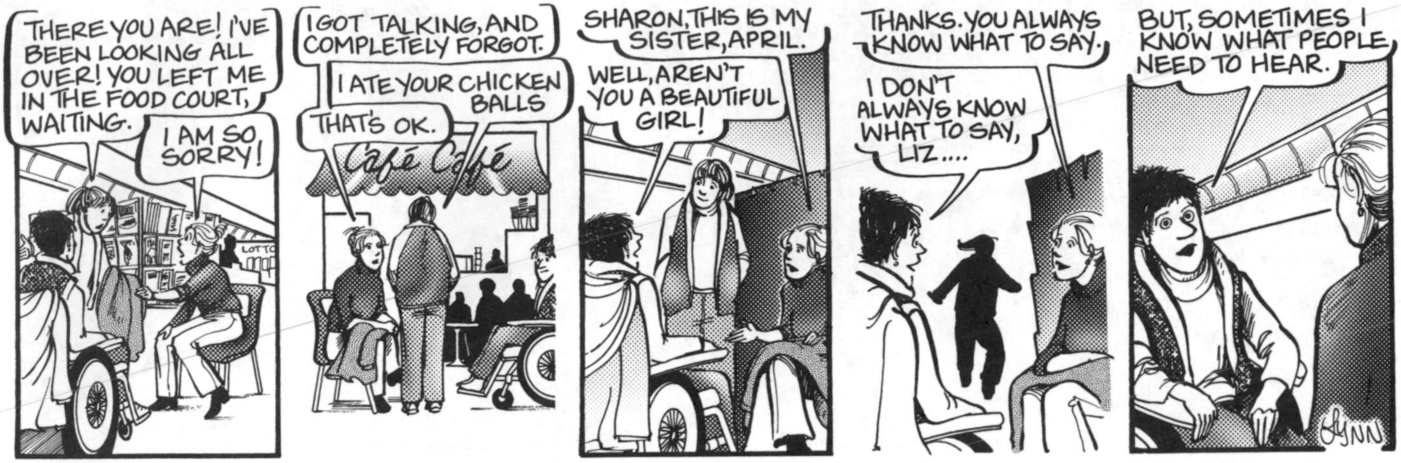
THERE YOU ARE! I'VE BEEN LOOKING ALL OVER! YOU LEFT ME IN THE FOOD COURT, WAITING.
I AM SO SORRY!
LOTTO
I GOT TALKING, AND COMPLETELY FORGOT.
I ATE YOUR CHICKEN BALLS
THAT'S OK.
Café Coffé
SHARON, THIS IS MY SISTER, APRIL.
WELL, AREN'T YOU A BEAUTIFUL GIRL!
THANKS. YOU ALWAYS KNOW WHAT TO SAY.
I DON'T ALWAYS KNOW WHAT TO SAY, LIZ....
BUT, SOMETIMES I KNOW WHAT PEOPLE NEED TO HEAR.
LYNN

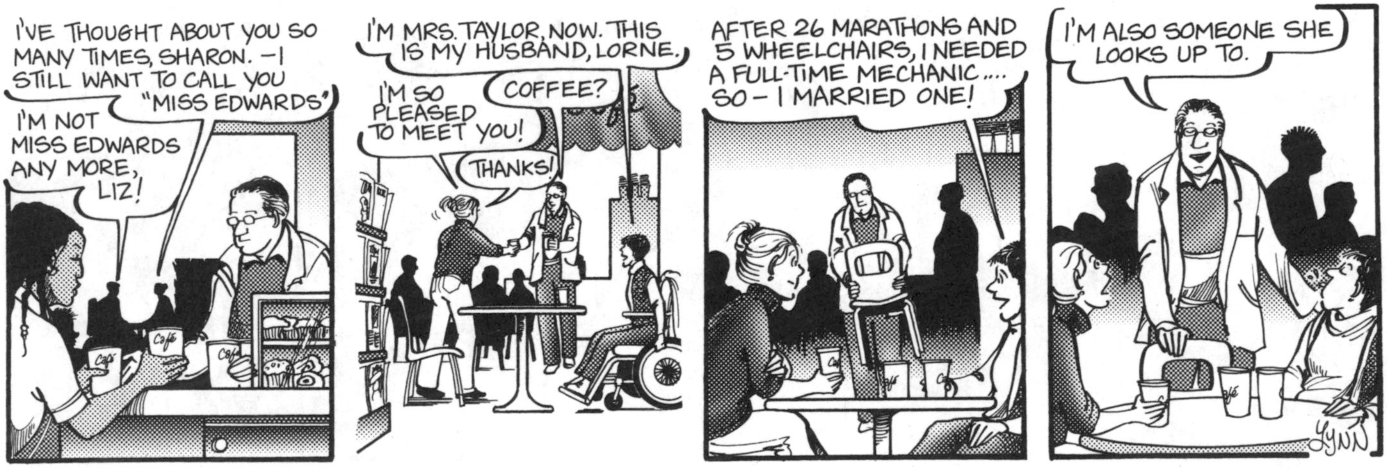
I'VE THOUGHT ABOUT YOU SO MANY TIMES, SHARON. —I STILL WANT TO CALL YOU "MISS EDWARDS"
I'M NOT MISS EDWARDS ANY MORE, LIZ!
I'M MRS. TAYLOR, NOW. THIS IS MY HUSBAND, LORNE.
I'M SO PLEASED TO MEET YOU!
COFFEE?
THANKS!
AFTER 26 MARATHONS AND 5 WHEELCHAIRS, I NEEDED A FULL-TIME MECHANIC.... SO – I MARRIED ONE!
I'M ALSO SOMEONE SHE LOOKS UP TO.
LYNN

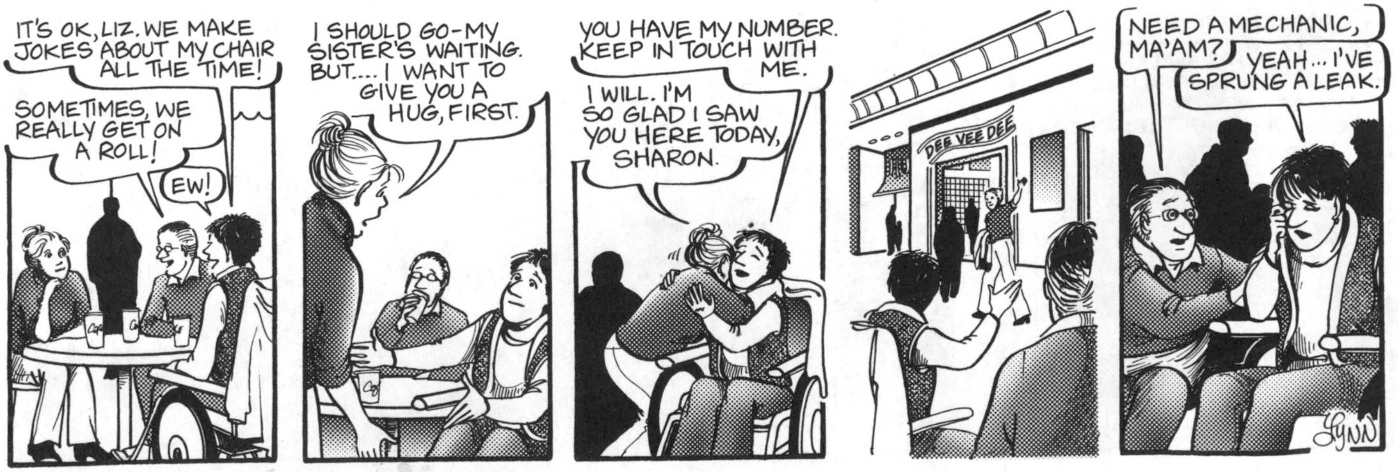
IT'S OK, LIZ. WE MAKE JOKES ABOUT MY CHAIR ALL THE TIME!
SOMETIMES, WE REALLY GET ON A ROLL!
EW!
I SHOULD GO–MY SISTER'S WAITING. BUT.... I WANT TO GIVE YOU A HUG, FIRST.
YOU HAVE MY NUMBER. KEEP IN TOUCH WITH ME.
I WILL. I'M SO GLAD I SAW YOU HERE TODAY, SHARON.
DEE VEE DEE
NEED A MECHANIC, MA'AM?
YEAH... I'VE SPRUNG A LEAK.
LYNN

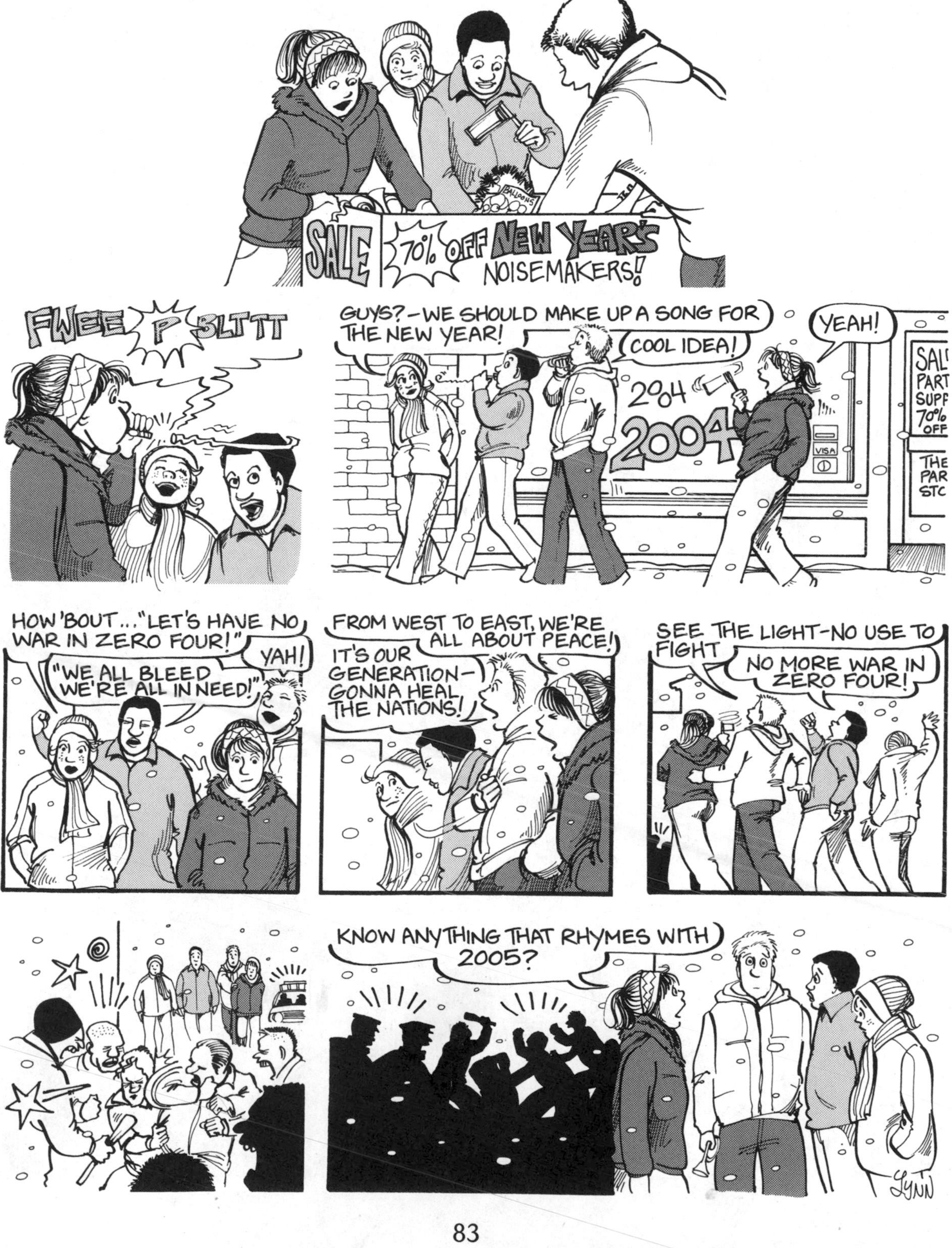
SALE
70% OFF NEW YEAR'S NOISEMAKERS!
FWEE P SLTTT
GUYS? - WE SHOULD MAKE UP A SONG FOR THE NEW YEAR!
COOL IDEA!
YEAH!
2004
HOW 'BOUT ... "LET'S HAVE NO WAR IN ZERO FOUR!"
"WE ALL BLEED WE'RE ALL IN NEED!"
YAH!
FROM WEST TO EAST, WE'RE ALL ABOUT PEACE!
IT'S OUR GENERATION— GONNA HEAL THE NATIONS!
SEE THE LIGHT-NO USE TO FIGHT
NO MORE WAR IN ZERO FOUR!
KNOW ANYTHING THAT RHYMES WITH 2005?
LYNN

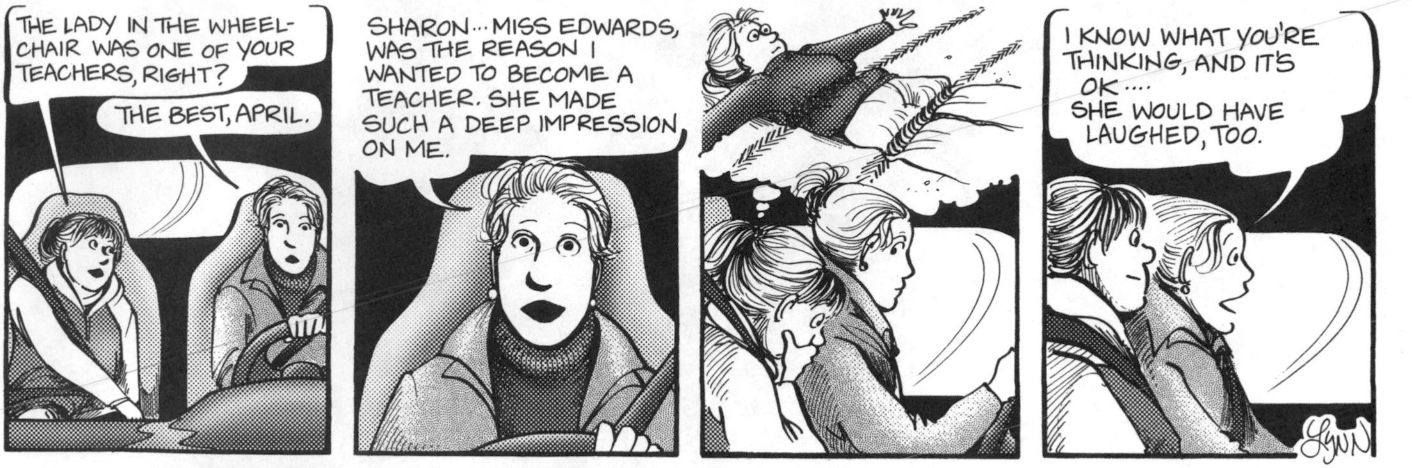
THE LADY IN THE WHEEL-CHAIR WAS ONE OF YOUR TEACHERS, RIGHT?
THE BEST, APRIL.
SHARON... MISS EDWARDS, WAS THE REASON I WANTED TO BECOME A TEACHER. SHE MADE SUCH A DEEP IMPRESSION ON ME.
I KNOW WHAT YOU'RE THINKING, AND IT'S OK....
SHE WOULD HAVE LAUGHED, TOO.
LYNN

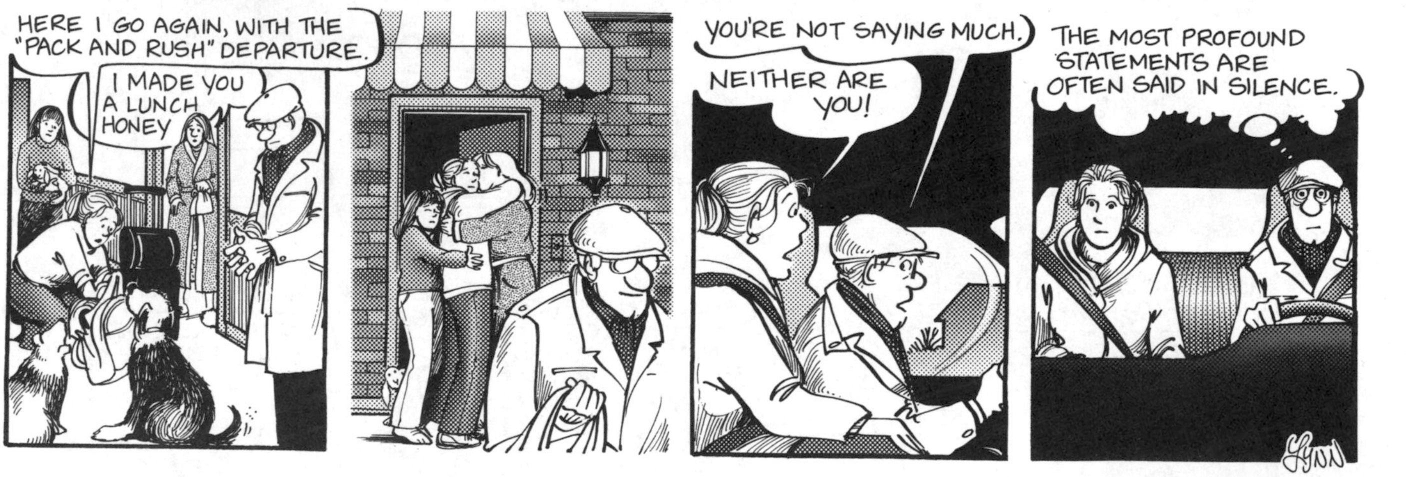
HERE I GO AGAIN, WITH THE "PACK AND RUSH" DEPARTURE.
I MADE YOU A LUNCH HONEY
YOU'RE NOT SAYING MUCH.
NEITHER ARE YOU!
THE MOST PROFOUND STATEMENTS ARE OFTEN SAID IN SILENCE.
LYNN

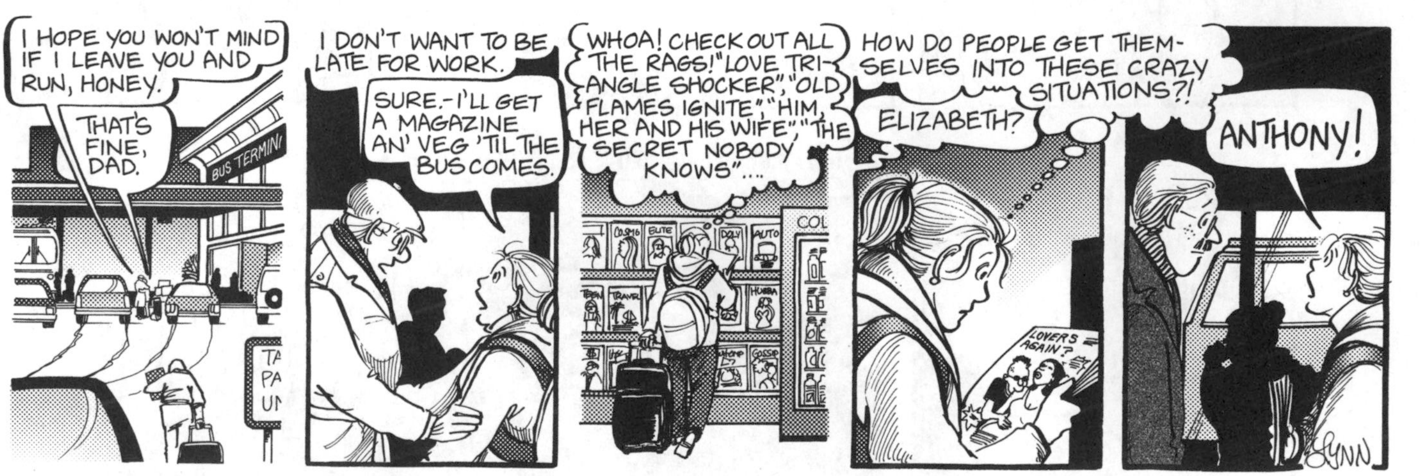
I HOPE YOU WON'T MIND IF I LEAVE YOU AND RUN, HONEY.
THAT'S FINE, DAD.
I DON'T WANT TO BE LATE FOR WORK.
SURE.-I'LL GET A MAGAZINE AN' VEG 'TIL THE BUS COMES.
WHOA! CHECK OUT ALL THE RAGS! "LOVE TRI-ANGLE SHOCKER", "OLD FLAMES IGNITE", "HIM, HER AND HIS WIFE", "THE SECRET NOBODY KNOWS"....
HOW DO PEOPLE GET THEM-SELVES INTO THESE CRAZY SITUATIONS?!
ELIZABETH?
LOVERS AGAIN?
ANTHONY!
LYNN

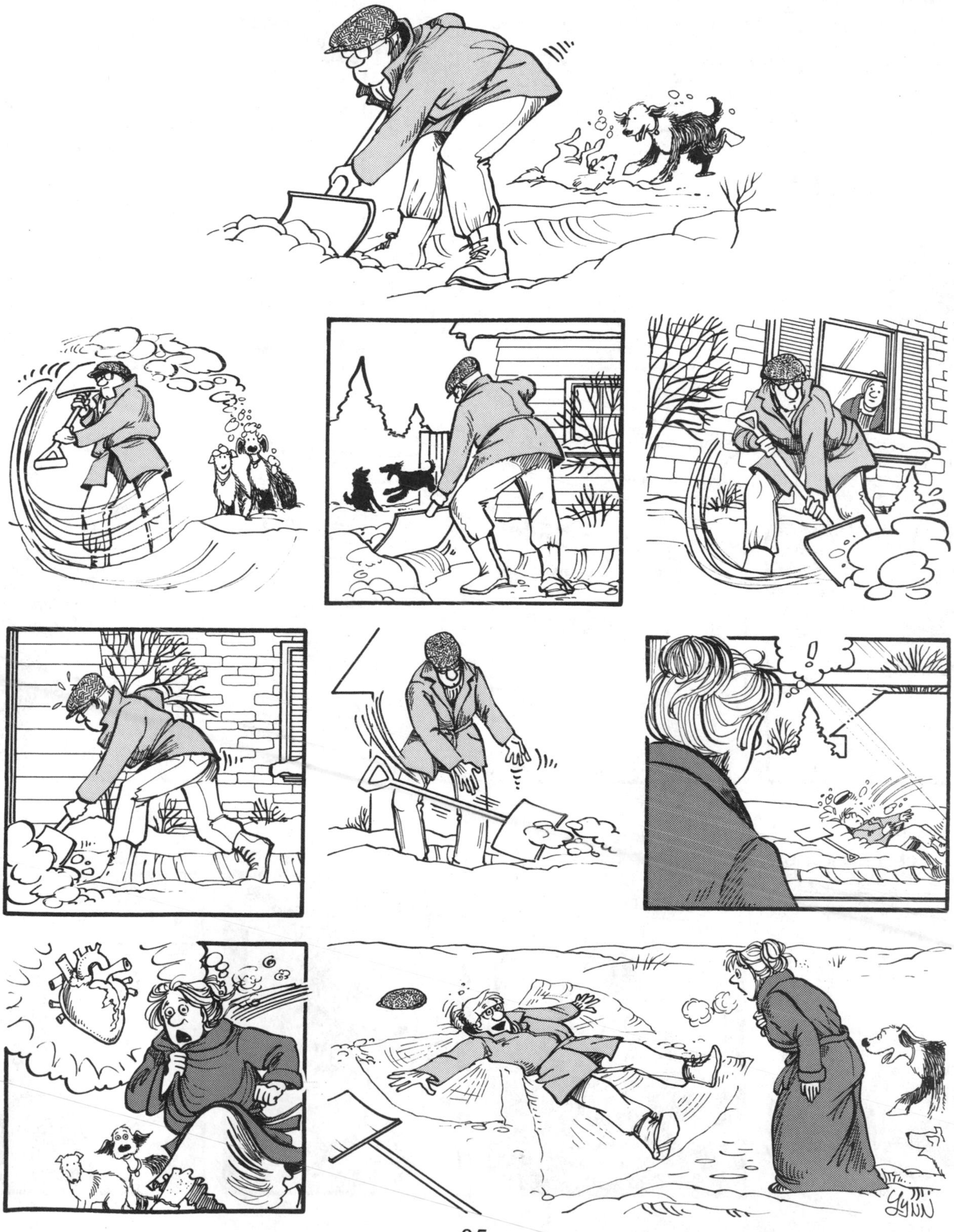
!

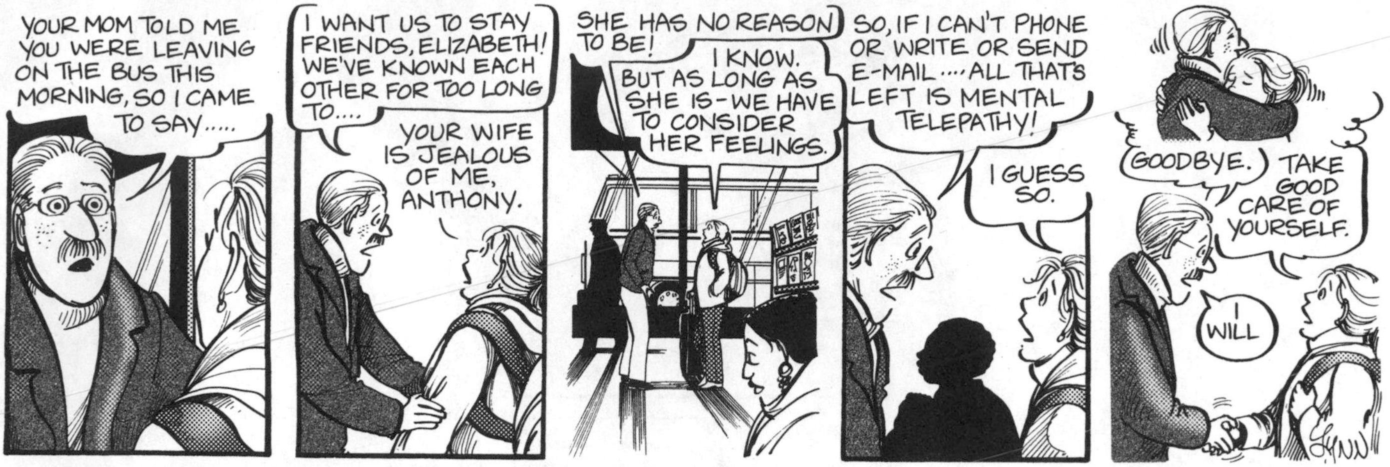
YOUR MOM TOLD ME YOU WERE LEAVING ON THE BUS THIS MORNING, SO I CAME TO SAY.....
I WANT US TO STAY FRIENDS, ELIZABETH! WE'VE KNOWN EACH OTHER FOR TOO LONG TO....
YOUR WIFE IS JEALOUS OF ME, ANTHONY.
SHE HAS NO REASON TO BE!
I KNOW. BUT AS LONG AS SHE IS–WE HAVE TO CONSIDER HER FEELINGS.
SO, IF I CAN'T PHONE OR WRITE OR SEND E-MAIL.... ALL THAT'S LEFT IS MENTAL TELEPATHY!
I GUESS SO.
GOODBYE.
TAKE GOOD CARE OF YOURSELF.
I WILL
LYNN

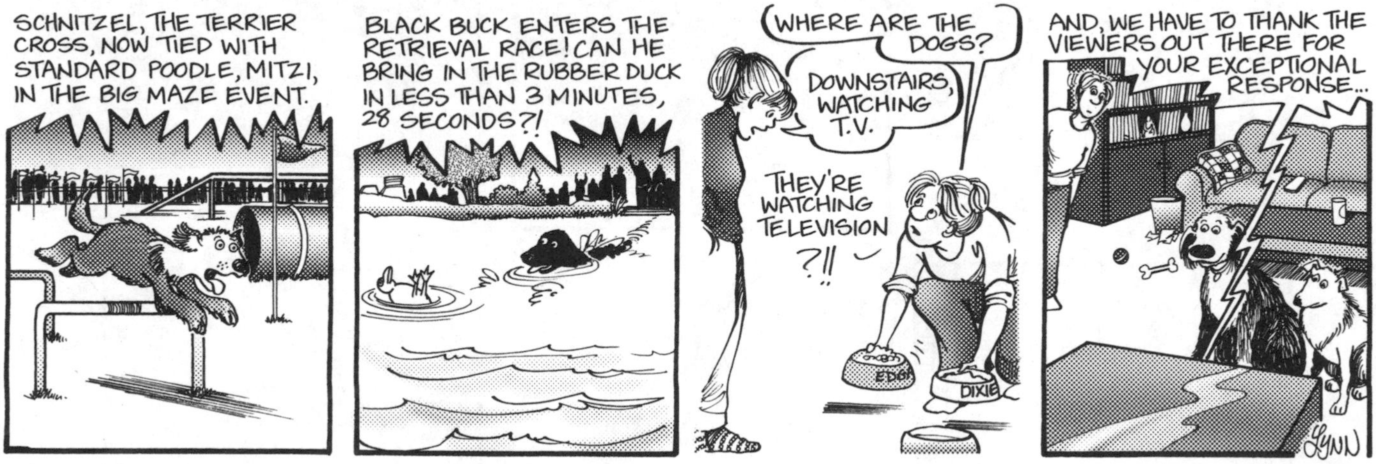
SCHNITZEL, THE TERRIER CROSS, NOW TIED WITH STANDARD POODLE, MITZI, IN THE BIG MAZE EVENT.
BLACK BUCK ENTERS THE RETRIEVAL RACE! CAN HE BRING IN THE RUBBER DUCK IN LESS THAN 3 MINUTES, 28 SECONDS?!
WHERE ARE THE DOGS?
DOWNSTAIRS, WATCHING T.V.
THEY'RE WATCHING TELEVISION ?!!
DIXIE
AND, WE HAVE TO THANK THE VIEWERS OUT THERE FOR YOUR EXCEPTIONAL RESPONSE...
LYNN

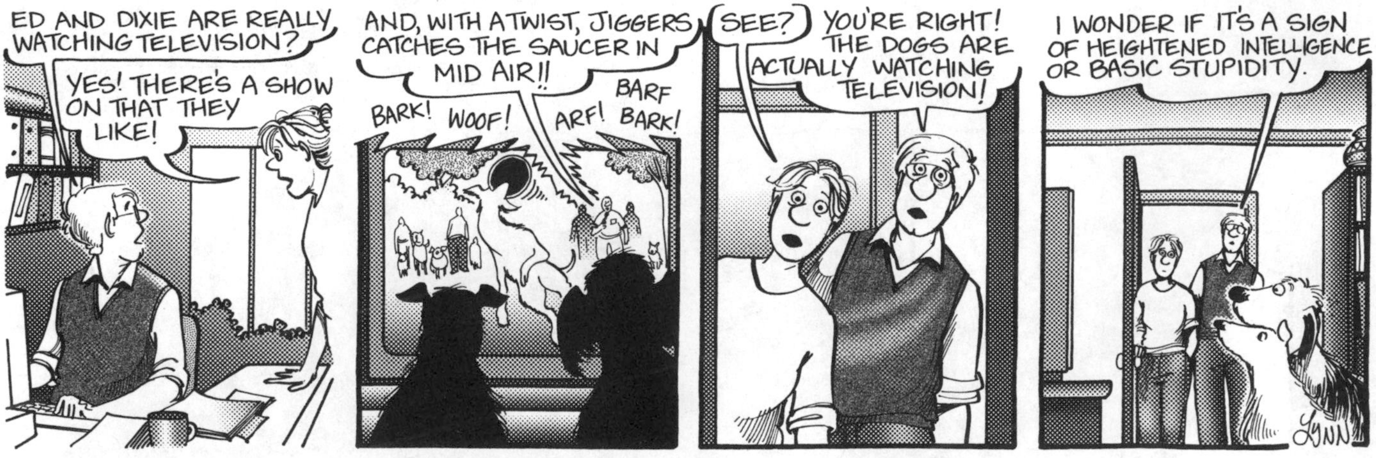
ED AND DIXIE ARE REALLY WATCHING TELEVISION?
YES! THERE'S A SHOW ON THAT THEY LIKE!
AND, WITH A TWIST, JIGGERS CATCHES THE SAUCER IN MID AIR!!
BARK! WOOF! ARF! BARF BARK!
SEE?
YOU'RE RIGHT! THE DOGS ARE ACTUALLY WATCHING TELEVISION!
I WONDER IF IT'S A SIGN OF HEIGHTENED INTELLIGENCE OR BASIC STUPIDITY.
LYNN

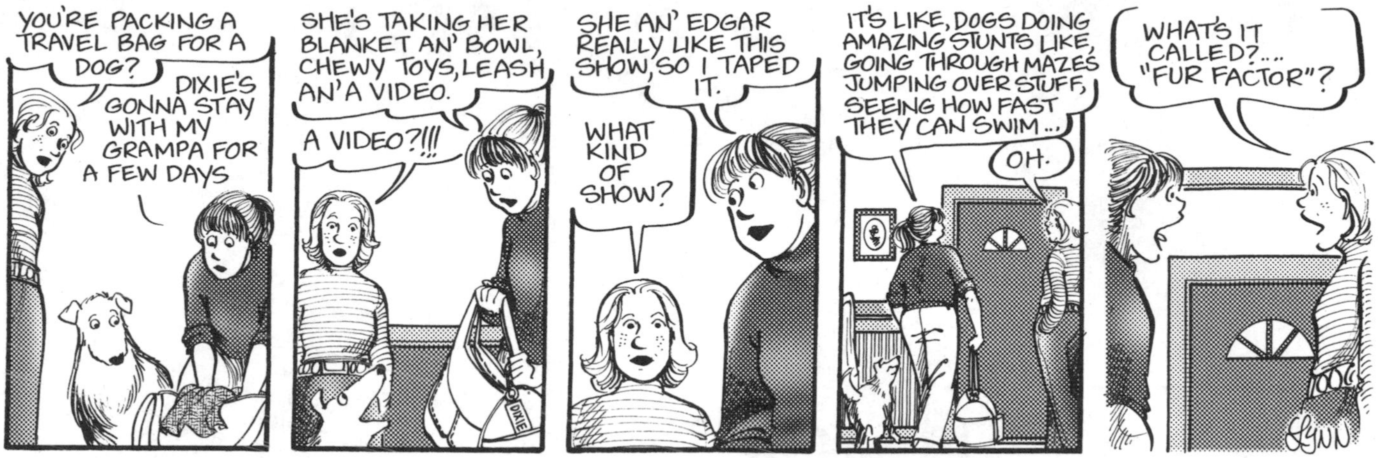
YOU'RE PACKING A TRAVEL BAG FOR A DOG?
DIXIE'S GONNA STAY WITH MY GRAMPA FOR A FEW DAYS
SHE'S TAKING HER BLANKET AN' BOWL, CHEWY TOYS, LEASH AN' A VIDEO.
A VIDEO?!!!
SHE AN' EDGAR REALLY LIKE THIS SHOW, SO I TAPED IT.
WHAT KIND OF SHOW?
IT'S LIKE, DOGS DOING AMAZING STUNTS LIKE, GOING THROUGH MAZES JUMPING OVER STUFF, SEEING HOW FAST THEY CAN SWIM...
OH.
WHAT'S IT CALLED?... "FUR FACTOR"?
LYNN

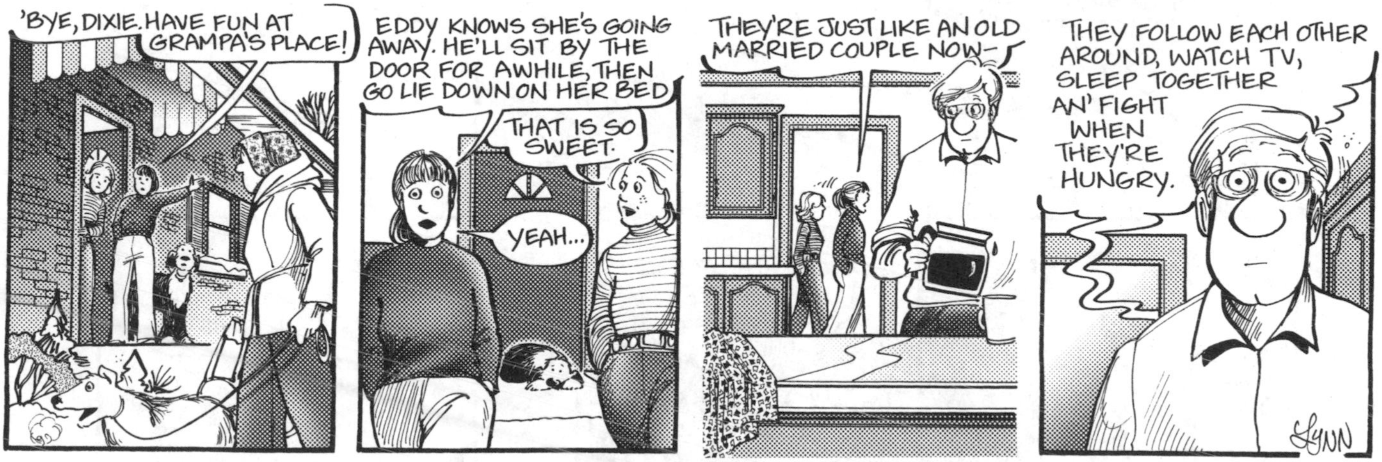
'BYE, DIXIE. HAVE FUN AT GRAMPA'S PLACE!
EDDY KNOWS SHE'S GOING AWAY. HE'LL SIT BY THE DOOR FOR AWHILE, THEN GO LIE DOWN ON HER BED
THAT IS SO SWEET.
YEAH...
THEY'RE JUST LIKE AN OLD MARRIED COUPLE NOW–
THEY FOLLOW EACH OTHER AROUND, WATCH TV, SLEEP TOGETHER AN' FIGHT WHEN THEY'RE HUNGRY.
LYNN

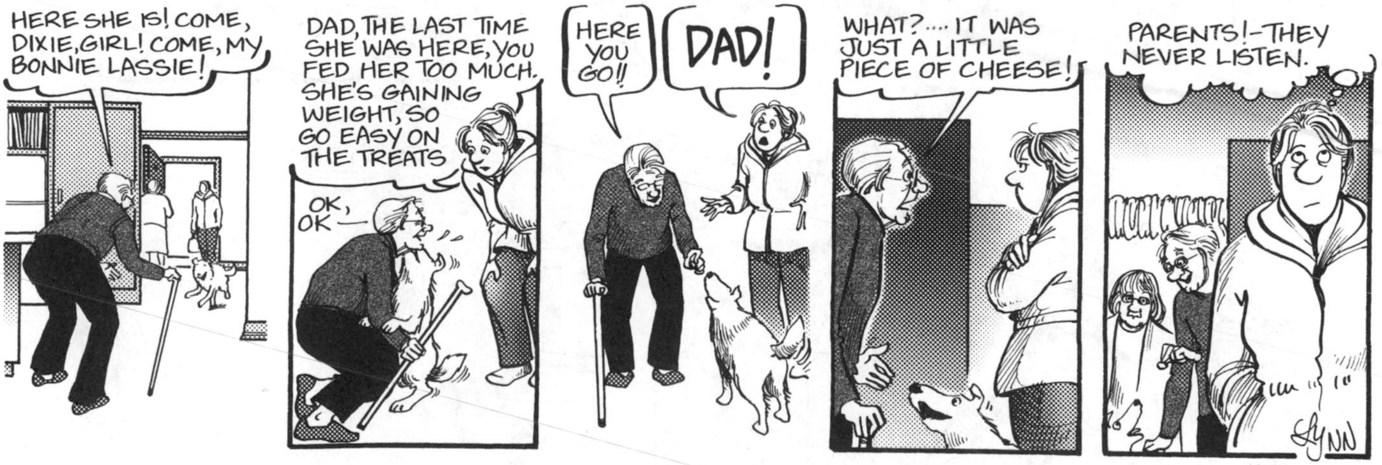
HERE SHE IS! COME, DIXIE, GIRL! COME, MY BONNIE LASSIE!
DAD, THE LAST TIME SHE WAS HERE, YOU FED HER TOO MUCH. SHE'S GAINING WEIGHT, SO GO EASY ON THE TREATS
OK, OK
HERE YOU GO!!
DAD!
WHAT?.... IT WAS JUST A LITTLE PIECE OF CHEESE!
PARENTS! – THEY NEVER LISTEN.
LYNN

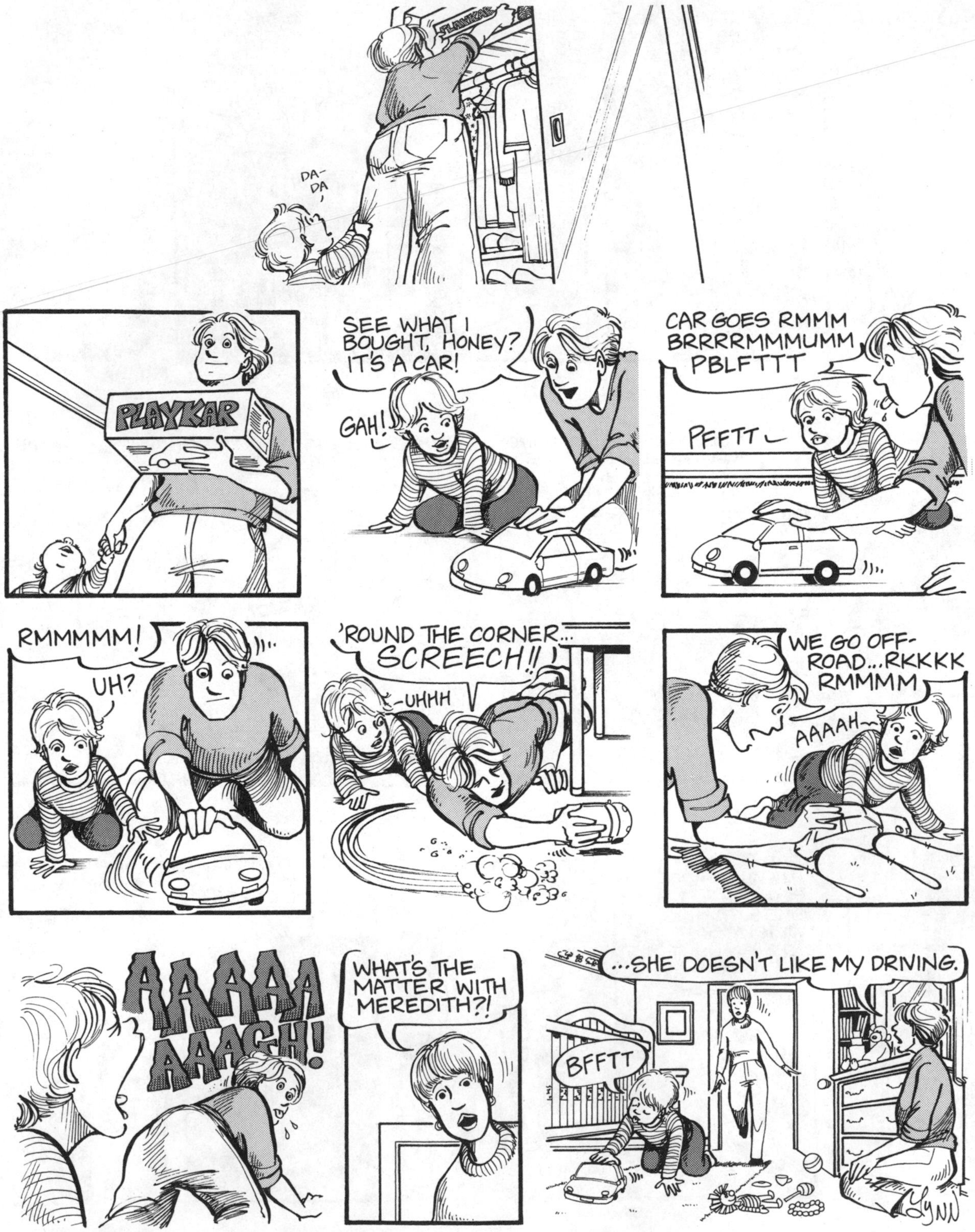

PLAYKAR
DA-DA
PLAYKAR
SEE WHAT I BOUGHT, HONEY? IT'S A CAR!
GAH!
CAR GOES RMMM BRRRRMMMUMM PBLFTTT
PFFTT
RMMMMM!
UH?
'ROUND THE CORNER... SCREECH!!
-UHHH
WE GO OFF-ROAD...RKKKK RMMMM
AAAAH
AAAAA AAAGH!
WHAT'S THE MATTER WITH MEREDITH?!
...SHE DOESN'T LIKE MY DRIVING.
BFFTT
Lynn

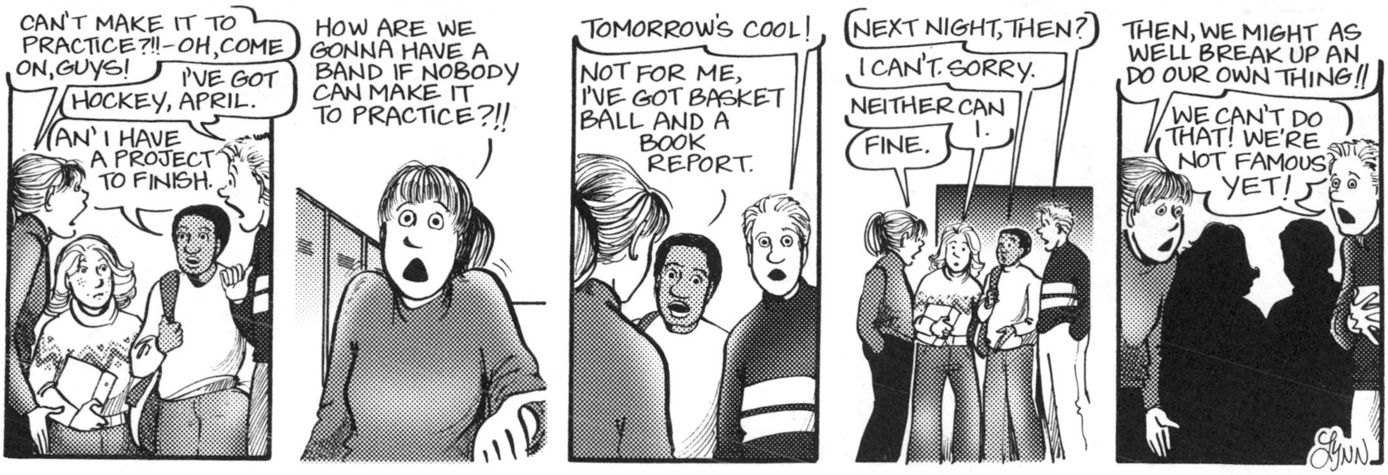
CAN'T MAKE IT TO PRACTICE?!!–OH, COME ON, GUYS!
I'VE GOT HOCKEY, APRIL.
AN' I HAVE A PROJECT TO FINISH.
HOW ARE WE GONNA HAVE A BAND IF NOBODY CAN MAKE IT TO PRACTICE?!!
TOMORROW'S COOL!
NOT FOR ME, I'VE GOT BASKET BALL AND A BOOK REPORT.
NEXT NIGHT, THEN?
I CAN'T. SORRY.
NEITHER CAN I.
FINE.
THEN, WE MIGHT AS WELL BREAK UP AN DO OUR OWN THING!!
WE CAN'T DO THAT! WE'RE NOT FAMOUS YET!
LYNN

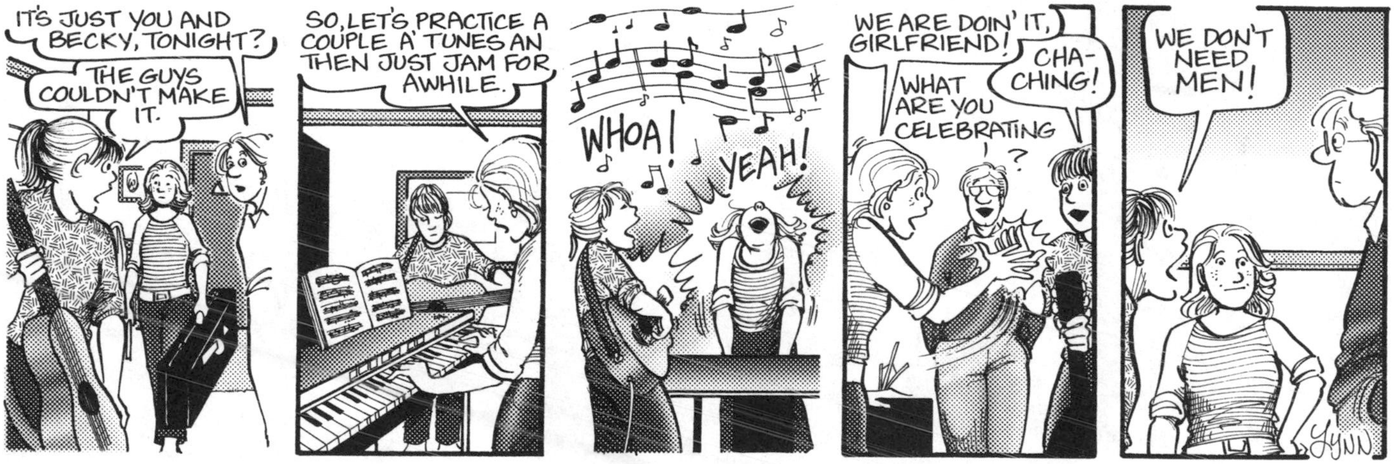
IT'S JUST YOU AND BECKY, TONIGHT?
THE GUYS COULDN'T MAKE IT.
SO, LET'S PRACTICE A COUPLE A' TUNES AN THEN JUST JAM FOR AWHILE.
WHOA!
YEAH!
WE ARE DOIN' IT, GIRLFRIEND!
CHA-CHING!
WHAT ARE YOU CELEBRATING?
WE DON'T NEED MEN!
LYNN

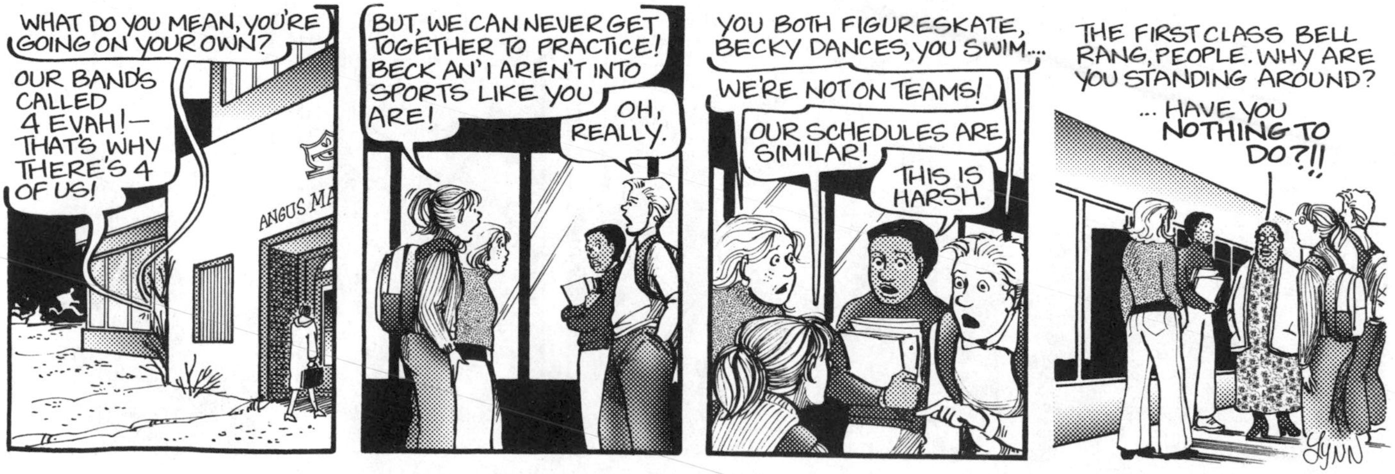
WHAT DO YOU MEAN, YOU'RE GOING ON YOUR OWN?
OUR BAND'S CALLED 4 EVAH!— THAT'S WHY THERE'S 4 OF US!
ANGUS MA
BUT, WE CAN NEVER GET TOGETHER TO PRACTICE! BECK AN' I AREN'T INTO SPORTS LIKE YOU ARE!
OH, REALLY.
YOU BOTH FIGURESKATE, BECKY DANCES, YOU SWIM....
WE'RE NOT ON TEAMS!
OUR SCHEDULES ARE SIMILAR!
THIS IS HARSH.
THE FIRST CLASS BELL RANG, PEOPLE. WHY ARE YOU STANDING AROUND?
... HAVE YOU **NOTHING** TO DO?!!
LYNN

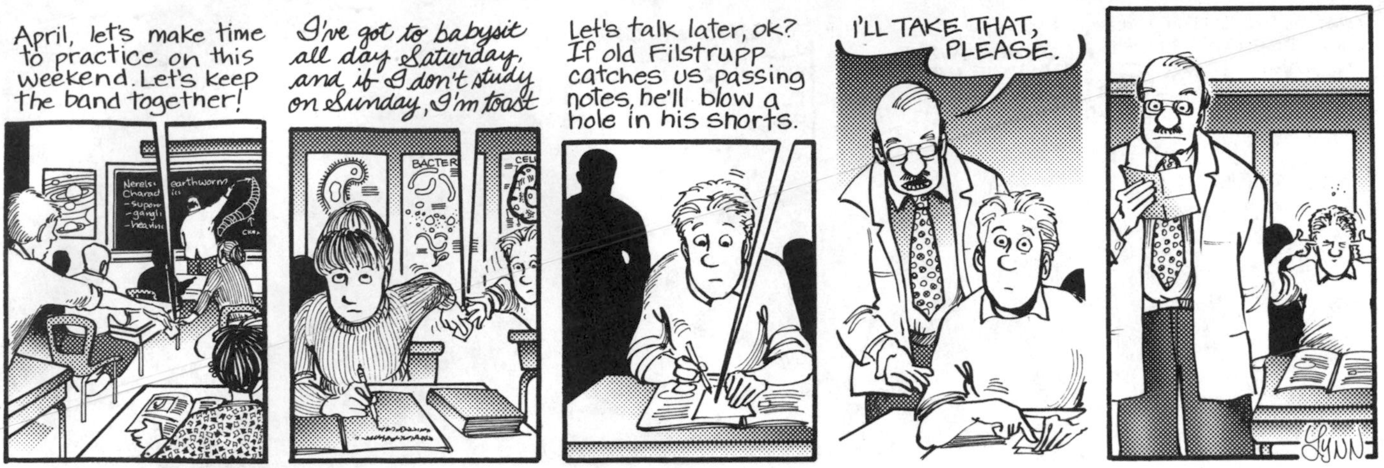
April, let's make time to practice on this weekend. Let's keep the band together!
I've got to babysit all day Saturday, and if I don't study on Sunday, I'm toast
Let's talk later, ok? If old Filstrupp catches us passing notes, he'll blow a hole in his shorts.
I'LL TAKE THAT, PLEASE.
LYNN

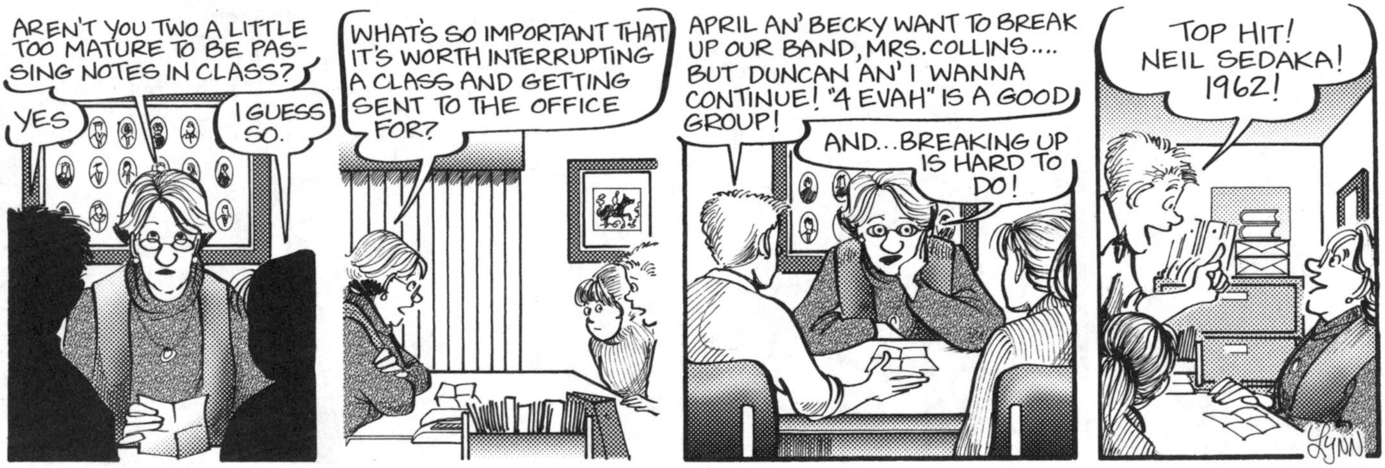
AREN'T YOU TWO A LITTLE TOO MATURE TO BE PASSING NOTES IN CLASS?
YES
I GUESS SO.
WHAT'S SO IMPORTANT THAT IT'S WORTH INTERRUPTING A CLASS AND GETTING SENT TO THE OFFICE FOR?
APRIL AN' BECKY WANT TO BREAK UP OUR BAND, MRS. COLLINS.... BUT DUNCAN AN' I WANNA CONTINUE! "4 EVAH" IS A GOOD GROUP!
AND...BREAKING UP IS HARD TO DO!
TOP HIT! NEIL SEDAKA! 1962!
LYNN

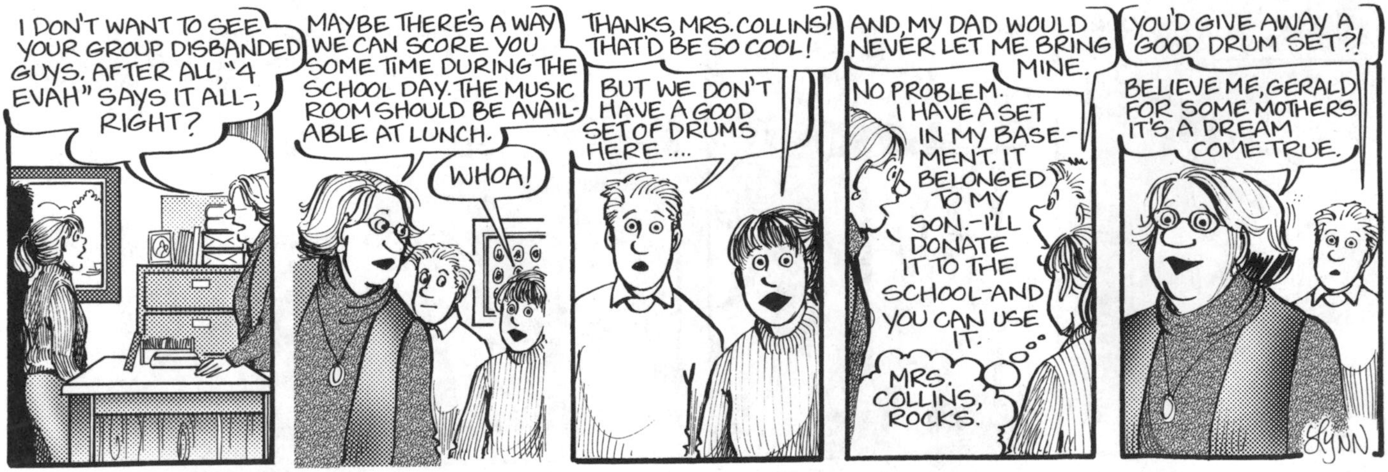
I DON'T WANT TO SEE YOUR GROUP DISBANDED GUYS. AFTER ALL, "4 EVAH" SAYS IT ALL- RIGHT?
MAYBE THERE'S A WAY WE CAN SCORE YOU SOME TIME DURING THE SCHOOL DAY. THE MUSIC ROOM SHOULD BE AVAILABLE AT LUNCH.
WHOA!
THANKS, MRS. COLLINS! THAT'D BE SO COOL!
BUT WE DON'T HAVE A GOOD SET OF DRUMS HERE....
AND, MY DAD WOULD NEVER LET ME BRING MINE.
NO PROBLEM. I HAVE A SET IN MY BASEMENT. IT BELONGED TO MY SON.-I'LL DONATE IT TO THE SCHOOL-AND YOU CAN USE IT.
MRS. COLLINS, ROCKS.
YOU'D GIVE AWAY A GOOD DRUM SET?!
BELIEVE ME, GERALD FOR SOME MOTHERS IT'S A DREAM COME TRUE.
LYNN

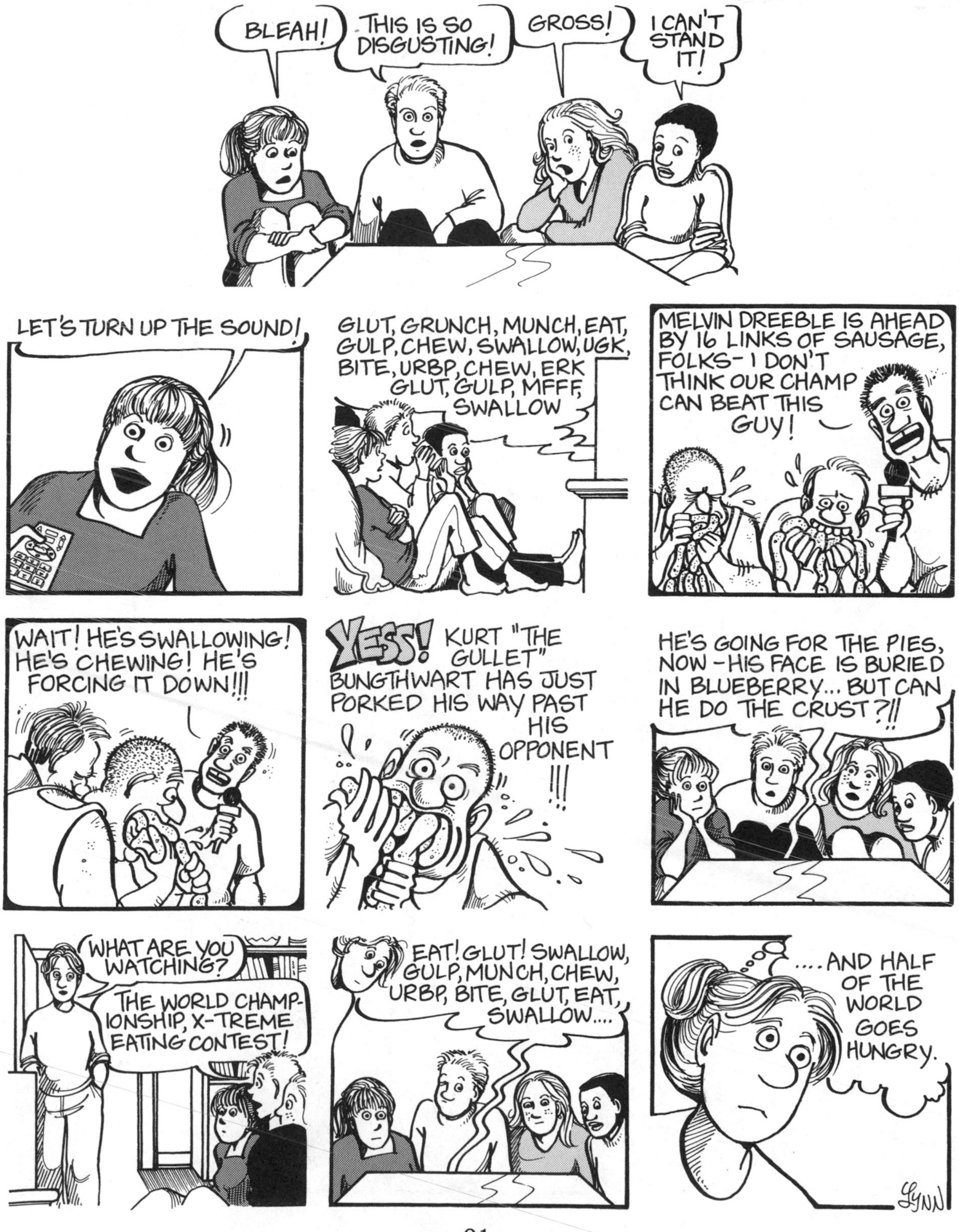
BLEAH!
THIS IS SO DISGUSTING!
GROSS!
I CAN'T STAND IT!
LET'S TURN UP THE SOUND!
GLUT, GRUNCH, MUNCH, EAT, GULP, CHEW, SWALLOW, UGK, BITE, URBP, CHEW, ERK GLUT, GULP, MFFF, SWALLOW
MELVIN DREEBLE IS AHEAD BY 16 LINKS OF SAUSAGE, FOLKS- I DON'T THINK OUR CHAMP CAN BEAT THIS GUY!
WAIT! HE'S SWALLOWING! HE'S CHEWING! HE'S FORCING IT DOWN!!!
YESS! KURT "THE GULLET" BUNGTHWART HAS JUST PORKED HIS WAY PAST HIS OPPONENT !!!
HE'S GOING FOR THE PIES, NOW - HIS FACE IS BURIED IN BLUEBERRY... BUT CAN HE DO THE CRUST?!!
WHAT ARE YOU WATCHING?
THE WORLD CHAMPIONSHIP, X-TREME EATING CONTEST!
EAT! GLUT! SWALLOW, GULP, MUNCH, CHEW, URBP, BITE, GLUT, EAT, SWALLOW....
....AND HALF OF THE WORLD GOES HUNGRY.
LYNN

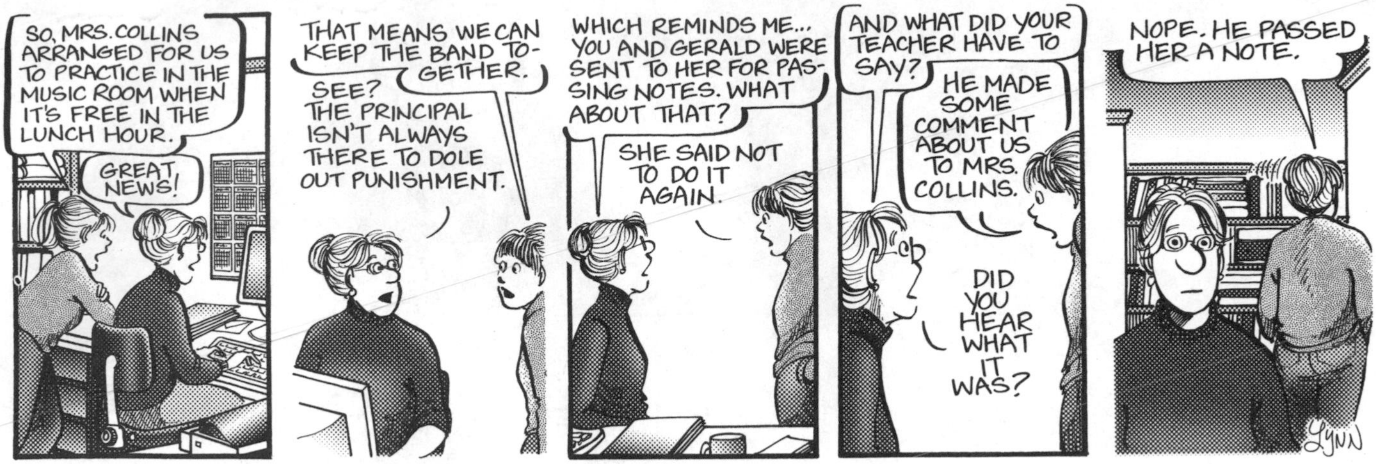
SO, MRS. COLLINS ARRANGED FOR US TO PRACTICE IN THE MUSIC ROOM WHEN IT'S FREE IN THE LUNCH HOUR.
GREAT NEWS!
THAT MEANS WE CAN KEEP THE BAND TOGETHER.
SEE? THE PRINCIPAL ISN'T ALWAYS THERE TO DOLE OUT PUNISHMENT.
WHICH REMINDS ME... YOU AND GERALD WERE SENT TO HER FOR PASSING NOTES. WHAT ABOUT THAT?
SHE SAID NOT TO DO IT AGAIN.
AND WHAT DID YOUR TEACHER HAVE TO SAY?
HE MADE SOME COMMENT ABOUT US TO MRS. COLLINS.
DID YOU HEAR WHAT IT WAS?
NOPE. HE PASSED HER A NOTE.
LYNN

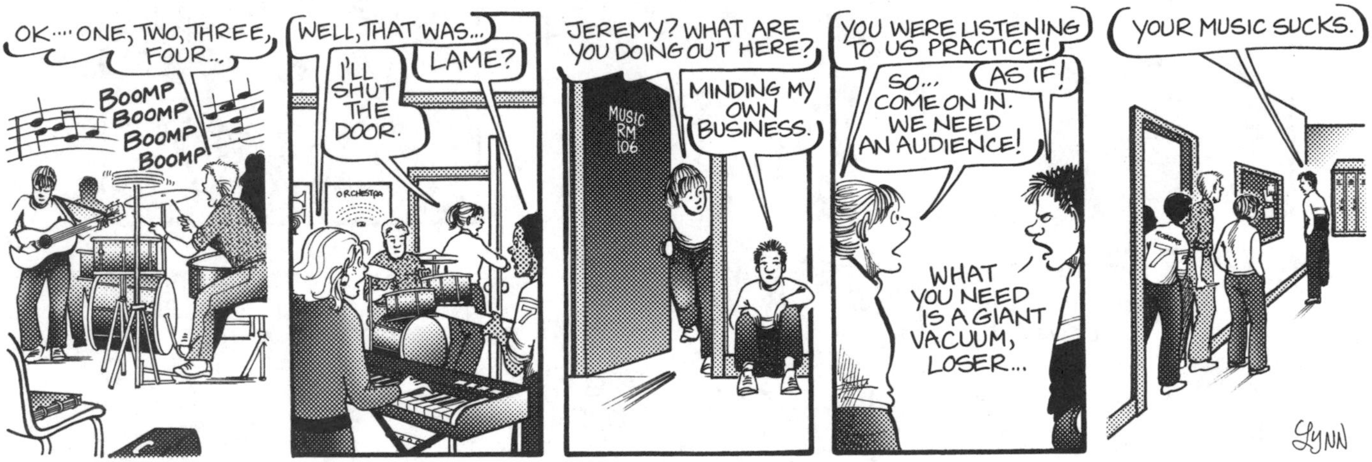
OK.... ONE, TWO, THREE, FOUR...
BOOMP BOOMP BOOMP BOOMP
WELL, THAT WAS...
LAME?
I'LL SHUT THE DOOR.
ORCHESTRA
JEREMY? WHAT ARE YOU DOING OUT HERE?
MUSIC RM 106
MINDING MY OWN BUSINESS.
YOU WERE LISTENING TO US PRACTICE!
AS IF!
SO... COME ON IN. WE NEED AN AUDIENCE!
WHAT YOU NEED IS A GIANT VACUUM, LOSER...
YOUR MUSIC SUCKS.
LYNN

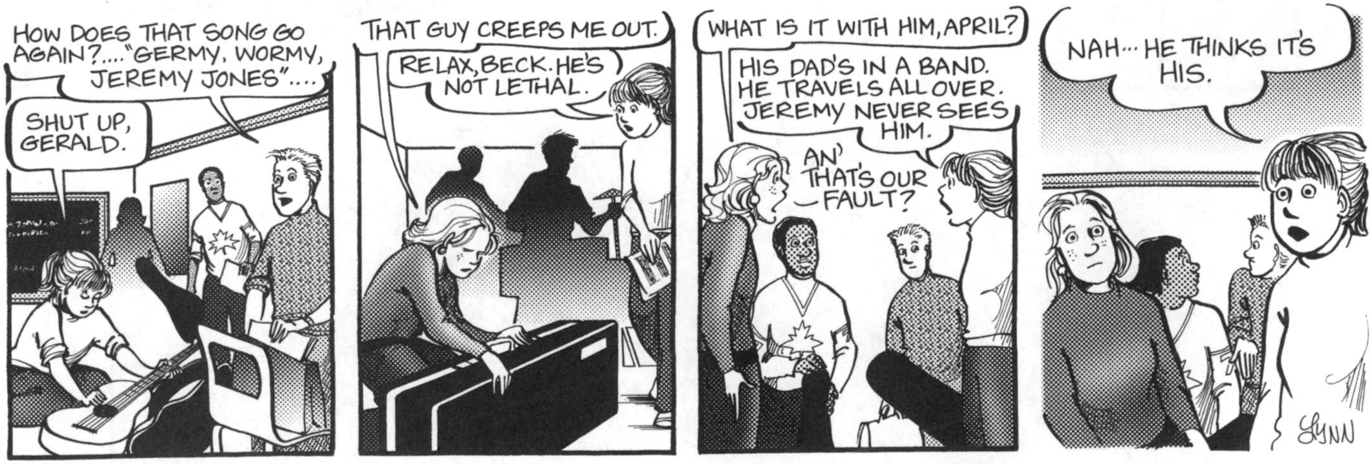
HOW DOES THAT SONG GO AGAIN?...."GERMY, WORMY, JEREMY JONES"....
SHUT UP, GERALD.
THAT GUY CREEPS ME OUT.
RELAX, BECK. HE'S NOT LETHAL.
WHAT IS IT WITH HIM, APRIL?
HIS DAD'S IN A BAND. HE TRAVELS ALL OVER. JEREMY NEVER SEES HIM.
AN' THAT'S OUR FAULT?
NAH... HE THINKS IT'S HIS.
LYNN

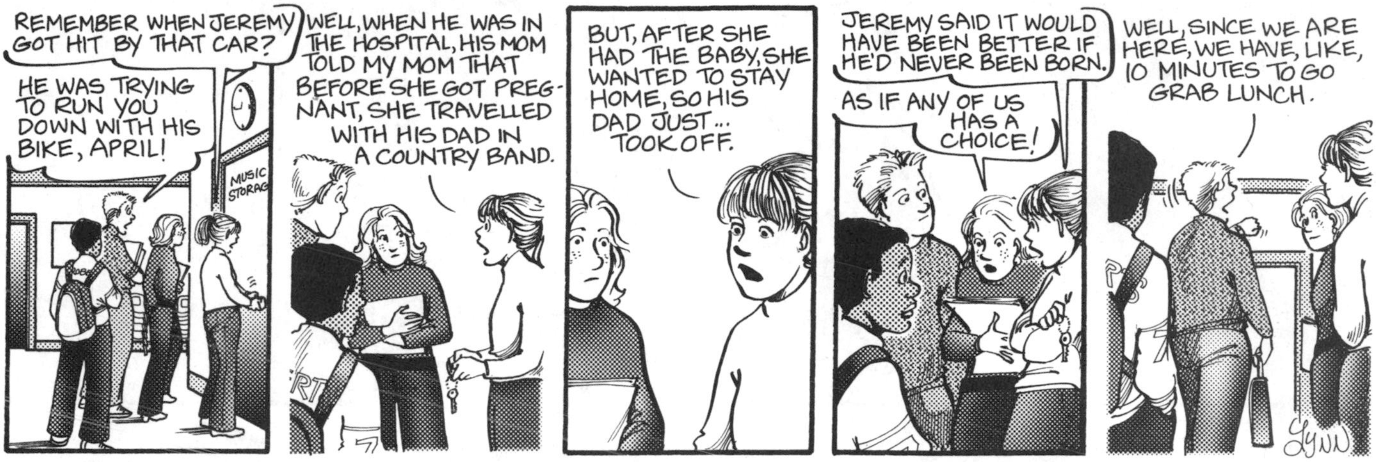
REMEMBER WHEN JEREMY GOT HIT BY THAT CAR?
HE WAS TRYING TO RUN YOU DOWN WITH HIS BIKE, APRIL!
MUSIC STORAG
WELL, WHEN HE WAS IN THE HOSPITAL, HIS MOM TOLD MY MOM THAT BEFORE SHE GOT PREG-NANT, SHE TRAVELLED WITH HIS DAD IN A COUNTRY BAND.
BUT, AFTER SHE HAD THE BABY, SHE WANTED TO STAY HOME, SO HIS DAD JUST... TOOK OFF.
JEREMY SAID IT WOULD HAVE BEEN BETTER IF HE'D NEVER BEEN BORN.
AS IF ANY OF US HAS A CHOICE!
WELL, SINCE WE ARE HERE, WE HAVE, LIKE, 10 MINUTES TO GO GRAB LUNCH.
LYNN

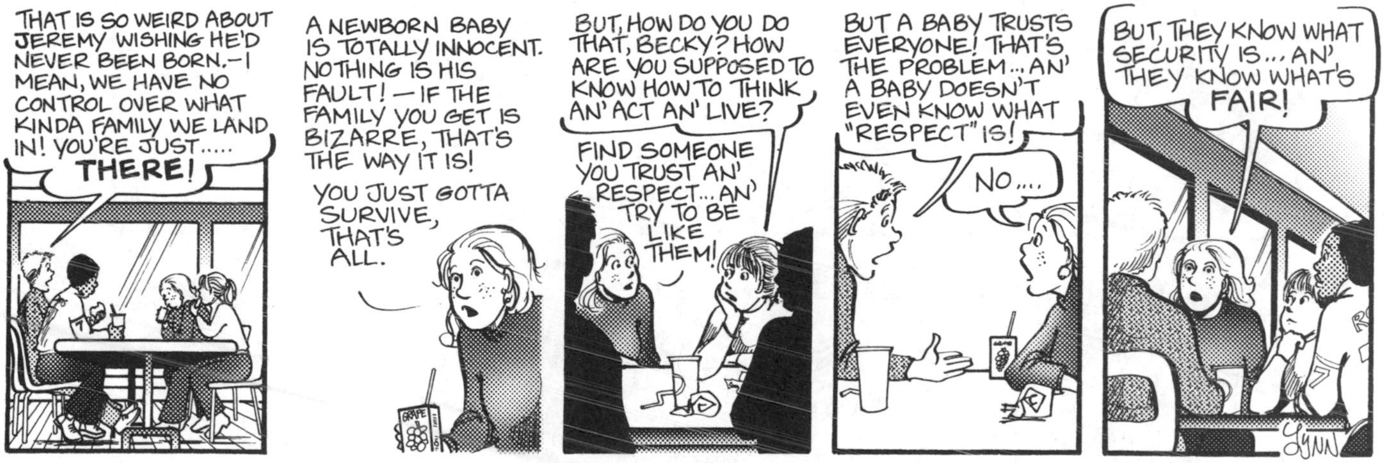
THAT IS SO WEIRD ABOUT JEREMY WISHING HE'D NEVER BEEN BORN.—I MEAN, WE HAVE NO CONTROL OVER WHAT KINDA FAMILY WE LAND IN! YOU'RE JUST..... THERE!
A NEWBORN BABY IS TOTALLY INNOCENT. NOTHING IS HIS FAULT! —IF THE FAMILY YOU GET IS BIZARRE, THAT'S THE WAY IT IS!
YOU JUST GOTTA SURVIVE, THAT'S ALL.
GRAPE
BUT, HOW DO YOU DO THAT, BECKY? HOW ARE YOU SUPPOSED TO KNOW HOW TO THINK AN' ACT AN' LIVE?
FIND SOMEONE YOU TRUST AN' RESPECT... AN' TRY TO BE LIKE THEM!
BUT A BABY TRUSTS EVERYONE! THAT'S THE PROBLEM... AN' A BABY DOESN'T EVEN KNOW WHAT "RESPECT" IS!
NO....
BUT, THEY KNOW WHAT SECURITY IS... AN' THEY KNOW WHAT'S FAIR!
LYNN

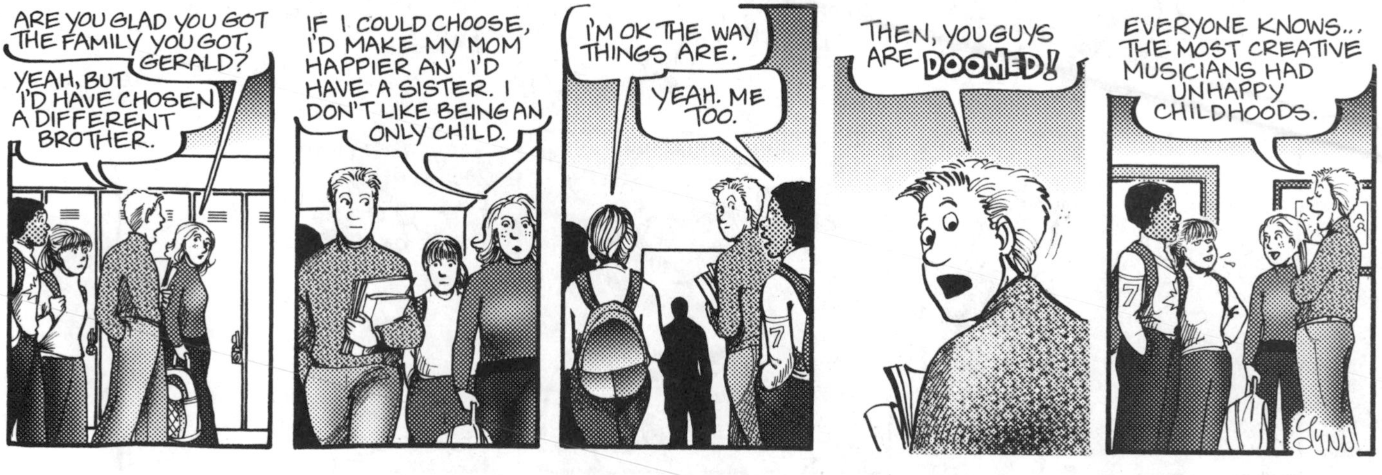
ARE YOU GLAD YOU GOT THE FAMILY YOU GOT, GERALD?
YEAH, BUT I'D HAVE CHOSEN A DIFFERENT BROTHER.
IF I COULD CHOOSE, I'D MAKE MY MOM HAPPIER AN' I'D HAVE A SISTER. I DON'T LIKE BEING AN ONLY CHILD.
I'M OK THE WAY THINGS ARE.
YEAH. ME TOO.
THEN, YOU GUYS ARE DOOMED!
EVERYONE KNOWS... THE MOST CREATIVE MUSICIANS HAD UNHAPPY CHILDHOODS.
LYNN

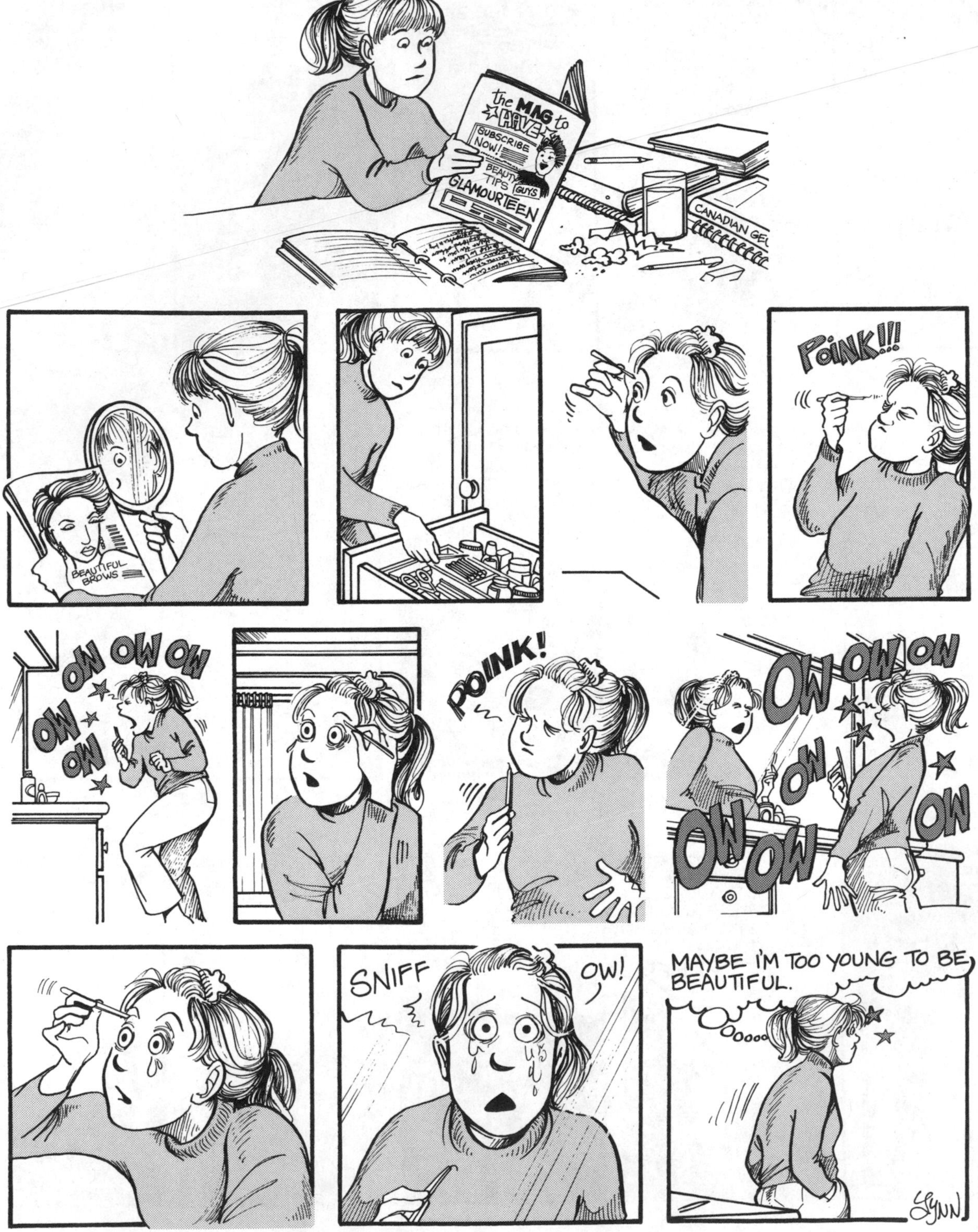
the MAG to HAVE
SUBSCRIBE NOW!
BEAUTY TIPS
GUYS
GLAMOURTEEN
CANADIAN GE
BEAUTIFUL BROWS
POINK!!!
OW OW OW OW
OW
OW
POINK!
OW OW OW
OW
OW
OW OW
OW
SNIFF
OW!
MAYBE I'M TOO YOUNG TO BE BEAUTIFUL.
LYNN

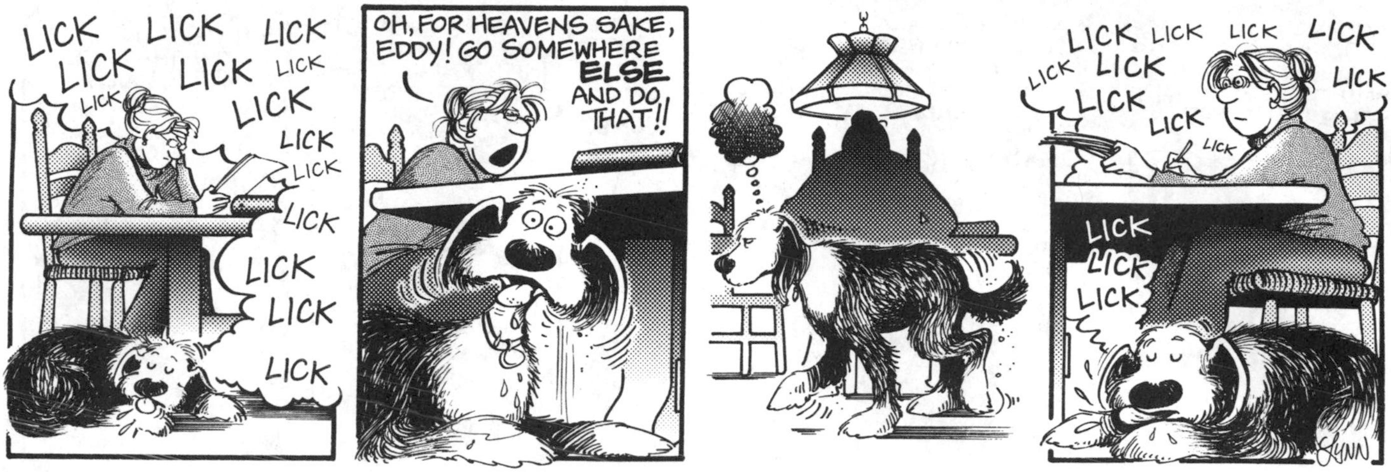
LICK LICK LICK LICK LICK LICK LICK LICK LICK LICK LICK LICK LICK LICK LICK
OH, FOR HEAVENS SAKE, EDDY! GO SOMEWHERE ELSE AND DO THAT!!
LICK LICK LICK LICK LICK LICK LICK LICK LICK LICK
LICK LICK LICK
LYNN

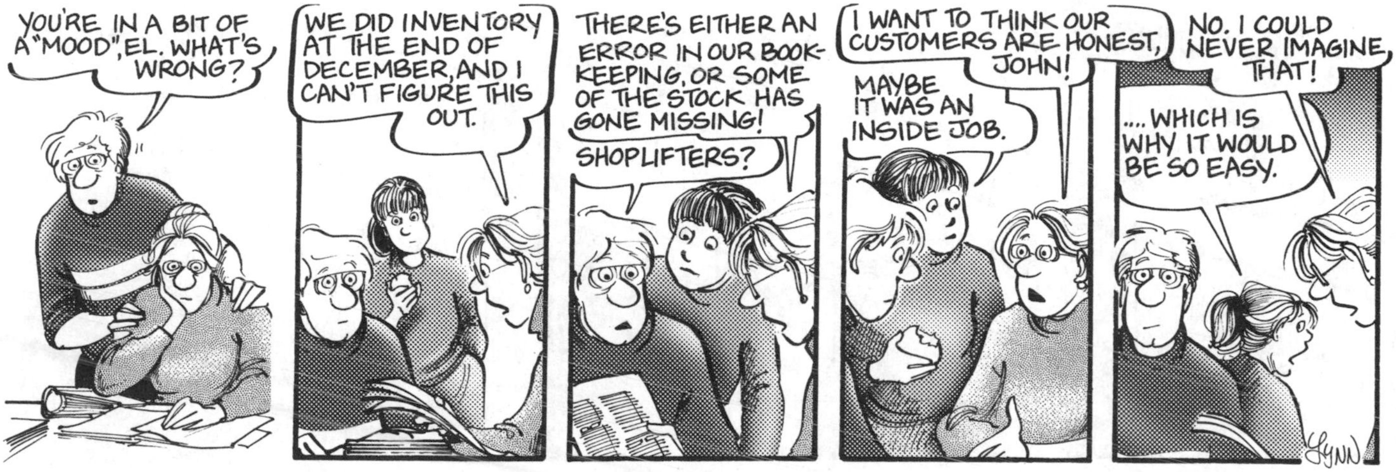
YOU'RE IN A BIT OF A "MOOD", EL. WHAT'S WRONG?
WE DID INVENTORY AT THE END OF DECEMBER, AND I CAN'T FIGURE THIS OUT.
THERE'S EITHER AN ERROR IN OUR BOOK-KEEPING, OR SOME OF THE STOCK HAS GONE MISSING!
SHOPLIFTERS?
I WANT TO THINK OUR CUSTOMERS ARE HONEST, JOHN!
MAYBE IT WAS AN INSIDE JOB.
NO. I COULD NEVER IMAGINE THAT!
....WHICH IS WHY IT WOULD BE SO EASY.
LYNN

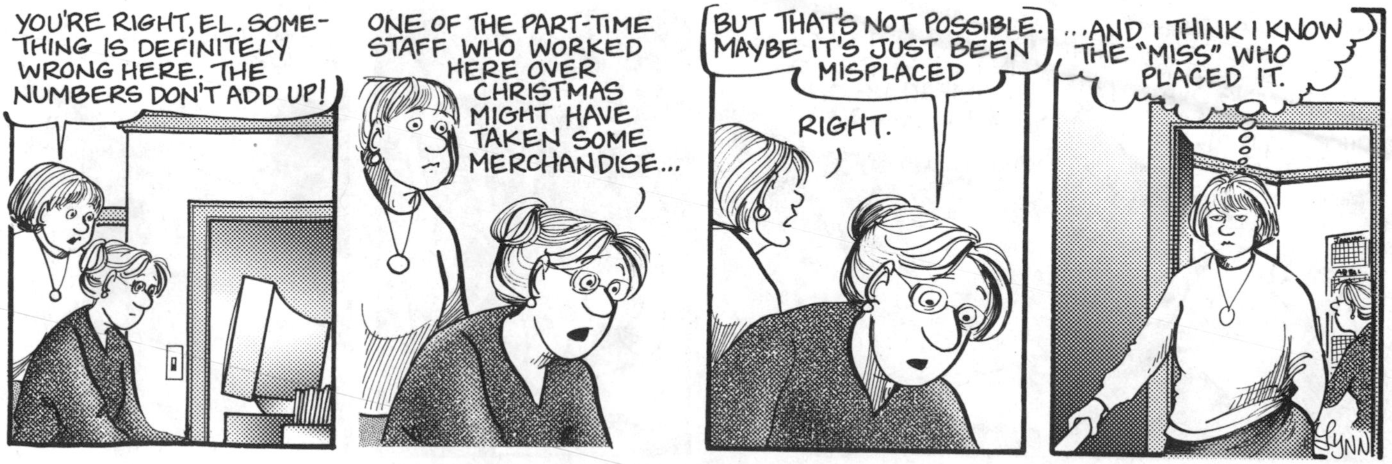
YOU'RE RIGHT, EL. SOME-THING IS DEFINITELY WRONG HERE. THE NUMBERS DON'T ADD UP!
ONE OF THE PART-TIME STAFF WHO WORKED HERE OVER CHRISTMAS MIGHT HAVE TAKEN SOME MERCHANDISE...
BUT THAT'S NOT POSSIBLE. MAYBE IT'S JUST BEEN MISPLACED
RIGHT.
...AND I THINK I KNOW THE "MISS" WHO PLACED IT.
LYNN

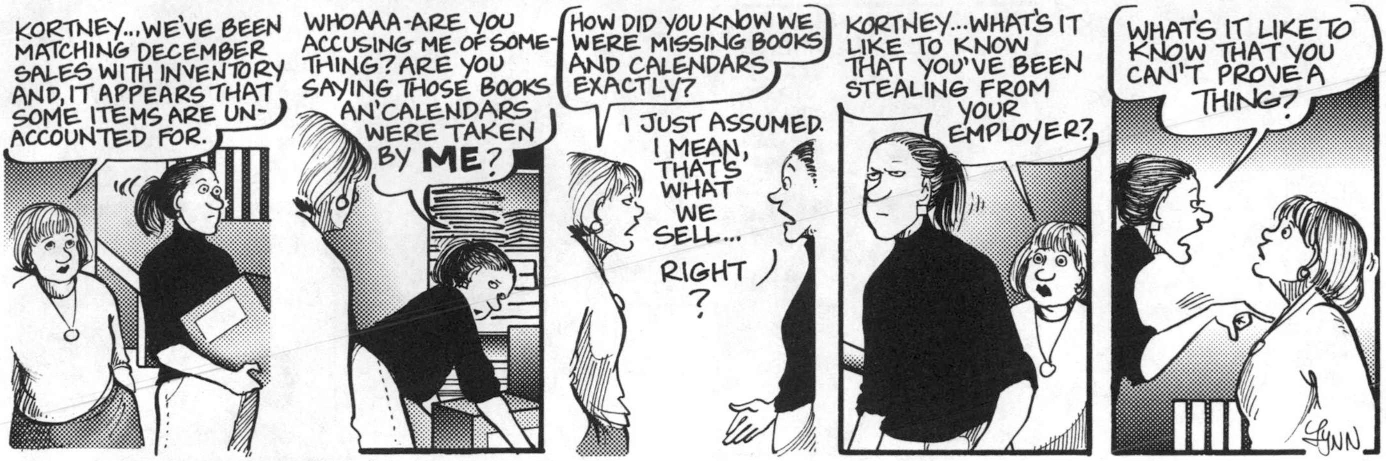
KORTNEY... WE'VE BEEN MATCHING DECEMBER SALES WITH INVENTORY AND, IT APPEARS THAT SOME ITEMS ARE UN-ACCOUNTED FOR.
WHOAAA-ARE YOU ACCUSING ME OF SOME-THING? ARE YOU SAYING THOSE BOOKS AN' CALENDARS WERE TAKEN BY ME?
HOW DID YOU KNOW WE WERE MISSING BOOKS AND CALENDARS EXACTLY?
I JUST ASSUMED. I MEAN, THAT'S WHAT WE SELL... RIGHT?
KORTNEY... WHAT'S IT LIKE TO KNOW THAT YOU'VE BEEN STEALING FROM YOUR EMPLOYER?
WHAT'S IT LIKE TO KNOW THAT YOU CAN'T PROVE A THING?
LYNN

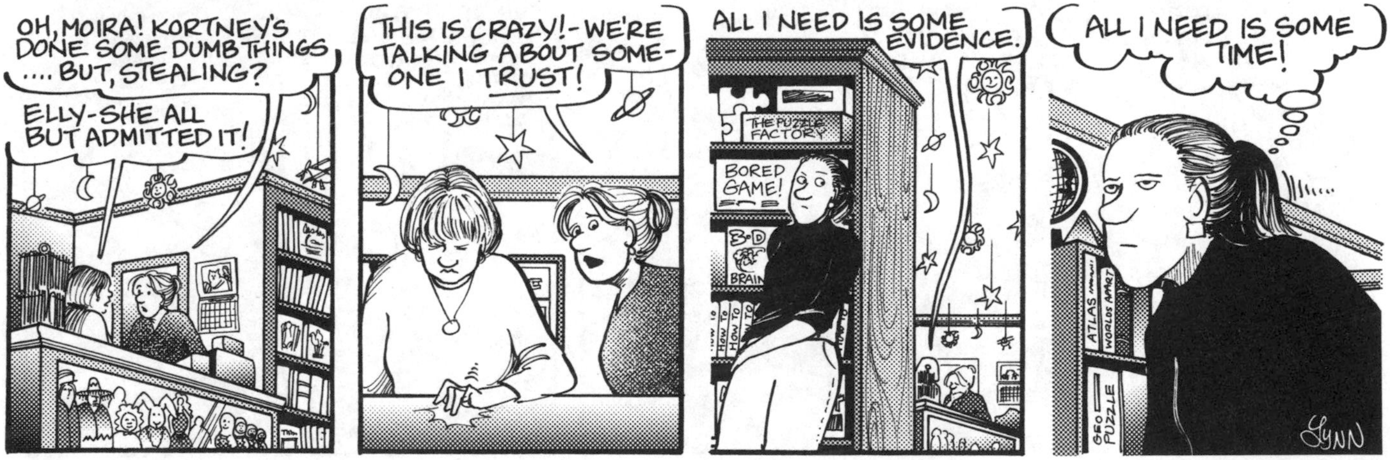
OH, MOIRA! KORTNEY'S DONE SOME DUMB THINGS .... BUT, STEALING?
ELLY-SHE ALL BUT ADMITTED IT!
THIS IS CRAZY! - WE'RE TALKING ABOUT SOME-ONE I TRUST!
ALL I NEED IS SOME EVIDENCE.
THE PUZZLE FACTORY
BORED GAME!
ALL I NEED IS SOME TIME!
ATLAS
WORLDS APART
GEO PUZZLE
LYNN

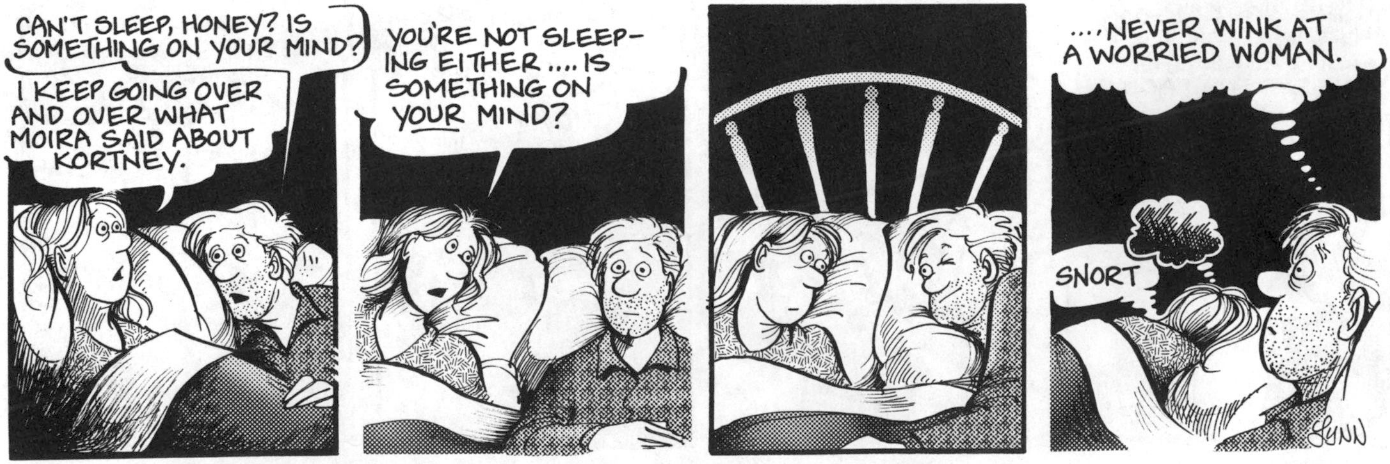
CAN'T SLEEP, HONEY? IS SOMETHING ON YOUR MIND?
I KEEP GOING OVER AND OVER WHAT MOIRA SAID ABOUT KORTNEY.
YOU'RE NOT SLEEP-ING EITHER .... IS SOMETHING ON YOUR MIND?
...., NEVER WINK AT A WORRIED WOMAN.
SNORT
LYNN

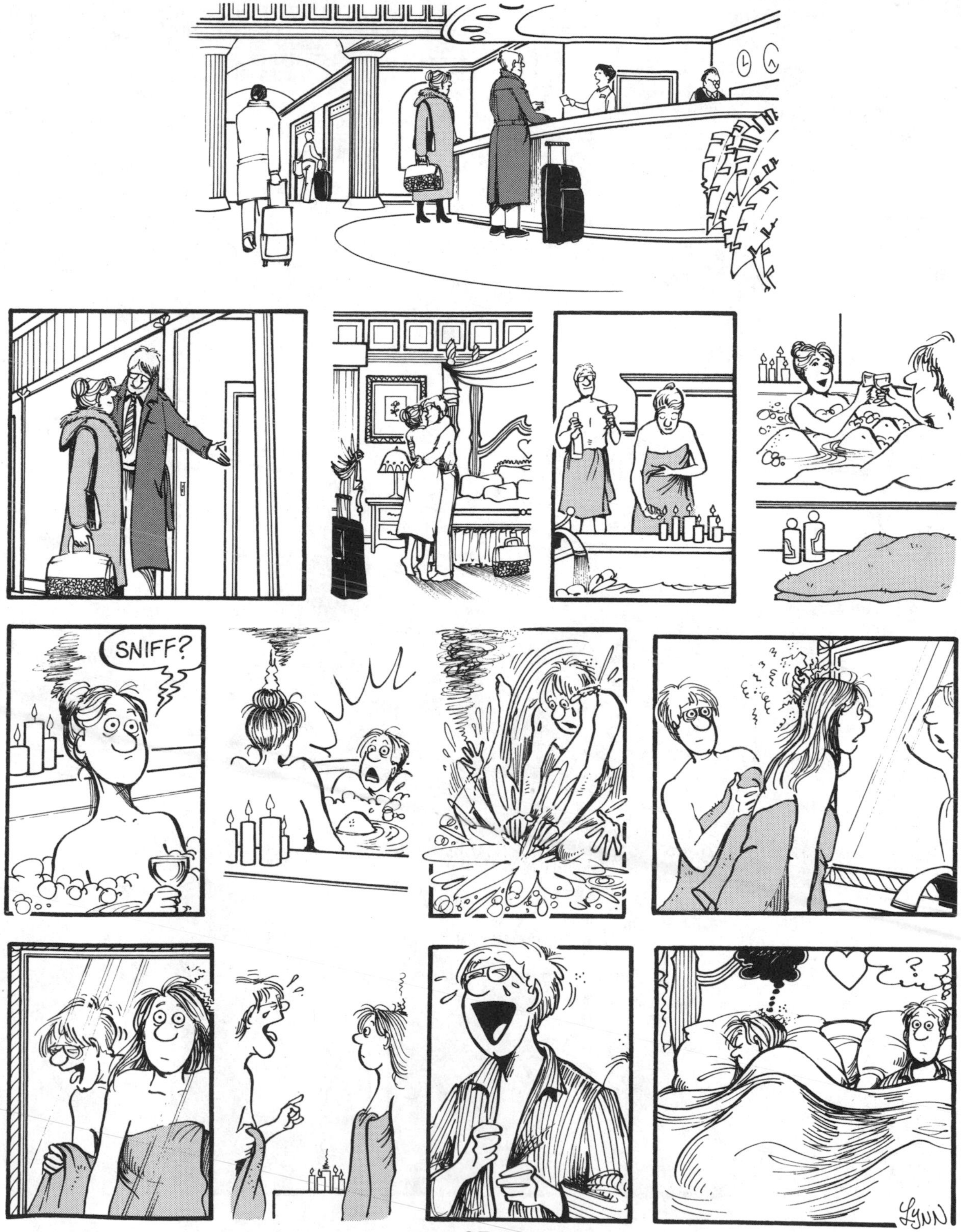
SNIFF?
LYNN

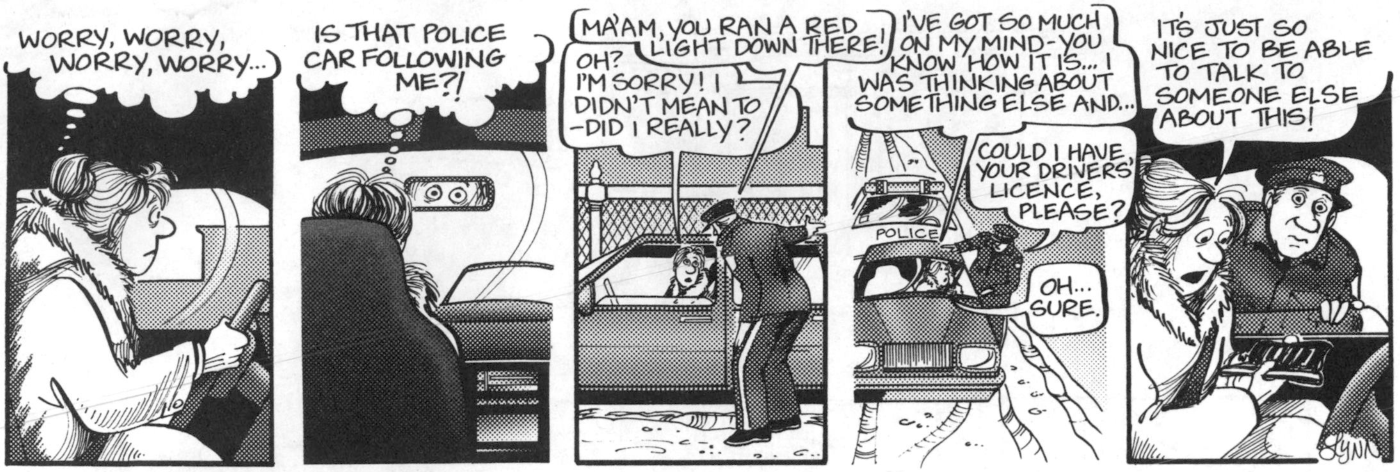
WORRY, WORRY, WORRY, WORRY...
IS THAT POLICE CAR FOLLOWING ME?!
MA'AM, YOU RAN A RED LIGHT DOWN THERE!
OH? I'M SORRY! I DIDN'T MEAN TO -DID I REALLY?
I'VE GOT SO MUCH ON MY MIND-YOU KNOW HOW IT IS... I WAS THINKING ABOUT SOMETHING ELSE AND...
POLICE
COULD I HAVE YOUR DRIVERS' LICENCE, PLEASE?
OH... SURE.
IT'S JUST SO NICE TO BE ABLE TO TALK TO SOMEONE ELSE ABOUT THIS!
LYNN

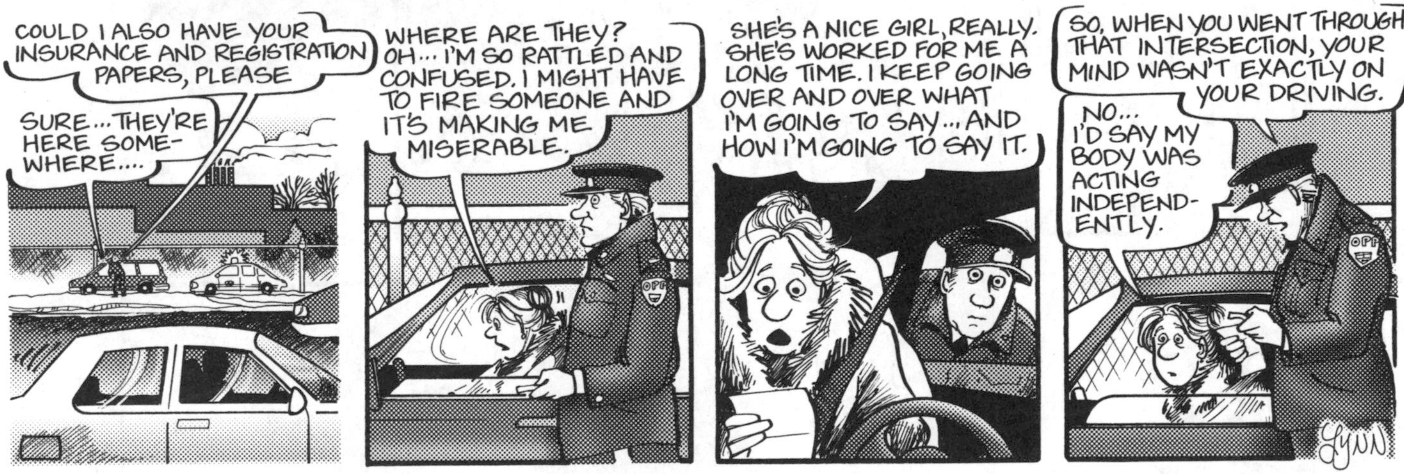
COULD I ALSO HAVE YOUR INSURANCE AND REGISTRATION PAPERS, PLEASE
SURE... THEY'RE HERE SOME-WHERE....
WHERE ARE THEY? OH... I'M SO RATTLED AND CONFUSED. I MIGHT HAVE TO FIRE SOMEONE AND IT'S MAKING ME MISERABLE.
SHE'S A NICE GIRL, REALLY. SHE'S WORKED FOR ME A LONG TIME. I KEEP GOING OVER AND OVER WHAT I'M GOING TO SAY... AND HOW I'M GOING TO SAY IT.
SO, WHEN YOU WENT THROUGH THAT INTERSECTION, YOUR MIND WASN'T EXACTLY ON YOUR DRIVING.
NO... I'D SAY MY BODY WAS ACTING INDEPEND-ENTLY.
LYNN

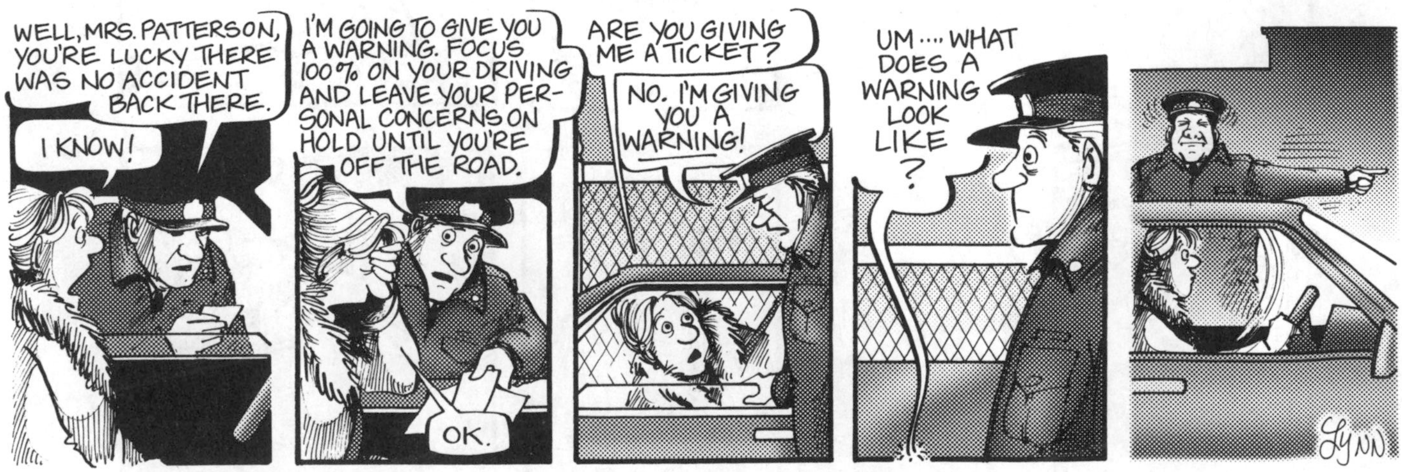
WELL, MRS. PATTERSON, YOU'RE LUCKY THERE WAS NO ACCIDENT BACK THERE.
I KNOW!
I'M GOING TO GIVE YOU A WARNING. FOCUS 100% ON YOUR DRIVING AND LEAVE YOUR PER-SONAL CONCERNS ON HOLD UNTIL YOU'RE OFF THE ROAD.
OK.
ARE YOU GIVING ME A TICKET?
NO. I'M GIVING YOU A WARNING!
UM.... WHAT DOES A WARNING LOOK LIKE ?
LYNN

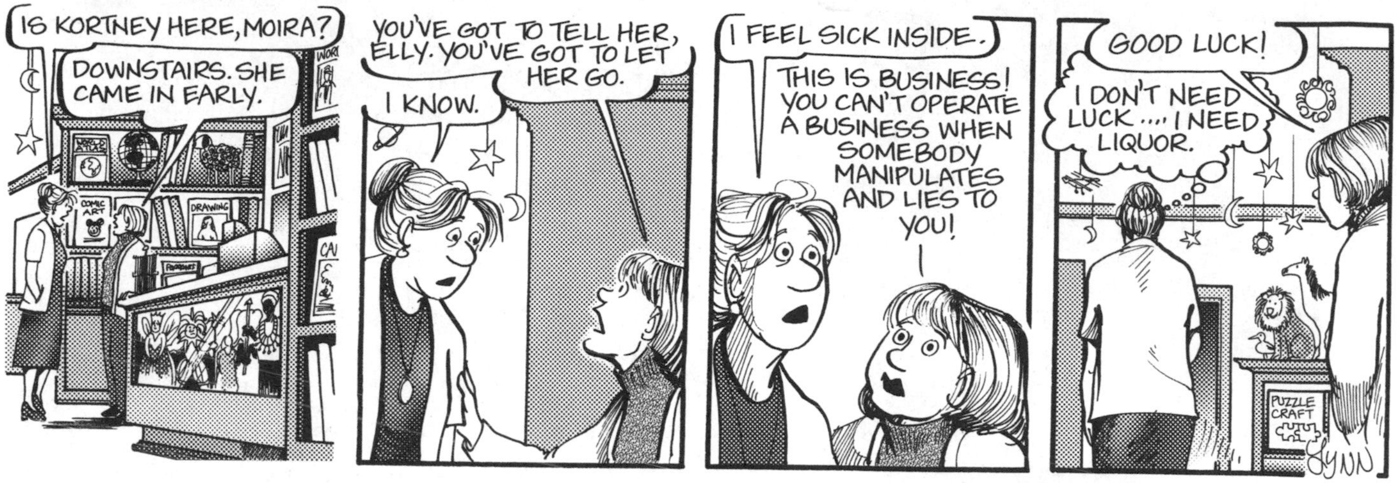
IS KORTNEY HERE, MOIRA?
DOWNSTAIRS. SHE CAME IN EARLY.
YOU'VE GOT TO TELL HER, ELLY. YOU'VE GOT TO LET HER GO.
I KNOW.
I FEEL SICK INSIDE.
THIS IS BUSINESS! YOU CAN'T OPERATE A BUSINESS WHEN SOMEBODY MANIPULATES AND LIES TO YOU!
GOOD LUCK!
I DON'T NEED LUCK.... I NEED LIQUOR.
PUZZLE CRAFT
LYNN

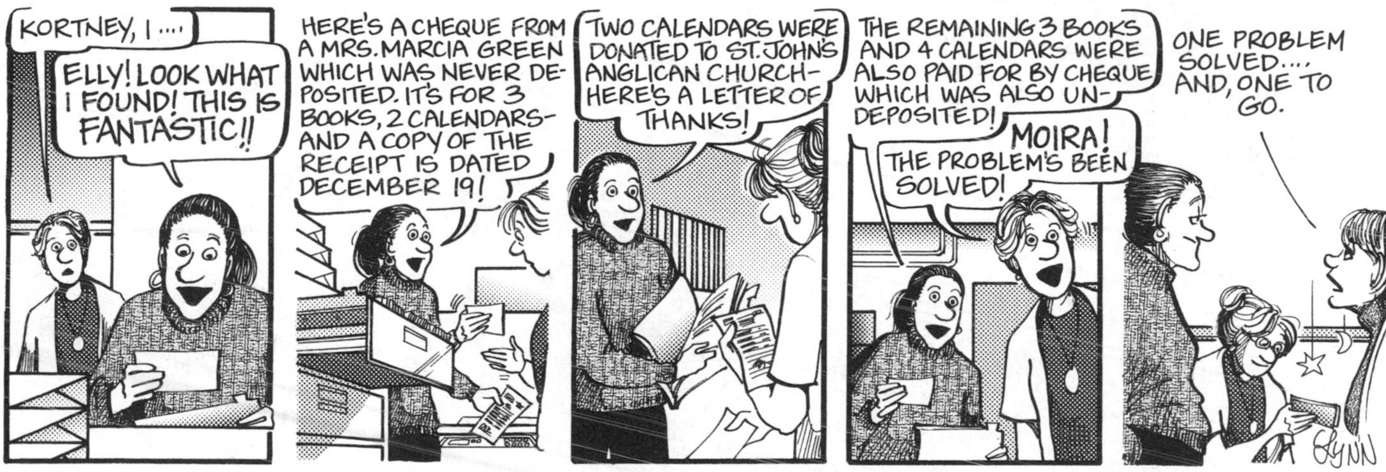
KORTNEY, I....
ELLY! LOOK WHAT I FOUND! THIS IS FANTASTIC!!
HERE'S A CHEQUE FROM A MRS. MARCIA GREEN WHICH WAS NEVER DEPOSITED. IT'S FOR 3 BOOKS, 2 CALENDARS - AND A COPY OF THE RECEIPT IS DATED DECEMBER 19!
TWO CALENDARS WERE DONATED TO ST. JOHN'S ANGLICAN CHURCH - HERE'S A LETTER OF THANKS!
THE REMAINING 3 BOOKS AND 4 CALENDARS WERE ALSO PAID FOR BY CHEQUE WHICH WAS ALSO UNDEPOSITED!
MOIRA! THE PROBLEM'S BEEN SOLVED!
ONE PROBLEM SOLVED.... AND, ONE TO GO.
LYNN

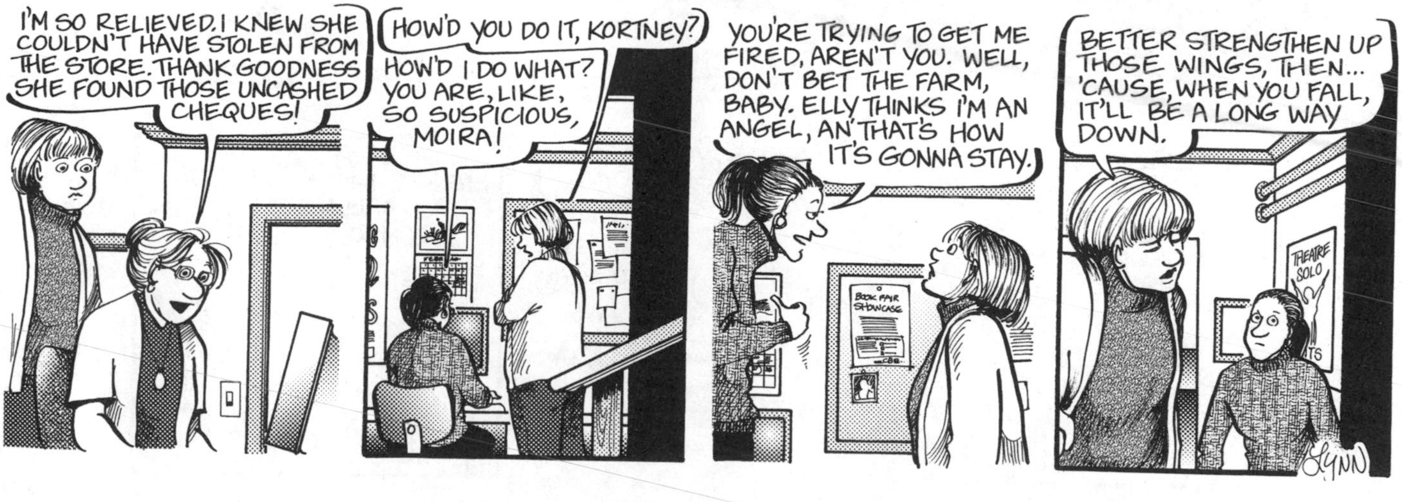
I'M SO RELIEVED. I KNEW SHE COULDN'T HAVE STOLEN FROM THE STORE. THANK GOODNESS SHE FOUND THOSE UNCASHED CHEQUES!
HOW'D YOU DO IT, KORTNEY?
HOW'D I DO WHAT? YOU ARE, LIKE, SO SUSPICIOUS, MOIRA!
YOU'RE TRYING TO GET ME FIRED, AREN'T YOU. WELL, DON'T BET THE FARM, BABY. ELLY THINKS I'M AN ANGEL, AN' THAT'S HOW IT'S GONNA STAY.
BOOK FAIR SHOWCASE
BETTER STRENGTHEN UP THOSE WINGS, THEN... 'CAUSE, WHEN YOU FALL, IT'LL BE A LONG WAY DOWN.
THEATRE SOLO
LYNN

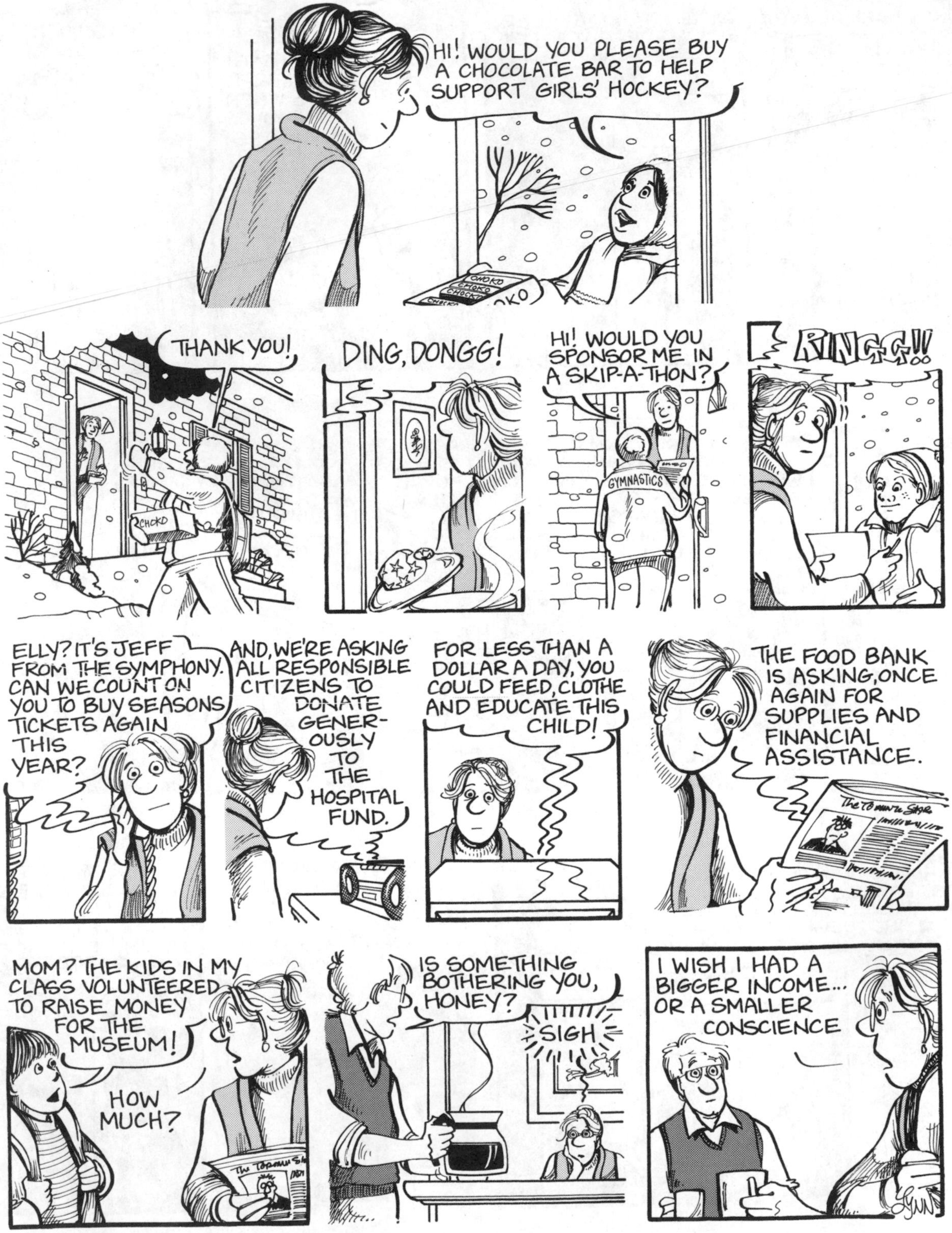
HI! WOULD YOU PLEASE BUY A CHOCOLATE BAR TO HELP SUPPORT GIRLS' HOCKEY?
CHOKO
THANK YOU!
CHOKO
DING, DONGG!
HI! WOULD YOU SPONSOR ME IN A SKIP-A-THON?
GYMNASTICS
RINGG!!
ELLY? IT'S JEFF FROM THE SYMPHONY. CAN WE COUNT ON YOU TO BUY SEASONS TICKETS AGAIN THIS YEAR?
AND, WE'RE ASKING ALL RESPONSIBLE CITIZENS TO DONATE GENEROUSLY TO THE HOSPITAL FUND.
FOR LESS THAN A DOLLAR A DAY, YOU COULD FEED, CLOTHE AND EDUCATE THIS CHILD!
THE FOOD BANK IS ASKING, ONCE AGAIN FOR SUPPLIES AND FINANCIAL ASSISTANCE.
MOM? THE KIDS IN MY CLASS VOLUNTEERED TO RAISE MONEY FOR THE MUSEUM!
HOW MUCH?
IS SOMETHING BOTHERING YOU, HONEY?
SIGH
I WISH I HAD A BIGGER INCOME... OR A SMALLER CONSCIENCE
LYNN

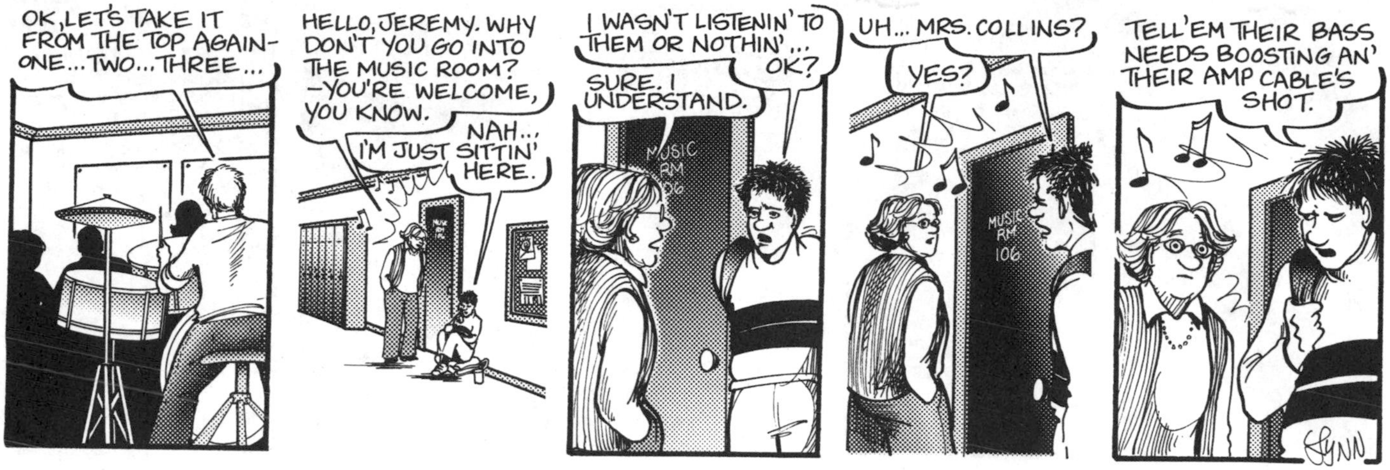
OK, LET'S TAKE IT FROM THE TOP AGAIN-ONE... TWO... THREE...
HELLO, JEREMY. WHY DON'T YOU GO INTO THE MUSIC ROOM? -YOU'RE WELCOME, YOU KNOW.
NAH... I'M JUST SITTIN' HERE.
I WASN'T LISTENIN' TO THEM OR NOTHIN'... OK?
SURE. I UNDERSTAND.
MUSIC RM 106
UH... MRS. COLLINS?
YES?
MUSIC RM 106
TELL'EM THEIR BASS NEEDS BOOSTING AN' THEIR AMP CABLE'S SHOT.
LYNN

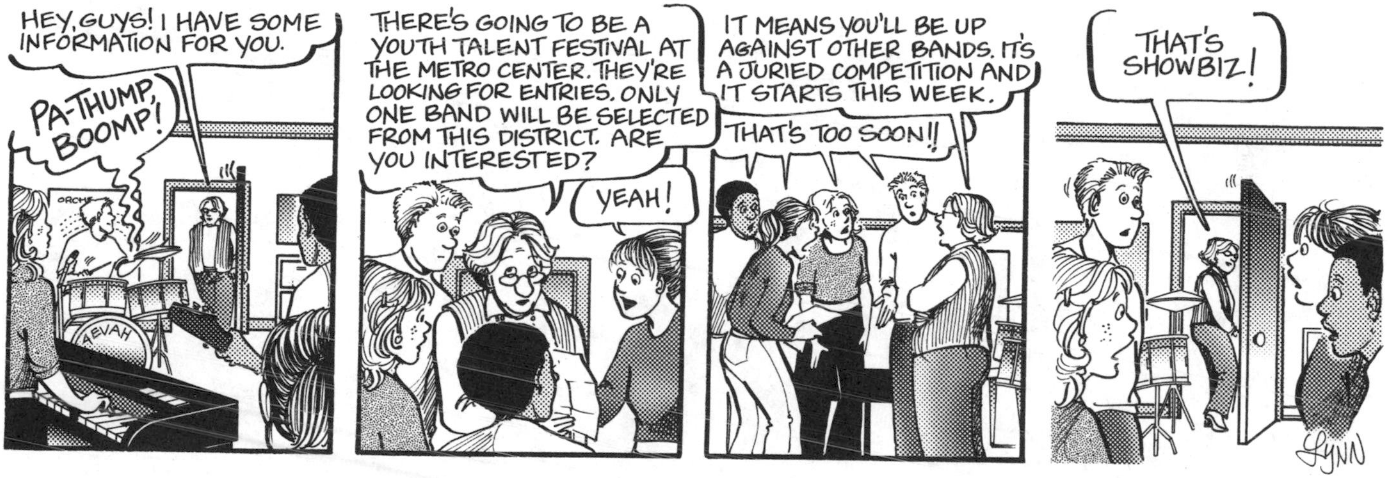
HEY, GUYS! I HAVE SOME INFORMATION FOR YOU.
PA-THUMP, BOOMP!
4 EVAH
THERE'S GOING TO BE A YOUTH TALENT FESTIVAL AT THE METRO CENTER. THEY'RE LOOKING FOR ENTRIES. ONLY ONE BAND WILL BE SELECTED FROM THIS DISTRICT. ARE YOU INTERESTED?
YEAH!
IT MEANS YOU'LL BE UP AGAINST OTHER BANDS. IT'S A JURIED COMPETITION AND IT STARTS THIS WEEK.
THAT'S TOO SOON!!
THAT'S SHOWBIZ!
LYNN

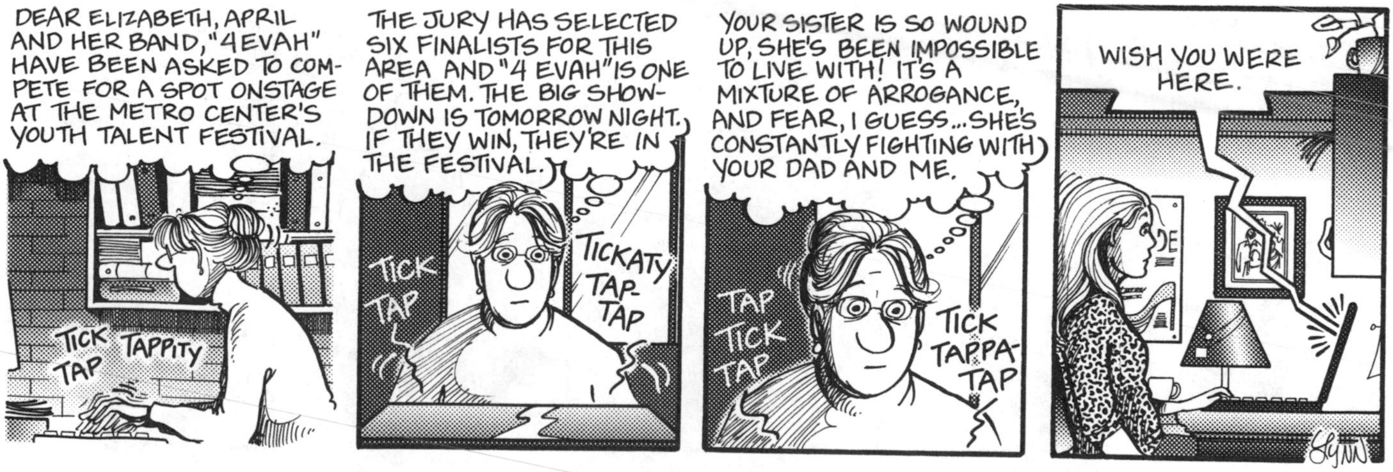
DEAR ELIZABETH, APRIL AND HER BAND, "4 EVAH" HAVE BEEN ASKED TO COMPETE FOR A SPOT ONSTAGE AT THE METRO CENTER'S YOUTH TALENT FESTIVAL.
TICK TAP TAPPITY
THE JURY HAS SELECTED SIX FINALISTS FOR THIS AREA AND "4 EVAH" IS ONE OF THEM. THE BIG SHOWDOWN IS TOMORROW NIGHT. IF THEY WIN, THEY'RE IN THE FESTIVAL.
TICK TAP
TICKATY TAP-TAP
YOUR SISTER IS SO WOUND UP, SHE'S BEEN IMPOSSIBLE TO LIVE WITH! IT'S A MIXTURE OF ARROGANCE, AND FEAR, I GUESS... SHE'S CONSTANTLY FIGHTING WITH YOUR DAD AND ME.
TAP TICK TAP
TICK TAPPA-TAP
WISH YOU WERE HERE.
LYNN

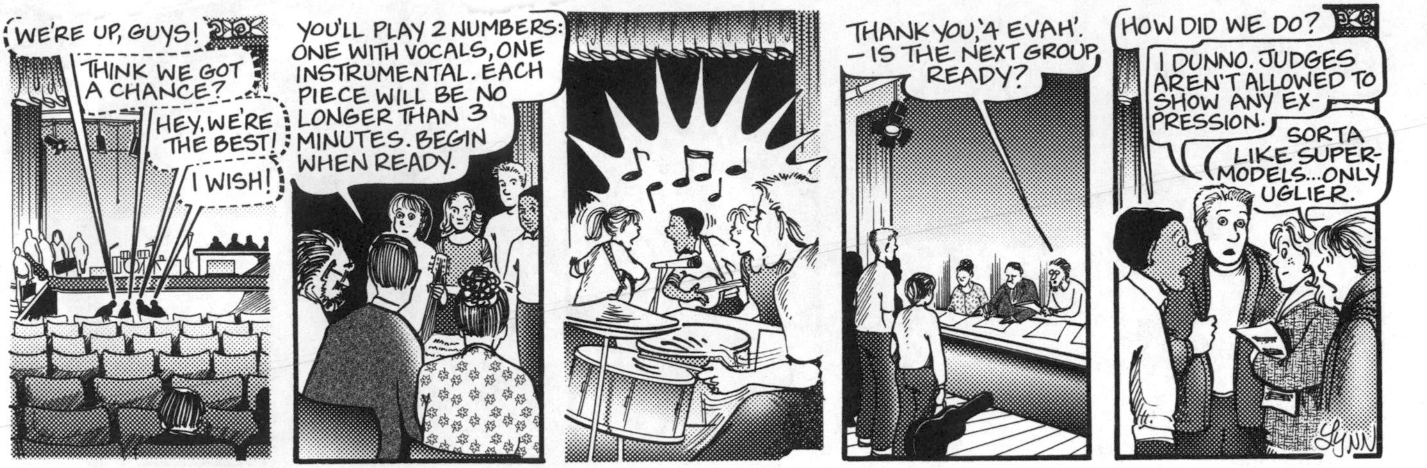
WE'RE UP, GUYS!
THINK WE GOT A CHANCE?
HEY, WE'RE THE BEST!
I WISH!
YOU'LL PLAY 2 NUMBERS: ONE WITH VOCALS, ONE INSTRUMENTAL. EACH PIECE WILL BE NO LONGER THAN 3 MINUTES. BEGIN WHEN READY.
THANK YOU, '4 EVAH'. - IS THE NEXT GROUP READY?
HOW DID WE DO?
I DUNNO. JUDGES AREN'T ALLOWED TO SHOW ANY EXPRESSION.
SORTA LIKE SUPERMODELS...ONLY UGLIER.
LYNN

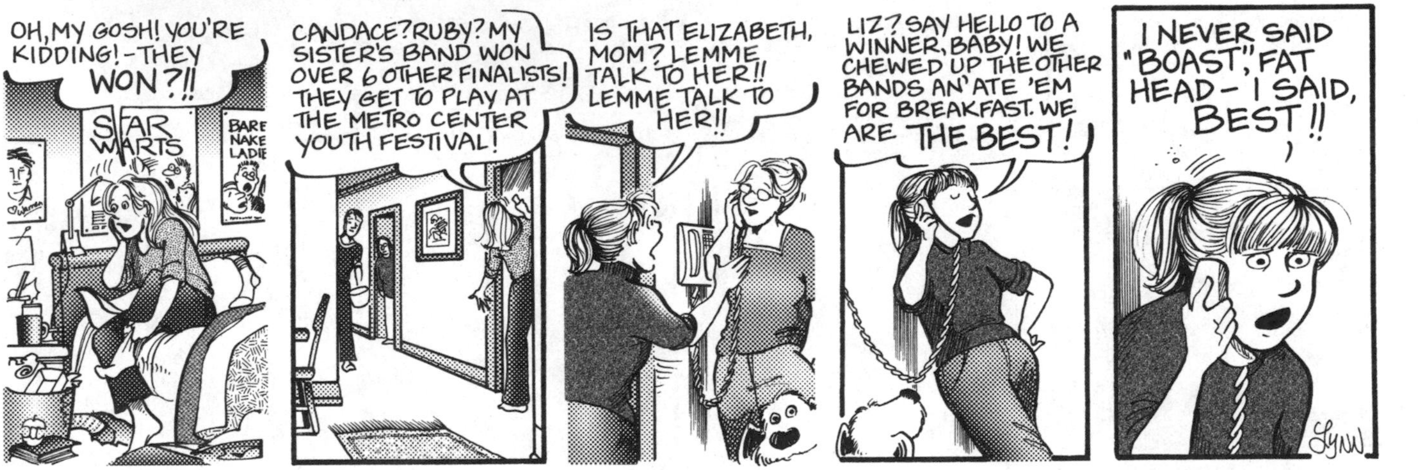
OH, MY GOSH! YOU'RE KIDDING! - THEY WON?!!
STAR WARTS
BARE NAKE LADIE
CANDACE? RUBY? MY SISTER'S BAND WON OVER 6 OTHER FINALISTS! THEY GET TO PLAY AT THE METRO CENTER YOUTH FESTIVAL!
IS THAT ELIZABETH, MOM? LEMME TALK TO HER!! LEMME TALK TO HER!!
LIZ? SAY HELLO TO A WINNER, BABY! WE CHEWED UP THE OTHER BANDS AN' ATE 'EM FOR BREAKFAST. WE ARE THE BEST!
I NEVER SAID "BOAST", FAT HEAD - I SAID, BEST!!
LYNN

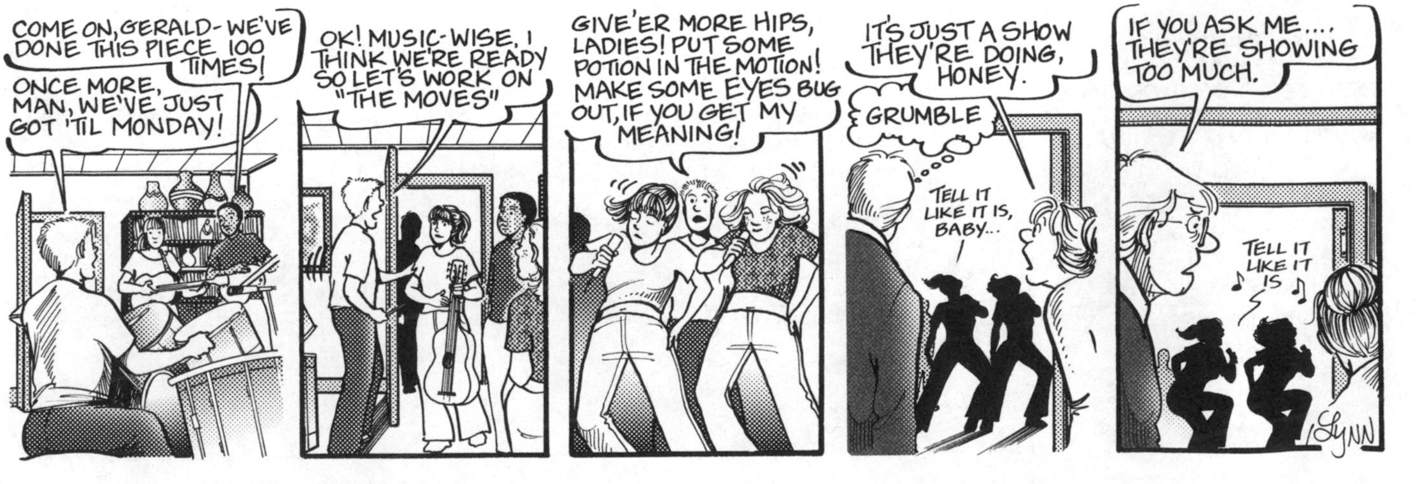
COME ON, GERALD - WE'VE DONE THIS PIECE 100 TIMES!
ONCE MORE, MAN, WE'VE JUST GOT 'TIL MONDAY!
OK! MUSIC-WISE, I THINK WE'RE READY SO LET'S WORK ON "THE MOVES"
GIVE 'ER MORE HIPS, LADIES! PUT SOME POTION IN THE MOTION! MAKE SOME EYES BUG OUT, IF YOU GET MY MEANING!
IT'S JUST A SHOW THEY'RE DOING, HONEY.
GRUMBLE
TELL IT LIKE IT IS, BABY...
IF YOU ASK ME.... THEY'RE SHOWING TOO MUCH.
TELL IT LIKE IT IS
LYNN

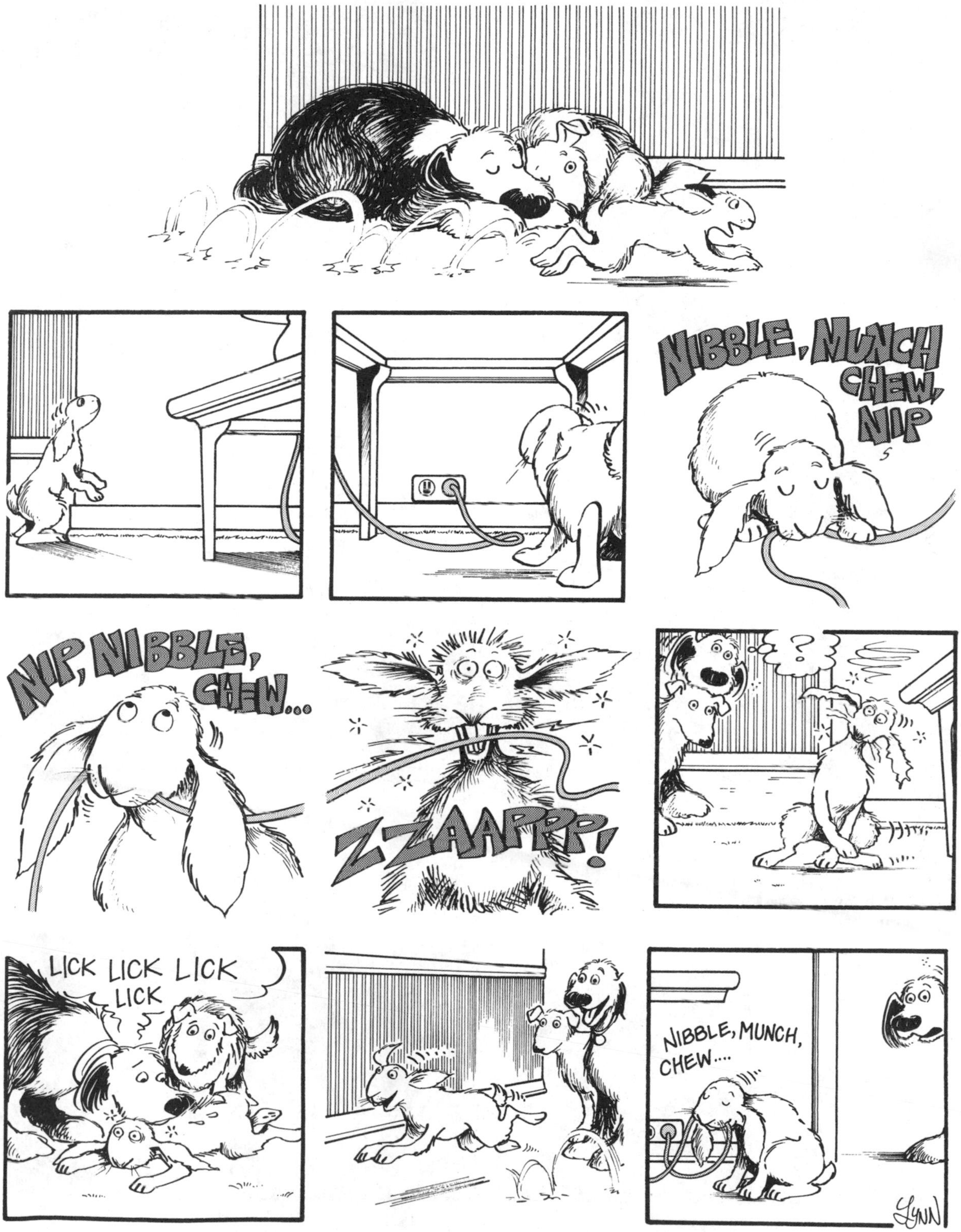
NIBBLE, MUNCH
CHEW,
NIP
NIP, NIBBLE,
CHEW...
ZZAAPPP!
?
LICK LICK LICK
LICK
LICK
NIBBLE, MUNCH,
CHEW....
LYNN

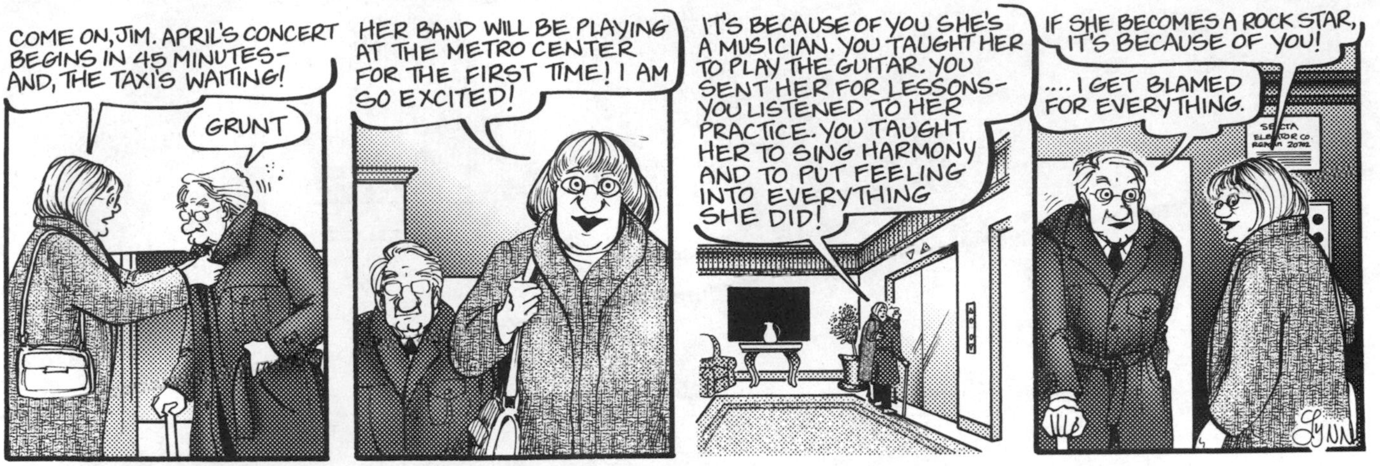
COME ON, JIM. APRIL'S CONCERT BEGINS IN 45 MINUTES– AND, THE TAXI'S WAITING!
GRUNT
HER BAND WILL BE PLAYING AT THE METRO CENTER FOR THE FIRST TIME! I AM SO EXCITED!
IT'S BECAUSE OF YOU SHE'S A MUSICIAN. YOU TAUGHT HER TO PLAY THE GUITAR. YOU SENT HER FOR LESSONS– YOU LISTENED TO HER PRACTICE. YOU TAUGHT HER TO SING HARMONY AND TO PUT FEELING INTO EVERYTHING SHE DID!
IF SHE BECOMES A ROCK STAR, IT'S BECAUSE OF YOU!
.... I GET BLAMED FOR EVERYTHING.
LYNN

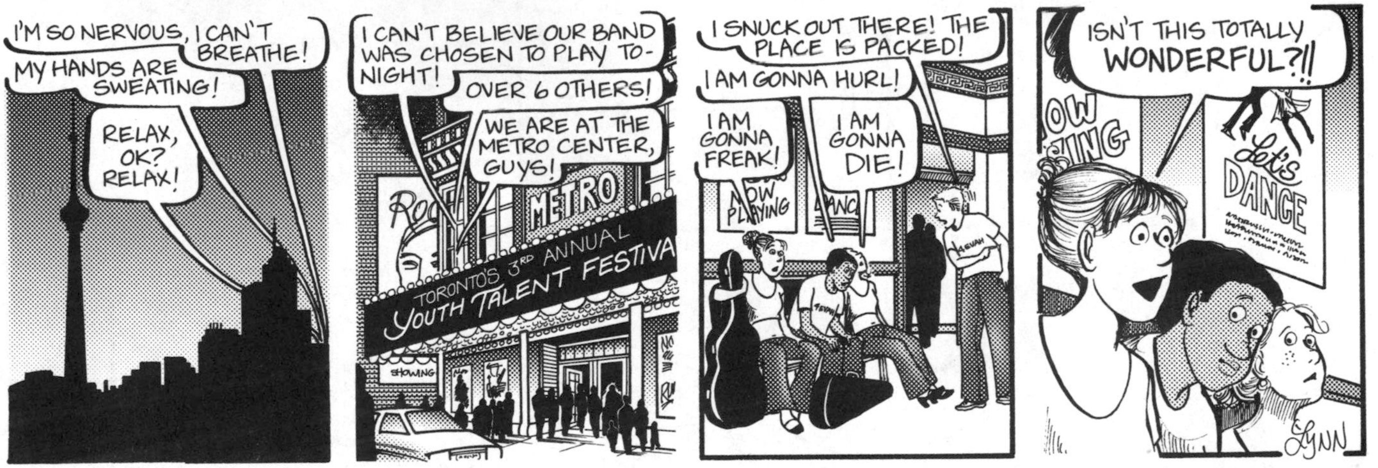
I'M SO NERVOUS, I CAN'T BREATHE!
MY HANDS ARE SWEATING!
RELAX, OK? RELAX!
I CAN'T BELIEVE OUR BAND WAS CHOSEN TO PLAY TO-NIGHT!
OVER 6 OTHERS!
WE ARE AT THE METRO CENTER, GUYS!
METRO
TORONTO'S 3RD ANNUAL YOUTH TALENT FESTIVA
SHOWING
I SNUCK OUT THERE! THE PLACE IS PACKED!
I AM GONNA HURL!
I AM GONNA FREAK!
I AM GONNA DIE!
NOW PLAYING
4EVAH
ISN'T THIS TOTALLY WONDERFUL?!!
Let's DANCE
LYNN

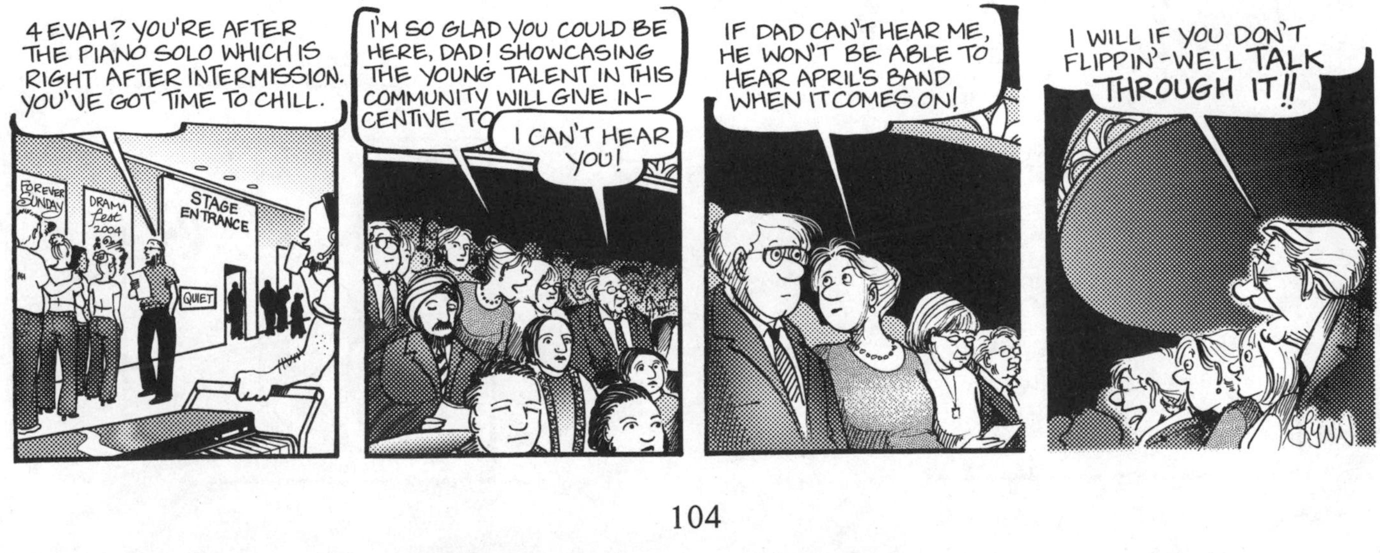
4 EVAH? YOU'RE AFTER THE PIANO SOLO WHICH IS RIGHT AFTER INTERMISSION. YOU'VE GOT TIME TO CHILL.
FOREVER SUNDAY
DRAMA fest 2004
STAGE ENTRANCE
QUIET
I'M SO GLAD YOU COULD BE HERE, DAD! SHOWCASING THE YOUNG TALENT IN THIS COMMUNITY WILL GIVE IN-CENTIVE TO
I CAN'T HEAR YOU!
IF DAD CAN'T HEAR ME, HE WON'T BE ABLE TO HEAR APRIL'S BAND WHEN IT COMES ON!
I WILL IF YOU DON'T FLIPPIN'-WELL TALK THROUGH IT!!
LYNN

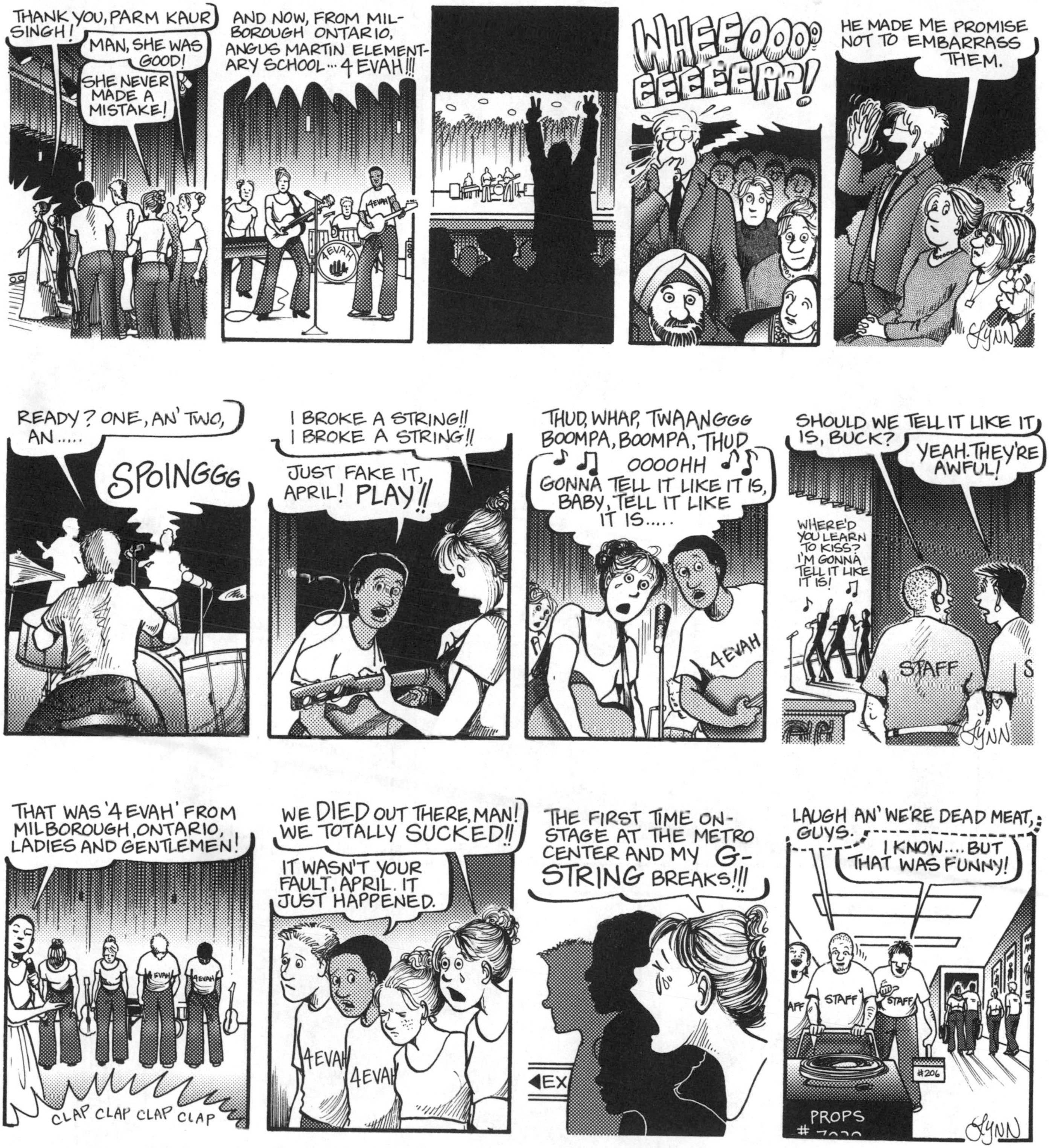
THANK YOU, PARM KAUR SINGH!
MAN, SHE WAS GOOD!
SHE NEVER MADE A MISTAKE!
AND NOW, FROM MIL-BOROUGH ONTARIO, ANGUS MARTIN ELEMENT-ARY SCHOOL... 4 EVAH!!!
4EVAH
4EVAH
WHEEOOO EEEEEPP!
HE MADE ME PROMISE NOT TO EMBARRASS THEM.
LYNN
READY? ONE, AN' TWO, AN.....
SPOINGGG
I BROKE A STRING!! I BROKE A STRING!!
JUST FAKE IT, APRIL! PLAY!!
THUD, WHAP, TWAANGGG BOOMPA, BOOMPA, THUD ♪♫ OOOOHH ♪♫ GONNA TELL IT LIKE IT IS, BABY, TELL IT LIKE IT IS.....
4EVAH
SHOULD WE TELL IT LIKE IT IS, BUCK?
YEAH. THEY'RE AWFUL!
WHERE'D YOU LEARN TO KISS? I'M GONNA TELL IT LIKE IT IS! ♫ ♪
STAFF
LYNN
THAT WAS '4 EVAH' FROM MILBOROUGH, ONTARIO, LADIES AND GENTLEMEN!
4EVAH
4EVAH
CLAP CLAP CLAP CLAP
WE DIED OUT THERE, MAN! WE TOTALLY SUCKED!!
IT WASN'T YOUR FAULT, APRIL. IT JUST HAPPENED.
4EVAH
4EVAH
THE FIRST TIME ON-STAGE AT THE METRO CENTER AND MY G-STRING BREAKS!!!
EX
LAUGH AN' WE'RE DEAD MEAT, GUYS.
I KNOW.... BUT THAT WAS FUNNY!
STAFF
STAFF
#206
PROPS
LYNN

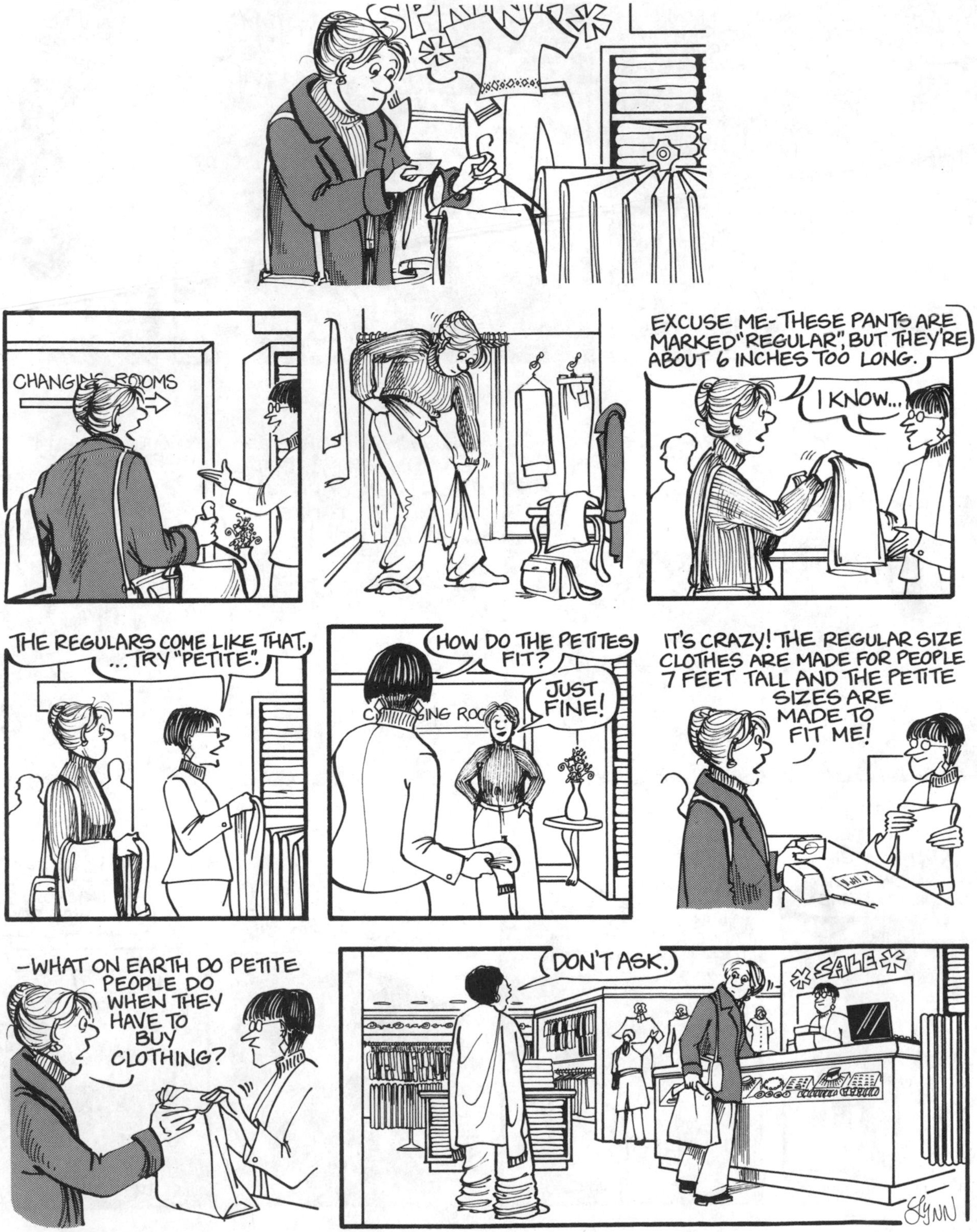
SPRING
CHANGING ROOMS
EXCUSE ME- THESE PANTS ARE MARKED "REGULAR", BUT THEY'RE ABOUT 6 INCHES TOO LONG.
I KNOW...
THE REGULARS COME LIKE THAT. ...TRY "PETITE".
HOW DO THE PETITES FIT?
JUST FINE!
IT'S CRAZY! THE REGULAR SIZE CLOTHES ARE MADE FOR PEOPLE 7 FEET TALL AND THE PETITE SIZES ARE MADE TO FIT ME!
-WHAT ON EARTH DO PETITE PEOPLE DO WHEN THEY HAVE TO BUY CLOTHING?
DON'T ASK.
SALE
LYNN

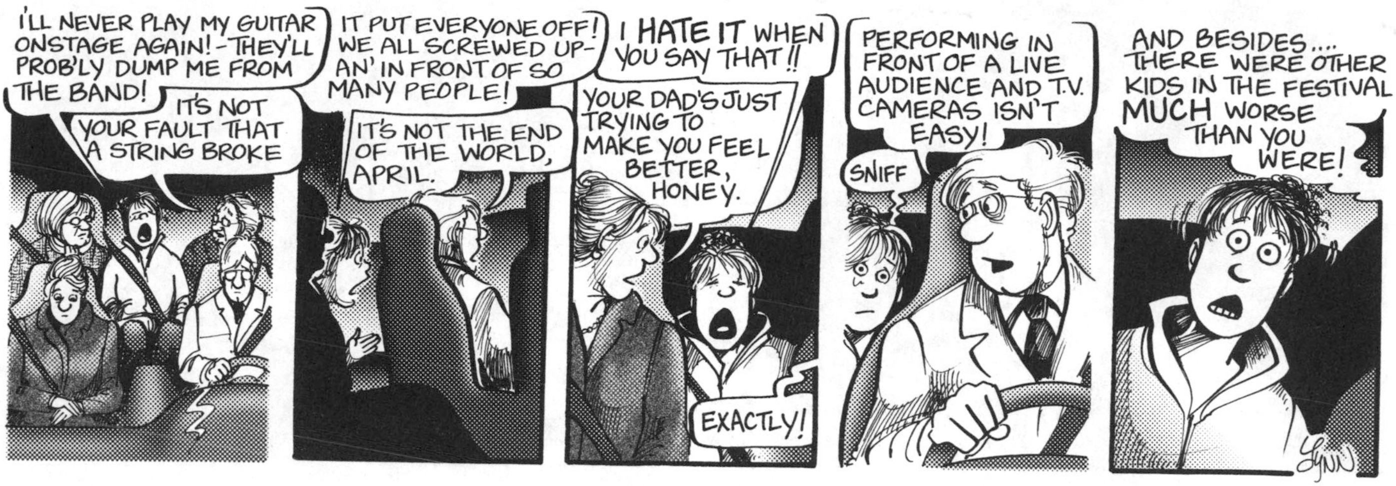
I'LL NEVER PLAY MY GUITAR ONSTAGE AGAIN! - THEY'LL PROB'LY DUMP ME FROM THE BAND!
IT'S NOT YOUR FAULT THAT A STRING BROKE
IT PUT EVERYONE OFF! WE ALL SCREWED UP- AN' IN FRONT OF SO MANY PEOPLE!
IT'S NOT THE END OF THE WORLD, APRIL.
I HATE IT WHEN YOU SAY THAT!!
YOUR DAD'S JUST TRYING TO MAKE YOU FEEL BETTER, HONEY.
EXACTLY!
PERFORMING IN FRONT OF A LIVE AUDIENCE AND T.V. CAMERAS ISN'T EASY!
SNIFF
AND BESIDES.... THERE WERE OTHER KIDS IN THE FESTIVAL MUCH WORSE THAN YOU WERE!
LYNN

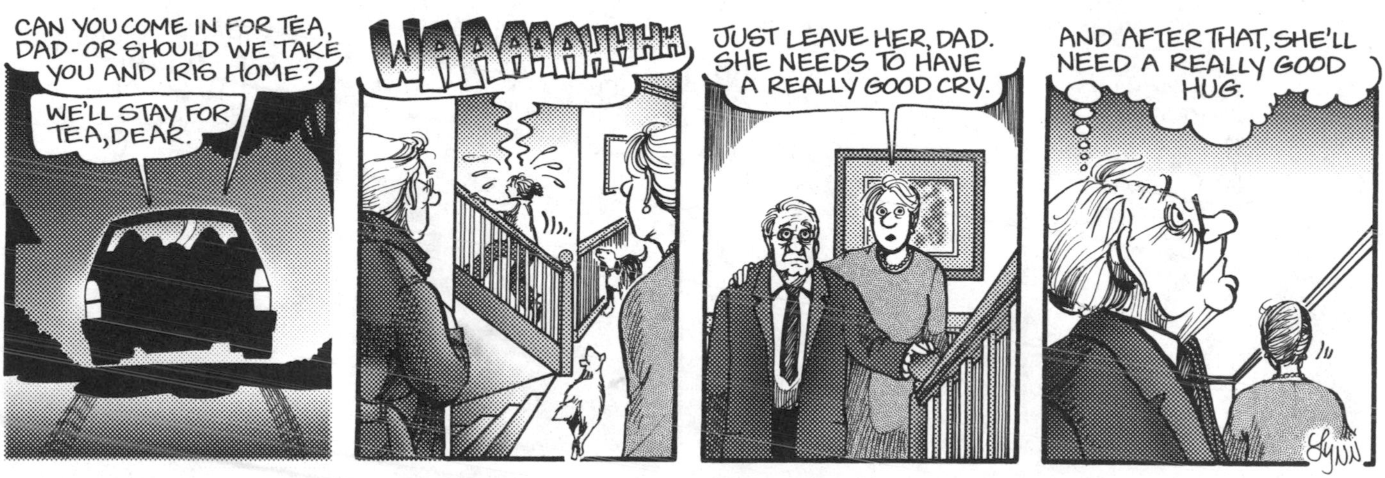
CAN YOU COME IN FOR TEA, DAD - OR SHOULD WE TAKE YOU AND IRIS HOME?
WE'LL STAY FOR TEA, DEAR.
WAAAAAHHHH
JUST LEAVE HER, DAD. SHE NEEDS TO HAVE A REALLY GOOD CRY.
AND AFTER THAT, SHE'LL NEED A REALLY GOOD HUG.
LYNN

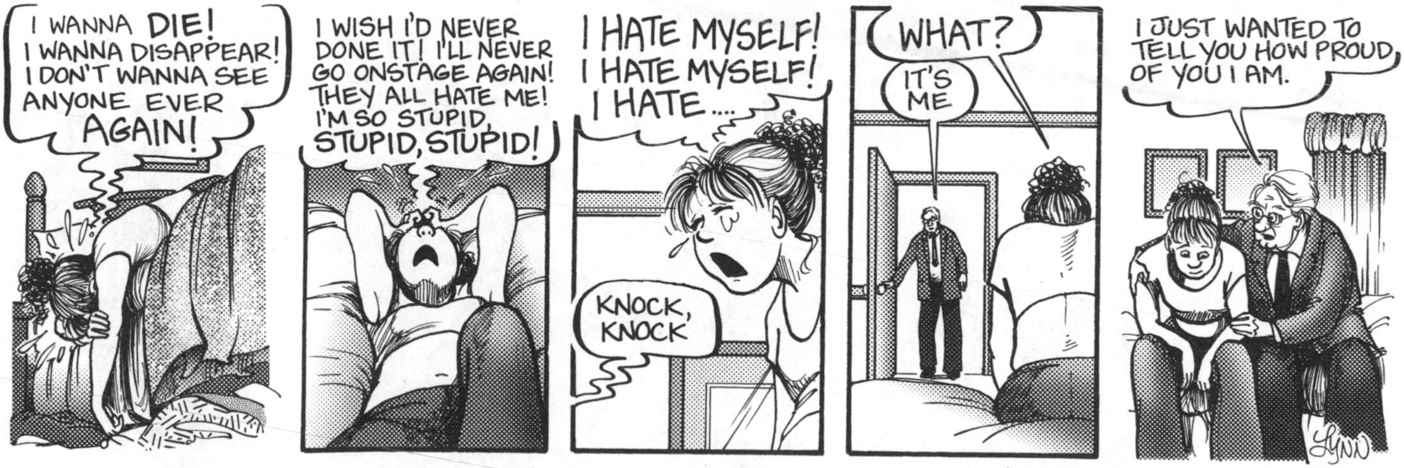
I WANNA DIE! I WANNA DISAPPEAR! I DON'T WANNA SEE ANYONE EVER AGAIN!
I WISH I'D NEVER DONE IT! I'LL NEVER GO ONSTAGE AGAIN! THEY ALL HATE ME! I'M SO STUPID, STUPID, STUPID!
I HATE MYSELF! I HATE MYSELF! I HATE....
KNOCK, KNOCK
WHAT?
IT'S ME
I JUST WANTED TO TELL YOU HOW PROUD OF YOU I AM.
LYNN

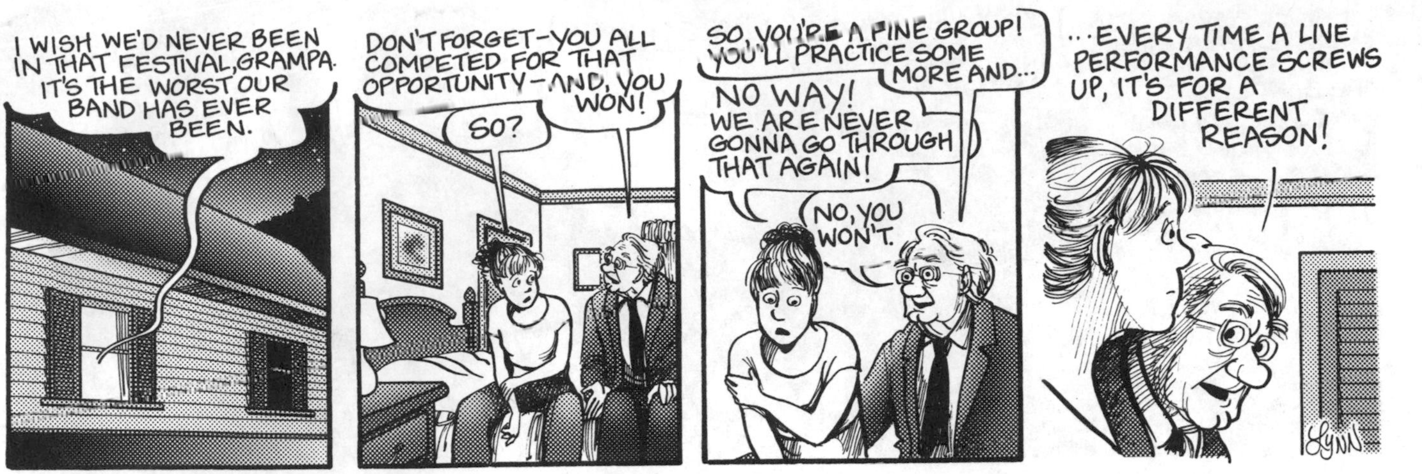

I WISH WE'D NEVER BEEN IN THAT FESTIVAL, GRAMPA. IT'S THE WORST OUR BAND HAS EVER BEEN.
DON'T FORGET—YOU ALL COMPETED FOR THAT OPPORTUNITY—AND, YOU WON!
SO?
SO, YOU'RE A FINE GROUP! YOU'LL PRACTICE SOME MORE AND...
NO WAY! WE ARE NEVER GONNA GO THROUGH THAT AGAIN!
NO, YOU WON'T.
...EVERY TIME A LIVE PERFORMANCE SCREWS UP, IT'S FOR A DIFFERENT REASON!
LYNN

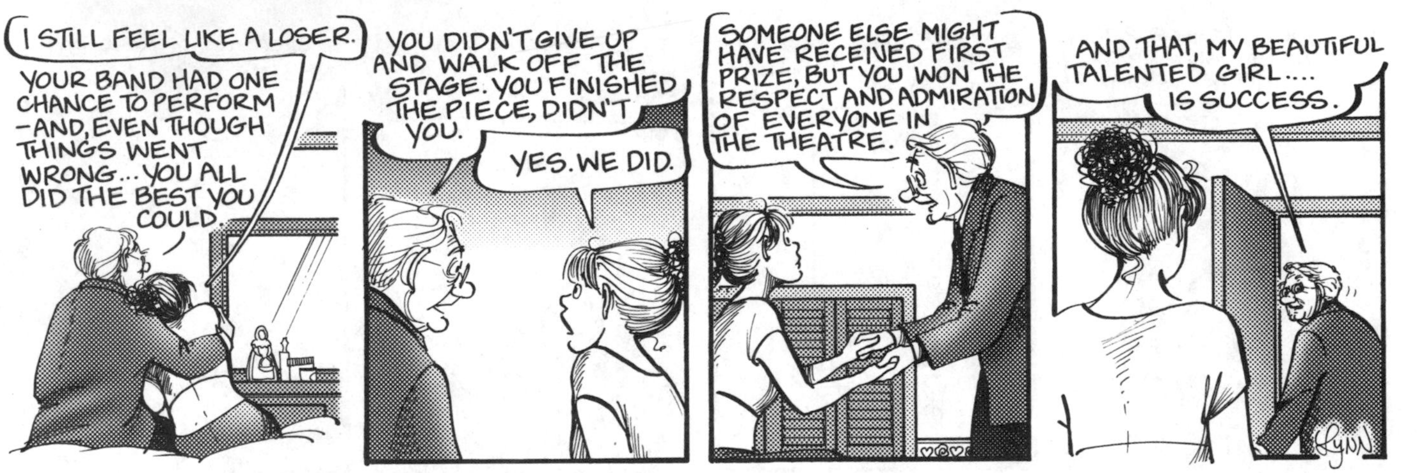

I STILL FEEL LIKE A LOSER.
YOUR BAND HAD ONE CHANCE TO PERFORM —AND, EVEN THOUGH THINGS WENT WRONG... YOU ALL DID THE BEST YOU COULD.
YOU DIDN'T GIVE UP AND WALK OFF THE STAGE. YOU FINISHED THE PIECE, DIDN'T YOU.
YES. WE DID.
SOMEONE ELSE MIGHT HAVE RECEIVED FIRST PRIZE, BUT YOU WON THE RESPECT AND ADMIRATION OF EVERYONE IN THE THEATRE.
AND THAT, MY BEAUTIFUL TALENTED GIRL....
IS SUCCESS.
LYNN

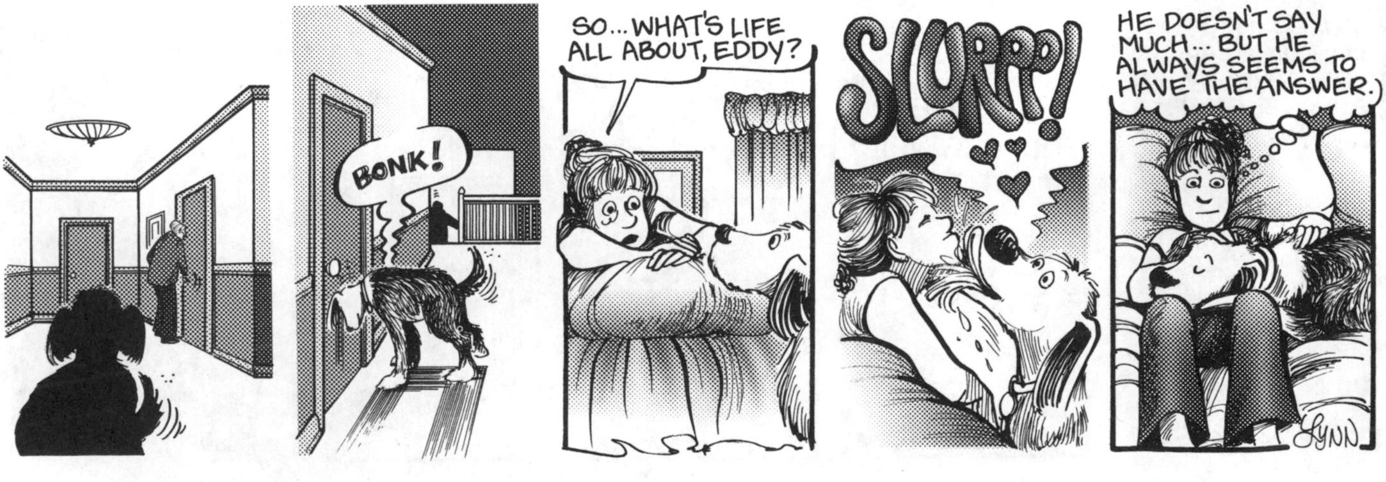

BONK!
SO... WHAT'S LIFE ALL ABOUT, EDDY?
SLURPP!
HE DOESN'T SAY MUCH... BUT HE ALWAYS SEEMS TO HAVE THE ANSWER.
LYNN

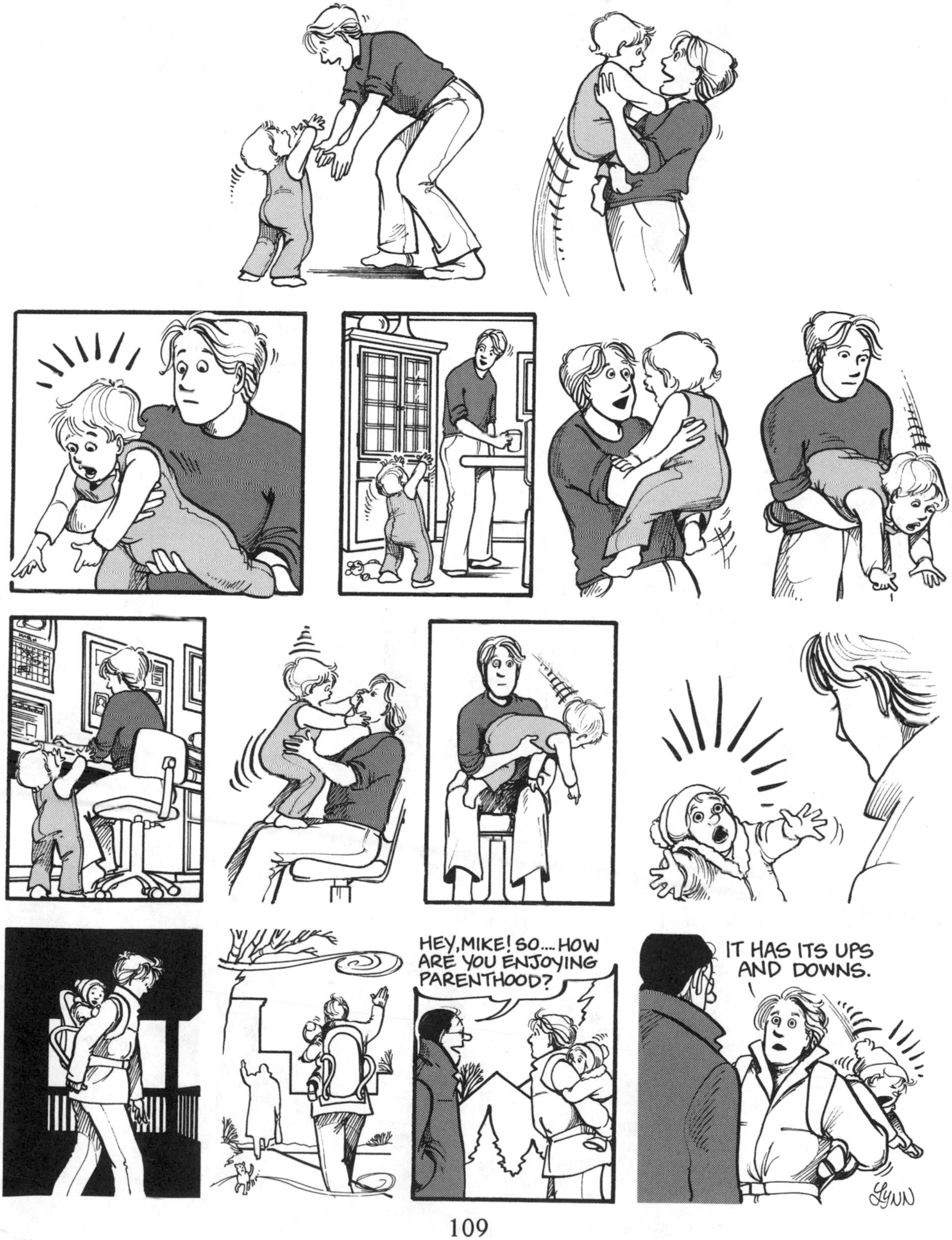
HEY, MIKE! SO.... HOW ARE YOU ENJOYING PARENTHOOD?
IT HAS ITS UPS AND DOWNS.
LYNN

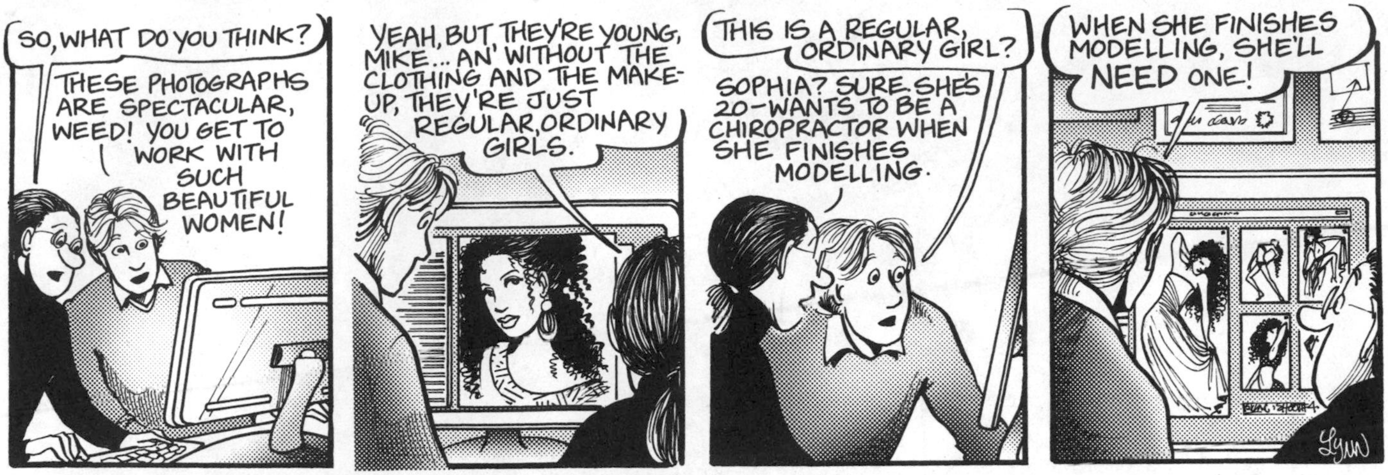
SO, WHAT DO YOU THINK?
THESE PHOTOGRAPHS ARE SPECTACULAR, WEED! YOU GET TO WORK WITH SUCH BEAUTIFUL WOMEN!
YEAH, BUT THEY'RE YOUNG, MIKE... AN' WITHOUT THE CLOTHING AND THE MAKE-UP, THEY'RE JUST REGULAR, ORDINARY GIRLS.
THIS IS A REGULAR, ORDINARY GIRL?
SOPHIA? SURE. SHE'S 20 - WANTS TO BE A CHIROPRACTOR WHEN SHE FINISHES MODELLING.
WHEN SHE FINISHES MODELLING, SHE'LL NEED ONE!
LYNN

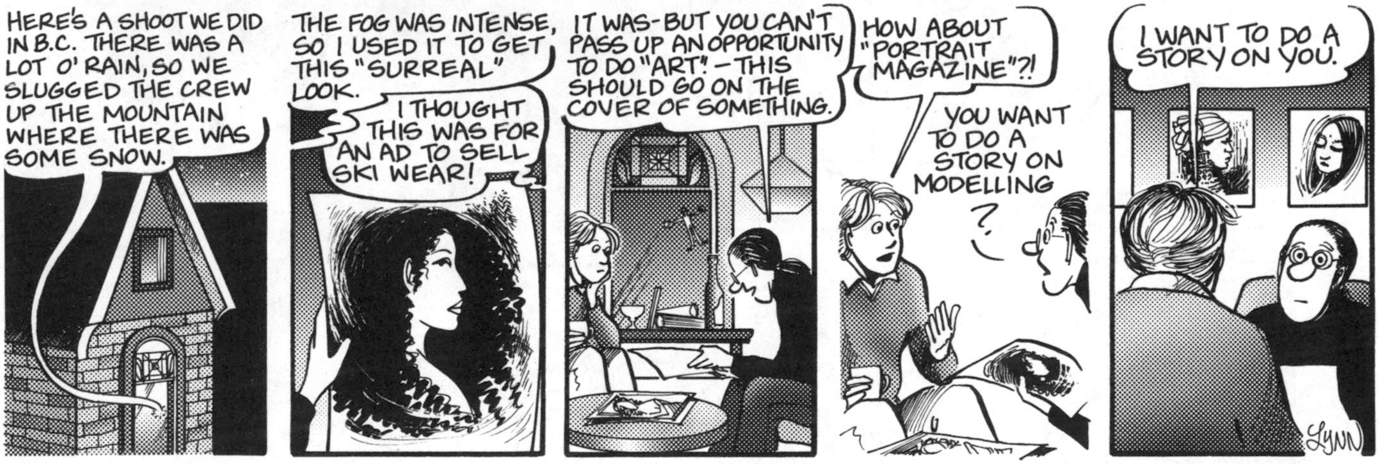
HERE'S A SHOOT WE DID IN B.C. THERE WAS A LOT O' RAIN, SO WE SLUGGED THE CREW UP THE MOUNTAIN WHERE THERE WAS SOME SNOW.
THE FOG WAS INTENSE, SO I USED IT TO GET THIS "SURREAL" LOOK.
I THOUGHT THIS WAS FOR AN AD TO SELL SKI WEAR!
IT WAS - BUT YOU CAN'T PASS UP AN OPPORTUNITY TO DO "ART"! - THIS SHOULD GO ON THE COVER OF SOMETHING.
HOW ABOUT "PORTRAIT MAGAZINE"?!
YOU WANT TO DO A STORY ON MODELLING
?
I WANT TO DO A STORY ON YOU.
LYNN

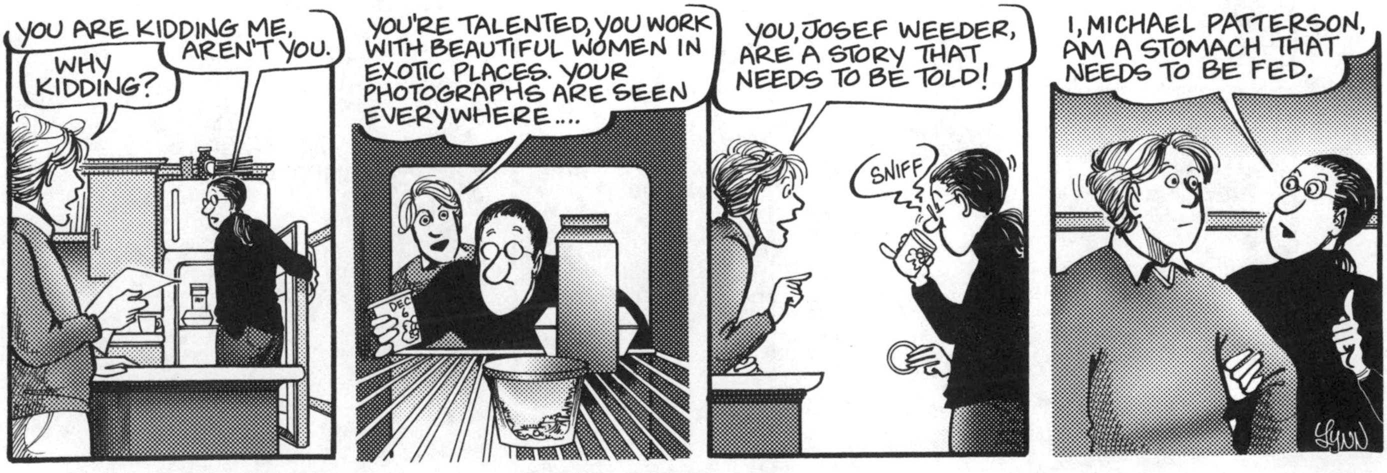
YOU ARE KIDDING ME, AREN'T YOU.
WHY KIDDING?
YOU'RE TALENTED, YOU WORK WITH BEAUTIFUL WOMEN IN EXOTIC PLACES. YOUR PHOTOGRAPHS ARE SEEN EVERYWHERE....
YOU, JOSEF WEEDER, ARE A STORY THAT NEEDS TO BE TOLD!
SNIFF
I, MICHAEL PATTERSON, AM A STOMACH THAT NEEDS TO BE FED.
LYNN

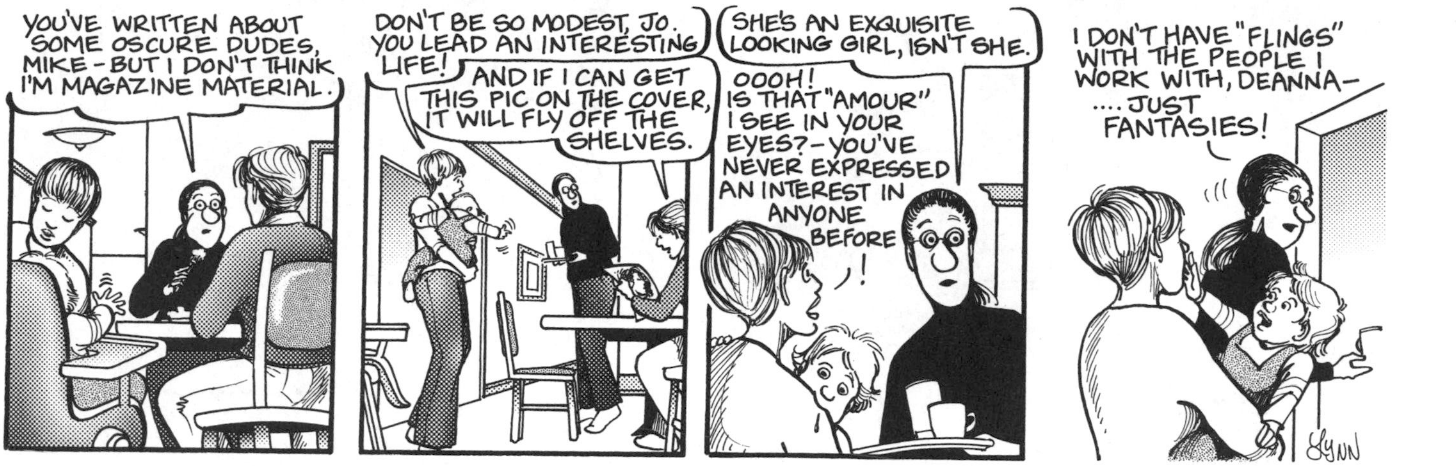
YOU'VE WRITTEN ABOUT SOME OSCURE DUDES, MIKE - BUT I DON'T THINK I'M MAGAZINE MATERIAL.
DON'T BE SO MODEST, JO. YOU LEAD AN INTERESTING LIFE!
AND IF I CAN GET THIS PIC ON THE COVER, IT WILL FLY OFF THE SHELVES.
SHE'S AN EXQUISITE LOOKING GIRL, ISN'T SHE.
OOOH! IS THAT "AMOUR" I SEE IN YOUR EYES? - YOU'VE NEVER EXPRESSED AN INTEREST IN ANYONE BEFORE
!
I DON'T HAVE "FLINGS" WITH THE PEOPLE I WORK WITH, DEANNA- .... JUST FANTASIES!
LYNN

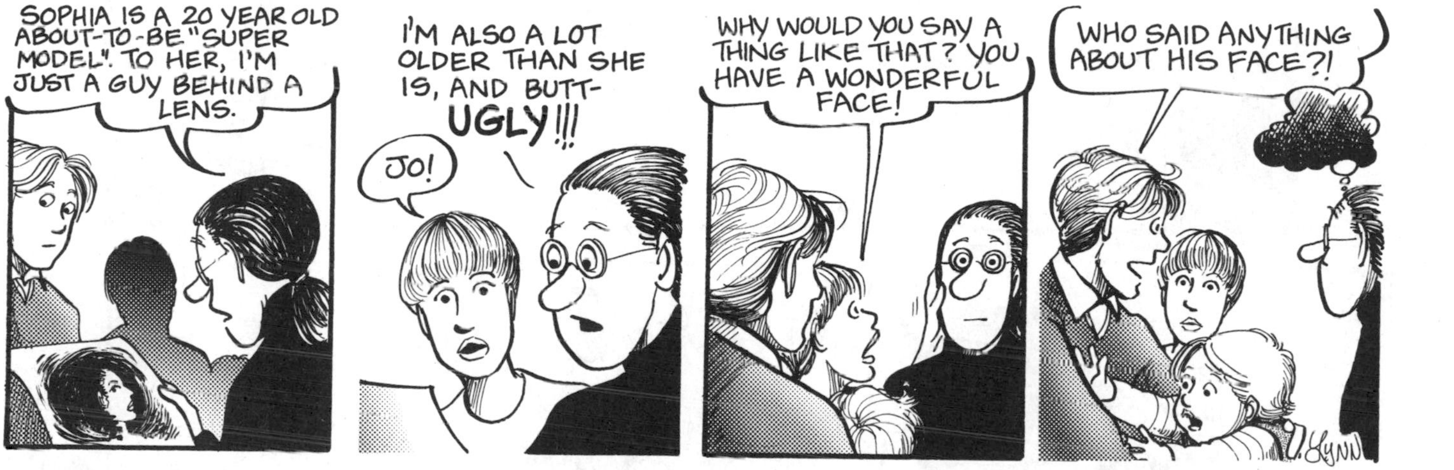
SOPHIA IS A 20 YEAR OLD ABOUT-TO-BE "SUPER MODEL". TO HER, I'M JUST A GUY BEHIND A LENS.
I'M ALSO A LOT OLDER THAN SHE IS, AND BUTT-UGLY!!!
JO!
WHY WOULD YOU SAY A THING LIKE THAT? YOU HAVE A WONDERFUL FACE!
WHO SAID ANYTHING ABOUT HIS FACE?!
LYNN

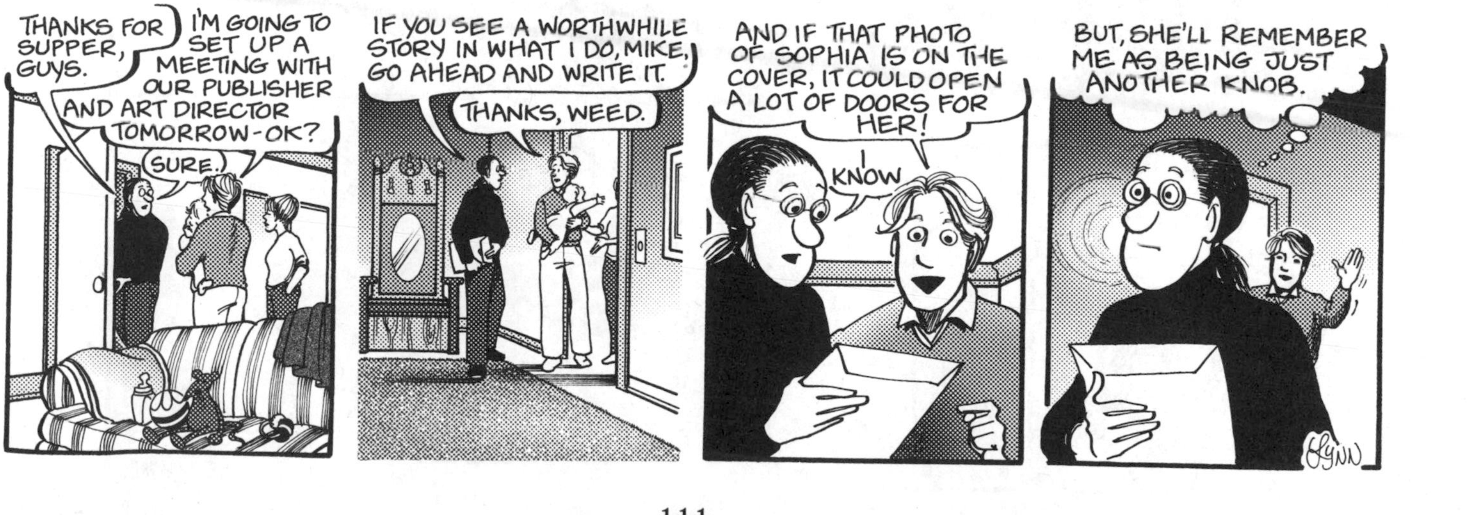
THANKS FOR SUPPER, GUYS.
I'M GOING TO SET UP A MEETING WITH OUR PUBLISHER AND ART DIRECTOR TOMORROW-OK?
SURE.
IF YOU SEE A WORTHWHILE STORY IN WHAT I DO, MIKE, GO AHEAD AND WRITE IT.
THANKS, WEED.
AND IF THAT PHOTO OF SOPHIA IS ON THE COVER, IT COULD OPEN A LOT OF DOORS FOR HER!
I KNOW
BUT, SHE'LL REMEMBER ME AS BEING JUST ANOTHER KNOB.
LYNN

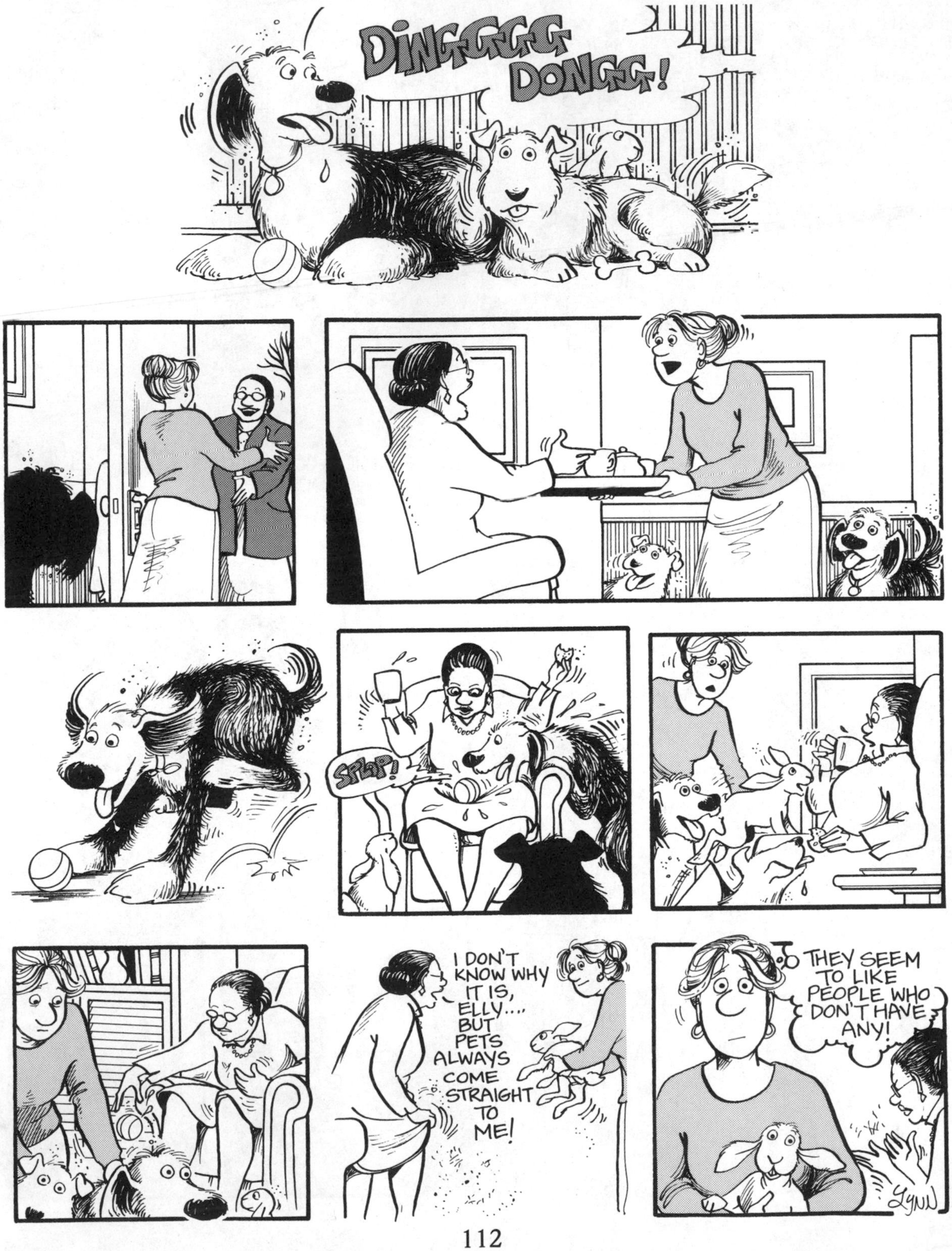
DINGGGG DONGGG!
SPLAP!
I DON'T KNOW WHY IT IS, ELLY.... BUT PETS ALWAYS COME STRAIGHT TO ME!
THEY SEEM TO LIKE PEOPLE WHO DON'T HAVE ANY!
LYNN

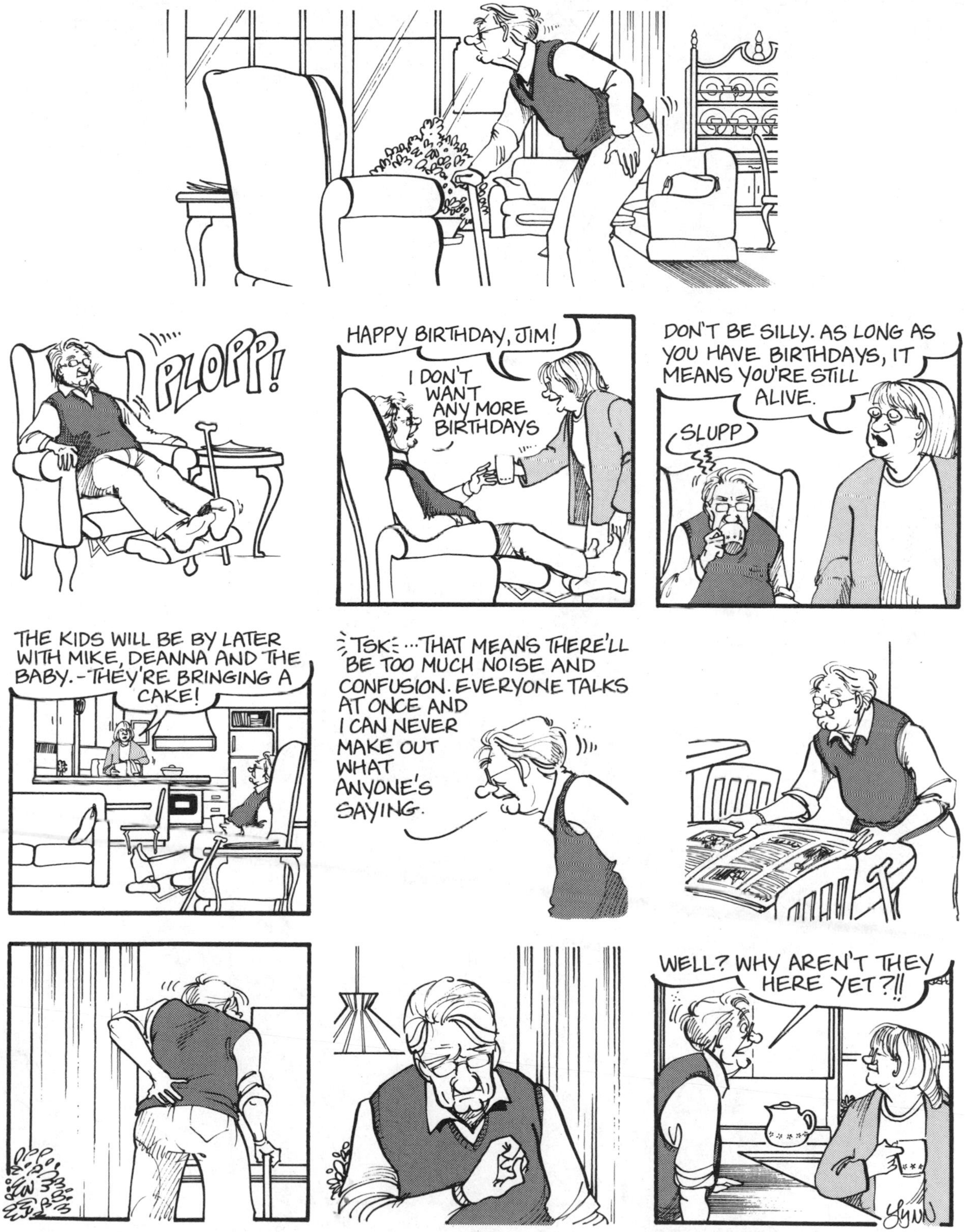
PLOPP!
HAPPY BIRTHDAY, JIM!
I DON'T WANT ANY MORE BIRTHDAYS
DON'T BE SILLY. AS LONG AS YOU HAVE BIRTHDAYS, IT MEANS YOU'RE STILL ALIVE.
SLUPP
THE KIDS WILL BE BY LATER WITH MIKE, DEANNA AND THE BABY.- THEY'RE BRINGING A CAKE!
TSK ... THAT MEANS THERE'LL BE TOO MUCH NOISE AND CONFUSION. EVERYONE TALKS AT ONCE AND I CAN NEVER MAKE OUT WHAT ANYONE'S SAYING.
WELL? WHY AREN'T THEY HERE YET?!!
LYNN

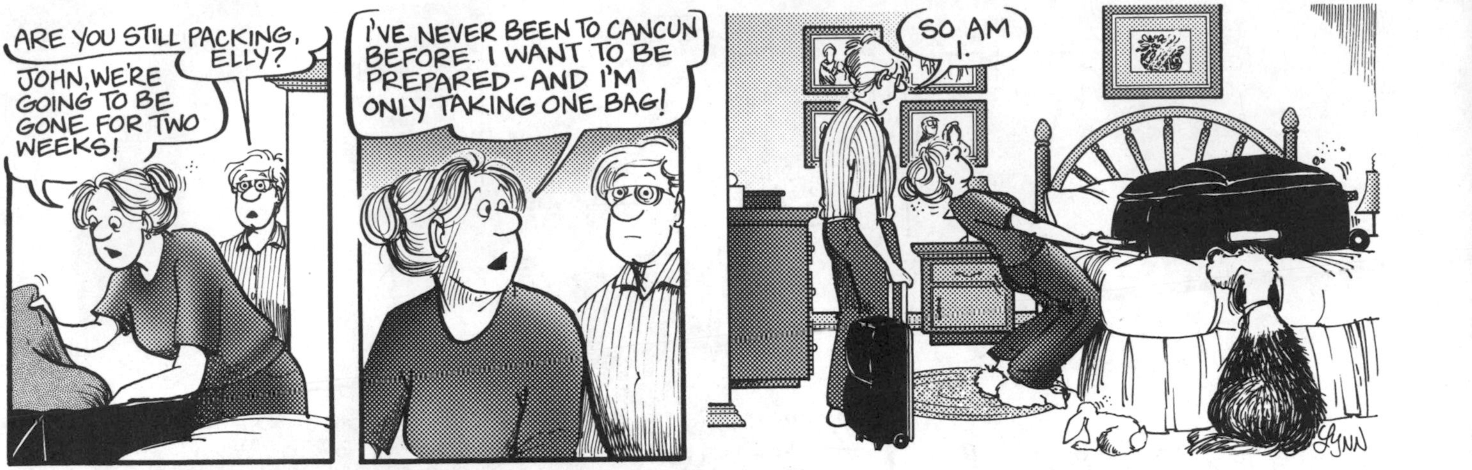

ARE YOU STILL PACKING, ELLY?
JOHN, WE'RE GOING TO BE GONE FOR TWO WEEKS!
I'VE NEVER BEEN TO CANCUN BEFORE. I WANT TO BE PREPARED - AND I'M ONLY TAKING ONE BAG!
SO AM I.
LYNN

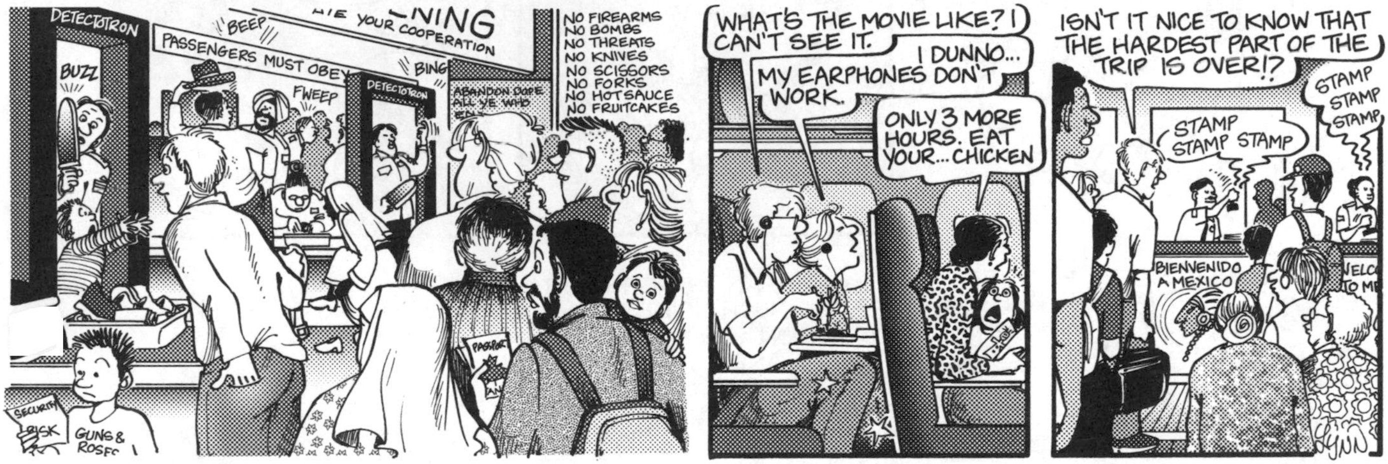

DETECTOTRON
BUZZ
BEEP
YOUR COOPERATION
PASSENGERS MUST OBEY
BING
FWEEP
DETECTOTRON
ABANDON DOPE ALL YE WHO
NO FIREARMS
NO BOMBS
NO THREATS
NO KNIVES
NO SCISSORS
NO FORKS
NO HOTSAUCE
NO FRUITCAKES
SECURITY RISK
GUNS &
WHAT'S THE MOVIE LIKE? I CAN'T SEE IT.
I DUNNO... MY EARPHONES DON'T WORK.
ONLY 3 MORE HOURS. EAT YOUR... CHICKEN
ISN'T IT NICE TO KNOW THAT THE HARDEST PART OF THE TRIP IS OVER!?
STAMP STAMP STAMP
STAMP STAMP STAMP
BIENVENIDO A MEXICO
LYNN

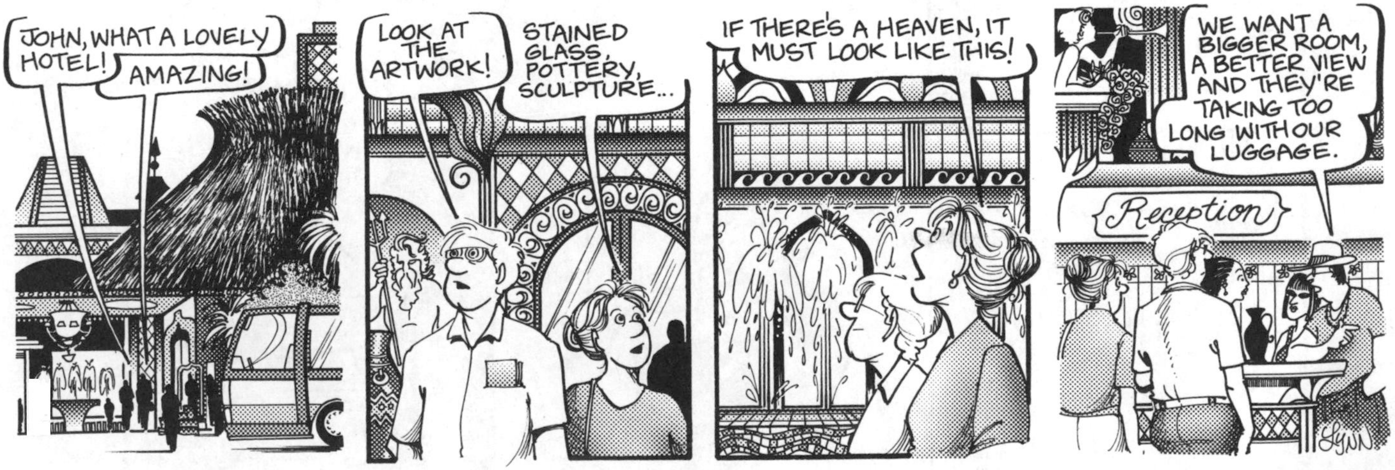

JOHN, WHAT A LOVELY HOTEL!
AMAZING!
LOOK AT THE ARTWORK!
STAINED GLASS, POTTERY, SCULPTURE...
IF THERE'S A HEAVEN, IT MUST LOOK LIKE THIS!
WE WANT A BIGGER ROOM, A BETTER VIEW AND THEY'RE TAKING TOO LONG WITH OUR LUGGAGE.
Reception
LYNN

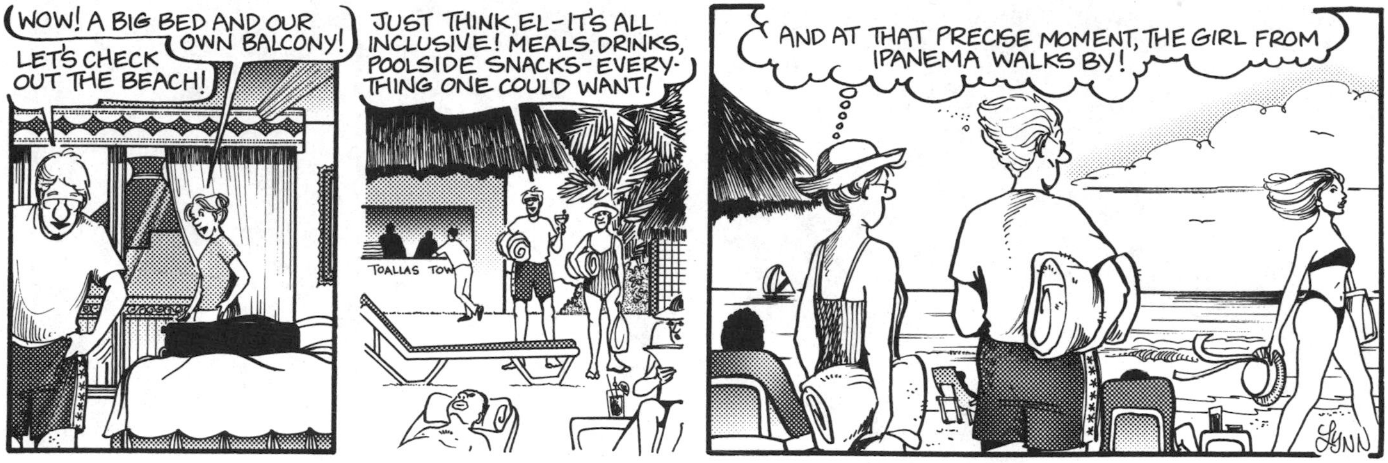
WOW! A BIG BED AND OUR OWN BALCONY!
LET'S CHECK OUT THE BEACH!
JUST THINK, EL - IT'S ALL INCLUSIVE! MEALS, DRINKS, POOLSIDE SNACKS - EVERYTHING ONE COULD WANT!
TOALLAS TOW
AND AT THAT PRECISE MOMENT, THE GIRL FROM IPANEMA WALKS BY!
LYNN

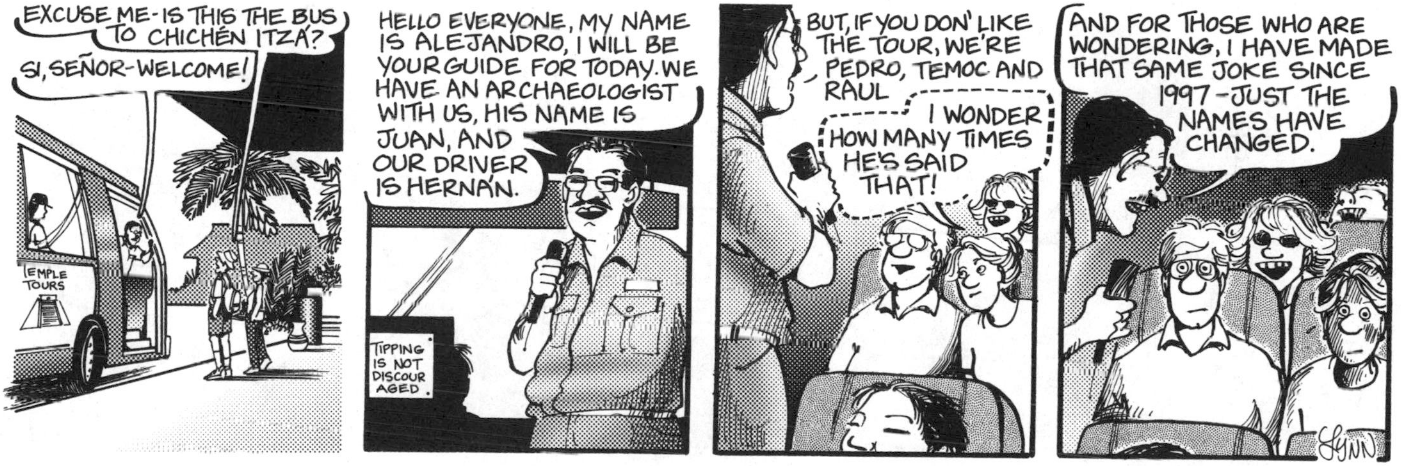
EXCUSE ME - IS THIS THE BUS TO CHICHÉN ITZÁ?
SI, SEÑOR - WELCOME!
TEMPLE TOURS
HELLO EVERYONE, MY NAME IS ALEJANDRO, I WILL BE YOUR GUIDE FOR TODAY. WE HAVE AN ARCHAEOLOGIST WITH US, HIS NAME IS JUAN, AND OUR DRIVER IS HERNÁN.
TIPPING IS NOT DISCOURAGED.
BUT, IF YOU DON' LIKE THE TOUR, WE'RE PEDRO, TEMOC AND RAUL
I WONDER HOW MANY TIMES HE'S SAID THAT!
AND FOR THOSE WHO ARE WONDERING, I HAVE MADE THAT SAME JOKE SINCE 1997 - JUST THE NAMES HAVE CHANGED.
LYNN

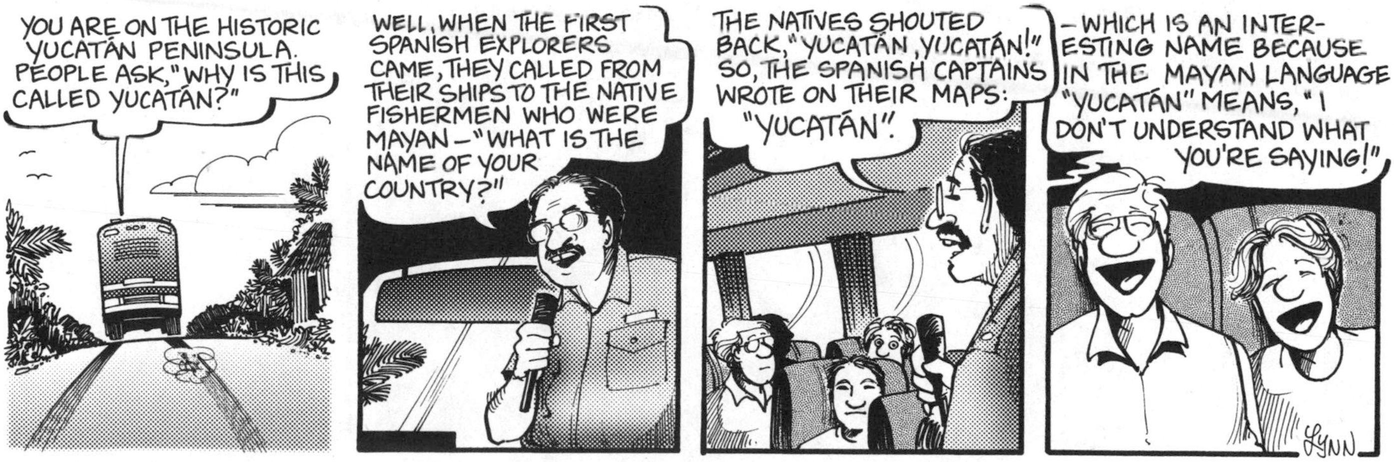
YOU ARE ON THE HISTORIC YUCATÁN PENINSULA. PEOPLE ASK, "WHY IS THIS CALLED YUCATÁN?"
WELL, WHEN THE FIRST SPANISH EXPLORERS CAME, THEY CALLED FROM THEIR SHIPS TO THE NATIVE FISHERMEN WHO WERE MAYAN - "WHAT IS THE NAME OF YOUR COUNTRY?"
THE NATIVES SHOUTED BACK, "YUCATÁN, YUCATÁN!" SO, THE SPANISH CAPTAINS WROTE ON THEIR MAPS: "YUCATÁN".
- WHICH IS AN INTERESTING NAME BECAUSE IN THE MAYAN LANGUAGE "YUCATÁN" MEANS, "I DON'T UNDERSTAND WHAT YOU'RE SAYING!"
LYNN

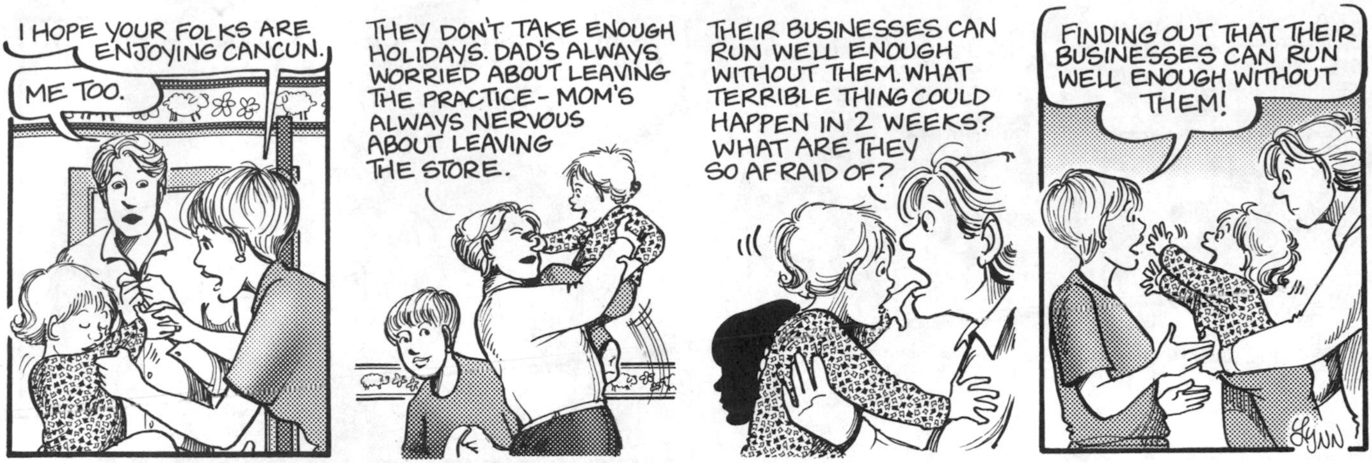
I HOPE YOUR FOLKS ARE ENJOYING CANCUN.
ME TOO.
THEY DON'T TAKE ENOUGH HOLIDAYS. DAD'S ALWAYS WORRIED ABOUT LEAVING THE PRACTICE - MOM'S ALWAYS NERVOUS ABOUT LEAVING THE STORE.
THEIR BUSINESSES CAN RUN WELL ENOUGH WITHOUT THEM. WHAT TERRIBLE THING COULD HAPPEN IN 2 WEEKS? WHAT ARE THEY SO AFRAID OF?
FINDING OUT THAT THEIR BUSINESSES CAN RUN WELL ENOUGH WITHOUT THEM!

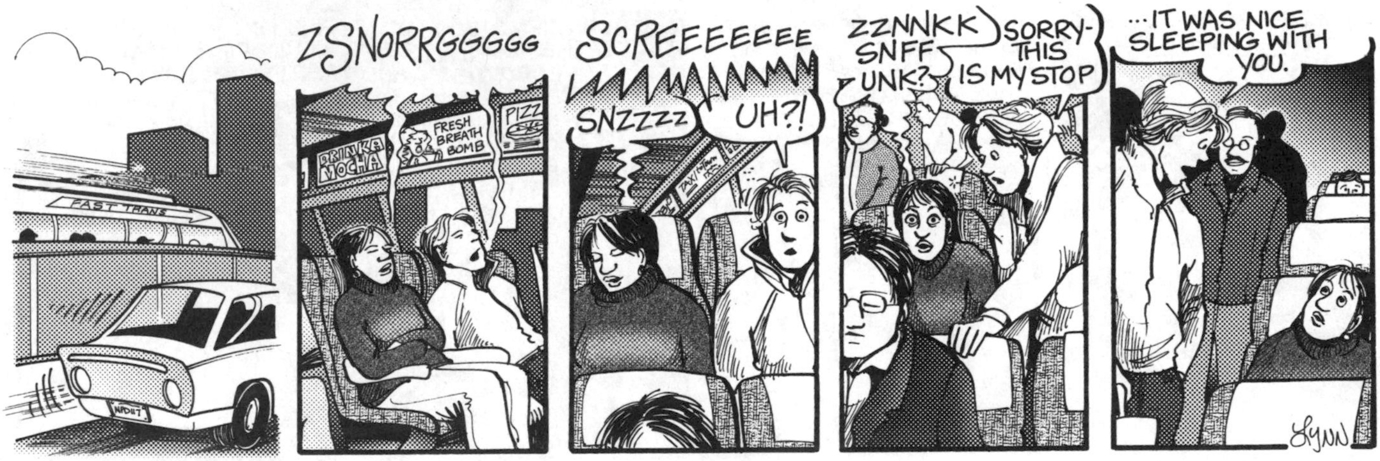
FAST TRANS
ZSNORRGGGGGG
DRINKA MOCHA
FRESH BREATH BOMB
SCREEEEEEEE
SNZZZZ
UH?!
ZZNNKK SNFF UNK?
SORRY- THIS IS MY STOP
...IT WAS NICE SLEEPING WITH YOU.

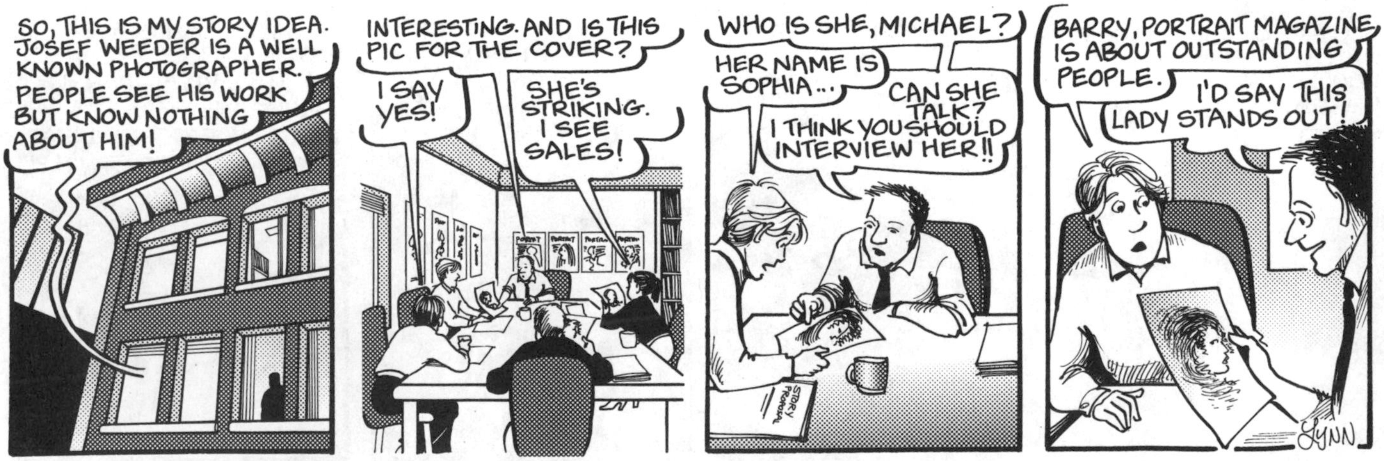
SO, THIS IS MY STORY IDEA. JOSEF WEEDER IS A WELL KNOWN PHOTOGRAPHER. PEOPLE SEE HIS WORK BUT KNOW NOTHING ABOUT HIM!
INTERESTING. AND IS THIS PIC FOR THE COVER?
I SAY YES!
SHE'S STRIKING. I SEE SALES!
WHO IS SHE, MICHAEL?
HER NAME IS SOPHIA...
CAN SHE TALK?
I THINK YOU SHOULD INTERVIEW HER!!
BARRY, PORTRAIT MAGAZINE IS ABOUT OUTSTANDING PEOPLE.
I'D SAY THIS LADY STANDS OUT!

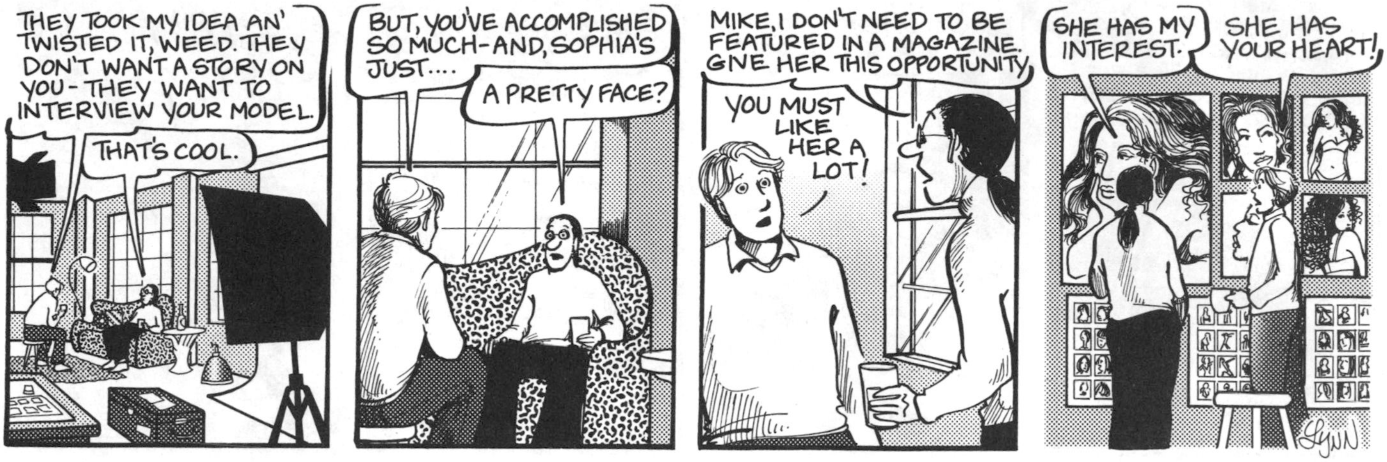
THEY TOOK MY IDEA AN' TWISTED IT, WEED. THEY DON'T WANT A STORY ON YOU - THEY WANT TO INTERVIEW YOUR MODEL.
THAT'S COOL.
BUT, YOU'VE ACCOMPLISHED SO MUCH - AND, SOPHIA'S JUST....
A PRETTY FACE?
MIKE, I DON'T NEED TO BE FEATURED IN A MAGAZINE. GIVE HER THIS OPPORTUNITY.
YOU MUST LIKE HER A LOT!
SHE HAS MY INTEREST.
SHE HAS YOUR HEART!
LYNN

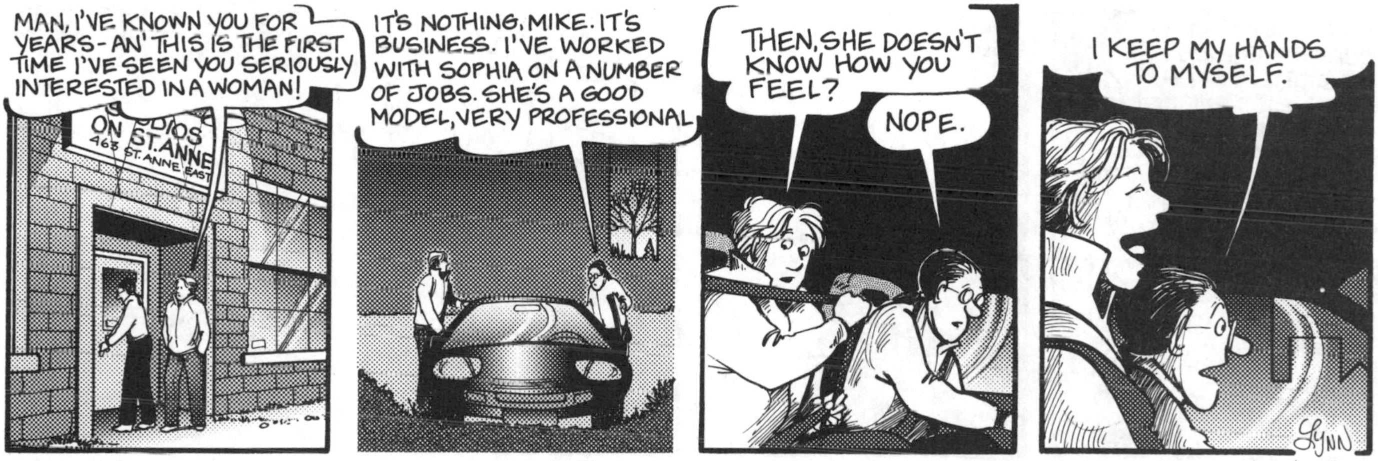
MAN, I'VE KNOWN YOU FOR YEARS - AN' THIS IS THE FIRST TIME I'VE SEEN YOU SERIOUSLY INTERESTED IN A WOMAN!
STUDIOS ON ST. ANNE
463 ST. ANNE EAST
IT'S NOTHING, MIKE. IT'S BUSINESS. I'VE WORKED WITH SOPHIA ON A NUMBER OF JOBS. SHE'S A GOOD MODEL, VERY PROFESSIONAL.
THEN, SHE DOESN'T KNOW HOW YOU FEEL?
NOPE.
I KEEP MY HANDS TO MYSELF.
LYNN

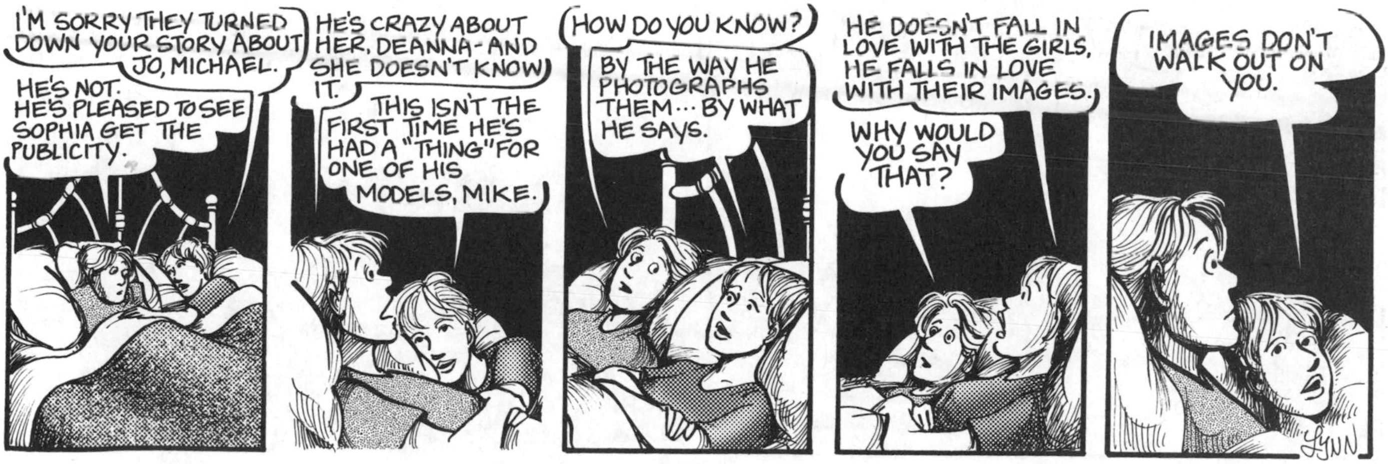
I'M SORRY THEY TURNED DOWN YOUR STORY ABOUT JO, MICHAEL.
HE'S NOT. HE'S PLEASED TO SEE SOPHIA GET THE PUBLICITY.
HE'S CRAZY ABOUT HER, DEANNA - AND SHE DOESN'T KNOW IT.
THIS ISN'T THE FIRST TIME HE'S HAD A "THING" FOR ONE OF HIS MODELS, MIKE.
HOW DO YOU KNOW?
BY THE WAY HE PHOTOGRAPHS THEM... BY WHAT HE SAYS.
HE DOESN'T FALL IN LOVE WITH THE GIRLS, HE FALLS IN LOVE WITH THEIR IMAGES.
WHY WOULD YOU SAY THAT?
IMAGES DON'T WALK OUT ON YOU.
LYNN

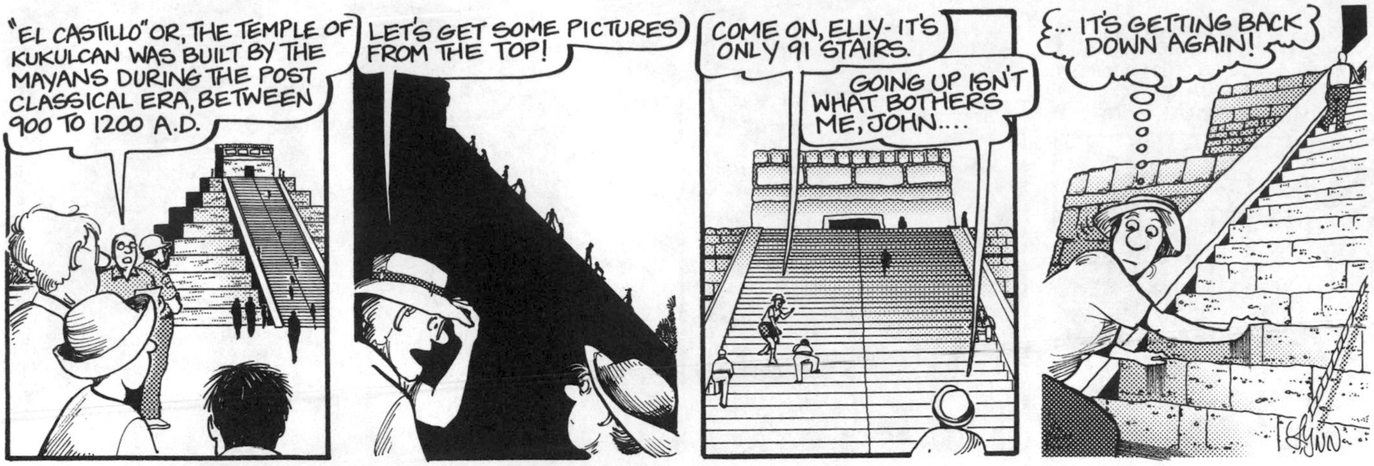
"EL CASTILLO" OR, THE TEMPLE OF KUKULCAN WAS BUILT BY THE MAYANS DURING THE POST CLASSICAL ERA, BETWEEN 900 TO 1200 A.D.
LET'S GET SOME PICTURES FROM THE TOP!
COME ON, ELLY- IT'S ONLY 91 STAIRS.
GOING UP ISN'T WHAT BOTHERS ME, JOHN....
...IT'S GETTING BACK DOWN AGAIN!
LYNN

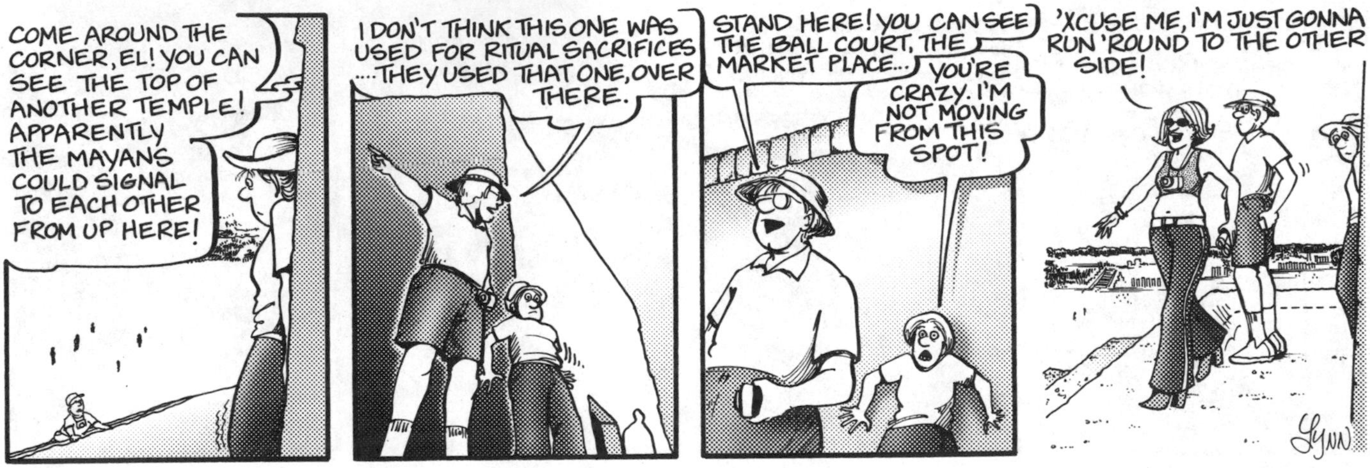
COME AROUND THE CORNER, EL! YOU CAN SEE THE TOP OF ANOTHER TEMPLE! APPARENTLY THE MAYANS COULD SIGNAL TO EACH OTHER FROM UP HERE!
I DON'T THINK THIS ONE WAS USED FOR RITUAL SACRIFICES ....THEY USED THAT ONE, OVER THERE.
STAND HERE! YOU CAN SEE THE BALL COURT, THE MARKET PLACE...
YOU'RE CRAZY. I'M NOT MOVING FROM THIS SPOT!
'XCUSE ME, I'M JUST GONNA RUN 'ROUND TO THE OTHER SIDE!
LYNN

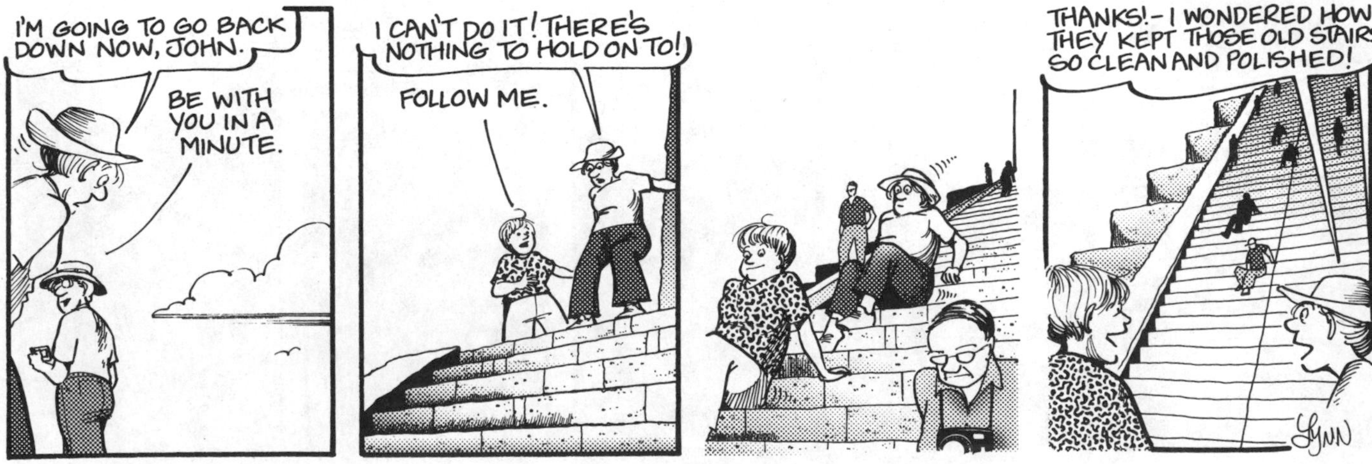
I'M GOING TO GO BACK DOWN NOW, JOHN.
BE WITH YOU IN A MINUTE.
I CAN'T DO IT! THERE'S NOTHING TO HOLD ON TO!
FOLLOW ME.
THANKS! - I WONDERED HOW THEY KEPT THOSE OLD STAIRS SO CLEAN AND POLISHED!
LYNN

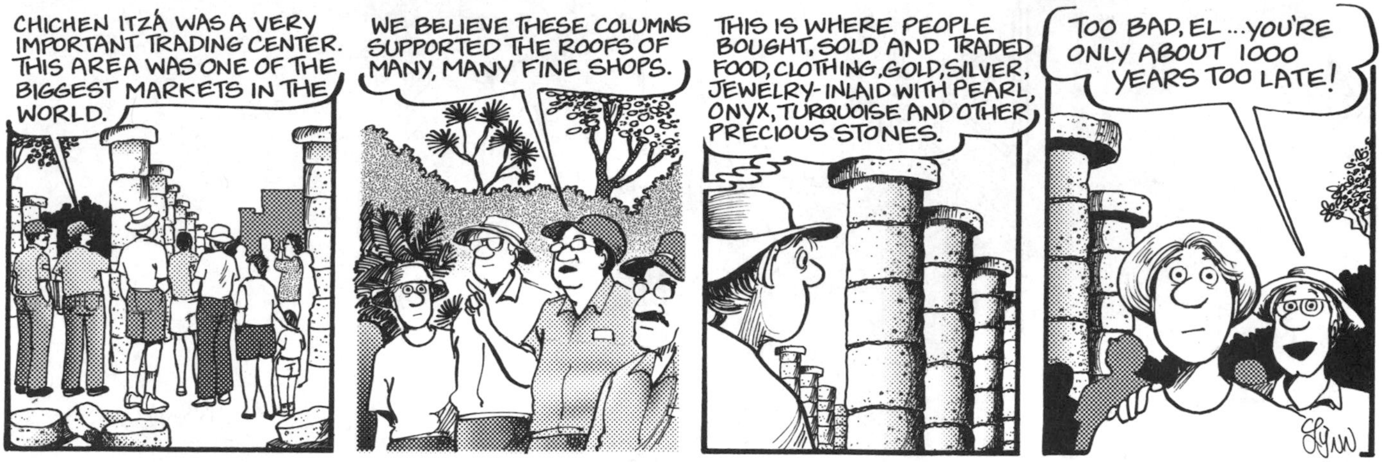

CHICHEN ITZÁ WAS A VERY IMPORTANT TRADING CENTER. THIS AREA WAS ONE OF THE BIGGEST MARKETS IN THE WORLD.
WE BELIEVE THESE COLUMNS SUPPORTED THE ROOFS OF MANY, MANY FINE SHOPS.
THIS IS WHERE PEOPLE BOUGHT, SOLD AND TRADED FOOD, CLOTHING, GOLD, SILVER, JEWELRY- INLAID WITH PEARL, ONYX, TURQUOISE AND OTHER PRECIOUS STONES.
TOO BAD, EL ...YOU'RE ONLY ABOUT 1000 YEARS TOO LATE!
LYNN

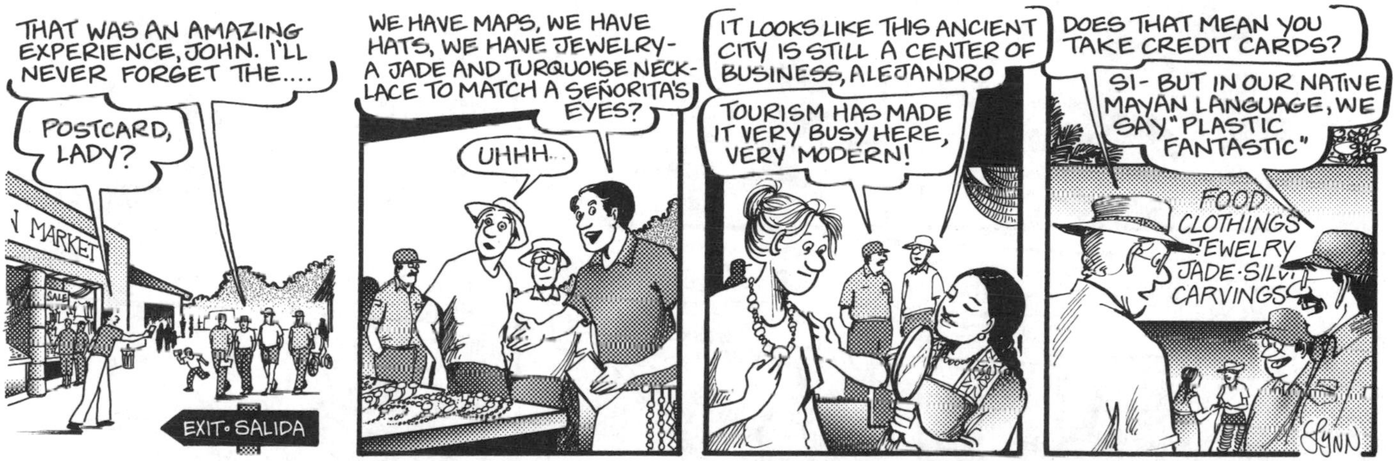

THAT WAS AN AMAZING EXPERIENCE, JOHN. I'LL NEVER FORGET THE....
POSTCARD, LADY?
N MARKET
SALE
EXIT • SALIDA
WE HAVE MAPS, WE HAVE HATS, WE HAVE JEWELRY- A JADE AND TURQUOISE NECKLACE TO MATCH A SEÑORITA'S EYES?
UHHH...
IT LOOKS LIKE THIS ANCIENT CITY IS STILL A CENTER OF BUSINESS, ALEJANDRO
TOURISM HAS MADE IT VERY BUSY HERE, VERY MODERN!
DOES THAT MEAN YOU TAKE CREDIT CARDS?
SI- BUT IN OUR NATIVE MAYAN LANGUAGE, WE SAY "PLASTIC FANTASTIC"
FOOD
CLOTHINGS
JEWELRY
JADE·SILV
CARVINGS
LYNN

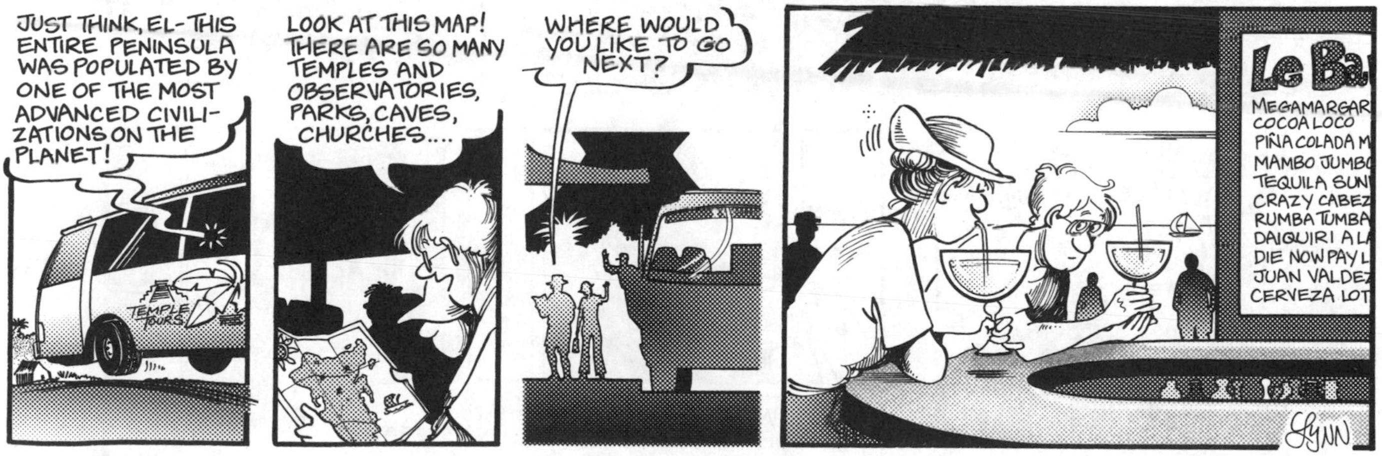

JUST THINK, EL- THIS ENTIRE PENINSULA WAS POPULATED BY ONE OF THE MOST ADVANCED CIVILIZATIONS ON THE PLANET!
TEMPLE TOURS
LOOK AT THIS MAP! THERE ARE SO MANY TEMPLES AND OBSERVATORIES, PARKS, CAVES, CHURCHES....
WHERE WOULD YOU LIKE TO GO NEXT?
Le Ba
MEGAMARGAR
COCOA LOCO
PIÑA COLADA M
MAMBO JUMBO
TEQUILA SUN
CRAZY CABEZ
RUMBA TUMBA
DAIQUIRI A LA
DIE NOW PAY L
JUAN VALDEZ
CERVEZA LOT
LYNN

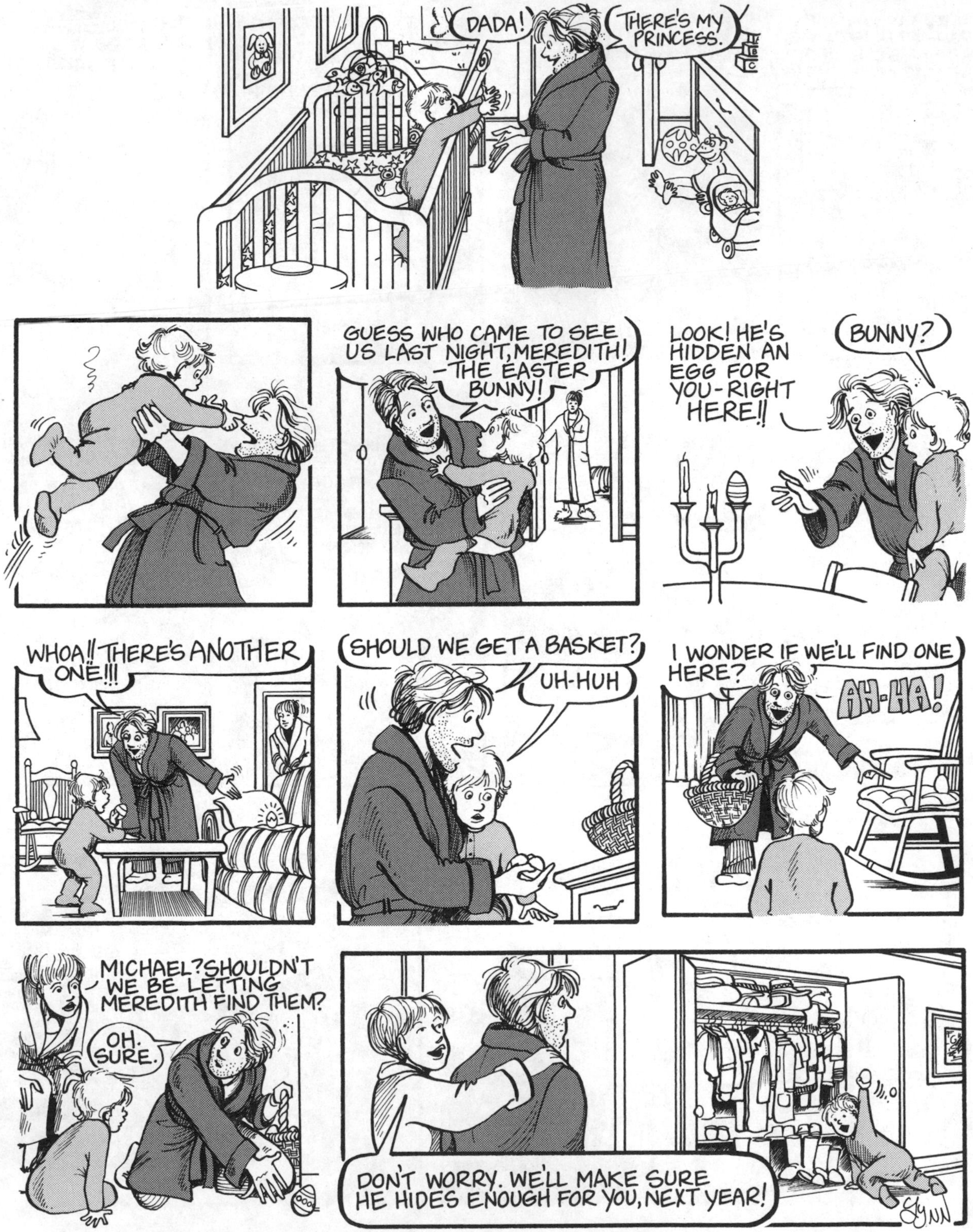
DADA!
THERE'S MY PRINCESS.
GUESS WHO CAME TO SEE US LAST NIGHT, MEREDITH! —THE EASTER BUNNY!
LOOK! HE'S HIDDEN AN EGG FOR YOU-RIGHT HERE!!
BUNNY?
WHOA!! THERE'S ANOTHER ONE!!!
SHOULD WE GET A BASKET?
UH-HUH
I WONDER IF WE'LL FIND ONE HERE?
AH-HA!
MICHAEL? SHOULDN'T WE BE LETTING MEREDITH FIND THEM?
OH. SURE.
DON'T WORRY. WE'LL MAKE SURE HE HIDES ENOUGH FOR YOU, NEXT YEAR!

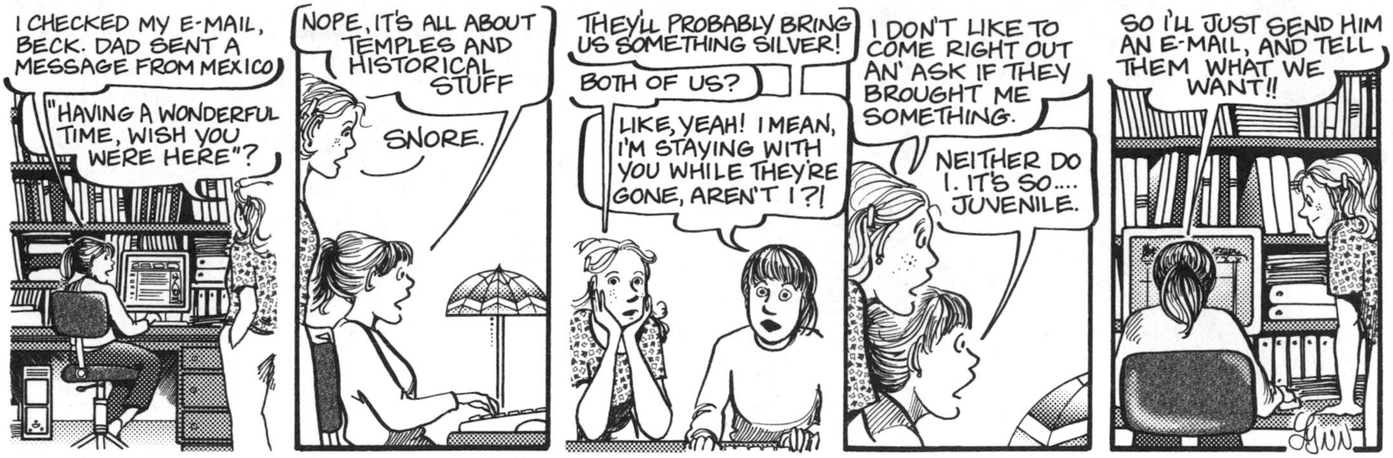
I CHECKED MY E-MAIL, BECK. DAD SENT A MESSAGE FROM MEXICO
"HAVING A WONDERFUL TIME, WISH YOU WERE HERE"?
NOPE, IT'S ALL ABOUT TEMPLES AND HISTORICAL STUFF
SNORE.
THEY'LL PROBABLY BRING US SOMETHING SILVER!
BOTH OF US?
LIKE, YEAH! I MEAN, I'M STAYING WITH YOU WHILE THEY'RE GONE, AREN'T I?!
I DON'T LIKE TO COME RIGHT OUT AN' ASK IF THEY BROUGHT ME SOMETHING.
NEITHER DO I. IT'S SO.... JUVENILE.
SO I'LL JUST SEND HIM AN E-MAIL, AND TELL THEM WHAT WE WANT!!
LYNN

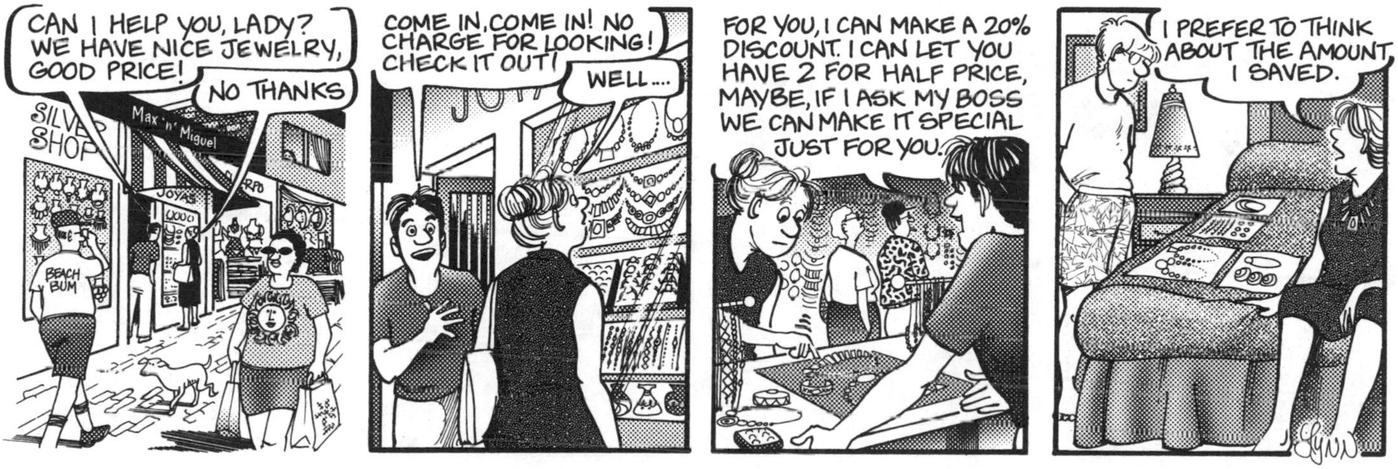
CAN I HELP YOU, LADY? WE HAVE NICE JEWELRY, GOOD PRICE!
NO THANKS
SILVER SHOP
Max 'n' Miguel
JOYAS
BEACH BUM
COME IN, COME IN! NO CHARGE FOR LOOKING! CHECK IT OUT!
WELL....
FOR YOU, I CAN MAKE A 20% DISCOUNT. I CAN LET YOU HAVE 2 FOR HALF PRICE, MAYBE, IF I ASK MY BOSS WE CAN MAKE IT SPECIAL JUST FOR YOU.
I PREFER TO THINK ABOUT THE AMOUNT I SAVED.
LYNN

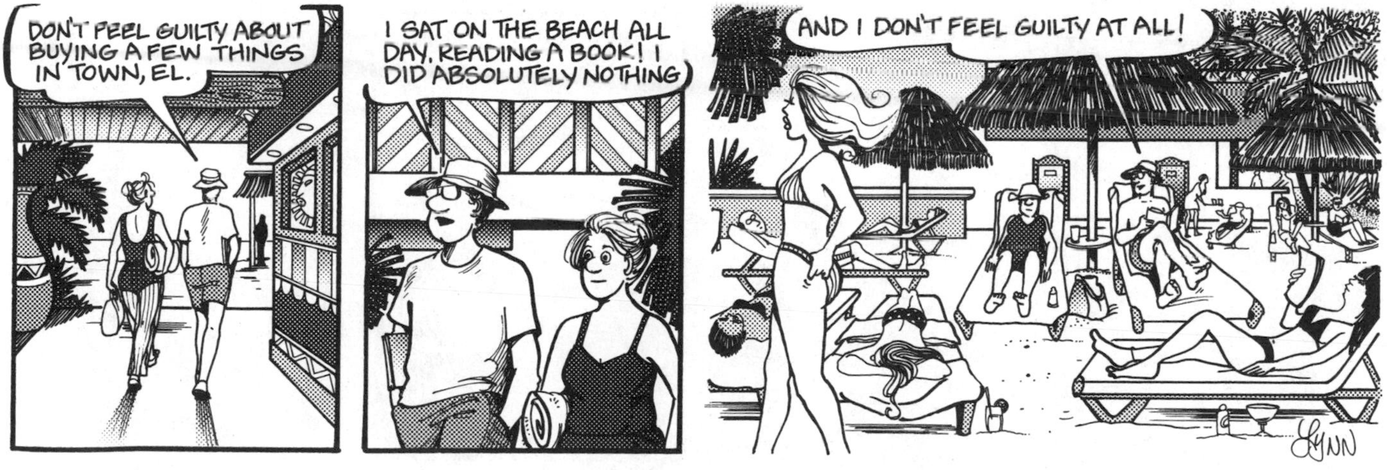
DON'T FEEL GUILTY ABOUT BUYING A FEW THINGS IN TOWN, EL.
I SAT ON THE BEACH ALL DAY, READING A BOOK! I DID ABSOLUTELY NOTHING
AND I DON'T FEEL GUILTY AT ALL!
LYNN

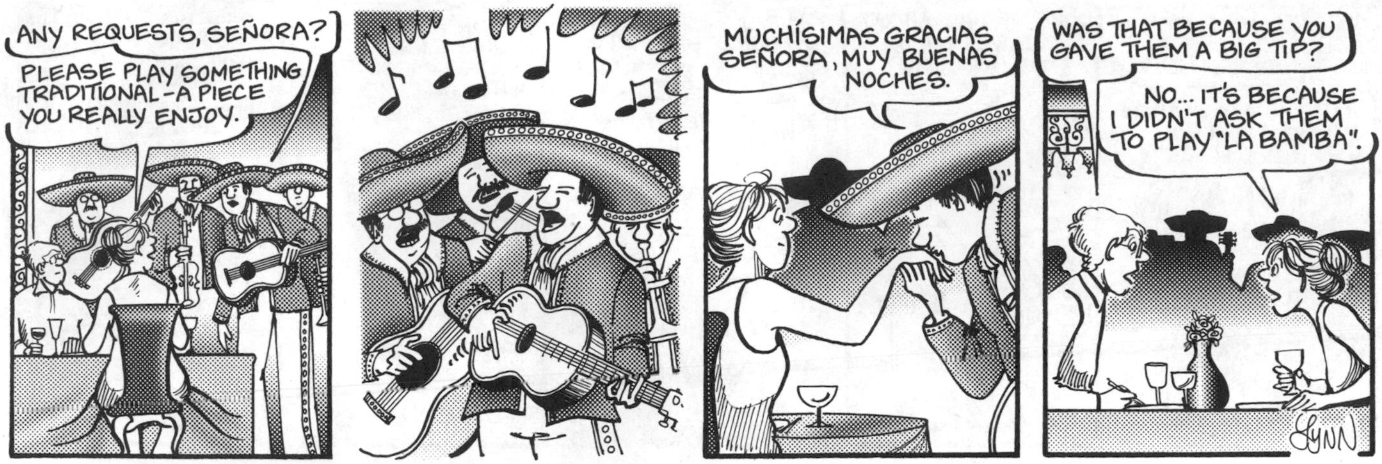
ANY REQUESTS, SEÑORA?
PLEASE PLAY SOMETHING TRADITIONAL - A PIECE YOU REALLY ENJOY.
MUCHÍSIMAS GRACIAS SEÑORA, MUY BUENAS NOCHES.
WAS THAT BECAUSE YOU GAVE THEM A BIG TIP?
NO... IT'S BECAUSE I DIDN'T ASK THEM TO PLAY "LA BAMBA".
LYNN

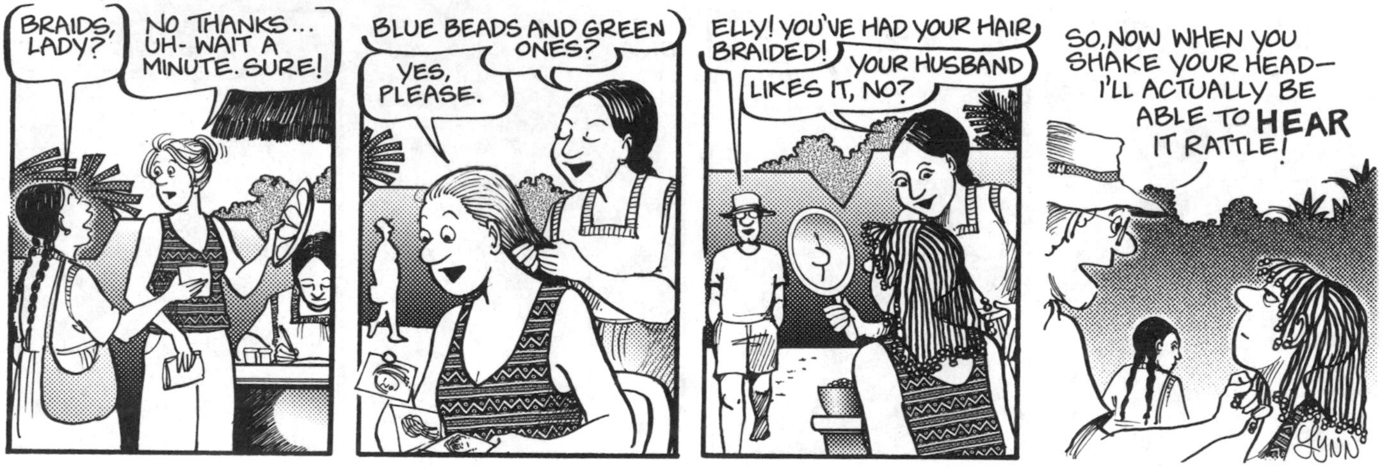
BRAIDS, LADY?
NO THANKS... UH- WAIT A MINUTE. SURE!
BLUE BEADS AND GREEN ONES?
YES, PLEASE.
ELLY! YOU'VE HAD YOUR HAIR BRAIDED!
YOUR HUSBAND LIKES IT, NO?
SO, NOW WHEN YOU SHAKE YOUR HEAD— I'LL ACTUALLY BE ABLE TO HEAR IT RATTLE!
LYNN

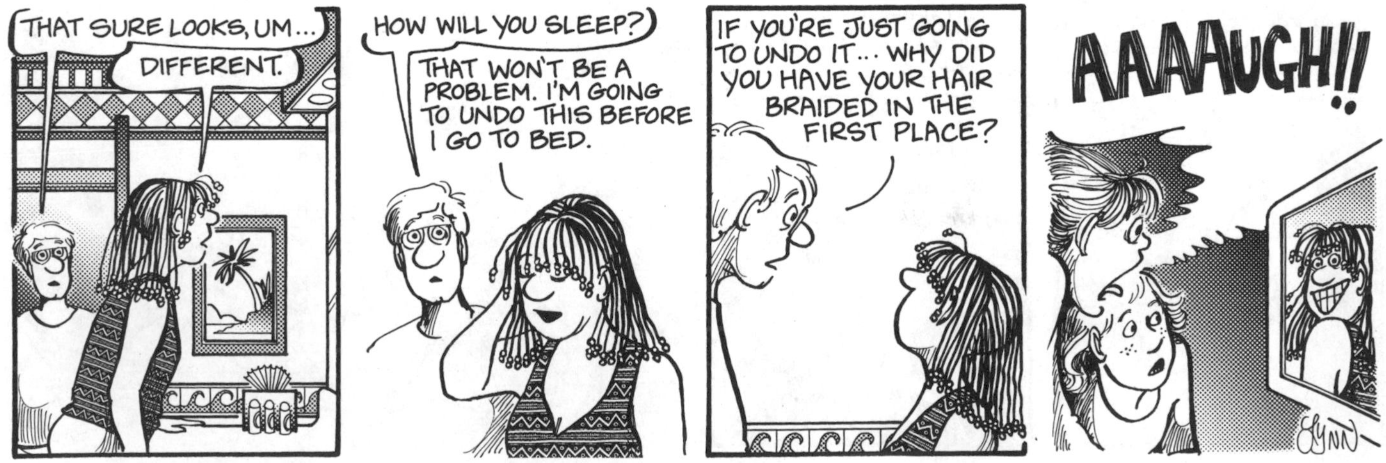
THAT SURE LOOKS, UM...
DIFFERENT.
HOW WILL YOU SLEEP?
THAT WON'T BE A PROBLEM. I'M GOING TO UNDO THIS BEFORE I GO TO BED.
IF YOU'RE JUST GOING TO UNDO IT... WHY DID YOU HAVE YOUR HAIR BRAIDED IN THE FIRST PLACE?
AAAAUGH!!
LYNN

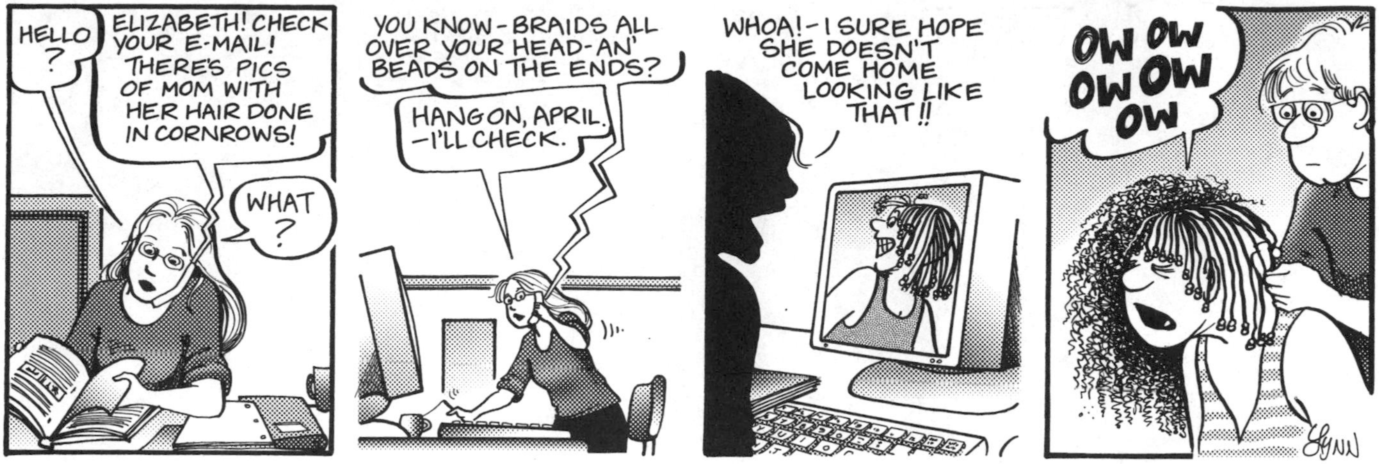
HELLO?
ELIZABETH! CHECK YOUR E-MAIL! THERE'S PICS OF MOM WITH HER HAIR DONE IN CORNROWS!
WHAT?
YOU KNOW - BRAIDS ALL OVER YOUR HEAD - AN' BEADS ON THE ENDS?
HANG ON, APRIL. - I'LL CHECK.
WHOA! - I SURE HOPE SHE DOESN'T COME HOME LOOKING LIKE THAT!!
OW OW OW OW OW
LYNN

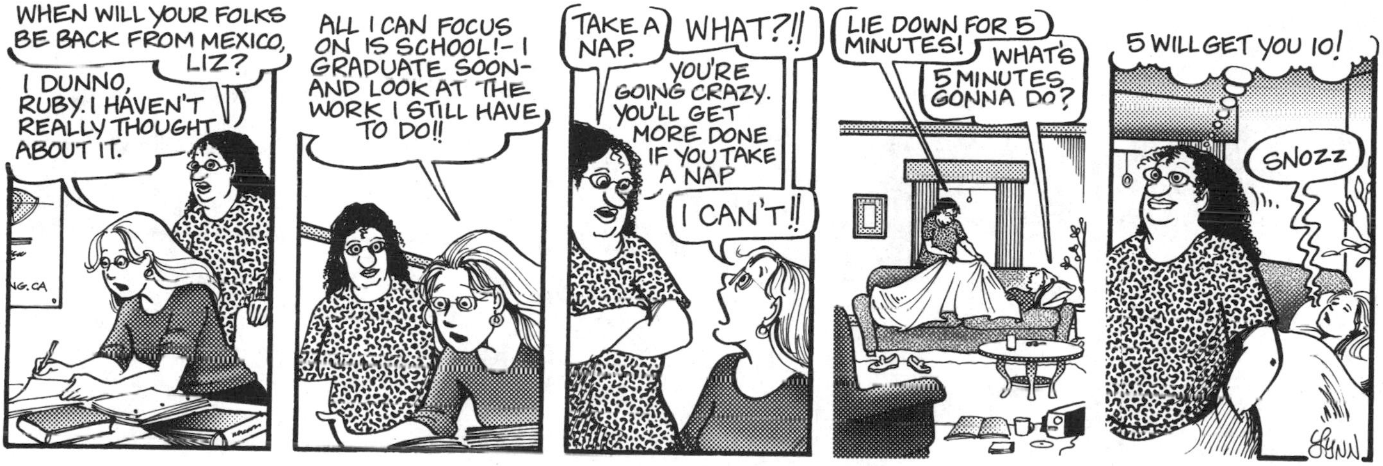
WHEN WILL YOUR FOLKS BE BACK FROM MEXICO, LIZ?
I DUNNO, RUBY. I HAVEN'T REALLY THOUGHT ABOUT IT.
ALL I CAN FOCUS ON IS SCHOOL! - I GRADUATE SOON - AND LOOK AT THE WORK I STILL HAVE TO DO!!
TAKE A NAP.
WHAT?!!
YOU'RE GOING CRAZY. YOU'LL GET MORE DONE IF YOU TAKE A NAP
I CAN'T!!
LIE DOWN FOR 5 MINUTES!
WHAT'S 5 MINUTES GONNA DO?
5 WILL GET YOU 10!
SNOZZ
LYNN

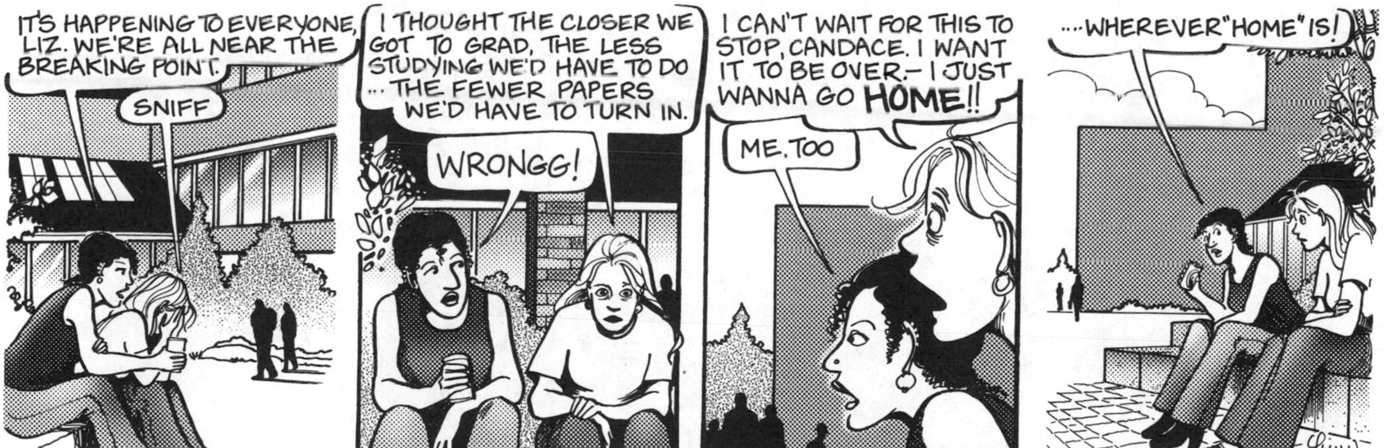
IT'S HAPPENING TO EVERYONE, LIZ. WE'RE ALL NEAR THE BREAKING POINT.
SNIFF
I THOUGHT THE CLOSER WE GOT TO GRAD, THE LESS STUDYING WE'D HAVE TO DO ... THE FEWER PAPERS WE'D HAVE TO TURN IN.
WRONGG!
I CAN'T WAIT FOR THIS TO STOP, CANDACE. I WANT IT TO BE OVER. - I JUST WANNA GO HOME!!
ME, TOO
....WHEREVER "HOME" IS!
LYNN

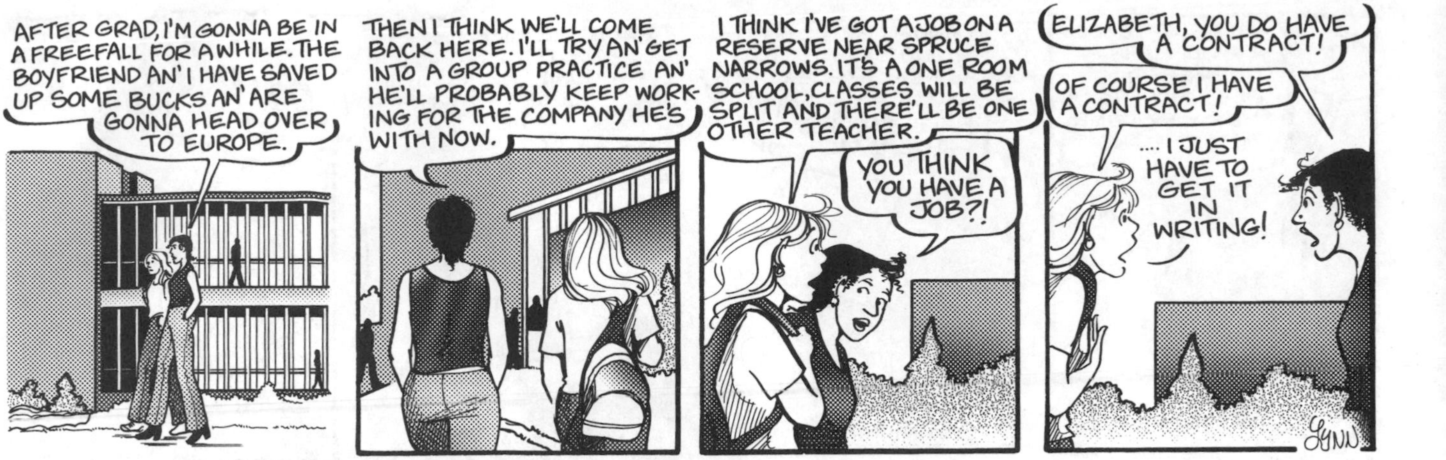
AFTER GRAD, I'M GONNA BE IN A FREEFALL FOR AWHILE. THE BOYFRIEND AN' I HAVE SAVED UP SOME BUCKS AN' ARE GONNA HEAD OVER TO EUROPE.
THEN I THINK WE'LL COME BACK HERE. I'LL TRY AN' GET INTO A GROUP PRACTICE AN' HE'LL PROBABLY KEEP WORKING FOR THE COMPANY HE'S WITH NOW.
I THINK I'VE GOT A JOB ON A RESERVE NEAR SPRUCE NARROWS. IT'S A ONE ROOM SCHOOL, CLASSES WILL BE SPLIT AND THERE'LL BE ONE OTHER TEACHER.
YOU THINK YOU HAVE A JOB?!
ELIZABETH, YOU DO HAVE A CONTRACT!
OF COURSE I HAVE A CONTRACT!
.... I JUST HAVE TO GET IT IN WRITING!
LYNN

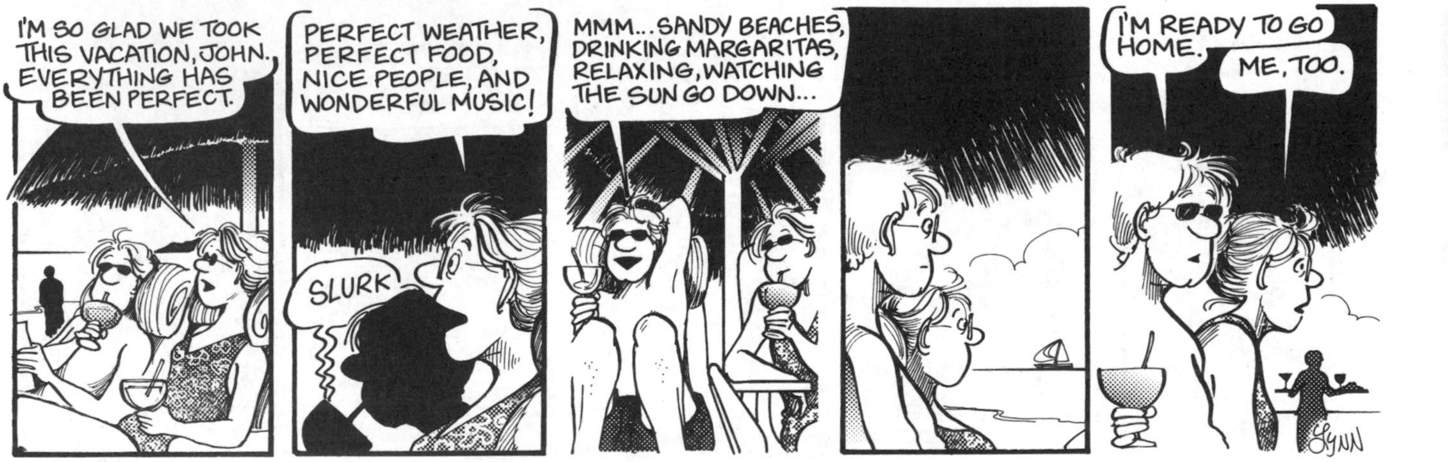
I'M SO GLAD WE TOOK THIS VACATION, JOHN. EVERYTHING HAS BEEN PERFECT.
PERFECT WEATHER, PERFECT FOOD, NICE PEOPLE, AND WONDERFUL MUSIC!
SLURK
MMM... SANDY BEACHES, DRINKING MARGARITAS, RELAXING, WATCHING THE SUN GO DOWN...
I'M READY TO GO HOME.
ME, TOO.
LYNN

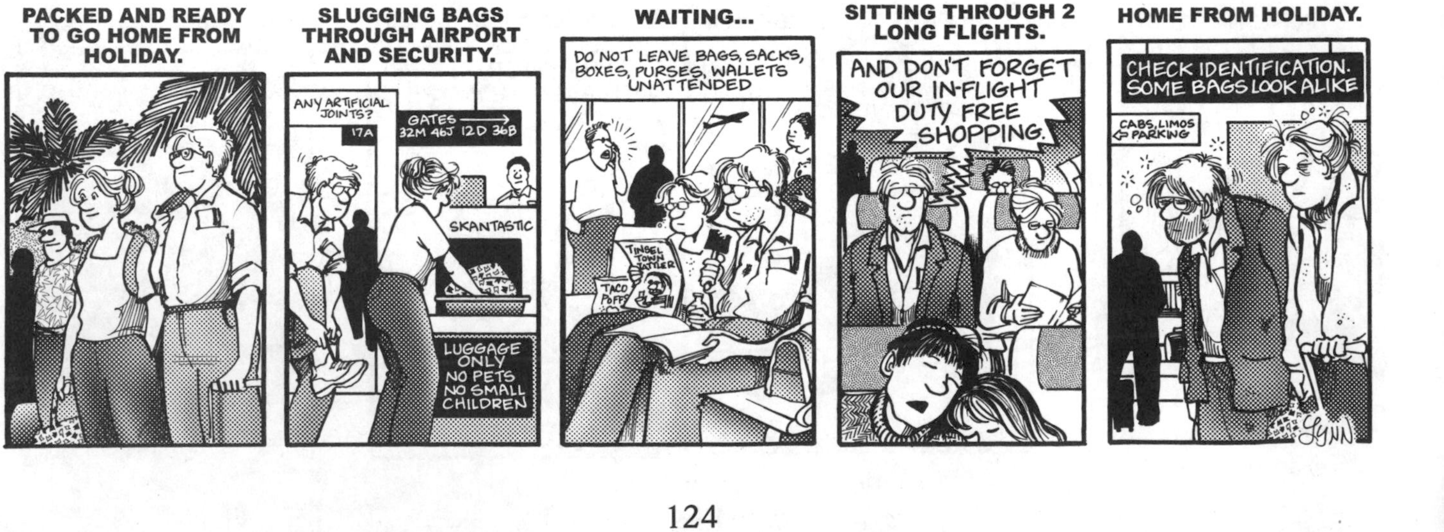
PACKED AND READY TO GO HOME FROM HOLIDAY.
SLUGGING BAGS THROUGH AIRPORT AND SECURITY.
ANY ARTIFICIAL JOINTS?
17A
GATES 32M 46J 12D 36B
SKANTASTIC
LUGGAGE ONLY NO PETS NO SMALL CHILDREN
WAITING...
DO NOT LEAVE BAGS, SACKS, BOXES, PURSES, WALLETS UNATTENDED
TINSEL TOWN TATTLER
TACO POFFS
SITTING THROUGH 2 LONG FLIGHTS.
AND DON'T FORGET OUR IN-FLIGHT DUTY FREE SHOPPING.
HOME FROM HOLIDAY.
CHECK IDENTIFICATION. SOME BAGS LOOK ALIKE
CABS, LIMOS PARKING
LYNN

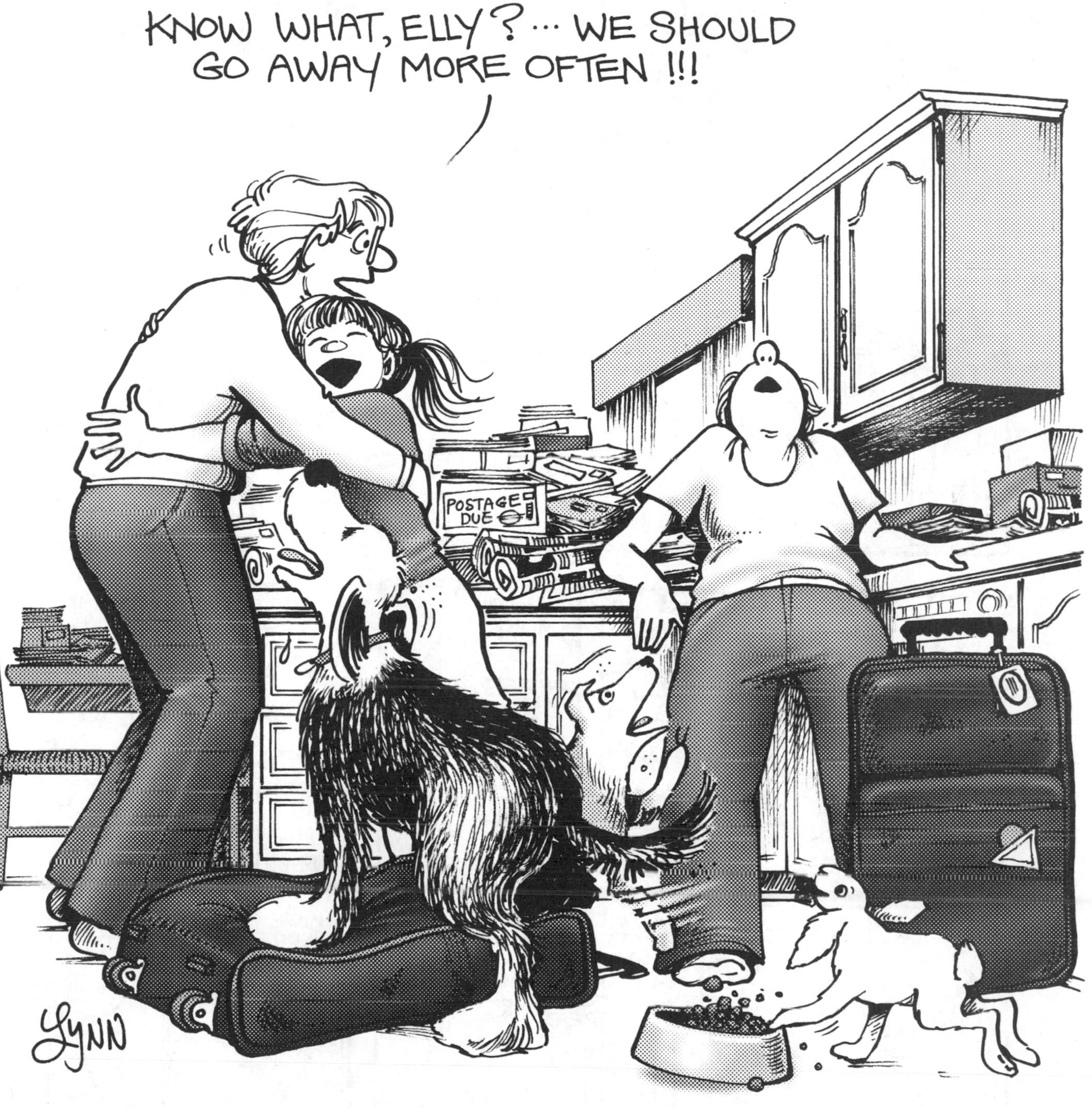
KNOW WHAT, ELLY?... WE SHOULD GO AWAY MORE OFTEN !!!
POSTAGE DUE
LYNN

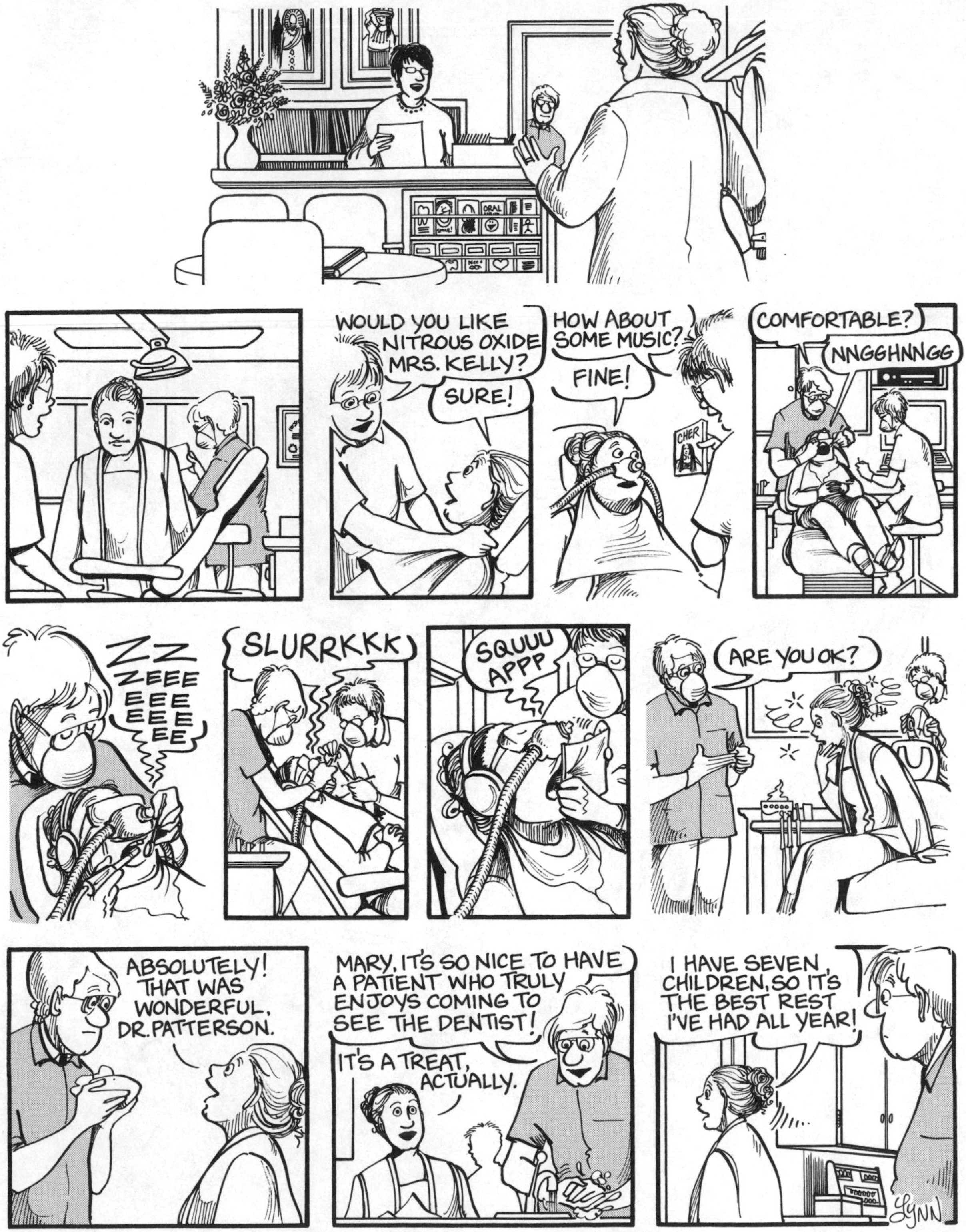

WOULD YOU LIKE NITROUS OXIDE MRS. KELLY?
SURE!
HOW ABOUT SOME MUSIC?
FINE!
CHER
COMFORTABLE?
NNGGHNNGG
ZZ ZEEE EEE EEE EEE EE
SLURRKKK
SQUUU APPP
ARE YOU OK?
ABSOLUTELY! THAT WAS WONDERFUL, DR. PATTERSON.
MARY, IT'S SO NICE TO HAVE A PATIENT WHO TRULY ENJOYS COMING TO SEE THE DENTIST!
IT'S A TREAT, ACTUALLY.
I HAVE SEVEN CHILDREN, SO IT'S THE BEST REST I'VE HAD ALL YEAR!
LYNN

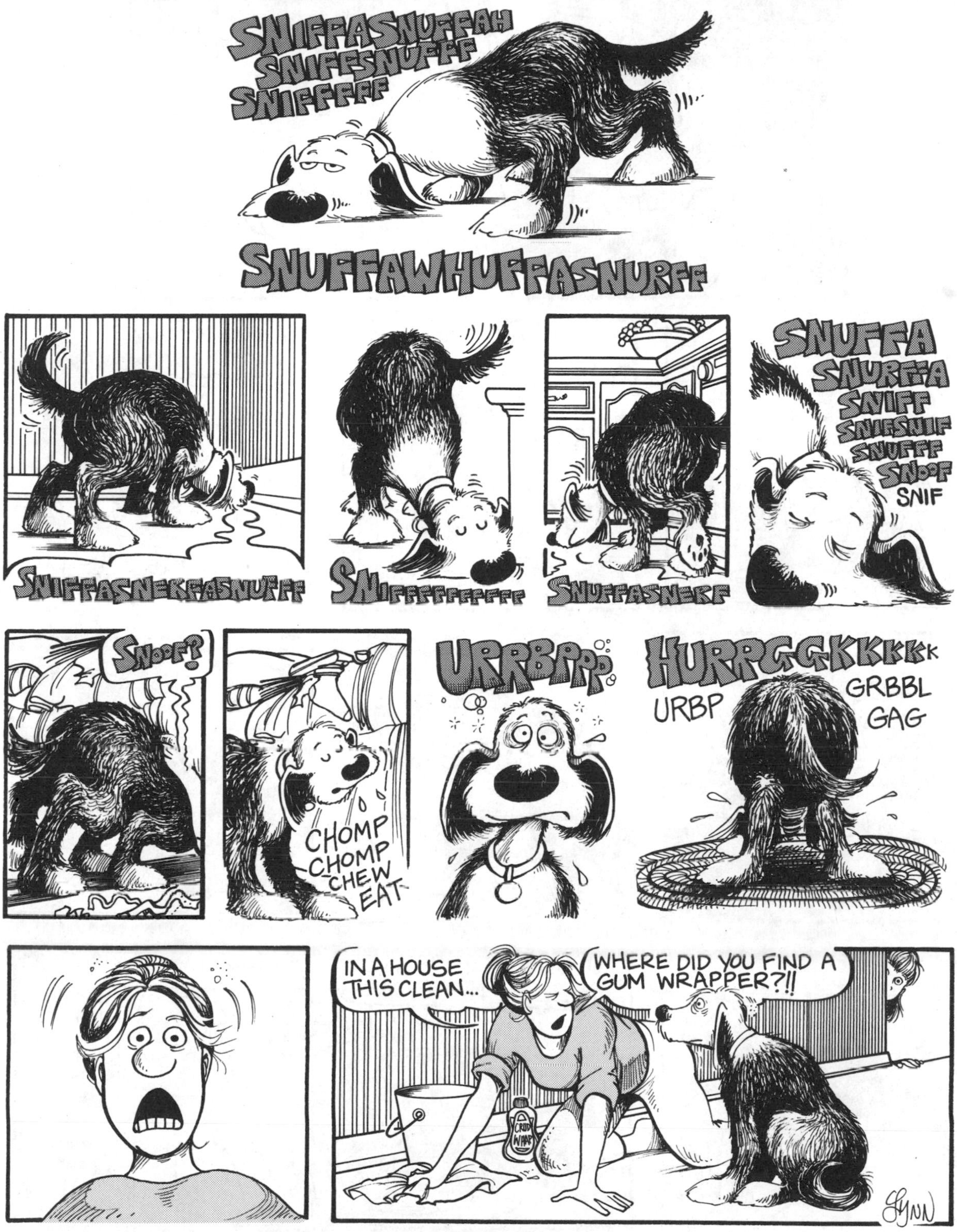
SNIFFASNUFFAH
SNIFFSNUFFF
SNIFFFFF
SNUFFAWHUFFASNURFF
SNIFFASNERFASNUFFF
SNIFFFFFFFFFFF
SNUFFASNERF
SNUFFA
SNURFFA
SNIFF
SNIFSNIF
SNUFFF
SNOOF
SNIF
SNOOF?
CHOMP
CHOMP
CHEW
EAT
URRBPPP
HURRGGKKKKKK
URBP
GRBBL
GAG
IN A HOUSE THIS CLEAN...
WHERE DID YOU FIND A GUM WRAPPER?!!
LYNN

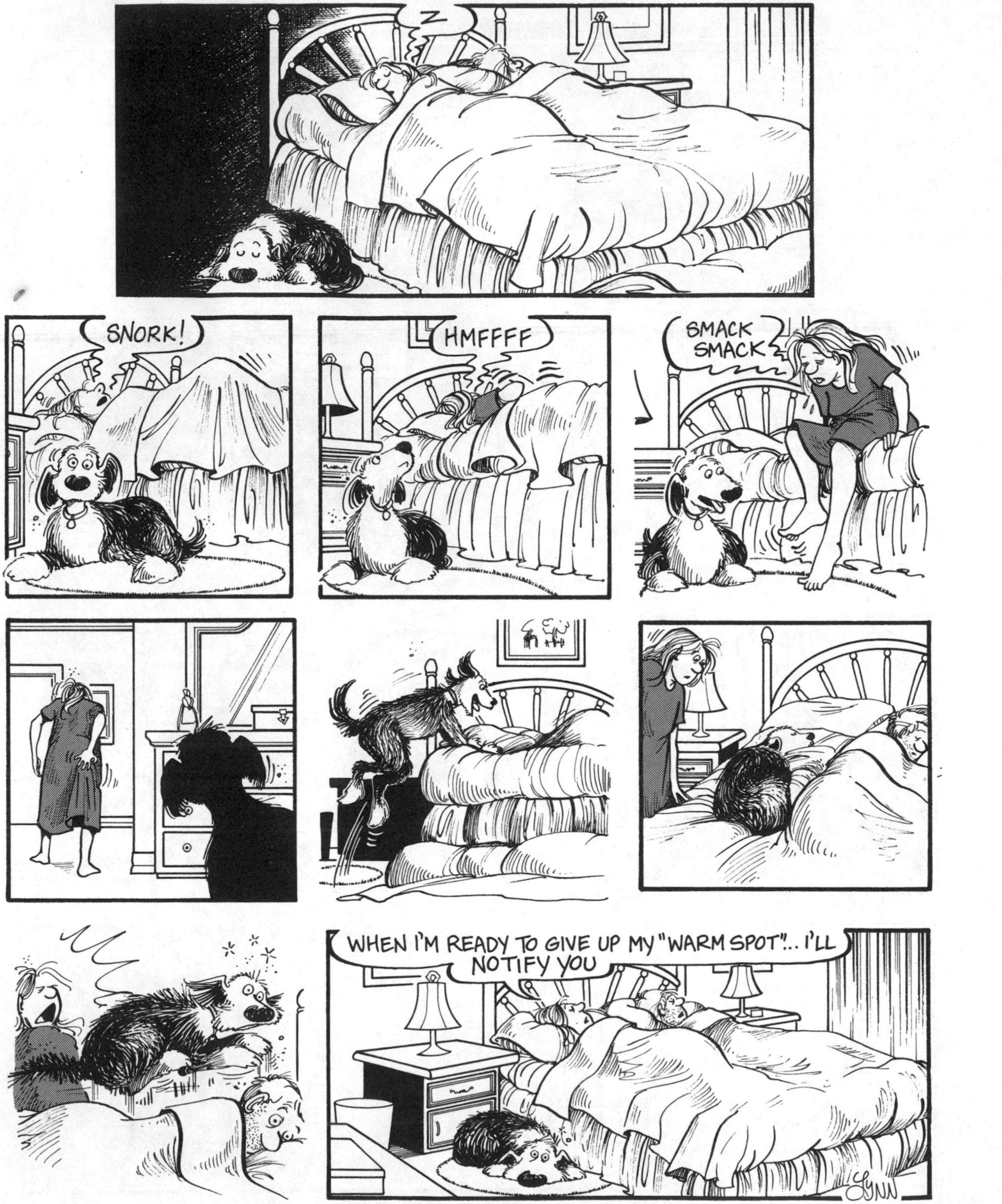

SNORK!
HMFFFF
SMACK SMACK
WHEN I'M READY TO GIVE UP MY "WARM SPOT"... I'LL NOTIFY YOU
LYNN